"*O'Meara's work is the perfect supplem* [the Goddess of Complete Being", shedd] *where Hughes's penetrating lens finally appears to aim. [This work] utterly clear light on the path of understanding we may re-win with regard to myth, forcing the reader to face the incredible starkness of the prospect we face—and the lack of options—ever closing in—and also giving the reader the necessary clues to follow, particularly Barfield, Shakespeare and Rudolf Steiner.*"

> Richard Ramsbotham, author of *Who Wrote Bacon?*
> *William Shakespeare, Francis Bacon and James I*

"*Very interesting stuff. Particularly where you parallel the break through the tragic dead end to the transcendental-redemptive solution—that I follow from "Macbeth" through "Lear" to the last plays—with the Steinerian view of the same progress.*"

> Ted Hughes on *Othello's Sacrifice*, from Letter to
> John O'Meara, 21 November, 1996, in the Ted Hughes
> Archives, Emory University, Atlanta, Georgia

This volume brings together virtually all of the published shorter critical work of John O'Meara, gathered from over 30 years of production. What emerges is an extensive, uniquely challenging interpretation of the evolution of, for the most part English, literary history, from Shakespeare's time to our own.

"*excellent Shakespearean explorations . . . The idea of Lutheran depravity without Lutheran grace or Lutheran-Calvinist justification is very strong and original . . .*"

> Anthony Gash, author of *The Substance of Shadows:*
> *Shakespeare's Dialogue with Plato*

"*O'Meara sets out to demonstrate . . . the essential fact that "full encounter with human depravity" was[/is] a necessary step in the attaining of true* [otherworldly] *Imagination.*"

> Eric Philips-Oxford on *The New School of the Imagination,*
> from the Sektion fur Schone Wissenschaften, the
> Goetheanum, *Newsletter*, Issue No. 3,
> Winter/Spring 2008-2009

* * *

On *Otherworldly Hamlet*:

"a remarkable and provocative contribution to Shakespeare Studies."
Corona Sharp, *English Studies in Canada*,
December 1993

"most interesting in the suggestive way it points forward to the structure of the Romantic text . . ."
Ruth Vanita, *Hamlet Studies*, Vol. 16, 1994

"I found much of interest, and especially upon re-reading the most complex sections"
Joost Daalder, *Review of English Studies*,
Vol. XLVIII, November 1997

On *Othello's Sacrifice*:

"O'Meara's analysis of previous critics provides new insight into both the potential and the limitations of Romanticism as an interpretive tool: it opens new vistas of further critical inquiry"
Elizabeth Anne Macdonald-Murray,
Canadian Book Review Annual,
Vol. 23, July, 1998

"O'Meara offers a thesis of evolution in which Shakespeare's concern with the ego and libido . . . is freed by the use of imagination and, in later stages, by inspiration and intuition . . ."
Arthur F. Kinney, *English Language Notes*,
September, 1998

Also by
JOHN O'MEARA

OTHERWORLDLY HAMLET

OTHELLO'S SACRIFICE:
Essays on Shakespeare and Romantic Tradition

THE MODERN DEBACLE
AND OUR HOPE IN THE GODDESS

THE THINKING SPIRIT:
RUDOLF STEINER AND ROMANTIC THEORY:
A Collection of Texts with Notes

SHAKESPEARE, THE GODDESS, AND MODERNITY

JOHN O'MEARA

iUniverse, Inc.
Bloomington

Shakespeare, the Goddess, and Modernity

iUniverse books may be ordered through booksellers or by contacting:

iUniverse
1663 Liberty Drive
Bloomington, IN 47403
www.iuniverse.com
1-800-Authors (1-800-288-4677)

ISBN: 978-1-4697-4627-2 (sc)
ISBN: 978-1-4697-4628-9 (hc)
ISBN: 978-1-4697-4629-6 (ebk)

Printed in the United States of America

iUniverse rev. date: 02/10/2012

CONTENTS

Foreword

I

II

III

Appendix:
Tony Gash's letter about Shakespeare's Muse

Endnotes

Acknowledgments

Cover Image

The Goddess

(detail)

from

The Destruction of the Giants by Jove's Thunderbolt,

by Giulio Romano,

Sala dei Giganti, the Pallazo da Te, Mantua

I record my indebtedness to Richard Ramsbotham, to Anthony Gash and to Eric Oxford for their faithful reading, over years, of many of the texts that are included here, and for their enthusiastic approbation in one respect and another, without which I could not have proceeded as I have.

Chapter 10, "On *King Lear*", appears here for the first time. Chapter 9 reproduces an article published in *English Language Notes*, Volume XXVIII, Number 1, September 1990. All other chapters have appeared previously under separate cover, each with its own characteristic design, and effect.

Chapter 3, "On Luther", and chapter 7, "Visionary Miraculism", have appeared under the imprint of *HCP* (Heart's Core Publications), Ottawa, Canada. The excerpt that constitutes Chapter 4 is taken from *Othello's Sacrifice, Guernica Editions,* Toronto, Canada. All remaining chapters have appeared under the imprint of *iUniverse*, Lincoln, Nebraska, and Bloomington, Indiana.

Only as much of *Myth, Depravity, Impasse* has been reproduced in Chapter 1 as seemed to fit the proper contours of the present volume. Interested readers may wish to consult the original (in its 2nd revised edition) for a further, comparative discussion of *Keats's* relationship to the Goddess and to modernity. Likewise with *The New School of the Imagination*, in Chapter 6, only as much of that work has been reproduced as seemed appropriate to the present volume's proper range of subjects. Revisions and emendations have generally been introduced into all of the texts as reproduced here in order to bring out more clearly the argument of this *oeuvre* seen as a whole.

Among other acknowledgments, the author also wishes to thank Adam Bittleston, for his superior translation of Rudolf Steiner's Mystery Plays (Rudolf Steiner Press), as well as Princeton University Press, for permission to reproduce pictures from *The Great Mother* and *Hero With a Thousand Faces*. The *Burial of the Count Orgaz*, by El Greco, is from the church of S. Tomé, Toledo, Spain.

this record of my life's work
is dedicated to

ALINE
FRANCOEUR

my
co-creator

Foreword

This volume brings together virtually all of my published shorter critical work gathered from over 30 years, in each case of about 70 pages or less, some of this work having appeared in the vulnerable form of booklets. It seemed the right thing to collect this shorter work for two reasons: there was the fear that some of it, being in such a small format, would get lost on the shelves of university libraries; and here was a chance to look at what all of it seen together amounted to as a more or less unified contribution to our understanding of (for the most part, English) literary history. Beyond the work represented here are what may be properly considered my books, which are more specialized elaborations, along some of the lines of enquiry as outlined in this volume. These comprise *Otherworldly Hamlet*, *Othello's Sacrifice* (on Shakespeare and Romantic Tradition); *The Thinking Spirit* (on Rudolf Steiner); and *The Modern Debacle*.

The present volume for the greatest part showcases studies on Shakespeare, bearing tangentially at one end on the Goddess-theme, especially as brought forward in our time by Robert Graves, and at the other end on the further large issue of the relationship between Romanticism and Modernity. Precisely how Graves comes to acquire the prominence he is assigned in my work is to a large extent explained by the extensive, if still very selective, treatment of modern authors that I provide in *The Modern Debacle*, in which Graves appears as the main hero. There I bring out merely one significant event in the very great complex that we know as modern literature. This event concerns the emphasis put on the Goddess, who emerges over the course of the development of modern literature as a unifying figure, and with whom Graves is pre-eminently associated. In this line of development the Goddess, as an inspirational force, appears as a form of answer to a widespread sense over this period that civilization has reached dead-end in its capacity for Imaginative experience, overwhelmed as it is, and indeed dictated to, by the accumulating effects, over centuries, of *Realpolitik*, or the politics of power.

Not only Robert Graves but Ted Hughes also has argued eloquently on behalf of the Goddess's immediate presence and influence in our lives, and for better or for worse I have allowed myself to be drawn into their discussion, especially as this bears at a certain point directly on Shakespeare. Shakespeare begins his career, in fact, in the midst of a theistic world-view and, only by degrees does he render himself up to a form of evolution that brings him into relation with the Goddess as his principal divinity. What we are to make of this astounding division in the sensibility of our greatest author I must leave to the reader to decide. A whole new theology, positing a further relationship between God and Goddess, and between God and the Sophia, would have to be conceived, and an issue is thus raised that lies beyond the scope of my present work to determine. But to highlight the issue, I have rounded out this volume with those pieces in which I have most faithfully explored Shakespeare's immersion in the theistic world-view (in Chapters 7 and 8).

My use of the insights provided by Rudolf Steiner in my work as a whole necessitates a word here also about my involvement with this great modern visionary, who ought to be known to many more readers today. After relying, in *Othello's Sacrifice*, on Steiner to account for the precise nature of Shakespeare's evolution through tragedy, I made sure to offer my reader a compendium of Steiner's thought in my edited collection of his work, published under the title, *The Thinking Spirit*. More about his thought may also be found in *Othello's Sacrifice*. The reader is therefore advised to turn to this other material for further insight into this complex thinker. In Steiner's truly prodigious outpouring the reader will find, apart from the elucidations that will serve to relate especially God and the Sophia, a view also of how, since medieval times, one period of time has grown out of the other, including, in his Mystery Plays, acute insights into our modern condition which show us more precisely what it now devolves upon us to work through if we are indeed to overcome the sense that we have reached dead-end in our Imaginative experience.[1]

For the most part a critic will be impelled to write about this or that subject, or in this or that area of literature, as his desire happens to dictate at any given time, but with every critic over time a pattern or patterns are created that define some very particular concerns, or it may be obsessions, that come to mark the limits of the contribution that critic has made. The predominant concerns or obsessions of this critic the reader will be able to fathom for him/herself as he/she reaches conclusion. But let me point out the one concern of which I have been the most conscious myself as I was going along, apart from my insistent emphasis on the total extent of Shakespeare's absorption in human depravity. That concern has to do with what we can think is possible as a form of breakthrough *into* a visionary otherworld, especially as regards an objectively *particular* revelation that may be bestowed from such a world, or the prospect of an actual otherworldly *justification* of one's experience. On this level, my study of Graves continues a line of enquiry that has engaged me from the time I first began writing on Shakespeare many years ago. A view of my work as a whole, extending through section II of this volume, will confirm that this always was the case.

Finally, to address the question of gender that will inevitably crop up as an import of the studies that follow. It seems clear that Shakespeare, like Graves, had one basic view of it: Man has brought down; Woman will bring up again. Nevertheless, virtually all of what follows reflects primarily a view of the matter as narrated by men; there would still be a need for the additional input that a woman's perspective would have to offer on their understanding, whether in confirmation or not, with the larger dialectic of views such an input is bound to open up as a matter of course as we move on into a difficult future together.

Otherwise, the main consideration when reading through this volume bears on the fact that only from the middle of Chapter 4 am I in any position to begin to make good on what I promise the reader that concerns the "progress" Shakespeare makes through tragedy.

JOM

As [a man] progresses in the slow initiation which is life, the form of the goddess undergoes for him a series of transfigurations: she can never be greater than himself, though she can always promise him more than he is yet capable of comprehending. She lures, she guides, she bids him burst his fetters . . .

if (only) he (could)match her import . . .
                                        —Joseph Campbell

                                *   *   *

                        for thou shalt hear that I
            Knowing . . . that the oracle
            Gave hope thou wast in being, have
                                preserved
            Myself to see the issue.
                                        —Hermione, to Perdita,
                                        from *The Winter's Tale*[2]

1

From

Myth, Depravity, Impasse:

On Graves, Hughes, and Shakespeare

I

THE MYTHIC GROUND

In a public lecture[1] given at the Y.M.H.A. Centre in New York in 1957, Robert Graves directly addressed the ground of his mythical faith with the potentially explosive question:

Do I think that poets are literally inspired by the White Goddess?

From the context of his address it is clear that Graves was not led to this question himself. It is prefaced by a remark that indicates it is being aired in response to signs of disbelief in his audience that he could be taking his claims so far. Graves's response to his question is a carefully crafted piece of evasive affirmation:

Some of you are looking queerly at me. Do I think that poets are literally inspired by the White Goddess? That is an improper question. What would you think, should I ask you if, in your opinion, the Hebrew prophets were literally inspired by God? Whether God is a metaphor or a fact cannot be reasonably argued; let us likewise be discreet on the subject of the Goddess.

Rarely was Graves so circumspect in his proclamation of his great Theme. His confidence on this occasion is, in a somewhat unusual way, tempered by the doubt he is addressing in his immediate audience. His subdued tone reflects also the bafflement he appears to have felt about a critique that had been made of his presentation of the White Goddess, in a recent review by Randall Jarrell, the American poet.[2] Jarrell had argued that Graves's picture of the White Goddess was merely a projection of his own personal fantasy. Thus both Jarrell and Graves's audience combine to confront him with an image of the opposition he might expect to find to the *kind* of claims he was making, with their unquestioned assumption about the literal existence, in some sense, of the White Goddess. In the face of this opposition Graves momentarily dampens his claims in respect to how far they might be taken.

I linger over this episode because it points the issue of what someone who claims to have found a literal connection with the mythical will face in his sceptical and uncomprehending audience. With that is raised the whole question of what the ground of a mythical faith can be. One may claim of Graves's lecture as a whole, in comparison with his many other pronouncements, a kind of retreat in the face of the enemy's display of its forces. Thus, for the most part here, he is content to reiterate that aspect of his Theme that is primarily historical. That approach is emphasized by way of making the point that

> *Mr. Jarrell cannot accuse me of **inventing** the White Goddess . . .*

Hence, also, his further statement that

> *It is enough for me to quote the myths and give them historical sense . . .*

And it is with this less-than-muted sense of being in the presence of the enemy that Graves proffers what is for him the comparatively reduced declaration, intended to set him on safe ground, that

> *I hold that critical notice should be taken of the Goddess.*

"Notice" of this kind is due because of the coherent "grammar of poetic myth" that Graves was known to have derived from his historical studies of the Goddess cult. Even Jarrell acknowledges that he is grateful for it, for on the basis of this "grammar" Graves was able to write poems that Jarrell describes as "some of the most beautiful poems of our time."[3] Especially is it a matter for Graves of taking notice of the "poetry which deeply affects readers", and how it comes to be. The answer is in "the persistent survival", among the "Muse-poets", of "faith" in the White Goddess—which may be conscious or unconscious. Their "imagery" can be proven to be "drawn" directly from Her cult, and the "magic" of their poems shown to be dependent on "its closeness to her mysteries."

Graves's account, bold as it is, still begs the question of what the ground of this "faith" might be, but, in this lecture at least, he is as sly as his enemy is unyielding. Primarily, he *reverts* (from the claim of literalness) to the view that

> *In scientific terms, no god at all can be proved to exist,*
> *but only beliefs in gods, and the effects of such beliefs on*
> *worshippers.*

Such a view, Graves maintains, applies as much to the Christian belief in a Father God as to the Jewish belief in the God of the prophets, and, therefore, can apply as much to a belief in the Goddess, whose religion can be attested to on the same grounds. Graves is as uncompromising about his own historical emphasis:

> *The most important single fact in the early history of*
> *Western religion and sociology was undoubtedly the gradual*
> *suppression of the Lunar Mother-goddess's inspiratory cult,*
> *and its supercession by ... the busy, rational cult of the Solar*
> *God Apollo.*

Of the Goddess's presence in the religion of former times, and of its stubborn survival against the odds into modern times, there can be no doubt, and since poetic inspiration remains, in scientific terms, an undisclosed mystery:

> *... why not attribute inspiration to the Lunar Muse, the*
> *oldest and most convenient European term for the source in*
> *question?*

It is a triumphant gambit, because of the appeal, in "the *oldest . . .* European term", to priority in this case. However, Graves goes farther: he implies that, as "Protestant Doctors of Divinity ... posit the literal existence of an all-powerful God"—claiming for themselves proofs of "supernatural happenings" in spite of these being "ill-attested" by science—adherents of the Goddess might do the same. There is also the argument from precedent and tradition (a very long tradition in this case), in which Graves deliberately milks the present perfect tense: "In fact, the Goddess has always been . . . . The Muse-poets have always recognized" etc. And it is only *after* Graves has pursued this whole elaborate strategic disarming of the enemy, that we find him shifting back to a claim about the Goddess's literal role in the lives of poets:

> *By ancient religious theory the White Goddess becomes*
> *incarnate in her human representative—a priestess, a*
> *prophetess, a queen-mother. No Muse-poet can grow*
> *conscious of the Muse except by experience of some woman in*
> *whom the Muse-power is to some degree or other resident.*

From a claim from "ancient religious theory", Graves shifts here to a present *actuality*—"No Muse-poet *can*"—and this shift is now sustained. Finally, we hear from him again in the forthright mode in which his auditors had been accustomed to hearing from him before he came face to face with the opposition his claims provoked:

> *But the real, perpetually obsessed Muse-poet makes*
> *a distinction between the Goddess as revealed in the*
> *supreme power, glory, wisdom and love of woman, and*
> *the individual woman in whom the Goddess may take up*
> *residence for a month, a year, seven years, or even longer.*
> *The Goddess abides; and it may be that he will again*
> *have knowledge of her through his experience of another*
> *woman . . .*

*   *   *

Graves's case is among the most extraordinary instances in modern times of a claim to literalness in the experience of myth, and it is for this reason that I choose to focus on him here. His case is the more extraordinary just because—in his comportment and in his whole manner of expressing himself—he is in every other respect the model of level-headedness, and is so to a fault (which has made him an easy object of caricature). I have also *begun* with the episode of the lecture because *it* represents, on the other side of the issue, a somewhat extreme instance of disobligingness when it comes to responding to a claim of literalness. Between these two extremes the issue of the *ground* of myth is thus raised. The encounter between the two here is not exactly what one would call fruitful; the issue degenerates into polemics, the appeal to "faith" appearing as the appeasing counter to be mutually appropriated by both sides. Perhaps in the case of

Graves's audience nothing short of the grossest scientific "proof" would have satisfied the sense of "reality" that needed to be appeased, where only a more subtle order of metaphysical proof could be provided.

The same could hardly be said of Jarrell, however, who is ready in his critique to credit Graves with "poems that almost deserve the literal *magical*"[4]. Only, Jarrell does not intend by "magical" the literal sense that Graves does, where for instance *he* writes, at the beginning of *The White Goddess*, "European poetic lore . . . is ultimately based on magical principles."[5] In his way of offering praise of Graves's poems—"*almost . . . the literal* magical"—Jarrell mischievously approaches Graves's sense while clearly intending another, very much more restricted one. Jarrell's use of "magical" intensifies the issue in yet another way, inasmuch as our use of the term allows us to draw on a literal connotation of the word where we do not in fact intend one—which we would scrupulously deny if ever held to account for it. Certainly we do not normally intend by it the literal rendering that Graves continues to proclaim, e.g., in his new Foreword to *The White Goddess*, written a few years after the critique by Jarrell:

> *My thesis is that the language of myth anciently current in*
> *the Mediterranean and Northern Europe was a magical*
> *language bound up with popular religious ceremonies in*
> *honour of the Moon-Goddess, or Muse . . . and that this*
> ***remains** the language of true poetry . . .*

And *because* it remains so, Graves was concerned that "poetry of a magical quality" should not continue merely as an incidental or haphazard achievement, the result of "an inspired, almost pathological, reversion to the original language", but should rather be strenuously researched and cultivated, on the clear basis of "a conscientious study of its grammar and vocabulary".

*   *   *

But it may be well to continue by looking at the poems by Graves that Jarrell himself describes as "magical"—what he calls the "mythical-archaic poems", among which are two of the best known, "The White Goddess" and "To Juan at the Winter Solstice". Thus we shall put off saying, for the moment, in what a mythical "faith" may be said to consist, or on what "ground" it may be said to be predicated, to consider first what *kind* of world it could be said to proclaim, or what world-view Graves can be said to have committed to on the basis of his experience of the ancient mythical material. We shall, in doing so, also be giving ourselves a chance to see precisely what kind of grammar and vocabulary we can expect to be dealing with.

Much of what Graves understood as to how the Goddess figures in our lives can be said to be contained in these two poems, which we may see as two parts of one whole, with "The White Goddess" (though second in composition) playing the first part to "To Juan". It is the forthrightness of his claims that impress themselves upon us in "The White Goddess". This forthrightness belies the strenuous effort that has been made first to disassociate from the main Western cultural attitudes that have obstructed a proper approach to the Goddess. These are gone into at great length in Graves's book, *The White Goddess*, and they are summarized in Graves's poem as the ascetic attitude associated with Christianity as well as Western Apollonian rational philosophy. The Goddess, among other things, demands one's engagement *with* the world; it could never be with Her a case of turning away from what the world has fully to offer, also to one's bodily experience and, from within that experience, to one's consciousness.

At the same time, the idea proposed as to how the Goddess is to be "found" has less to do with the typical mythical journey of the past than with a way of living into Nature that has much in common with latter-day Romantic experience. Thus Jarrell's term, "archaic", does not fit altogether. One need not go far either across the world or back into time to be able, in Graves's view, to "celebrate" the Goddess's presence; one need only be able to live one's "way" fully into Spring as well as into all of the rest of the natural year.[6] Here is where the peculiar attitude involved in making the right approach to the Goddess makes itself felt. It must be, if one is to find Her, a matter of living fully into the *whole cycle* of the year, and so *quite as much* into Fall and Winter as into Spring and Summer. That thought defies one's imagination, as much as does the thought that one is to find Her "at the volcano's head" or "Among pack ice", or that, in aspiring to know Her *through* this kind of engagement, one risks, by one's unworthiness, being mentally struck down as by lightning ("the next bright bolt"). Graves reserves the certainty of being so much in tune with the essential Goddess Who lies behind Her natural manifestations—blessed, as he is, "with so huge a sense/Of her *nakedly* worn magnificence"—the possibility of being favored and supported in this venture seems within reach. As Graves puts it, in "'To Juan", "fear" is to be countered by trust in the dependability of the Goddess's "love"; this "love", from Her side, the Goddess bestows for the "life" that is given over to Her. The "fear" Graves addresses is what haunts one from knowing that one must, in the end, *go* to one's death. Nature in its foreboding and destructive aspect speaks ultimately of the death one must endure. But the hope lies in the "love" that is tendered *out* of this prospect, which will *return* one from that great "ocean" or "sea" of death into which one plunges. We are reborn into a new life (for Graves, we eventually re-incarnate) because we are *in* the Goddess, Who reserves to Herself the *power* to return, from the great "grapple" with death which, sooner or later, engages us along with Her. And so She is presented towards the end of Graves's poem, Herself continually resurrecting from death.[7]

Submission to the dark, material side of the Goddess's Creation *as mythically rendered* is the aspect of Graves's presentation that has met with the most extreme resistance. Resistance has come because of the literal emphasis Graves gives to this rendering. This reaction is especially strong in relation to his portrayal of the White Goddess or Mother of All-Living as "the ancient power of fright and lust—the female spider, the queen bee whose embrace is death."[8] Often, in his poems, Graves paints pictures of the Goddess in her dark, dreadful claim on him. She appears in this guise in "She Is No Liar", with

Honey from her lips, blood from her shadowy hand.

Graves presents the Goddess as One Who *generally* submits her devotee to violent dispossession, but in "Lion Lover" Graves depicts himself as only ready to accept this "doom". Graves knows himself to be caught up in his flesh-bound nature and its confounding depravation bearing on death. Yet in his submission to this doom he will often be re-paid, the sight of Her "love" appearing to him as a result of his strenuous refusal of all eluding tendencies, rationalistic and otherwise. Thus the Goddess appears to him in this poem once again, Her "eyes naked with love", as she triumphantly rides the lion of his own "beasthood", as in one of those many artistic renderings of the Goddess that have survived out of the ancient and classical pasts[9].

It is precisely this readiness, in the face of all deterrents, to *continue* to think himself in a relationship with His Creatress that explains Graves's great success, by moments, in thinking himself into the Goddess's order, however darkly problematic his expression of that order often appears to be. One may, indeed, speak in connection with his more successful efforts of an extraordinary *congruity* between his own consciousness and the mythical material he is proclaiming. In making his own individual approach to the Goddess's world, it almost seems at times as if the ancient material comes to meet Graves's efforts independently. Nowhere is this more dramatically so than where his efforts to reach out to the Goddess bring on *pictorial* manifestations: pictures of the Goddess that, as in "The White Goddess" and in "To Juan", suddenly appear out of their own inner Imaginative space—as if independent manifestations of a living Being:

> *Whose broad high brow was white as any leper's,*

> *She in her left hand bears a leafy quince;*
> *When with her right she crooks a finger, smiling,*

> *Her sea-grey eyes were wild,*

Here the personal and the mythical dimensions have merged. The mythical images seem to come of their own accord and from their own dimension, as if independently of Graves's conscious intention, as if they had, that is, their own intrinsic value in relation to the personal experience he is having. If so, they are not then to be discounted as "merely" mythical, or metaphorical. They seem rather to represent the pictorial *equivalent* of that which is being projected *out* of that otherworldly order into which Graves has succeeded in personally penetrating.

II

Accounts of the mythical process contemporary with Graves, even in their most radical expressions, never go as far as to proclaim the immediate possibility of recovering the mythical world in the extraordinary form Graves's production attests to. This is so even in the case of Mircea Eliade, with whose accounts one may note the closest similarities in tendency. Eliade himself focuses on gods and the "Supernaturals" generally, rather than on the Goddess, but in Eliade also there is, seemingly, complete literalness in the approach to myth, so that we find in treatments of his work the very same rationally-justified, astounded critique as was levelled at Graves:

> *What sort of scholar would talk with apparent credulity*
> *about the Creation as if it really happened, about some myths*
> *'participating' in others, about the gods as if they really*
> *worked **in illo tempore**, about myths as if they really arose*
> *in moments of actual release from history and sacramentally*
> *produced such moments for their devotees?*[10]

Eliade himself can attest to the experience, through myth, of "an encounter with a transhuman reality—which gives birth to the idea that something *really exists*"[11], and it is, moreover, in his view, "through the objects of this present world" that "one perceives traces of the Beings and powers of another world."[12] However, it is also clear that Eliade attributes that experience *strictly* to "[t]he man of the societies in which myth is a living thing"[13], or, as he puts it famously, "the man of the archaic societies"[14], who thrived in the remote past. Out of *that* context Eliade brings forward his ultimate view of a World that literally "'speaks' to man", and that "to understand [that World's] language [man] needs only to know the myths and decipher the symbols."[15] All of these descriptions *could* apply to Graves's own experience, except that nowhere does Eliade assume the possibility of such an experience in the modern present. On the contrary, that present is defined by Eliade as, uniquely, a time of deep historical subjection, cut off as it is from all the advantages of transcendence that derive from mythical experience, as these were formerly available to archaic man.

For Eliade—as indeed for all of the great artists and thinkers of his time[16], the modern present involves us in a world that, in its very nature, is metaphysically inconsequential, defined (to quote his own Camusian turn of phrase) principally by that temporal rhythm "in which we are condemned to live and work".[17] Misfortune and death in that context become themselves "absurd"[18], and Eliade has been seen as resorting, in his response to that condition, to the classic attitude of his own Mioritic hero of folk tradition. He imposes a meaning on the absurd by viewing the tragedy of the modern age not "as a personal historical event but as a sacramental mystery"[19], a low-point, as it were, of "Chaos" that *must* be "followed by a new Creation", of a sort that can eventually be "homologized with a cosmogony".[20] Eliade is already pointing the way to that cosmogony through his own "nostalgia" for the archaic.[21] In the meantime, he could recognize, especially in the area of modern literature, "a revolt against historical time",[22] and especially against what he alludes to as "certain contemporary philosophies of despair".[23] That revolt is achieved paradoxically through the creation of closed, hermetic universes—Eliade cites the pre-eminent case of *Finnegan's Wake* by Joyce. These "cannot be entered except by overcoming immense difficulties, like the initiatory ordeals of the archaic and traditional societies."[24] In this way the opportunity for a new "initiatory gnosis" is created that is built up from the "ruins and enigmas" of modern existence—the Waste Land, so to speak—that Eliade sees as the first phase in the return to cosmogony. No doubt he would have seen in Graves's own work some "initiatory gnosis" of the sort, especially in the case of Graves's monumental prose work, *The White Goddess*, which T.S. Eliot described as a "monstrous, stupefying, indescribable book"—echoing his earlier comments on *Finnegan's Wake* as "a monstrous masterpiece". What Eliade would *not* have allowed, however, is a possibility of recovering the mythical experience of archaic man immediately and directly in the modern present, as Graves was also claiming to do.

In fact, the modern theory of myth is almost uniformly based on an *acceptance* of our separation from the mythical experience, even where that experience *seems* to be fully grasped as a radical alternative. In the case of Ernst Cassirer, for instance, an account is offered of the nature of mythic thinking especially powerful for the way it brings out the radical kind of metaphorical *identification* mythic thinking involves. Cassirer could see very clearly that

> *for mythic thinking there is much more in metaphor than*
> *a bare "substitution", a mere rhetorical figure of speech;*
> *that what seems to our subsequent reflection as a sheer*
> *transcription is mythically conceived as a genuine and direct*
> *identification.*[25]

Were we to assume a recovery of mythic thinking in our own time, one could refer this account to the metaphors Graves himself applies to the Goddess in speaking of *the dark edge of her double-axe* or *blood from her shadowy hand*. However, like Eliade, Cassirer was elaborating on what he saw as an *archaic* mode of thinking, very distant from our own time. In contrast with that former mode, modern thinking thrives on its unique *separation* from "the hard realistic powers"[26] of the mythic image. In the modern-day production of Holderling and of Keats particularly, "the mythic power of insight breaks forth again in its full intensity and objectifying power"[27], but it does so in "the world of poetry . . . as a world of illusion and fantasy".[28] Cassirer sees this ultimately as "liberation", since word and mythic image are now used by the mind as "organs of its own, and [the mind] thereby recognizes them *for what they really are*: forms of its own self-revelation."[29]

From this last remark, one sees where Cassirer finally stands. It had always been for him, as he insinuates elsewhere, a matter of "the direction of the subject's interest"[30], even where it *looks* like objectivity has been conferred on the mythic process, as where he says of it:

> *all spontaneity is **felt as** receptivity, all creativity as being, and every product of subjectivity **as so much** substantiality . . .* [31]

One needs to bring out the emphasis that is implicitly made here. It was for Cassirer a necessity for humankind, in its archaic experience, to *assume* an objective presence behind its mythical invention, for only in that way could an idealization of spiritual reality be conceived that would justify all future expression of the human spirit and its ever-progressive elaboration; thus

> *the Word **has** to be conceived, in the mythic mode, as a substantive being and power, before it can be comprehended as an ideal instrument, an organon of the mind, and as a fundamental function in the construction and development of spiritual reality.* [32]

In this way mythic thinking is finally rationalized to fit in fully with our modern experience, and it is in the spirit ultimately of a *modern* teleology, in diametric contrast with Eliade's direction, that Cassirer involves us in his extraordinary accounts of the power of mythic identification, paradoxically among the most aesthetically satisfying formulations we have.[33] The effect is ambiguous to the point where we can speak of a philosophical *tour de force*. Cassirer continues to the end to insist on the radical uniqueness of mythic thinking, but from a point of view that, paradoxically, affirms his and our hard-earned separation and freedom from its peculiarly captive mode of operating.

*   *   *

Like Cassirer, Owen Barfield also welcomed our necessary freedom from the phenomenal experience with which archaic man originally identified both at the level of the mythic image and of the word. It was part of *his* view, however, that what archaic man was about was not just mythical invention:

> *Men do not invent those mysterious relations between*
> *separate external objects, and between objects and feelings*
> *or ideas . . . The language of primitive man reports them as*
> *direct perceptual experience.*[34]

It was Barfield's special purpose (at a time contemporary with Cassirer) to claim that *originally* an objective presence does indeed lie behind the mythic image. This view is at the basis of his statement that "Mythology is the ghost of concrete meaning."[35] Barfield grounded this view on an elaborate etymological approach to the history of words, from which we gather that archaic man *must* have been involved in the phenomena, and in the representation of the phenomena, in the direct way Barfield describes:

> *you may imply, if you choose . . . that the earliest words in*
> *use were 'the names of sensible, material objects' and nothing*
> *more; only, in that case, you must suppose the 'sensible objects'*
> *themselves to have been something more; you must suppose*
> *that they were not, as they appear to be at present, isolated*
> *or detached from thinking and feeling.*[36]

Archaic representation involves, in fact, a whole *different* figuration, one that reflects "an awareness which we no longer have, of *an extra-sensory link* between the percipient and the representations."[37] Such a link (referred to 'mana' or 'waken') is "anterior to the individuality of [both] persons and objects"[38]—it presupposes originally "experiencing the phenomena [themselves] as representations"[39]. On that basis Barfield fills out the corollary understanding, that "This extra-sensory participation of the percipient in the representation involves a similar link between the representations themselves and of course between one percipient and another."[40] Barfield, quoting Durkheim, takes it still farther back to

> *collective mental states of extreme emotional intensity, in*
> *which representation is as yet undifferentiated from the*

movements and actions which make the communion towards
which it tends a reality to the group. Their participation in
it is so effectively lived that it is not yet properly imagined.[41]

Like Cassirer, Barfield sees a long progression in freedom from these
phenomenally captive origins. We have, in the meantime, separated out
from this experience, and a concomitant of the process has been that the
phenomena themselves have detached from the original element in which
both humankind and the phenomena were at one time involved. Thus,

As consciousness develops into self-consciousness, the [now]
remembered phenomena become detached and liberated from
their originals and so, as images, are in some measure at
man's disposal.[42]

From here Barfield plots out two courses. On the one hand, there is the
direction of modern-day science, which today dictates experiencing the
phenomena "non-representationally, as objects in their own right, existing
independently of human consciousness".[43] This leads to the idea of the
manipulation of nature as just so many objects, to be tossed about at will,
and to what Barfield calls "idolatry", "involving in the end the elimination
of those last vestiges of original participation, which . . . survive [even] in
our language".[44] There is, however, another direction that follows from
understanding that, as humankind was *once* involved (without its will) in
the phenomena, so (on the basis of freedom) it can be *again*. This leads
to the equally extraordinary idea—at the other extreme from scientific
manipulation—of a new Creation in which "man himself now stands in a
'directionally creator relation'"[45] to the phenomena.

Something of *this* direction is already suggested, Barfield claims, in a
"high" or "prophetic" art, in those instances where "a real analogy" is pursued
"between metaphorical usage and original participation".[46] However, one is
only able to *build* on this analogy

if, but only if, we admit that in the course of the earth's
history, something like a Divine Word has been gradually
clothing itself with the humanity it first gradually
created—so that what was first spoken by God may
eventually be respoken by man.[47]

And for this to be the case, Nature, and not my own fancy, must be my representation, for then,

> *I know that what so stands is not my poor temporal*
> *personality, but the Divine Name in the unfathomable*
> *depths behind it. And if I strive to produce a work of art, I*
> *cannot then do otherwise than strive humbly to create more*
> *nearly as that creates*[48]

Barfield thus brings us back, ultimately, to a cosmogony that would open the door for someone like Graves to find acceptance for the relationship to Nature that *he* claimed, except that what Barfield had in mind was a creative direction that was but "rudimentary as yet" and "mainly impulsive so far".[49] It is unlikely that he would have seen even in Graves's extraordinary output evidence of the "final" participation Barfield could look forward to. In the meantime, the creation of poetry, though implicitly *involved* in such a prospect, would seem to continue to import our present distance from it:

> *For it is the peculiarity of metaphorical language that, at*
> *first sight, it does often resemble very closely the language of*
> *participation; though upon closer examination its existence is*
> *seen to depend precisely on the absence of participation.*[50]

It was as far as the modern theory of myth would go to support Graves in his claim.

*   *   *

There was, what's more, to be direct *opposition* to Graves's claim, from another area of the modern theory of myth, where the science of psychoanalysis comes into it. That Graves's poetic creation was centred in the Goddess made complete sense in the natural-cosmological terms of myth, but all that had, in turn, been fully rationalized by the psychoanalysis that confidently proclaimed these terms mere projections of the unconscious. In the natural-cosmological terms in which Graves pursues his production, to embrace death, as his solar hero embraces death, is to embrace the power to return from death: a goal that psychoanalysis could easily refer to the need in every man to sublimate an unconscious desire for incest with the Mother. As Jung explains:

*sun myths and rebirth myths devise every conceivable kind of
mother-analogy for the purpose of canalizing the libido into
new forms and effectively preventing it from regressing to
actual incest.*[51]

Freud and Jung could also explain Graves's emphasis on the darker
problematic aspect of the Goddess and Her Creation and why it *must*
figure in his representation, for the Mother has the power both to give and
to take away, as Randall Jarrell was especially intent on pointing out:

*That all affect, libido, mana should be concentrated in this
one figure of the Mother-Muse; that love and sexuality
should be inseparably intermingled with fear, violence,
destruction in this "female spider"—that the loved one should
be, necessarily, the Bad Mother who, necessarily, deserts and
destroys the child; that the child should permit against her
no conscious aggression of any kind, and intend his **cruel,
capricious, incontinent,** his **bitch, vixen, hag,** to be neither
condemnation nor invective, but only fascinated description
of the loved and worshiped Mother and Goddess, She-Who-
Must-be-Obeyed—all this is very interesting and very
unoriginal. One encounters a rigorous, profound, and quite
unparalleled understanding of such cases as Graves's in the
many volumes of Freud . . . [and] . . . in Volume VII of Jung's
Collected Works, in the second part of the essay entitled "The
Relations between the Ego and the Unconscious."*[52]

Even the 'objectivity' that could be claimed for the independent power
of Graves's images, seeming as they do to come from an otherworld of
their own accord, is accounted for, in the psychoanalytic view, by the nature
of the "archetypes" that offer themselves as "analogies" to the instinctual
processes, for

*The archetypes are the numinous, structural elements of the
psyche **and possess a certain autonomy** and specific energy
which enables them to attract out of the conscious mind those
contents which are best suited to themselves.*[53]

The *individual* archetypal symbol—whether sea-serpent, or subjected lion, or even the bloody hand of Graves's Goddess—according to Jung

> *carries conviction and at the same time expresses the content*
> *of that conviction. It is able to do this because of the numen,*
> *the specific energy stored up in the archetype.*[54]

Not that the creation of these analogies does not constitute

> *a serious problem because, as we have said, they must be*
> *ideas which attract the libido.*[55]

Hence, the tremendous significance Jung attaches to the creative fantasy, which

> *is continually engaged in producing analogies to instinctual*
> *processes in order to free the libido from sheer instinctuality*
> *by guiding it towards analogical ideas.*[56]

In the end such creation, according to Jung, will also *necessarily* produce faith, for

> *Experience of the archetype is not only impressive, it*
> *seizes and possesses the whole personality, and is naturally*
> *productive of faith.*[57]

*   *   *

No less than Jung was Joseph Campbell ready to allow for the psychic inevitability of the initiatory images that were formerly supplied from myth. So much so that without the supports from myth, these images *must* be reproduced in dream, for the same reason that Jung cites, that otherwise there could only be instinctual regression.[58] It was *also* Campbell's view, however, that a crucial distinction would have to be introduced between the *sources* of dream and those of myth (a view that is paralleled in the distinction Graves introduces between poems and dreams[59]):

*But if we are to grasp the full value of the materials,
we must note that myths are not exactly comparable to
dream ...*

*we are in the presence rather of immense consciousness than
of darkness ...*

controlled and intended statements *of certain spiritual
principles ....* [60]

What's more, on the basis of his own vast research into these mythological materials, Campbell could bring himself to the point of formulating the one great principle that underlies them all:

*Briefly formulated, the universal doctrine teaches that all the
visible structures of the world—all **things** and beings—are
the effects of a ubiquitous **power** out of which they rise,
which supports and fills them during the period of their
manifestation, and back into which they must ultimately
dissolve.* [61]

One notes in this passage the focus on "all *things* and beings" that are "the effects" of this "ubiquitous power". *Objectivity* is, in this way, restored to the mythical process. And it is in this spirit that Campbell throws himself into his own engagement with the mythical experience, insofar as this touches on the Goddess:

*the meeting with the goddess (who is incarnate in every
woman) is the final test of the talent of the hero ... She ...
is the life of everything that lives ... the death of everything
that* dies *... The whole round of existence is accomplished
within her sway .... Thus she unites the "good" and the
"bad", exhibiting the two modes of the remembered mother,
not as personal only, but as universal .... not primarily
as "good" and "bad" with respect to his childlike human
convenience, his weal and woe, but as **the law and image of
the nature of being**.* [62]

At another point, Campbell will describe it as an evolutionary passage

> *from the infantile illusions of "good" and "evil" to an*
> *experience of the majesty of* **cosmic law**, *purged of hope and*
> *fear, and at peace in the understanding of the revelation of*
> *being.*[63]

Here, we will feel, is all the confirming support Graves would have needed for his own strong claims, for like him Campbell assumes that is it both possible and imperative to recover the mythical experience now. Campbell was pursuing his own view at this time altogether independently of Graves, who had published *The White Goddess* only a year before Campbell himself brought out *The Hero with a Thousand Faces* (from which these excerpts are taken.) The concurrence is extraordinary and might have given pause to Jarrell when he brought forward his critique of Graves some seven or eight years later. An entirely independent case had been made for the objectivity of the process that Jarrell, following Jung, had preconcluded to be purely subjective. In fact, with Campbell, as with Graves, it is precisely the point that the psychoanalytic patient must learn to transcend his own personal situation by entering fully into the universal process. (For Graves it is the poet's task to lead him there.) Then he would see that the "good" and the "bad" that so obsess and tie down his mind, and that are the basis of his "hope" and "fear", arise as the principles upon which the order of Nature itself is founded. Unity, if anywhere, will be found there. This was already understood in the Romantic context out of which Graves was writing: "fear" (in "To Juan") being ultimately subsumed in "love". It is how Wordsworth himself presents it, who also saw it as a case of refusing the regression back to death; only in Wordsworth, it is the universal forms of Nature that assure his passage through:

> [I] *rather did with jealousy shrink back*
> *From every combination that might aid*
> *The tendency, too potent in itself,*
> *Of habit to enslave the mind, I mean*
> *Oppress it by the laws of vulgar sense,*
> *And substitute a universe of death,*
> *The falsest of all worlds, in place of that*
> *Which is divine and true. To fear and love,*
> *To love, as first and chief, for there fear ends,*

> Be this ascribed; to early intercourse,
> In presence of sublime and lovely Forms,
> With the adverse principles of pain and joy,
> Evil, as one is rashly named by those
> Who know not what they say. From love, for here
> Do we begin and end, all grandeur comes,
> All truth and beauty, from pervading love,
> That gone, we are as dust.[64]

Campbell himself assumes an ultimate peace from the unity of the two experiences as these come together in the Mothering Goddess. Likewise, in "To Juan" as we have seen, Graves assumes an ultimate unity, but in him the duality persists, if only because *he* was working this experience out immediately and directly through the form of being he saw himself as having at that moment. Hence the persistence in *his* representations of the Goddess of the dual aspect of Her involvement with him. It was in any case Graves's view (at least for the longest time; there would be a further evolution in his view towards the end of his career[65]) that man had always been and would have to remain in a dualistic relationship with his Creatress, for

> Man is a demi-god: he always has either one foot or the
> other in the grave; woman is divine because she can keep
> both her feet always in the same place, whether in the sky, in
> the underworld, or on this earth. Man envies her and tells
> himself lies about his own completeness, and thereby makes
> himself miserable; because if he is divine she is not even a
> demi-goddess—she is mere nymph and his love for her turns
> to scorn and hate.[66]

III

What are we to make, then, of the insistent efforts of Campbell and Graves to announce the prospect of a new mythical experience in the modern world, one founded on the basis of Nature, in defiance of the rigidly qualifying strictures of the many acknowledged modern theorists of myth? In Graves's view, inability, or unwillingness, to recognize that the time was ripe for a fresh breakthrough into mythical experience has a clear historical explanation. It is the end-result of an intellectual pretension to resolve the almost intolerable duality in which man is naturally placed, by which he has, over centuries, rationalized himself outside the sphere of Nature, and so outside the Goddess's order.[67] Referring himself directly to the mythical record, Graves put it as follows:

> [man] *is divine not in his single person but in his twinhood.*
> *As Osiris, the Spirit of the Waxing Year, he is always*
> *jealous of the weird, Set, the Spirit of the Waning Year, and*
> *vice-versa; he cannot be both of them at once except by an*
> *intellectual effort that destroys his humanity, and this is the*
> *fundamental defect of the Apollonian or Jehovistic cult.*[68]

By this "cult" Graves had in mind the longstanding effects of the decisive intervention over the course of the 1st millennium B.C. of patriarchal influences that had been slowly seeping into both the Hellenic and Hebraic cultures, from which our own Western experience derives. War had been declared in Heaven with the conflict between Jehovah and the Great Goddess of 7th century B.C. Jerusalem, which led to Her displacement by this Universal God, and

> [t]*he result of envisaging this God of pure meditation, the*
> *Universal Mind still premised by the most reputable modern*
> *philosophers, and enthroning him above Nature as essential*
> *Truth and Goodness was not an altogether happy one.*[69]
>
> *Then came the early Greek philosophers who were strongly*
> *opposed to magical poetry as threatening their new religion*
> *of logic, and under their influence a rational poetic language*
> *(now called the Classical) was elaborated in honour of their*
> *patron Apollo and imposed on the world as the last word in*
> *spiritual illumination.*[70]

Not that the elaborate indictment of Western tradition that we get from Graves in *The White Goddess* does not still leave him with the challenge of effectively harnessing the energy associated with his engagement with the Goddess. For without a deliberate, conscious reining of this energy, the need for which Graves himself acknowledges, there is the real danger of being destroyed by it, as Graves's poems themselves bear witness.[71] The purpose of the post-Exilic religious reformation that substituted Jehovah for the Goddess had been precisely to disassociate man from the destructive influence of his commitment to the 'darker' side of the Goddess's claims on him. Thus a recent reader of Graves, considering the challenge of this crucial opposition, between the "voracious life-giving energy" on the one hand and "the rationalizing element" on the other, concludes:

> *the issue is how successfully the two key elements can be*
> *accommodated without the energy being destroyed.*[72]

One keeps this universal energy of Nature under control, according to this reader, "through mythic or religious ritual".[73] Ted Hughes, a modern poet whom one should be linking with Graves, is further recruited on behalf of this view.[74] However, it is truer to say that this force of mythic or religious ritual, if it is effective, must *by its own operation* control the energy. We have an especially powerful instance of the operation of this force (of mythic ritual) in Graves's poem, "She Is No Liar":

> *She is no liar, yet she will wash away*
> *Honey from her lips, blood from her shadowy hand,*
> *And, dressed at dawn in clean white robes will say,*
> *Trusting the ignorant world to understand:*
> *'Such things no longer are; this is today.'*

*   *   *

"Such things no longer are;"—Graves's view was that modern man had come into a new age in which all that had formerly obstructed the Goddess's power to direct his life had been left behind. Graves's faith that this was so was categorical, and the situation could not be reversed for him. With a characteristic freedom from the effects of history, he could say with complete assurance and with a complete finality, in "The End of Play":

> *We have reached the end of pastime . . .*
> *. . . . .*
> *We have at last ceased idling . . .*
> *. . . . .*
> *We tell no lies now, at last cannot be*

> *The rogues we were—so evilly linked in sense*
> *With what we scrutinized . . .* [75]

One is astounded by the unitary view Graves takes of history, which allowed him to affirm this faith and to install himself, very simply, without any further sense of any conflict that might subvert or continue to wear away at his vision.[76] It is the measure of a formidable single-mindedness in Graves that in this view he stands perhaps alone.[77] All had been for him a matter of the suppression merely of the Goddess-culture, which had remained inexpungeable and irrepressible, so that it was only a matter of time before that culture would openly affirm itself again. Hence the account of his purposes as Graves shared this with his audience in his 1957 Y.M.H.A. lecture:

> *It is enough for me to quote the myths and give them*
> *historical sense: tracing a certain faith through its historical*
> *vicissitudes—from when it was paramount, to when it*
> *has been driven underground and preserved by witches,*
> *travelling minstrels, remote country-folk and a few secret*
> *heretics to the newly established religion.*[78]

This faith had been restored again in the twentieth century principally through Graves himself, though Graves further cites, as indirect evidence, the fact that the Virgin Mary could now in the established religions "legitimately be saluted as 'the Queen of Heaven'—the very title borne by Rahab (the Goddess Astarte), against whom the prophet Jeremiah declaimed in the name of his monotheistic Father-god Jehovah."[79]

Graves's assurance in proclaiming this faith is in large part a feature of its surviving power as he saw this operating especially in British culture. Thus he emphasizes that "the Queen of Heaven with her retinue of female saints had a far greater hold in the popular imagination between the Crusades and the Civil War than either the Father or the Son."[80] This Thunder-God, as Graves presents Him, did get re-instated at the time of the Puritan Revolution in England, but it is characteristic of Graves that he sees this God's triumph as "short-lived"; it could never have withstood "the stubborn conviction" among the British that Britain was "a Mother Country, not a Father-land".[81] Writing out of this view as well as the power of his own experience, Graves has simply no inclination to consider that perhaps Western civilization as a whole had been through a deeper conflict and a deeper agony. However, Ted Hughes, who was (up to a point) a professed disciple of Graves, took a very different view of the matter in his book, *Shakespeare and the Goddess of Complete Being.* There it is Hughes's special insistence that man *continues* in conflict with himself over the Goddess, and no one saw that this would be so with greater clarity than did Shakespeare, whose case *about* the conflict, according to Hughes, has still to be heard—through his plays.[82] It is the conflict of the Reformation itself, behind which Hughes, like Graves, sees the conflict of Jehovah and the great Goddess of 7th century B.C. Jerusalem.[83] It is, according to Hughes, the *one* conflict in which Shakespeare was engaged from the beginning of his career to its end.

Macbeth, for Hughes, is the play in which this conflict comes to fullest expression, being also the turning point in Shakespeare's own dealings with it. In his earlier tragedies, including *Hamlet* and *King Lear*, Shakespeare had already dramatized the process by which his heroes suddenly succumb to the "delusion"[84] of thinking their beloved ones unholy. In this they pretend to do *without* the Goddess's all-supporting life by charging *Her*, as it were, with dark and unholy motives. Now, in *Macbeth*, the nature of this charge is fully exposed for the erroneous "Tarquinian" madness that it represents, for which the hero must be destroyed. It is the hero's rational "Adonis" world of "Puritan-style ideals"[85]—which underlies that madness—that must be destroyed, by the irrepressible life of the Goddess. Macbeth's real crime in this respect precedes his appearance in the play and is the measure of his value as a representation of the more recent Shakespearean tragic heroes who precede him. Macbeth must be set right by being driven to destroy his Adonis-nature, murdering Duncan and seeking to murder Banquo in the process, only because all are guilty of rejecting the Goddess. However, up to that point Shakespeare's heroes have *thought* themselves justified in their charge, and it is the power that this thought exercises over them that so impresses Hughes and (so Hughes supposes) Shakespeare:

> *Even after it has been capsized in spectacular fashion by that*
> *irrational secret-sharer [Tarquin] rising from beneath it,*
> *that point of view, of the Adonis ego, though it no longer has*
> *any control over its actions, always retains the ability, like*
> *a ship's gimbal, to think itself rational (at least, it does so*
> *up to the point at which the ego is destroyed, and a new self,*
> *neither Adonis nor Tarquin, emerges—as begins to happen*
> *in* **King Lear**).

It is Hughes's argument that Western man continues to lie somewhere in the general area in which Shakespeare's tragic heroes find themselves before *Macbeth* comes through to set right all delusion. The challenge for Hughes lies in the fact that rational man must learn to see him*self* in Macbeth and indeed in every Shakespearean tragic hero who comes before him. Shakespeare had given direct and complete expression to Western man's judgment of the Goddess, only to bring out, in fact, the *tragedy* in that judgment:

> *What Shakespeare* **goes on** *to reveal is that in destroying her* [the Goddess] *he destroys himself and brings down Heaven and Earth in ruins.*[86]

But this is, for Hughes in any case

> *the inevitable crime of Civilization, or even the inevitable crime of consciousness.*[87] *Certainly the crime of the Reformation—the "offense/From Luther until now/That has driven a culture mad" as Auden phrased it.*[88]

But what if this sudden shift in consciousness in the hero, into judgment, turned out *not* to be some misguided "offense" stemming from "delusion", whether this is seen as criminal or tragic (which is to say, in the latter case, stemming from "error"), but a new *objective* development, which Shakespeare took that seriously because it seemed to him it *had* become the reality. Everything *had*, disastrously, fallen apart, and all because the kind of "love" Shakespeare's tragic hero had known with his beloved *had* failed and a new perception of the extent of human depravity come into view. If this is so, the story would not then be (as it appears to be on the surface) about "rejection of the Female" or "the Puritan fear of female sexuality", but about some still *deeper* failure or change, something still *more* to reckon with than either Graves or Hughes seemed ready to acknowledge: a matter of coming to terms with a deeper degree of depravity than we had supposed ourselves subject to and that could, therefore, potentially only confound us the more. This is to shift the focus I have been pursuing thus far into a still more problematic depth—"fear", as in the case of Macbeth, originating, in this conception, from a deeper instability and a deeper derangement. I shall thereby be raising a still *further* issue that would seem to arise from the course Western experience has taken, which throws into doubt whether Graves's (and Hughes's) conception of "love" and of the "Female" or Goddess takes us far enough or as far as we need to take ourselves, if we are to avoid any deeper subversion than what Hughes claimed has characterized Western experience thus far.[89]

II

THE WORST OF DEPRAVITY

For, what shall we say *is* Macbeth's "fear" and *what* the violence of conception that takes him over, to the point where, it would seem, he has *no choice but* to yield?

> ***why** do I yield to that suggestion*
> *Whose horrid image doth unfix my hair*
> *And make my seated heart knock at my ribs*
> *Against the use of nature?*

Hughes and Graves would have us believe that this is the Goddess taking Macbeth over, possessing him in order to avenge Herself against him for the crime he has committed against Her.[1] Macbeth's crime lies in rejecting the Goddess by turning away from Her sensual creation, for which *he* has judged Her unholy. But does Macbeth, when viewed more closely, represent the *judgment* of sensuality, or does he not rather represent the complete *indulgence* of it, along with Lady Macbeth, and indeed all the characters in this play, with whom he is united in a complete sensual ambition? To what extent all are immersed in the darkest sensuality in *Macbeth* can be gleaned from what James Calderwood has to say about the opening battle scene in which a universal ambition is drastically played out:

> *As priestly leaders of the royal forces Macbeth and Banquo*
> *preside over a ceremony in which the Scots are purged and*
> *exalted by the shedding of sacred blood in the King's cause*
> *even as mankind was once purged by the shedding of Christ's*
> *sacred blood on Golgotha. Only men in battle, who bathe in*
> *their own and their enemies' blood, are able to partake bodily*
> *and symbolically in the divinity of the state. As Christ's*
> *blood streaming in the firmament offers everlasting life to*

> *the worshiper, so the sacred blood of battle yields immortality*
> *to Macbeth and Banquo as Bellona's deathless bridegrooms*
> *and as participants in the greater life of the state (Macbeth*
> *will be king, Banquo will beget kings).*[2]

We are, with *Macbeth*, in a world that, in its original situation—before the tragic breakdown—is complete as perhaps no other is in Shakespeare. It is a complete world because of the *grounds* of its justification, archaic as those grounds certainly are, involving human nature as they do in the complete depth of its violent sensuality. From *this* starting position (in itself an extraordinary feat of cultural anamnesis on his part) Shakespeare had a point to make, as we shall see. As Calderwood explains, war is intrinsic to this archaic world, being literally its means of divination and of sanctification, for,

> *It enables kings to look into the entrails of violence and see if*
> *they are still sacred to the gods.* [3]

The Challenger in this world is thus the King's necessary and welcome counterpart, since *he* raises, by his own daring rebellion, the issue of the king's sacredness, which must be continually justified anew, and in this sense

> *each fight with a challenger who would kill him is a test of*
> *the king's sacredness: will the golden bough remain on its*
> *branch? Will the god's strange heart still beat within him?* [4]

The seemingly complete extent of the violence, as we have it in *Macbeth*, represents the fullest measure of that justification. In fact, so complete is the violence at a certain point we are *un*able to distinguish the king's challenger from his defender. As Calderwood puts it, "it is a scene of undifferentiated brutality" for "all are bloodily one in battle".[5] But this is as it ideally should be, for only out of the deepest engagement in these terms—the deepest violence and the deepest effort of will on both sides, will justification come. Thus in the context of this battle

> *violence erodes cultural distinctions, even the fundamental*
> *distinction between "us" and "them", yet its function is*

> *to reaffirm and recreate distinctions by singling out, not*
> *scapegoat victims, but heroic survivors.*[6]

For in this context, "surviving is a sacred achievement".[7]

It is the chief value of the warrior in this world that he can survive this scene of battle, as Macbeth and Banquo survive it, and in doing so justify himself. The king's justification thus follows from the warrior's own. If the warrior is happy to serve his king, this is because, as Harry Berger Jr. points out, it is the king who provides him with the "bloody occasions"—and so "the reputation and honors" that follow from success on those "occasions"—by which the warrior seeks to prove and to justify himself.[8] It is easy to see, at the same time, the constant threat that might be posed to the king by the pride of the warrior on whose extreme prowess the king must rely for his justification.[9] We can see how ideas of service and love would then enter into this context, to safeguard against overweening pride, and as it were to sublimate the threat of violence. It was the view of Johannes Huizinga that these ideas come into play in the time of the Middle Ages (in which Shakespeare's action is set) as a purely formal code of conventions, deliberately constructed and imposed on a tendency to ferocious passion that is everywhere present at that time because of its reigning quality of pride.[10] Thus

> *Love has to be elevated to the height of a rite. The*
> *overflowing violence of passion demands it. Only by*
> *constructing a system of forms and rules for the violent*
> *emotions can barbarity be escaped.*[11]

> *The passionate and violent soul of the age . . . could not*
> *dispense with the severest rules and the strictest formalism.*
> *All emotions required a rigid system of conventional forms,*
> *for without them passion and ferocity would have made*
> *havoc of life.*[12]

And so we may approach those extraordinary moments in Shakespeare's play when Macbeth and Lady Macbeth formally express their obeisance to Duncan in spite of Macbeth's extreme achievement in battle that seems to redound more to his own honor:

Duncan.   *O worthiest cousin!*
The sin of my ingratitude even now
Was heavy upon me: thou art so far before,
That swiftest wing of recompense is slow
To overtake thee. Would thou hadst less deserved,
That the proportion both of thanks and payment
Might have been mine! only I have left to say,
More is thy due than more than all can pay.

Macbeth.   *The service and the loyalty I owe,*
In doing it, pays itself. Your highness' part
Is to receive our duties: and our duties
Are to your throne and state children and servants;
Which do but what they should, by doing every thing
Safe toward your love and honour.

Duncan.   *Welcome hither:*
I have begun to plant thee, and will labour
To make thee full of growing.

*   *   *

Duncan. *See, see, our honoured hostess!*
The love that follows us sometime is our trouble,
Which still we thank as love . . .

Lady Macbeth.   *All our service*
In every point twice done, and then done double,
Were poor and single business to contend
Against those honours deep and broad wherewith
Your majesty loads our house: for those of old,
And the late dignities heaped up to them,
We rest your hermits.

We are setting aside for the present the effect on these moments (in the way *we* actually see them) of the evil intention in Macbeth and in Lady Macbeth that has *also* disturbingly penetrated this world. Here I wish to propose that the play's original experience transcends Huizinga's notion of a deliberately constructed culture, as if sentiments of love and service were for the most part, as he argues, only put on, only moving *towards* being essential, if no *less* crucial for that.[13] On the contrary, there seems a case for saying that service and love are themselves an intrinsic part of the unified whole of the original *Macbeth*-world—as *much* a feature of what holds that world together and makes it complete, as the extreme violence on which that world is predicated. It is a logical predication, for if it *is* the extreme violence that makes the *Macbeth*-world complete—because only such violence creates the necessary basis for a complete justification—so too must the love that finally supports that justification be complete.

We are to imagine an *original* condition of culture in which utmost sensual depths of dark violence are perfectly expressed and perfectly contained by the love and service that support and motivate that violence. It is what we glimpse in those moments of obeisance that unite Macbeth and Lady Macbeth in the same expression of will. These moments present the characters in the image of what they *were* until now, borne up by love and service. Only, the characters have now separated out from the reality and so give us merely the image. So too was Macbeth in battle at one time borne up by love and service, until things changed, though we are only given insight into Macbeth's love in hypocritical fashion later, in the words he uses to justify slaying Duncan's guards *after* he has murdered Duncan:

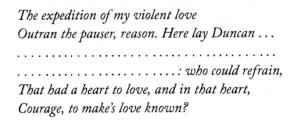

The expedition of my violent love
Outran the pauser, reason. Here lay Duncan . . .
. . . .
. . . .*: who could refrain,*
That had a heart to love, and in that heart,
Courage, to make's love known?

Here is our glimpse into the principal original motive of this world, now gone preternaturally awry. All *was* formerly a unity—the violence and the love quite *one*, until the supporting love goes out of it. Macbeth finds himself in battle immersed in an extreme violence, fighting the King's cause suddenly *without* the love that had borne him up in his will to that point. That fact is momentously registered through the contrast with Banquo *who himself has battled no less fiercely or completely* but who comes away from his engagement as Macbeth could have expected to—supported still by love.[14] Herein lies the horror of the separation of "foul" from "fair" from the former unity in which they lay; what was "fair" and should have remained "fair", and does remain "fair" for Banquo (the "foul" being incorporated into *it* for

him) has become simply "foul" for Macbeth. His complete violence of will
has been released from the supporting reality of love, with the effect that,
without its support and without its defense, he is now overwhelmed by the
violence of his will. In this complete world, Macbeth's will has identified
with the King in fighting his cause; stripped now of any further underlying
motive of love, Macbeth *becomes* in his will the very King with whom he
is identified in his defense. His very identity has gone over to *being* King,
and he meets the recognition from the Witches that this is so with fear
because in that moment for the first time he consciously recognizes that
this is so. His displacement of Duncan as King has already taken place and
so *must* lead to murder.

What Calderwood's account overlooks is that the situation in *Macbeth*
has altered—preternaturally so, so that we view all that we are given in the
beginning of the play as it were in double form. We see on the one hand
what the *Macbeth*-world is originally constituted of and at the same time
measure a seismic alteration in it, which has everything, in fact, different
and looking different. That effect extends to the imagery of Golgotha that
the Sergeant elaborates in his account of the battle, which *seems* to positively
identify the blood of the battling warriors with that of Christ, but *in fact*
registers an effect wildly inappropriate. Calderwood himself acknowledges
the association as a "grotesque collusion".[15] This is generally the case with
all that is presented in the play's opening scenes. A new *difference* has come
into it and to some extent come into the consciousness of all the characters
who have witnessed Macbeth's action on the battlefield, though, being
unused to any other world, none are in the position to recognize what that
difference imports. Nevertheless, it is clearly present in the consciousness of
the *effect* of Macbeth's deeds, which project him as bearing the very identity
of the Rebel or Challenger with whom he has literally united in battle, and
who, by this perverted route, through Macbeth, has *become* King:

> Ross. *The king hath happily received, Macbeth,*
> *The news of **thy** success: and when he reads*
> ***Thy personal venture in the rebels' fight**,*
> *His wonders and his praises do contend*
> ***Which should be thine or his**: silenced with that,*
> *In viewing o'er the rest o' the selfsame day,*
> *He finds thee in the stout Norweyan ranks,*
> *Nothing afeard of what thyself didst make,*
> ***Strange images** of death. As thick as hail*

Came post with post, and every one did bear
Thy *praises in his kingdom's great defence,*
And poured them down before him.

Macbeth is originally identified with a form of extreme expression in violent will that has been the supporting power of his society until now while the substance of love also motivated it. The sudden *withdrawal* of this substance of love now leaves the will to operate on its own. Macbeth is suddenly left without any defense against that will, which being as extreme as the love that contained it, cannot be resisted. The human will has come free in its essential depravity, and no defense in human nature is able to protect against it. Thus the horror and the fear that overcome Macbeth who is left grappling helplessly with himself, for the utmost violence of his will is bound to overpower him. It is the measure Shakespeare has taken of the depths of human depravity; he has traced it back to this original situation when love had all in check. Then, dramatizing the moment in which the primal human will separates out from love, he shows with a perfect horror how little power human nature on its own can have over this will. To make the point with an even greater effect of horror, he then brings into his exposition the power that the *ideal* of love might still be thought to have over the will—for love has now *become* an ideal, is no longer the governing reality. This is where Macbeth imagines the angels judging his murderous intentions before he gets down to the murder. Here Shakespeare brings love back into it, with all the power it could exercise over the mind *as* an ideal, and bringing it back he demonstrates how the ideal in this case can have no power over that will. Macbeth's most evolved Imaginations of that ideal, by which his projected deed is judged, do have the effect of rousing his conscience but can have no effect in keeping him from seeing the deed through.[16]

What can Shakespeare's purpose have been in depicting this primal scene if not to cite, as evidence, the sheer extent of violent sensuality that is there deep down in the human make-up, if only as an atavistic survival today? Starting from an archaic world, which Shakespeare in his own way recovers, he shows how sensuality in this degree would *have* to be restrained by a power of love that is there originally in the same degree. He assumes, as his own mythographer of the archaic, that formerly this was so, and then deliberately takes us back, to that fateful moment when separation from love is brought about. The sensuality that had until then been kept in check now subverts disastrously from the sheer extent of its expression, its completeness. Having once subserved the "mana" of love, it is now exposed for the horrible depravity it constitutes when left to its own purposes and acts in its own right. It has the power of a pure unchecked somatic *disturbance* that can only take Macbeth away with itself in his mind.[17] This is what absorbs him in fear from the start, and what keeps him in fear throughout. And so his famous visions, which only have the *content* of moral imagination when in *substance* they are woven out of his disturbance, so that the imagination of Duncan in his virtues *must* give way to those of the daggers that rush him into the murder without impediment. Those visions continue, of course, beyond the murder, and are continually at play in Macbeth[18], until, by the sheer force of his destructive will, he manages in a sense to kill them, destroying his whole human nature in the process. In comparison with Macbeth, Lady Macbeth one might say has only "played" at being possessed, is not as fully engaged, is herself in dismay at the diabolic visions that continue in her husband.[19] She goes mad ultimately less from the influence of demonic possession than from her horror of Macbeth's complete separation from her, the only person with whom, in this world of violent debacle, she could have retained *any* form of hopeful human complicity.

II

The action in *Macbeth* is only the most extreme and the most horrid case of a tragic pattern in Shakespeare that is typical of this phase. We feel the connection back to the other tragedies especially where Macbeth and Lady Macbeth are suddenly presented to us, at the scene of the murder, in their fundamental innocence. It is the effect that so impressed John Middleton Murry:

> *That a man and woman should, in the very act of heinous*
> *and diabolical murder, reveal themselves as naïve and*
> *innocent, convulses our morality and awakens in us thoughts*
> *beyond the reaches of our souls.*[20]

Innocence is the fundamental condition of Shakespeare's tragic characters, when one compares them to the villains via whom their destinies are galvanized. Villains though they have *become*, Macbeth and Lady Macbeth are still innocent, and so tragic, and the lesson they dramatize is therefore the more horrifying because of that. Their fate is typical of the Shakespearean tragic action: innocent as they are, they are now subverted by their own sensuality, which they had *thought* love, and which was indeed love until their condition altered. The reality of sensual life has suddenly become pretension, and we see now that they are *composed* of sensuality and are judged for it. Sensuality, separated from love, turns into depravity.

The moment when this alteration takes place is the moment of evil, which strikes like lightning, immediately and with an overwhelming violence, because, at any and every cost, the separation from sensuality must now take place—for whatever evolutionary reasons we may divine. The Shakespearean villain, from this perspective, is merely party to the process, a mechanism merely who adds to the effect of the process that must now go forward. Shakespeare's tragic characters remaining, as they do, profoundly attached to the sensuality and to the love that they have known, which is the only love they *can* know, the effect of separation is world-altering; but it is now what *has* to be borne, for human sensuality can only subvert now.[21] How dismal a process this is the plays bear witness to, for Shakespeare's tragic characters remain profoundly implicated. And in this they are the image of what *we* might be if we thought ourselves into, or pretended to live out, our own sensuality, in the complete and unthinking way we might wish to.

Lear is only slightly less horrid as presentation in this respect than is *Macbeth*. Lightning strikes here in the same way—the scene altering instantaneously, and with a complete irreversibility. A love that was until then supported in its sensuality now converts, disastrously—into hate, from the influence of a sensuality now become depravity:

> *For by the sacred radiance of the sun*
> *The mysteries of Hecate, and the night;*
> *By all the operation of the orbs*
> *From whom we do exist and cease to be;*
> *Here I disclaim all my paternal care,*
> *Propinquity and property of blood,*
> *And as a stranger to my heart and me*
> *Hold thee from this forever. The barbarous Scythian*
> *Or he that makes his generation messes*
> *To gorge his appetite, shall to my bosom*
> *Be as well neighboured, pitied, and relieved,*
> *As thou my sometime daughter.*

No villain is required to help subvert things here, unless that villain might be Cordelia. It will seem outlandish to say so, but this is nevertheless in a certain sense the case. Of the perversely sensual basis of Lear's love of Cordelia there is no doubt, but to the extent that Cordelia is involved in this love, who can say that she herself does not *share* in that sensuality or express *herself* in it? Cordelia balking at the profession of her love for Lear in the ritual, from this point of view, can be seen as a deliberate effort to repress her own involvement in that sensuality, which she finds she cannot openly express herself in, from a reticence she cannot control, which itself converts to pride. [I elaborate further on this viewpoint in the chapter "On King Lear" below.] Evil has entered the *Lear*-world as it were through this back route. Pride of this kind can easily be seen as hate; and so Lear sees it; he sees, also, the evil at work through it, and on that basis must react in his turn, for he can only reject Cordelia for it. That reaction is repeated later when Lear sees it in Goneril:

> *Darkness and devils!*

Only, by comparison of course, Cordelia is relatively far more innocent. It is principally through Lear that the subversion by sensuality takes place and depravity is exposed. As the passage quoted above shows, the breakdown is as great, and as profoundly sensual in its turn, as the borne-up experience of love that had sustained it until this moment. But what can we imagine Cordelia's perception of Lear to be at this moment, or of her own love shared with him up to now? As far as I know, no commentary exists on what we may suppose Cordelia is experiencing through the extensive silence that marks her response to Lear's outburst at this point. But we can surely imagine that, among other feelings, Cordelia would be wondering about the basis of the love shared with him until now, and feeling some guiltiness about it. Not in the sense that she wonders how she could love this man, but that she wonders on what grounds she herself has been having this love, since it was love partaken of *with* him. When she and Lear meet again later in the play, after much suffering, both have by then been largely purged of the sensual basis of the love that they once shared.[22]

As I have shown in my work as a whole, no one is spared the judgement. I have elsewhere [in "Shakespeare's Muse" and "On *Othello*" below] gone in some depth into the basis of guilt also in Desdemona, after Othello himself breaks down. The sensuality that absorbs *them* from the beginning needs no elucidation, and it becomes the doorway into a view of the depravity that is thought to lurk in these characters as an essential condition—tragically so in light of how they otherwise appear to us on the surface, as perhaps Shakespeare's greatest romantic lovers. The breakdown from sensuality into depravity is overwhelmingly clear in the case of Othello, but Shakespeare's vision of fundamental depravity extends in the play, as I show, to Desdemona herself. It is a measure of the universal import of what we may call the Shakespearean doubt at this time; it is a doubt that Shakespeare had carried over to *Othello* from *Hamlet*. Human nature is seen in *Hamlet* as *determined* by lust, this being the reigning view of human nature on which Shakespeare was then acting, which he had derived from Luther.[23] Even if we feel that Shakespeare stands finally for something else, something ultimately beyond this pessimism, it would seem that he assumed this view of human nature to be fundamentally true, and it is how his characters are shown to us, after falling from their formerly protected sphere in a world where lust and a general sensuality are originally absorbed in a certain *order* of love. Love in the tragedies is presented by Shakespeare in those terms, and it is *this* original ordering love that now goes; when it does, the subversion by sensuality is overwhelming—virtually everyone will and must die from it, in one elaborate way or another.[24]

Hamlet's subversion by sensuality is in his mind, but the subversion is no less real for that. The picture of lust that presents itself to him from his world derives not only from what he sees in the relationship between Claudius and his mother, but also from the relationship between his mother and his father:

> *why, she would hang on him,*
> *As if increase of appetite had grown*
> *By what it fed on*:

Originally, Hamlet's picture incorporates this sensuality of his parents into an idea of their love, in keeping with the fundamental pattern of experience in Shakespeare's tragedies, and Hamlet's own love of his father is bound up with this picture. But with the Ghost's revelation about his condition in the afterlife, the lust (typically) separates out from that picture as its own force, for which his father is now suffering punishment in the otherworld. His father's murder at Claudius's hands is in this respect but the image of the former's condemnation of himself, as if in his own lustful relationship to his wife lay the seeds of her further relationship to his murderer Claudius, who *is* the demonic extension of himself.[25]

Soon Hamlet is bitterly generalizing this condition of lust about everyone. If what his mother has made of herself with Claudius, or what Claudius himself represents of the grossest sensuality, so subverts Hamlet's mind, it is because they have become the images of a universal human condition that Hamlet can now see also touches him, and he is now himself subverted:

> *for virtue cannot so inoculate our old stock but we shall relish*
> *of it*

> *for the power of beauty will sooner transform honesty from*
> *what it is to a bawd than the force of honesty can translate*
> *beauty into his likeness: this was sometime a paradox, but*
> *now the time gives it proof.*

It is the same view of a now *altered* condition of love that Iago expounds upon at length in *Othello*, that condition being (appallingly) the natural ground for his own introduction onto this scene. Addressing a love *thus altered*, Iago can now confidently proclaim of *it*:

> *It is merely a lust of the blood and a permission of the will.*[26]

III

To return to the model put forward by Graves and by Hughes—I see a very different picture emerging from Shakespeare's presentation. An *original* picture presents itself—an original archaic world—in which love, in various forms, does indeed reign over all and have all in hand, and we can certainly conceive of *this* totality as expressing the Goddess's primal hold over Her indulged creation. Lust and a *general* sensuality that makes room for self-indulgence, ferocious character, and even violence—all this may be said to have had at one time an assigned place within an order principally directed by love. But then this indulgent and supporting love withdraws, and all is as if poured out, in a way that seems to confirm directly all that Luther had said[27] was true about human nature: that it is fundamentally, grossly and hopelessly depraved:

ARTEMIS
Stone, Italy, 500 B.C.

> *A serving-man, proud in heart and mind; that curled my*
> *hair; wore gloves in my cap; served the lust of my mistress'*
> *heart and did the act of darkness with her . . . one that slept*
> *in the contriving of lust and waked to do it . . . false of heart,*
> *light of ear, bloody of hand; hog in sloth, fox in stealth, wolf*
> *in greediness, dog in madness, lion in prey.*

Edgar's speech, as Poor Tom, catalogues it all. Humankind has been left to itself alone, subject to almost any subversion by its own sensuality, and with no further defense against itself, save for what it might find of support from whatever might come of this situation. If we are to speak of any further *return* to the Goddess, surely it would have to be with reference ultimately to *all* that we may suppose human nature to be composed of, as Shakespeare saw it. And, coming away from Shakespeare, it will boggle our minds to imagine the kind of confidence that would allow us the total leap in human experience that Graves for one proposed.

We may suppose that what Shakespeare thought of human nature would have some bearing on what we consider Imaginatively possible today, and Ted Hughes certainly assumed this, though I would propose a different lesson to be derived from what Shakespeare presents. The problem of our re-uniting with the Goddess necessitates for Hughes a complex evolution *with* Shakespeare, through the whole of the rest of the work that follows from his great tragedies. It is therefore in no simple sense that Hughes wishes to propose our extrication from the consequences that have followed from Man's historical rejection of the Female, as he sees the problem.[28] Only, the fear in Shakespeare, the pity and the terror, would seem to stem from a deeper source than simply the fear of female sexuality. It is fear of an actual and a complete depravity reigning potentially in us all, to which even woman in her relative innocence is subject. That is the full extent of the Shakespearean despair: all are overwhelmed, and moreover with a violence that does not appear to have limits, except that Shakespeare's characters bear it all in their deaths. From the Shakespearean account, there would seem to be far more in human nature to contend with that would need watching over, some still deeper influence or threat in the blood than what either Graves or Hughes seems ready to acknowledge—some graver menace that Shakespeare would have thought should concern us from our continued embroilment in a fundamental sensuality that defines us all.[29]

Of all the ways in which human nature may be menaced, the experience of subverted love may well be the worst. In Shakespeare the experience is conceived in the absolute terms of our separation from an original, archaic condition of love, which has left us utterly vulnerable. Thus Shakespeare could not see any hope *in the immediate term* except directly through our suffering of that separation, or our suffering through it. All the best characters of his imagination are sacrificed to this idea, in the literal sense that all go to their deaths consequentially, and that *would* have to drive him further to wonder if this could be all. His coming through beyond this point, as it were back to unity in the Goddess, was as hard a route as any could take, and hardly how we would wish to imagine our way through. Shakespeare's route represents how we would have to come through if we were to act on our hope for ourselves immediately, in our total psychological condition at present, and the cost of that immediate venture is consequently as great as it can be. The tremendously arduous route Shakespeare took from here must for that reason stand *also* in the nature of a warning, as to what we might wish to pretend to from a misplaced idea of our capacities at present.

In comparison with the Shakespearean venture, Graves's venture builds on a peculiar *acceptance* of his immediate condition, and that is Graves's strength. One could hardly deny to him, as we have seen, a profound power to mediate the Goddess's order. He himself involves us in the total reaches of that order, in which the whole range of natural experience is accounted for. But it seems that it is enough for him that he has visited that order and that he can fitfully and every so often visit it again, and in the meantime is content to think himself very simply into a proper alignment with the Goddess's purposes. This is at the cost, however, of facing more *directly* the greater range of passions with which a man can yet imagine himself contending, it might seem to him hopelessly.[30] Recovering the totality of experience is recognized by Graves as the end goal, but with an *acceptance* of the way things are at present, so long as a proper alignment with this goal is maintained. This perfectly nice, if perfectly profound, adaptation to his situation is what led Hughes to bewail Graves's too strict limitations as a poet, as one critic has pointed out:

> *For all the excitement of the chase, there is something*
> *distancing and detached in Graves's evocation of the*
> *Goddess. Take, for example, the first line of the dedicatory*
> *poem with which the book (**The White Goddess**) opens: "All*
> *saints revile her, and all sober men." This is measured, cool,*
> *and polished, and virtually lacks any pulse at all. It is as if*
> *this control of the verse and the emotion behind it was part*

*of Graves's defense mechanism—a means of controlling the
threat of the energy. This may be what Hughes has in mind
when he writes of Graves's poetry operating at "some kind of
witty, dry distance".*[31]

There is more of careful rationality in Graves than one might have expected
of one who was otherwise so critical of Western rationalism. Hughes seems
to have felt that *he* took on more, was more aware also (after Reformation
man) of his own potential for rejection of the Goddess, was also more aware,
as Shakespeare was, that approach to the end-goal would have to involve
a greater and more immediate reckoning with those deeper passions that
Graves cavalierly puts away. I have quibbled with Hughes, however, for his
own relative degree of superficiality, when one refers him to Shakespeare,
because Hughes supposes that such passions as a man has to deal with are
merely the result of a mistaken perception of the corruption of his beloved
or his fear of the Female only.

Any illuminating process which might come to Shakespeare out of
humankind's immediate situation, as he understood it, could only come to
him by a process of self-growth that few will be able to manage for now.
That is because he took *on* more, far more than we are in any position to do
ourselves. He was unable to abandon his humankind to their experience,
could only see their tragedies through with every one of his ill-fated
characters and so, seeing these through, could re-emerge eventually with a
far greater perception of the restored mythical totality than even Hughes
was able to imagine of him. The corruption by evil is suffered totally, but
it is merely suffered; it is not to be understood in terms of any mistaken
psychology, hubris, or hamartia, however inevitable, or even as a simple
affront to the Goddess. A universal corruption is suffered through totally;
it has been the only means for bringing humankind as a whole out of
its former condition of sensual embroilment. The consequence of that
embroilment has been the extreme violent death of the beloved, marked as
this is also by the extreme despair of the hero through whom a prevailing
evil has come. The death of Desdemona, the death of Cordelia, as the final
consequence of evil: these are challenge enough for now. They are enough of
a measure of the tragic tendencies in human nature with which, according
to this presentation, we would have to reckon, before we could begin to
work our way back into any unity such as was formerly ours in the archaic
sphere. In comparison with Graves, Shakespeare offers a more complete
picture of what we can understand to be at stake. From Shakespeare's point

of view, there would appear to be far more of human nature to contend with, far more of a struggle with this nature to anticipate, and consequently more of a prospect following from our ultimate success with this struggle. It is a view that looks more boldly to the future on the basis of a far more courageous consideration of our whole nature as inherited from our archaic past. Contrastingly, Graves's view is of our situation in relation to the basic prospect, looking out from a standpoint somewhere between before and after, as it were out of our *present* embroilment in our sensual nature, to the limited extent that we may speak of our coming to terms with it.

Even so, Shakespeare could not *foresee* his re-emergence from tragedy. It was not as if he was conscious of any further illuminating power of vision which was his *before* he undertook the plunge into the totality of human errancy. He could not have predicted how things would develop, or even that they would. He had been overwhelmed himself, as could only be the case, with the series of deaths that had come from his imagination: Ophelia, Desdemona, Cordelia; from there, for many months it would seem, he lived with the death of the beloved as the symbolic end-consequence of human tragedy. Until, with *Pericles*, the light begins, faintly at first, to shine through again, though not without a drastic re-living, a necessary re-surfacing, of the quintessential tragedy—as this takes shape in the death of Thaisa. The experience of human tragedy *continues* in Shakespeare's mind, and when the mythical world finally does break in again on Shakespeare it does so within the terms of this experience. It breaks in on him for the first time when Thaisa recovers, or rather is recovered, from death—*with all that that symbolically implies* of a re-emergence for Shakespeare. In her very first words, as she returns to consciousness, Thaisa calls upon Diana, the Goddess as Virgin, as the ruling Spirit Who underlies this whole action. There is an experience of being supported again, from being *through* tragedy. And here *begins* the great experience of the recovery of unity to which Shakespeare's last plays bear witness as a whole. (*I* begin my account of this experience in this volume from Chapter 4 onwards, with some preliminary hint of it at the end of Chapter 2.) It is a long process, however, by which Shakespeare is brought back to unity. The whole range of the tragic experience he had seen through would have to be distributed over all of the last plays in order for that experience to be properly seen and dealt with. That effort, as we shall see, involves Shakespeare in a production over years. The studies brought forward in the rest of this volume have constituted an attempt to bring out in progressively greater depth what this long process of tragic suffering and recovery is all about.

2

Shakespeare's Muse:

An Introductory Overview

I

THE MUSE APPEARS

Recent interest in who Shakespeare's Muse may have been—his personal Goddess, so to speak—prompts one to come forth to dispel the drastically simplistic notions that have been brought forward. In Tom Stoppard's film script for *Shakespeare in Love*, we are asked to imagine Shakespeare as an author who, at a certain point in his career, has become creatively impotent because sexually and romantically dispossessed, and who is especially non-plussed by the overshadowing influence of Marlowe who is presented as actually dictating some of the material of *Romeo and Juliet*. Along comes a lady who, running against the mainstream of contemporary appreciation, is profoundly taken not with Marlowe's dramatic poetry but (of all things) with Shakespeare's. On his discovering this passion, she and Shakespeare fall head over heels in love, but because of their previous respective commitments in marriage, they cannot prosper, so that she must be ultimately cast as the Juliet to Shakespeare's now tragically unfortunate Romeo (each plays his/her respective part in the opening performance). Shakespeare is once again free to be creative also because Marlowe is now dead, and the former is presented as being responsible for the latter's murder (he has willed it and feels profoundly guilty for it). His lady must now leave him, to go overseas, but in departing from him she is transformed into a symbol of an indestructible creative energy that will never leave him. She will survive the great waters of tragic developments in which they are now immersed to return one day to his symbolic shores as the Viola of *Twelfth Night* (the name she actually bears in real life).

*   *   *

What are we to make of a view of Shakespeare's creative development that stops short halfway through his career, at *Twelfth Night*? It is true that the film's final symbolic sequence, depicting the flaying motions of bodies submerged in water, is intended to evoke not just the scene of *Twelfth Night* but also that of *The Tempest*. The suggestion perhaps (it is far from clear) is that Shakespeare is already in possession of a creative potential that will see him through the great tragic sequence that will engage him so profoundly in the long interval between one play and the other. Of this sequence one must say that there is nothing more tremendous or more tremendously distressing in any literature, and yet all this has been very conveniently left out of the presentation in this film, as if we were to understand that the tragic engagement was there to be gotten through but (once again) were not really ready to know it.

*   *   *

Stoppard's popularizing projection of what we may suppose was involved in Shakespeare's growth and transformation at a highly discrete moment of his career is clearly meant as "entertainment", and it is conveyed to us with a certain (large) measure of tongue-in-cheek license as well as some very deliberate over-dramatization. In that case, we must think the presentation all the more insidious as an influence, since it also purports to offer a serious view of Shakespeare's development (over-grand, one will think, in the case of the film's very last cut that shows Viola taking her very long walk up the beach on which she has landed). No doubt it is the view of Shakespeare's experience that will survive in the large portion of humankind that got to marvel at this film. Stoppard's presentation is full of the most perverse notions about Shakespeare's experience, and I will be addressing only three of these here before I go on to say where I believe our concern with Shakespeare should actually lie or what form of Muse we can suppose it was that commanded his development the way it did.

(1)

That Shakespeare was ever at a loss for creation, in any degree and at any time in his career, must be seen as a suggestion of total absurdity, and not even Marlowe's influence could keep him from continuing monumentally prolific, as from the first. By the time of the period in question, Shakespeare had produced as many as eight full plays over approximately a five year span, two long narrative poems as well as much of his Sonnet-sequence, and he was returning from a hiatus from the stage of almost two years on account of the plague, to immediately produce almost at one time three new plays in three separate genres: in comedy (*A Midsummer Night's Dream*), in tragedy (*Romeo and Juliet*), and in history (*Richard II*). At what point over this short period of time, and with what possible meaning, can we speak of a creative lapse? We may reasonably speak of a significant qualitative transformation in Shakespeare in the period he was away from the stage, and he returns to it with a renewed impulse of considerable power, as everyone will who has had the occasion to break away from some continuous activity for a while. He would have a similar break at the time of the accession of James I, and that moment would mark another highly significant point of transition: from the powerful, relatively static mode that we associate with *Hamlet* to the still more profoundly engaging, considerably more dynamic production represented by *Othello*, *King Lear*, and *Macbeth*.

(2)

In the meantime, the sudden absence of Marlowe from the theatrical scene certainly had something to do with the newly-found sense of freedom and release that appear to characterize Shakespeare's creative effort in the period of *Romeo and Juliet*, though it will strike us as paradoxical to say so. No doubt the sudden death of Marlowe, who was so tremendously gifted and so young at the time, would have had an impact of terrible grandeur, aggrandizing the already profound impression his genius had made on his contemporaries. Shakespeare's struggle with Marlowe would have been made all the *more* difficult by this death, which immediately immemorialized his achievement. However, that struggle went so very deep very simply it had to be deferred, since it had little to do with any usual sense of professional rivalry, by which Shakespeare does not seem to have been very affected.[1] In spite of Marlowe's decided advantage in respect of dramatic achievement at the time of his death, Shakespeare reserved quite enough sense of his own genius, which was already monumental and indeed momentous (his address to his personal daemon in the Sonnets bears this out dramatically). He seems to have been quite content to let his own destiny play itself out, and humbled as he may have been for the moment from the comparison with Marlowe, this was a part that otherwise suited him in light of the altogether singular way he was developing.

His own genius was leading him down a path that he sensed would only bear greater and greater fruit as he was going along. On the other hand, Marlowe's work laid down a challenge that Shakespeare would fully take up only in his great tragic period, which lay ten years away. That Shakespeare would require a full decade to come to terms is a measure of the tremendous depth of Marlowe's achievement, which extended from the combination of both *Tamburlaine* and *Dr. Faustus*, though especially from the latter. Shakespeare would not quite fully absorb the achievement in romantic grandeur of the former play until he finally came through with *Othello*. As for the latter play, and especially its ending, in its incomparable projection of the depths of human depravity, it set a standard that not even Shakespeare's great tragic plays from *Othello* onwards, or Donne's *Holy Sonnets* or Milton's *Paradise Lost* could displace. I shall have more to say about Marlowe's tremendous achievement below, but influence at that depth was not likely at any time to have kept Shakespeare from continuing strongly in his own development.

(3)

There can be no question that Shakespeare returned to the stage at the time of *Romeo and Juliet* personally transformed, and I too happen to believe that he had in the meantime fallen in love, but the evidence of the Sonnets suggests that he fell in love with a man and not with a woman, and in any case he had been transformed more from love of the eternal that this man represented, from love bred of the eternal, than for what this man represented in himself. Perhaps we may attribute to this love the strong development in the representation of (comic) romantic love that follows from *A Midsummer Night's Dream* through *Twelfth Night*, though highly different forms of love were involved. Shakespeare presents the love of the Sonnets as "builded far from accident" (see Sonnet 124); he seems to have come back to this saving love in the privacy of his time away from what must have been the trying vicissitudes of continual production in the theatre, among numerous other social responsibilities. He would have returned to this love quite as often from his work in the comedies as from his strenuous work in the histories, which also continued strongly at this time.

We have in any case always made too much of his so-called "happy" comedies and the supposed romantic inspiration that it is only too easy to associate with his dazzling work in the genre that has always made him so popular, overlooking that Shakespeare was also at this time profoundly engaged in a far broader course of development that was driving him into progressively less and less happy regions. He had always been critical, his romantic comedies themselves incorporating at every turn the sharpest critique of the "happy" world he was indulging, and that critique he was to unfold to the point where he would finally abandon writing comedies (there would be no more comedies written after *Twelfth Night*).

Very simply he had grown too serious for it. He had continued strongly over this same period with his monumental project of depicting the long, dark history of England after Richard II, and that project had involved him in a progressively deeper and deeper study of the great fall in human nature that he saw represented in the will to power. His more recent productions—especially *Henry IV, part one* and *Henry V*—had brought this study to marvellous consummation: his psychological technique especially he had brought to a point of great refinement, so that we have no trouble imagining from here the further leap to *Hamlet*. Here indeed is the great line of continuous development on which we should be insisting, in contradistinction to the usual romantic emphasis. What primarily absorbs Shakespeare in his long, ongoing career is a deeper and deeper study of the will to power, and Claudius would be his next major subject in *Hamlet*. The effects of this character's deeds he could now submit to the intense scrutiny of his own highly developed and refined consciousness as reflected in the figure of Hamlet. In respect of this enterprise, Shakespeare's comedies might be seen as a set of brightly lit candles hanging preciously over his work-desk, which might serve as a form of consolation in the face of the great darkness around him that he had now made his principal concern, but they had become in the meantime secondary, even adventitious accomplishments.

*　　*　　*

Something of the import of Shakespeare's development at this point may be gleaned from what is dramatized over the course of the Sonnets experienced as a totality. Right up to *Hamlet* Shakespeare maintains an especially resistant and rich connection with the universally beautifying capacities of his most intimate self, the ideal personalized daemon, if you will, who appears in the form of the immortalized young man of the Sonnets' first section. It is well-known that the many Sonnets to this young man break off suddenly to make room for a short sequence of intensely problematic Sonnets to a dark lady, which have baffled understanding. The labyrinthine efforts made over the years to seek to identify this dark lady have spelled nothing but futility, for the reason that she is an all-embracing, universal symbol and, unlike in the case of the young man, did not have biographical existence outside the scope of Shakespeare's mythical imagination.

Standing at the other extreme from the young man who concentrates Shakespeare's idealized spiritual self, Shakespeare's dark lady crystallizes all the length and breadth and abysmal depths of human perversity. Shakespeare imagines himself enthralled to her as to a kind of universal lover from whom he knows nothing good can come, though he remains wilfully hers. What can this import but that he was fated for a certain experience from which he could not extricate himself, even if he had wished to? This dark lady *is* the Muse to his now tragically beleaguered self—not being at all the kind of Muse popular imagination might have wished for its most celebrated author. It is as if Shakespeare had at a certain point, coincident with his turning to *Hamlet*, gathered up all the forces of his best spiritual self, only to be then bewitched and condemned to experience, in some sense for himself (in his mind), the very worst of which human nature could be thought capable. The Sonnets themselves speak of an absolute negation of any hope of redeeming himself in the terms Shakespeare had elaborated up to that point. The very power of self that the young man had inspired, as an eternal entity lying "beyond accident", has had to succumb to the greater force of experience that now overwhelms our great author, as in Sonnet 134:

> *Him have I lost, thou hast both him and me;*
> *He pays the whole, and yet I am not free.*

II

LINKING UP TO LUTHER

One could well imagine Shakespeare pursuing his studies in the will to power in the histories quite on his own, without substantial recourse to any other major thinker of the time, unless that might be Machiavelli. However, in extending his growing understanding of the will to power into areas that now included (more fully than ever before) the whole psychology and metaphysics of lust (beginning with *Hamlet*), Shakespeare reflects back to us a highly significant deference to Luther—the figure who, after Marlowe, exercised the most significant influence on him at any time in his career. The extent of Shakespeare's reference to the dramatic details of Luther's life in *Hamlet* has been well documented[2]; the elaborate correspondence points to the crucial place Luther continued to hold in the cultural make-up of post-Reformation England. This is in spite of what has been pointed out as the decline of Lutheranism, as a devotional church, in Shakespeare's time. Luther remained, in spite of this, the great hero of the European Reformation to which England, as a Protestant nation, belonged. He continued to maintain, in spite of the strong independence of the English Church from its very outset, a pre-eminent position as the central figure who binds together at every juncture the great effort of the Reformation as recounted by John Foxe in his *Acts and Monuments*, the book that after the Bible was the most widely read in Shakespeare's England.

Precisely how far Shakespeare's reading of Luther extends is impossible to say, though numerous translations of Luther's work in English already existed in Shakespeare's day, so that one could imagine these setting him off on a more elaborate line of research that no doubt also included everything he might glean from what others could tell. (By Shakespeare's day, an almost perfect intercourse with Europe had become the norm both by open and by devious means, since, given the political-religious instability of the time, it had become crucial, from early on, to know all that had been and continued to be imagined, thought out, etc.). Shakespeare's dramatizations from *Hamlet* onwards in any case bear witness to a profound intellectual engagement with the great Protestant leader's appalling view of human nature, amidst which one thought in particular seems to represent Shakespeare's obsessive preoccupation at this time, namely the view that "nothing can cure libido".

I imagine Shakespeare taking up this thought in particular (from Luther's commentary on *Genesis*) with appalled abandon. He does so, however, from a point of view that requires some elucidation, since at no point does he embrace this thought as a Lutheran—except perhaps, in a highly qualified sense, initially with *Hamlet*. It was especially devastating for Shakespeare to think this thought, precisely because he was not Lutheran and so did not have to hand the further elaborate consolations that Lutherans can claim in the face of it. He seems to have come to this thought with the idea that it must be true, or any rate ready to think it true[3], precisely with that full dramatic power of thinking thoughts through that of course belonged only to him. If this thought, which he seemed to have grasped as the worst of thoughts, did indeed account for human nature, then he would have to take hold of that thought in all its potential reality to see what could be made of it. If one were in the meantime disposed at all to thinking well of human nature, let alone idealizing it, one would have first to find a way of disposing of this thought. And so, at a certain point it seemed all that Shakespeare was ready to think or could think of human nature, like the figure of Hamlet himself, with whom Shakespeare first undertakes his quest.

Over the course of his tragic period Shakespeare would not in fact be able to resolve this thought, which seemed altogether irreducible. At a certain point he seems to have suffered from it without consolation, via all of the tragic figures that now come from his hand, who seem progressively to add to it the sense of greater and greater capacity for moral perversity. So that we may imagine him carrying on as a great Lutheran would, though without the consolations of grace that also awaited the Lutheran faithful. These in any event Shakespeare was not ready to admit into his inquiry as to what might be thought to be the innate potential of humanity. Luther's terrible injunction, which compelled the moral imagination to peer into the very depths of human depravity, and which we may see as driving Shakespeare, must have appeared all the more grandly and distressingly terrible to the author who was to penetrate more deeply into human nature than any other writer before or since:

> Come, accept. Be a sinner! "Esto peccator!" And don't do the thing by halves; sin squarely and with gusto, "pecca fortiter!" Not just playful sins. No, but real, substantial, tremendous sins!

Not that Shakespeare was alone in this investigation. The dramatists who were his immediate contemporaries in the time of James would also add to the inquiry, offering their own spectacular representations of horrible forms of human perversity, so that the question arose as to whether there could be any other way of checking these tendencies than by some severe manner of moral imposition, of the kind finally proposed in plays such as Marston's *The Malcontent* or Tourneur's *Revenger's Tragedy*, or Shakespeare's own *Measure for Measure*. These plays put forward models of moral solution that reflect something of the severe moral repression practised by James, who would have thought such interventions laudable (missing out on the irony of the dramatists' representations). Luther would have judged such an approach to the problem typical of "the ways of the Romanizing oppressors" from whose hands he had come to set humanity free. In Luther's view, it could only be by a free act of the imagination that humanity could turn from an intense absorption in its own innate depravity to the grace-bestowing God on whose "justification" the Lutheran community attended in its hopeful faith. In the meantime, Shakespeare had left aside any and every such faith, so full is his association with our humanity he could not imagine any prospect of hope other than one which might arise from within humanity's own nature.

III

MARLOWE'S ROUTE

Years earlier, Christopher Marlowe had come to his own proud reckoning with the Protestant experience. His Faustus (ironically dressed in black and from Wittenberg, as Luther was) initially makes short shrift of it. The view that humanity was radically or fundamentally depraved, so that it could not in the last analysis escape judgment, is dismissed out of hand as irrelevant. Humanity would in any case only wish to venture out for itself when confronted with such a prospect. Thus Faustus is presented as the hero who in choosing a path of magic has come to lead a subjected Europe out of the superimposed Hell of the Protestant judgment:

> *And I, that have with subtle syllogisms*
> *Gravelled the pastors of the German Church*
> *And made the flowering pride of Wittenberg*
> *Swarm to my problems as the infernal spirits*
> *On sweet Musaeus when he came to hell,*
> *Will be as cunning as Agrippa was,*
> *Whose shadow made all Europe honour him.*

The magic is seen as building upon the great sense of worldly promise forecast for humanity from a magnificent understanding of its own powerful graces. Marlowe, in this way, projects another potential *romantic* Wittenberg out of the narrowly oppressed and oppressive historical one. Insistent is his vision of the infinite range of action that was thought to be available:

> *All things that move between the quiet poles*
> *Shall be at my command. Emperors and kings*
> *Are but obeyed in their several provinces.*
> *Nor can they raise the wind or rend the clouds.*
> *But his dominion that exceeds in this*
> *Stretcheth as far as doth the mind of man;*
> *A sound magician is a demi-god.*
> *Here tire my brains to get a deity.*[4]

The terms of Faustus's quest necessitate that he resolutely stand by his view that the projection of a judgmental hell is a fictive illusion. This would have to be the case when Mephistopheles and Lucifer finally do appear, in all their terrible, compulsive grandeur (appearances that are absolutely extraordinary in themselves). What are we to make, then, of the fact that within a mere scene of the first encounter with Mephistopheles, in which Faustus expresses himself admirably in this resolution, and before we are even out of Act One, he should immediately collapse and is thinking himself already damned from his confrontation with these dark forces?

> *Now, Faustus, must thou needs be damned?*
> *And canst thou not be saved?*
> *What boots it then to think on God or heaven?*[5]

While Faustus returns to his initial faith in this same scene, what the rest of the play dramatizes (beyond the elaborate forms of escape of his actions with Mephistopheles) is a progressively greater and greater intensification of forces of despair in him—until we reach the play's monumentally terrible ending.

In this ending the whole Protestant angst of being hopelessly fallen is concentrated without relief, as Faustus seems destined for damnation in a strictly literal sense. Sensationally enough, he has by then swung over entirely to the opposite experience from the one in which he initially bases himself, an about-face that seems to represent an extraordinary capitulation of sorts. There are the most desperate efforts to work a way out of the entrapment. Faustus calls on time to stop still and for mountains to come and fall on him:

> *Stand still, you ever-moving spheres of heaven,*
> *That time may cease and midnight never come.*

Fair nature's eye, rise, rise again, and make
Perpetual day. Or let this hour be but a year, a month,
a week, a natural day,
That Faustus may repent and save his soul ...

Mountains and hills, come, come, and fall on me,
And hide me from the heavy wrath of God.
. . . . .
Earth, gape! ....
You stars that reigned at my nativity,
. . . . .
Now draw up Faustus ....

So attuned is Marlowe to the terms of the Lutheran experience, he dramatizes in this same moment much of the terrible incomprehensibleness of that paradoxical turning back to God that Luther was saying was still possible to our humanity in spite of the fundamental condition of depravity in which it would remain right up to the moment of death, inasmuch as one remained bound to the flesh:

Oh, I'll leap up to my God: who pulls me down?
See, see, where Christ's blood streams in the firmament.
One drop would save my soul, half a drop. Ah, my Christ.
Rend not my heart for naming of my Christ!
Yet will I call on him. Oh, spare me, Lucifer!
Where is it now? 'Tis gone:
And see where God stretcheth out his arm,
And bends his ireful brows.

Donne, deliberately building on Marlowe's Faustus, would dramatize this acutely strained hope throughout his *Holy Sonnets*, but without the full terror of 'knowing', as Faustus does, that damnation is a certainty. And that 'knowledge' of course is what explains the unsurpassable power of Marlowe's ending and what made it so continually haunting to those who came after him:

The clock strikes twelve.
Oh, it strikes, it strikes! Now body turn to air,
Or Lucifer will bear thee quick to hell.

Thunder and lightning.
Oh soul, be changed into little water drops
And fall into the ocean, ne'er be found.
Thunder. Enter the Devils.
My God, my God, look not so fierce on me.
Adders and serpents, let me breathe awhile.
Ugly hell, gape not, come not, Lucifer!
I'll burn my books. Ah! Mephistopheles!

*   *   *

Marlowe's overwhelming projection of defeat in *Dr. Faustus* takes on a profounder cast the moment one gets behind the apparent impression created to the actual intention of its author, which was heterodoxical in a deeper way than has been supposed. Certainly the play and its ending were bound to be referred to the overriding concern with depravity and damnation that so fanatically mark the epoch in which Marlowe lived and over which Luther had cast a shadow that would not lift. The fear of damnation had never been so real, and Marlowe was playing directly into this fear by dramatically inverting the longstanding Morality-play tradition on which he was drawing, a tradition in which Everyman, hopelessly perverse as he had been, had always been saved.

A new element has obtruded itself, however, in the further concern with magic—a bold stroke that was bound to raise the heat of theological concern of those times. Conventionally-speaking, it would have been too easy to draw the conclusion that such was the fate that awaited one who presumed through magic to circumvent the intentions of a God who could not be gainsaid. It is indeed doubtful that Marlowe would have accomplished the goals that he reserved if he had not first carefully appealed to this response, both in the play's opening Chorus and in his Epilogue. What he presents within these confines, however, puts an altogether different spin on the action, rendering Chorus and Epilogue ambiguous in turn. All hinges on the dramatic reversal that Faustus undergoes within a mere scene of his first encounter with Mephistopheles.

There is nothing to suggest that, before this moment, Faustus does not fully maintain himself in the resolution he expresses initially to see his way past the illusory thought of hell. From Faustus's assumption, that there could be no reality to a notion of hell for the human spirit, it follows that he must look upon all that Mephistopheles imports as itself an effect of illusion. Hence the contemptuous superiority Faustus expresses about the despair Mephistopheles reveals over losing the joys of heaven, which appears to Faustus either as feigned or the effect of a spirit itself suffering from illusion:

> *What, is great Mephistopheles so passionate*
> *For being deprived of the joys of heaven?*
> *Learn thou of Faustus manly fortitude.*
> *And scorn those joys thou never shalt possess.*

In this scene Faustus continues strongly in his views:

> *This word "damnation" terrifies not me,*
> *For I confound hell in Elysium.*

Then follows the breakdown I have mentioned, without extenuation, the very next time we see him:

> *Now, Faustus, must thou needs be damned?*
> *And canst thou not be saved?*
> *What boots it then to think on God or heaven?*

This extraordinary about-face is the more unbelievable in that Faustus returns to his initial resolution within the action of this same scene, as if he had never known of the breakdown he has only just experienced:

> *Come, I think hell's a fable.*
> . . . .
> *Why, dost thou think that Faustus shall be damned?*
> . . . .
> *Think'st thou that Faustus is so fond to imagine*
> *That after this life there is any pain?*

It should be clear that in the intervals between his conscious dealings with Mephistopheles Faustus is in the process of being possessed, is indeed already profoundly possessed from the first by those dark forces that Mephistopheles and Lucifer represent. This is happening in a part of Faustus that he does not appear to know about, developments that contrast sharply with the control he assumes he actually possesses over both Mephistopheles and "that Lucifer" who is presumed to be Mephistopheles's master:

> *Did he not charge thee to appear to me?*
> . . . .
> *Did not my conjuring speeches raise thee?*

Faustus enters into his dealings assuming (as Blake would, two hundred years later[6]) that he will have the better of these dark forces that only *appear* to him in the guise of Mephistopheles and Lucifer; hence, the distance he assumes from the names they possess:

> *Tell me, what is **that** Lucifer, thy lord?*

Marlowe's working assumption is that it is in the power of these forces to overwhelm with the illusion of hell, and he has Faustus confidently suppose that he will outwit them from the sheer strength of his better knowledge. (That Marlowe should have assumed it possible to summon these forces to manifestation is altogether extraordinary in itself, especially in light of the fact that he did not think humanity ready for this occult fate, though it is a testimony to what he was seriously considering.) Faustus is dramatically unaware, however, that these very forces are, from his first dealings with them, already taking possession of him, for the most part in those dramatic interstices during which he is away from our view. Something of that power to overwhelm and possess is suggested in the first appearance of "that Lucifer" who overpowers precisely as an unrecognizable form:

> *Oh what art thou that look'st so terribly?*

His very form suggests the power of possession he is actually exercising, over an unsuspecting Faustus who is suddenly rendered defenseless:

> *Oh Faustus they are come to fetch away thy soul.*

The problem for Marlowe, then, lies not in any actual depravity that may be thought of human nature but in the fact that humanity is compelled to *think* depravity from a power of suggestion that he associates with dark forces who are in control and who limit human power in this way.[7] Marlowe's presentation goes so far as to insinuate that all the voices and visions that are represented in the play are the projected suggestions of those dark forces with which Faustus is in communication. This is the case from the very first appearance of Good Angel and Bad that sound as unheard voices to Faustus, as Mephistopheles confesses at the end:

> *when thou took'st the book*
> *To view the scriptures, then I turned the leaves*
> *And led thine eye.*

Even the Old Man who appears at the end and who would seem to offer the greatest impression of objectivity constitutes another of the manifold manifestations of these forces: if not, how is it that he appears fully aware of Faustus's dealings with these forces, when no one else has been made aware of them—a point that is emphasized in the scene between Faustus and the Scholars that follows?[8] In fact, none of the voices and visions that are obtruded into the play's scene have any other effect on Faustus than to combine in the most varied ways to compound and aggravate the progressive despair that has been so powerfully suggested to him, destabilizing him beyond any possible power of control over himself. In this way, Faustus is placed, at the end, at the centre of the most massive phantasmagoria of suggested despair this literature had ever seen and was to see for some time to come, which explains the tremendous status Marlowe's ending was to have for some of the greatest writers for years to come. Otherwise, Marlowe's presentation suggests, God is not there: there is no effective presence or reality to any such "God" or to the "heaven" that are spoken of so casually in this play, and humanity has in the meantime been left to itself, to deal with forces that can only get the better of a defenseless and unsuspecting human psyche.

IV

LUTHERAN HAMLET

It would take many years before Shakespeare could finally assimilate Marlowe's achievement in *Dr. Faustus* in respect of what it imports of a hopelessly overwhelmed humanity. Shakespeare would not come to terms fully until he came through with *Macbeth*, and in the meantime there was his own extremely complex route to this point from *Hamlet*—a route on which we find him struggling not only with Marlowe but also, profoundly, with Luther. *Hamlet*, as I have said, marks that extraordinary juncture in

Shakespeare's career at which, having gathered up the best of his own forces, he suddenly plunges into a Luther-like confrontation with the very worst of human nature. Something of those best forces are projected in the figure of Hamlet, who is described in terms that compare directly with those ascribed to the young man of the Sonnets:

> *The expectancy and rose of the fair state*
> *The glass of fashion and the mould of form*
> *Th'observed of all observers ...*

However, these forces are now overwhelmingly referred to the depravity that is supposed to dwell at the heart of human nature as its fundamental condition. This is a new direction in vision that we may see as the effect of the commanding action of the dark Muse to whom Shakespeare has been made accountable.

Hamlet's meeting with the Ghost of his dead father is in this respect a first initiation. He learns of the profound corruptive force of lust at work not only in his mother and in his uncle Claudius, but in his very father, who on account of it has already submitted to the universal judgment that awaits everyone, and so Hamlet himself (and Ophelia).[9] Needless to say Hamlet is greatly disturbed by this revelation, which he bears alone, overwhelmed and possessed by it as Faustus had been overwhelmed and possessed, though in Hamlet's case, unlike what Marlowe makes of Faustus's situation, *what* is revealed turns out to be really true. At the same time, as the product of a greater maturity, Hamlet has far greater resources for dealing with his experience. As I have suggested, *Hamlet* is the play in which Shakespeare comes closest to actually adopting a Lutheran standpoint inasmuch as the horror expressed about the extent of human degeneracy is complemented on the other side by a highly sophisticated effort to find some form of "justification" in the face of it. That effort of "justification" is expressed through the play's profound concern with Hamlet's striving after an otherworldly validation for revenge.[10] That prospect failing Hamlet, he is drawn down by the forces of despair that have otherwise possessed him, with fatal consequences for almost everyone concerned, at the other extreme from the otherworldly justification he has been seeking. We watch him vacillating violently between one extreme consideration and the other; the effect clearly recalls Faustus's analogous condition, though we are as yet, in fact, far from seeing our way through to the limits of the exploration of human nature on which Shakespeare was now bent.

V

THINKING DEPRAVITY

A significant gap interposes itself between *Hamlet* and *Othello*, during which period we may imagine Shakespeare going through a transformation of an intensity unlike any experienced by any artist before or since. Three years after *Hamlet*, and after almost a year away from the stage, he would return to produce in regular succession *Othello*, *King Lear* and *Macbeth*—incontestably the most intense works of literature we are ever likely to know. We grasp something of his monumental transformation in technique at this time from the fact that in *Othello* he now accomplishes in one scene (Act Three, scene three) what it had taken Marlowe five years to achieve—taking Othello the whole route from the tremendous heights of the Marlovian magnificence in which he initially invests his hero (and in this greatly outdoing Marlowe for the first time) right through to the abysmal depths of the possession, by Iago, in which we find Othello by the time the scene has closed, with extensive allusion made to the controlling power exercised by Mephistopheles over Faustus.

There is a crucial difference, however, bearing on the fact that, in between Marlowe and Shakespeare, Luther has interposed himself with his own great overweighing claim, so that it is not finally for Othello, as it is for Faustus with Mephistopheles, simply a matter of a self-created thinking gratuitously imposed by the dark forces with which Iago is aligned. Othello falls into the possession of Iago, thinking depravity of Desdemona, because Iago's suggestion is profoundly based in reality—not in that Desdemona is guilty of unfaithfulness of course, but in that depravity may be supposed *even of her*, in that it is possible to think it. The suddenly overwhelmingly sensual nature of her engagement with Othello, after a whole history of severe withdrawal from suitors, lends itself profoundly to the suggestion that it is her sexual will, which violently comes over her, that impels her in the first place.[11]

Shakespeare's working assumption in *Hamlet* was that all are steeped in lust at bottom (from the very fact that we are born of it). It is a matter in this play of an actual condition we all bear in us, even if Hamlet has much trouble thinking it. Something of this point of view is now carried over to *Othello*, with a similar application, if with a profounder irony. In a single passage in this new play, Shakespeare rehearses the material both of

Hamlet's confrontation with Ophelia (cf. Act Three, scene one) and his confrontation with Gertrude (cf. Act Three, scene four):

> Desdemona. *I hope my noble lord esteems me honest.*
> Othello. *O, ay, as summer flies are in the shambles,*
> *That quicken even with blowing . . . .*
> . . . .
> *. . . . would thou hadst never been born!*
> Desdemona. *Alas, what ignorant sin have I committed?*
> Othello. *Was this fair paper, this most goodly book,*
> *Made to write "whore" upon? What committed?*
> *Committed? O thou public commoner,*
> *I should make very forges of my cheeks*
> *That would to cinders burn up modesty,*
> *Did I but speak thy deeds. What committed?*
> *Heaven stops the nose at it, and the moon winks;*
> *The bawdy wind that kisses all it meets*
> *Is hushed within the hollow mine of earth*
> *And will not hear't. What committed?*[12]

In a later scene, Desdemona, by then overwhelmed by the influence of the profound suggestion at work in this play, will apply *to herself* the thought of her own depravity, in a way that we must see functions also apart from the force of Othello's imposition:

> Desdemona. *Am I that name, Iago?*
> . . . .
> *Such as she said my lord did say I was.*
> Emilia. *He called her whore . . . .*
> Iago. *Why did he so?*
> Desdemona. *I do not know; I am sure I am none such.*

This last statement especially should be seen as spoken in a tone that reveals Desdemona desperately wondering that it may somehow be true. We are returned at this point, in a way that forces the suggestion on us again, to the ambiguous circumstances of her initial choice of Othello, on which Iago had harped so strategically:

Emilia. *Hath she forsook so many noble matches,*
Her father and her country, and her friends,
To be called whore . . . .
Desdemona. *It is my wretched fortune.*

Thinking depravity of Desdemona, Othello is of course himself steeped in his own unconscious share in it, and in this way the thought of it in her profoundly taints him, as Hamlet himself was tainted. The spirit of revenge in Othello bears all the marks of being corrupted by the very vice it sets out to judge. This is unlike in the case of Hamlet who strives strenuously to keep free of that corruption, though he does so only with an ambiguous success. Othello, what is more, in his further deliberate killing of Desdemona goes far beyond the kind of judgment Hamlet expresses about Ophelia and at his mother, horrible as that is in itself. For the first time in Shakespeare in the fullest sense we may say that a hero whom we had thought inherently and profoundly noble is exposed to us in the irreversible depravity of his action.

However, Othello is still far from confronting the actual depravity of which he has become guilty. A very large gap remains between the new degree of depravity Shakespeare suddenly represents and any self-perception in the hero that we might suppose would accompany it, which might persuade us that the depravity has in some way been dealt with. Until this moment, Shakespeare's hero has for the most part been 'merely' thinking depravity, immersed in that thinking in a way that is profoundly disturbing. Now he is plunged into an actual depravity with which he appears, superficially at least, to be unable to come to terms at all.

Equally significant about *Othello* is the way in which Shakespeare for the first time foregrounds a character—in Desdemona—who comes right up to meet the thought about depravity head on. Ophelia is given something of this function in *Hamlet*, but she herself falls prey psychologically to the impact this thought makes through the figure of Hamlet. Strangely, it is Hamlet who in an initial phase bears Desdemona's function. *He* is Shakespeare's idealized self ("That unmatched form and feature of blown youth") submitting to the prospect of depravity that yawns before him. After that, Othello takes us fully into that abyss, relinquishing in doing so the kind of magnificent dignity he stands for. In the figure of Desdemona Shakespeare's idealized self returns yet again, pretending to balance out this prospect from the other side, for while her life may be defeated in the face of this prospect, not so, as she says, her love:

> *Unkindness may do much,*
> *And his unkindness may defeat my life,*
> *But never taint my love.*

Her love, however, will itself be of no immediate consequence at least in the face of the appalling, extreme violence with which she is finally done away with [on which more below in Chapter 3 and Chapter 4].

VI

DEFEATED LIFE

King Lear takes us one step further than *Othello* in respect of an actual depravity that is now fully expressed, by now by quite a sizable assortment of characters. That representation is, also, accompanied now by a more or less conscious perception in the hero of what is involved both in the scope and import of that depravity. *King Lear* is, in this respect, the play of greatest Lutheran reach and impact, taking us about as far into violent depravity as we can imagine. Speaking of Lear's daughters, Albany says:

> *Tigers, not daughters, what have you performed?*

And Lear too fully grasps the extent of their actions:

> *The fitchew, nor the soiled horse, goes to't*
> *With a more riotous appetite?*
> . . . .
> *But to the girdle do the gods inherit,*
> *Beneath is all the fiend's.*
> *There's hell, there's darkness, there is the sulphurous pit,*
> *Burning, scalding, stench, consumption; fie, fie, fie! pah,*
> *pah! Give me an ounce of civet, good apothecary, to sweeten*
> *my imagination . . .*

Of course Lear himself partakes in a very substantial degree in this depravity. There is his initial rejection of Cordelia in which he is overwhelmingly hideous and through which all are plunged into the unstemmable chaos of depraved motives that ensue:

> *The barbarous Scythian,*
> *Or he that makes his generation messes*
> *To gorge his appetite, shall to my bosom*
> *Be as well neighboured, pitied, and relieved,*
> *As thou my sometime daughter.*

And at the end of it all, Cordelia lies dead in Lear's arms, Lear inheriting the completeness of his rejection of her. All that Cordelia might have offered of hope in the face of the general depravity is crushed, and she herself has become in her death the profoundest symbol of life defeated by the grossest elements of human nature that prevail. It is the furthest point to which Shakespeare's dark Muse has led him. The further element of love, fitfully thrown up from the depths of Shakespeare's idealized self, is also wiped away by the sheer force of accumulated violence represented over the course of the play and the impact this violence has when Cordelia is herself done away with.

Beyond Lear Shakespeare imagines a still greater precipitation in depraved chaos such as we are given in Macbeth who will "tumble in confusion", as Marlowe puts it in *Dr. Faustus*. Macbeth is driven by a force of *actual* depravity that entirely overtakes and possesses him as the *thought* of depravity had once overtaken and possessed Faustus. Shakespeare had indeed taken on Luther's challenge to imagine real depravity to the fullest, while he had also fully incorporated Marlowe's lesson as to the part that would be played in human tragedy by the human psyche in thinking depravity in the first place. Indeed much of the power of "merely thinking" depravity goes into precipitating Macbeth deeper and deeper into his own tragedy. Such power of thinking is at work in Macbeth from the first, though it stems in his case, in an extraordinary way, from the violence of his actions on the battlefield. However, Shakespeare had by then already passed the point of greatest devastation, the farthest extremities of a stifled humanity, in the ending of *King Lear*. It is a wonder that Shakespeare had anywhere to go from there. Compelled ruthlessly by his dark Muse, and desperately following Luther's lead, he had brought himself to the point of imagining an action in which, as one critic has shown, horrible death finally prevails over "all forms of hope"[13]:

> *I know when one is dead and when one lives;*
> *She's dead as earth.*

> *Thou'lt come no more.*
> *Never, never, never, never, never.*

By no obvious route does Shakespeare then imagine his way beyond this point of utter hopelessness. He had done all that Luther could expect in the way of an imagination of human depravity and its devastating consequences. He had come to that point entirely on the strength of his own thinking, without further recourse to a faith that might either console him or allow him, by any mechanism of compensation, to come *away* from the spectacle of human depravity he had opened up. He had been brought to it by his Muse and by his unconscious will to prove the Lutheran indictment of human nature incomplete if not wrong. Could Shakespeare now show that he could plumb further than Luther ever supposed a human imagination might go? Could there be anything else or anything more than what Luther had spoken, about the irreclaimable hopelessness of human nature? Could Shakespeare, that is, pass beyond the worst hopelessness imaginable and, in doing so, thereby prove humanity capable of something by which it could redeem itself in the face of the spectacle of depravity by which it seemed otherwise inculpated? The process by which this prospect finally opens up must be counted amongst the greatest events in our literature and, as we shall see, expresses an almost supernatural faith in the power of human self-justification before the most withering indictment of human nature history had yet known.[14]

VII

THE TRANSMUTATION OF THE MUSE

With his seemingly interminable string of tragedies, which had run their course as far as *Timon of Athens*, it appeared for a while as if Shakespeare's career had come to an end. Tragedy in him had spent itself, without further recourse—or so it seemed. The obituary Alcibiades pronounces about Timon might almost apply to Shakespeare himself, who had gone as far in despair about human nature as one could go, far beyond what *we* might think ourselves capable of absorbing:

> *Though thou abhorred'st in us our human griefs,*
> *Scorned'st our brains' flow and those our droplets which*

From niggard nature fall, yet rich conceit
Taught thee to make vast Neptune weep for aye
On thy low grave,

It seems fitting that Shakespeare would see himself by the time of *Timon of Athens* as finally settled close up to the verge of that great "sea" of troubles of acutest human perversity into which he had peered more fearlessly than any author had before.

Then suddenly, with *Pericles*, a light appears out of the darkness as, out of that "sea" of ultimate tragedy by which Shakespeare had been claimed, there emerges, by an extraordinary turn, a new *transfigured* life, to replace that which was lost for good. Desdemona had gone down, as had Cordelia, and Shakespeare's tragic heroes with them. No further life could be supposed in those terms. Shakespeare would not in the least deny the ultimate power of tragedy: for him human tragedy finally focuses in the extremest form of violent death of the loved one. With that form of death the love that, out of Shakespeare's idealized self, goes out to meet tragedy is also wiped out. But beyond the extinction of Shakespeare's self in these terms lies the enduring power of Shakespeare's Muse who has led him this far *and who now transmutes in and through the death of the loved one.*

Structurally, the new developments are conveyed through the fact that the loved one—Thaisa in *Pericles*; Hermione in *The Winter's Tale*—now "returns" from death, having in some sense then "borne" that death, while leaving behind her in her sacrificial "bearing" a new redeeming power in the form of her "daughter" (Marina in *Pericles*; Perdita in *The Winter's Tale*). Pericles focuses around himself the impact human tragedy has made on Shakespeare in respect of our innocence of it—given the way it strikes without regard to our responsibility for it. It would take Shakespeare another two years to find a way of reconciling himself to his tragic imagination also in respect of all tragic guilt that would be incurred from the impact human perversity could have—this in *The Winter's Tale*. Between Pericles and Leontes (the tragic protagonist of *The Winter's Tale*), we read allegorically the sum total of tragic consequence as Shakespeare had imagined this over the course of his entire tragic period. He is by the time of the ending of *The Winter's Tale*, however, transcendentally restored by the power of his own Muse, who has borne, as "wife" and "mother", all of that tragedy with him, having bestowed upon him the power of an enduring self through which he has come through, with which we associate the "daughterly" force of Marina (in *Pericles*) and Perdita (in *The Winter's Tale*).

The Return (Ancient Rome)

The Tempest itself builds on the whole massive structure and content of the psychological experience I have just described, referring us to Shakespeare more openly and fully than before. For the death of Prospero's wife we read the multiple form of death as borne over the course of Shakespeare's entire tragic period by Shakespeare's own Muse. In this sense Prospero repeats in his own loss the loss of every other Shakespearean tragic hero that has gone before him, on which more below. By then, however, the force of enduring self Shakespeare's Muse has bestowed upon him has evolved, in the figure of Miranda, to the point of complete development—Miranda taking the power brought forth by Marina in a first stage and by Perdita in a second stage to the point of a third and final, fully formed achievement. How is that consummation of self-transcendent power achieved? As we shall see, by the final "sacrifice" that Shakespeare's Muse now performs, which seems to have taken the form of her actual "death" in his life. In *Pericles* and *The Winter's Tale* both, wife and mother are returned from death—i.e., Shakespeare's Muse continues to support him and to bear him up in his struggle to recover. In *The Tempest* wife and mother are *not* returned—i.e., his Muse has passed beyond him. She has left him to fare for himself, though with the ultimate gift of consummate enduring power as reflected in the figure of Miranda who has been left behind. That ultimate gift Shakespeare's Muse brings about by her own final "death" in his life. This further action of "sacrifice" corresponds to the difference between Shakespeare bearing the forces of self-transformation as a principle of integration in his mind alone and his finally bearing that integration in his very self as the possession of his own individual person. That difference may be summed up as a difference between the power of his creative thought and such thought become an actuating power in the world. It is the latter development that is reflected back to us in the figure and actions of Prospero, who now works in a supreme power of continual self-transformation symbolically represented to us in the figure of his daughter, Miranda. From her Prospero cannot be dissociated in his essence, while in her *own* person she stands to offer, by her marriage to the world (as represented by Ferdinand), to perform infinitely more for our humanity in the future.

* * *

Whoever Shakespeare's Muse may have been, we must suppose that she had everything to do with driving him along the whole strenuous route that I have traced, for now in preliminary form. His Muse drives Shakespeare along this route, initially at least, without either his will or his desire in the matter. From this extraordinary destiny we finally deduce purposes that are generally unknown today, inasmuch as a further *evolution* is supposed on the basis of the fullest possible engagement with the worst forces of our human nature. The challenge was laid down to Shakespeare to imagine the very worst of human nature, ultimately purely on behalf of our humanity and in an entirely experiential way. Thus "Know thyself" acquires, as the behest to Shakespeare of his Muse, the most terrible of implications. That the journey was worthwhile *The Tempest* will finally bear witness. Profoundly fitting it is that, when Prospero and Miranda finally do come forward, in their very first gesture, they should be looking out towards that whole destructive "sea" of ultimate tragedy they themselves have successfully braved. We imagine Miranda, as she stands looking out with Prospero, literally gathered to his bosom, for in one function she stands there as the innermost power of his very self, the very fruit of the whole tragic journey Shakespeare has taken. Shakespeare could not have imagined anything greater or imagined her by any other route than the one he was compelled to take, and she has become, via the self-sacrificing action of the Muse in which he has shared, the greatest gift he could finally have bequeathed to humankind.

SUGGESTED FURTHER READING

Brooke, Nicholas
"The Ending of *King Lear*" from *Shakespeare 1564-1964*, ed. Edward Brown, 1964.
"The Moral Tragedy of *Dr. Faustus*", *The Cambridge Journal, 1952*, reprinted in *Marlowe: "Dr. Faustus"*, A Casebook, ed. John Jump, 1969.

Dillenberger, John, ed.
Martin Luther: Selected Writings, 1961.

Granville-Barker, Harley
"From Henry V to Hamlet", British Academy Annual Shakespeare Lecture, 1925.

Haydn, Hiram
The Counter-Renaissance, 1950.
(see, especially, the sections on "The Romanticists" and "The Naturalists")

3

On Luther, *Measure for Measure,*
Good and Evil in Shakespeare, Comedy,
and the Evolution of Consciousness

On *Othello*

[*The following essay documents my reply to Anthony Gash and his response, in a letter to me, to 'Shakespeare's Muse'. (See the Appendix below for Tony Gash's letter.) Tony was no more that 3 years my senior when he was assigned to me as my doctoral supervisor 35 years ago, and he proved an inspiring influence on my only slightly more impressionable mind at the time. Ideally, I might have wished that he had taken me up with a further reply of his own, but the exigencies of work and the preoccupations of his life did not finally permit this. The reader can look forward to more from him and his own views in a book that has been promised for some time, and is shortly to appear, on "Shakespeare's Dialogue with Plato".*]

Dear Tony,

First, how to thank you for the way you have engaged with my work? and then to take the time to express something of your best self to me in response to the vision of Shakespeare's development I propound. What a privilege to have that from you and to be involved in an actual conversation about literature!

I am speaking of course of your response to my presentation in *Muse*.

To start with, I'm not altogether sure that you grasped, though I suppose that you did, that it is Luther and not I who said "nothing can cure libido". In any case let me here address your readiness to suppose that "Luther [did open] the tide of 'depravity' which Shakespeare, and Marlowe, dared to embody . . . as long as one doesn't accept the term 'depravity' oneself or assume that Shakespeare did." You go on to say that "One objection to its use is that the notion that sin is grounded in sexuality—"nothing can cure libido"—is neurotic, or heretical a theologian might say." Then you begin to give your arguments: "For sexual desire is necessary for reproduction, and according to Plato and others, is an unconscious expression of higher desires etc."

Your way of putting it about Luther, Shakespeare, and Marlowe I shall take as a kind of shorthand, for Luther didn't exactly "open the tide of depravity"; the depravity was already there, and he had the courage, as he saw it, to say so, and to exhort us to see it that way (in that sense alone he "opens the tide"). If we did not see it that way, that it is there, according to Luther we should be forever at the mercy of this depravity in our nature, and among other things find ourselves going straight to hell where we thought ourselves already in heaven (this is the way he saw it). Shakespeare and Marlowe "embody" this "tide" as you put it in very different ways. For Marlowe, as I say, it is a matter of the problem of "thinking" depravity, of being compelled to think it, by those negative supernatural forces Marlowe invokes in *Faustus*. These are not, incidentally, inconsistent with Luther's own direct experience of the devil, though in *his* view of those forces Marlowe is far more heterodoxical or heretical than even Luther. For Shakespeare, it is far more a case of realizing that depravity is real and not just something we compulsively think about ourselves (even if supernatural beings make us think it), and he does as much as, if not more than, any other writer to bring all that real depravity to us in the tragedies.

However, if Shakespeare dares to "embody" that tide of depravity that you speak of, it is not in the sense that he is ready to make himself into the depraved creature he is supposed to imagine he is, which is how your phrasing might be taken, but in the sense that he is ready to see this idea through imaginatively through the explorations of his drama. And seeing it through, he comes to see that it *is* true, or rather he has made it into something true outside himself, whatever he was personally inclined to believe about life. In thinking this idea through, Shakespeare gives himself up, I think very painfully, to a very pessimistic view. He manages (and this is the extraordinary thing) to dissociate himself at some point entirely from his own/our own ("happy—as you like it") view of what we might wish life to be about, which has been for some time now the most popular way of appreciating Shakespeare.

Now let me say that it is not *my* view, any more than it was initially at least Shakespeare's view—that we are essentially or substantially *defined* in our nature by an irreducible depravity or badness—though this *was* Luther's view. In *Sacrifice* I argue along the lines that one is bound to continue to think as one wills about life, and so was Shakespeare, irregardless of where his tragic explorations led him. I happen to think that Shakespeare at a certain point *altered* his fundamental view, accepting that it is *in fact* a case of badness, and of tragedy in that badness, but of course he himself could go on, comfortably it would seem, with his own life, even dying (more or less) wealthy etc . . . But in the meantime he had been through another experience in the depths of his being, and he must have been privately very much aware of it. This is to judge from how he proceeded in his plays (as I see it, of course). Let us suppose that it *is* a case of "the notion that sin is grounded in sexuality"; I do not myself experience sexuality in this way at all, and in fact experience it more along Plato's lines as you describe them. On the other hand I am not so sure that this experience of mine is altogether unalloyed with something baser in my will that does compromise me spiritually—which is precisely where Luther saw himself coming in.

There is, on the other hand, something counterproductive in insisting on our sexuality as a problem, to the extent that it is one. In fact, I do not personally have much patience for those who think themselves neurotically into their sexuality, for we still have to be as spiritually productive as we can be as soon as we rise again from our beds. However, I fully understand why Luther *could* come in and insist on the fact that our sexuality *is* fundamentally a problem, once we break through all the cob-webs of illusion, as he saw it. Various forms and degrees of neurosis have been attributed to him (Erikson himself speaks of a "critical area between neurosis and creativity"[1]) and he was of course *declared* heretical (the plan *was* to burn him for it). But in his essential view of it, *apart* from the additional neurosis and his deliberate heretical tendencies (these were designed to subvert the Catholic Church further once he saw what power he had mustered), Luther saw through to something that he thought was true and had been deemed true by others, by Augustine for example and by St. Paul. It was not a matter of sexuality as such; sexuality was an aspect of the more universally-based problem of our irreducible *sens*uality, of our condition of life in the flesh, which of course we cannot help till we die, and which we must reproduce ourselves in. But we are nevertheless not unaccountable for that. Or so Luther. We are accountable for it, according to Luther, in every moment of our lives.

*Un*like many of his followers, Luther was able to hold all of this in a workable balance (at least while he wasn't suffering from violent *im*balance, of which there is some record). *He* knew how to set up, in his mind, to accept that he had to live in the flesh and was bound to live in the flesh, all the while knowing that he faced damnation for it. Those who could *not* achieve the right balance in relation to the damning power of the flesh capitulated, indulging in brute violence against others or against themselves.[2] But Luther knew that to keep oneself in balance was to give oneself the only chance to make oneself ready (by the necessary faith that followed from knowing one *is* hopeless in oneself) for that further act of salvation that for Luther is accomplished gratuitously, by pure election by God, and this through what would *have* to be the last-minute saving action of Christ on the Cross at the moment of death (hence the basis of Faustus's last-minute hysterical effort to connect with Christ, for which in his case he has *not* made himself ready).

This leads me now to take up your point or points about Angelo in *Measure for Measure*, for I am not sure that you have grasped Luther's position, where you say, for example, that "Angelo . . . does . . . accept Luther's challenge ('Come accept! Be a sinner!')" and it is only because he does, because of his "incapacity to admit an experience of sexual desire as anything but sinful", that a tragic problem arises. You can see already what Luther meant when he exhorted everyone to accept being a sinner. For him one is *already* a sinner (by virtue of life in the flesh) and, it might be, a huge sinner, and if it did not appear that it was so, it would be necessary to whet one's imagination so one could think it so. That is how the exhortation to be a sinner comes into it, as in his famous view that one should 'sin strongly', "*pecca fortiter*". It was a meditative practice. And it should not have been difficult to imagine how depraved humankind was or could be, with the evidence of it around everywhere, except for the fact that one could live superficially, or hypocritically, or unconsciously, which for Luther meant disastrously, because one was then only "treading the primrose path to the everlasting bonfire", and all because the Catholic Church let you do so, by offering penances, indulgences etc . . . It might be very necessary in that case to imagine oneself in the power of humankind's depravity in order to remind oneself of the fact that one faced judgment in every moment—once again, not to despair about it, but to set oneself up as best one could in relation to that reality and in the hope of being saved. *Self-restraint was for Luther, in the last analysis, absolutely critical.* One would otherwise be plunging more deeply into sin. Angelo for his part capitulates and thus makes himself into a *worse* sinner by forcing himself upon Isabella. The problem is that *he* had pretended to be free of passion, and is now completely overwhelmed when it does come over him. It is the inverse problem of the Puritan, who would have appeared to Luther as no less under an illusion than the Catholic in pretending that he could ever have been free of passion, or remained free. The Puritan's error lay in going to the opposite extreme from the Catholic. But as for what Angelo *otherwise* argues about his passion when it does overtake him, or as an account of what *is* transpiring between himself and Isabella, his words are truth in Luther's sense. The truth about his passion, what's more, goes beyond what he formally acknowledges to the audience.

Superficially, Angelo judges it to be a case of *his* sinning; it is his fault etc . . . But this position, taken in relation to the audience in soliloquy, reduces the import of the question he has just framed. He properly leaves the matter open in his question:

Is this her fault or mine?
The tempter or the tempted, who sins most?

The answer he goes on to give ("Not she; nor doth she tempt: but it is I etc.") is a reduction of the case and is intended (by Shakespeare) to make him comprehensible to the audience, who could not otherwise grasp a situation so challenging and complex. Forgive me but I utterly believe that this is so, though you will have to bear me out on this. In spite of Angelo's self-judgment, ambiguity continually shows its ugly head, even in this soliloquy:

> *Can it be*
> *That modesty may more betray our sense*
> *Than woman's lightness?*

Consider also

> *Most dangerous*
> *Is that temptation that doth goad us on*
> *To sin in loving virtue;*

"[M]odesty" and "virtue" are the focus here, but they have been brought into a strong identity respectively with "betray" and "temptation". (There is a re-working here, surely, of Hamlet's "For the power of beauty will sooner transform honesty from what it is to a bawd than the force of honesty can translate beauty into his likeness." Except, of course, that Angelo's "honesty" has been a sham honesty, the Puritan honesty, and not the essential honesty Hamlet can still conceive of, for it was still possible for Shakespeare to think *it* at one time.) And it is in another sense (than the manifest one that Angelo intends for the audience) that we also hear

> *never could the strumpet ...*
> *Once stir my temper; but this virtuous maid*
> *Subdues me quite ...*

There is in fact much shifting about in this soliloquy, of course, so that Angelo also asks:

> *What, do I **love** her?*
> *That I desire to hear her speak again ...*

But "love", in the context of the whole soliloquy, with its rampant sense of Angelo's being already inwardly overcome and condemned, cannot have the positive implications you would wish to comb out of the situation. "Love" is identified here also with "desire", which has strong implications of brute sexual will in this period generally. Love, in your sense, has here become, in fact, an *alien* concept, in the overwhelming swirl of imputation of "temptation" that has identified Angelo to us as "betrayed" to "sin" and to a "desire" which is already "foul".

The *main* evidence, however, for concluding Angelo wrong in his manifest view of himself in his soliloquy comes from *inside* the actual encounter between Angelo and Isabella. And this we must follow closely. We must ask first: at what point is Angelo's armour broken through? And I think we can say with (near) certainty that it is broken through at the point where Isabella, sensing that Angelo cannot be moved, really 'turns it on', so to speak, with her "Could great men thunder" speech. We know this from Lucio's aside that follows ("He's coming; I perceive 't"), although the fresh onslaught on Angelo begins, in fact, in the speech that comes before this one: "So you must be the first … tyrannous etc". "Could great men thunder" is one of those anthology pieces submitted by everyone to memory and that everyone who hears that you have an interest in Shakespeare will cite to you at once (there are a few others) to show how much *they* appreciate Shakespeare and have always known him better than you do. In any case, we have been so taken up with the special content of this speech that we have failed to appreciate how Isabella actually comes across here (which is something you especially will appreciate as a theater director). What sort of emotion, or tactic, is driving her at this point? because it *is* a tactic at some level, teleologically *another* way of trying to break through, and perhaps the most extreme, certainly a last and total, effort in some sense.—And her tactic succeeds! She overwhelms Angelo, breaks through his armour. But it is not her *argument* that overwhelms him, although that is how one might be led to see the matter, and one would have textual evidence for this of course: "Why do you put these sayings upon me?" and "She speaks, and 'tis/Such sense that my sense breeds with it." But this is not the level at which the action is actually proceeding. The meaning of "sense" here is heavily weighted *toward* "sensuality", and the last quote in fact reads: "My sensuality breeds with hers", a meaning of "sense" that has been brought out from below the superficial effect the word "sense" registers of "argument" which has, in the meantime, become a purely irrelevant consideration.

For Isabella *has* come through, in fact in all the power of a *sensual* attempt to overwhelm with argument, her whole being *and so also her body* being in this appeal. And Angelo *is* overwhelmed, by her sensuality, which ironically is expressed in a novitiate nun who is otherwise virtuous and is also beautiful, which is *precisely* what renders that sensuality into the kind of temptation that cannot be resisted. (Cf. "For the power of beauty etc").

And we have to notice how the language itself in the rest of this scene breeds, from this new sensuality that has entered into it, a sexual intention. And let me emphasize that it is not Angelo who speaks Isabella's words here:

> Isabella. *Hark how I'll bribe you: good my lord, turn back.*
> Angelo. *How? bribe me?*
> Isabella. *Ay, with such gifts that heaven shall share with you.*
> Lucio. (aside) *You had marr'd all else.*

Isabella utters this language here because she has in the meantime *unconsciously* compromised herself, has been undermined *by her own libido*, and that process *continues* to be registered in the sexual ambiguity of her language which reaches (forgive the crude pun, but this is Shakespeare) rock bottom, in Isabella's next lines:

> *Not with fond sicles of the tested gold,*
> *Or stones whose rates are either rich or poor*
> *As fancy values them; but with true prayers . . .*

This we un-scramble easily enough: and so, "test"/"sicles", or "testicles" and its contemporary synonym, "stones". (I don't have to send you to the OED to authenticate the use of these associated terms in Shakespeare's day, but I have verified the matter again for myself, just to be quite sure!) There is then that further astonishing ironic shift (so typical of Shakespeare, who was addicted to such irony) back to "prayers", and so "heaven", "fasting" etc . . .

That Isabella *could* ransom her brother by satisfying Angelo sexually is thus an idea that *she* has sown in him. The idea is not originally of his conception. Not that Angelo ascribes the idea of sexual implication to Isabella as her conscious intention. The idea has simply (or not so simply) been sown between them, from the nature of their encounter, where an extremely intense communication of sensual appeal has come into it. That Isabella is fighting for her brother's *life* will explain why she becomes so extremely intense, and this intensity is, as I think, a measure also of her conceit of herself, as if she could not accept that Angelo could get the better of her. And she pays for it, for she consequently implicates herself. Isabella is a novice in a convent, and that of course is the whole point and why Shakespeare goes that far with Isabella's subversion by her sexual instinct.

Religion subverted by sexuality is *the* great development in Shakespeare's time as far as Shakespeare and his contemporary Jacobean dramatists are concerned. Not that Shakespeare took a simple view of the matter, and it is not at all, with Isabella, a case of crude reversal, but of the most subtle implication of herself, along the lines of Shakespeare's presentation of Ophelia, whose own libidinal drives, in spite of *her* innocent nature, are much exposed in her later scenes of madness, except that Isabella is a more mature young woman and so (biologically at least) can be imagined to have a more complex effect on Angelo than would Ophelia on Hamlet.

That Angelo could be properly in love with Isabella is completely pre-empted, in fact, by the *kind* of communication that has taken place between them, which is entirely on the level of being "stirred", or of roused "blood". The floodgates then open for him, on a scale that compares with the way Macbeth is overtaken by *his* evil conception (as I am sure you've noted). It is beyond his (and would be beyond anyone else's) capacity to withstand the attack:

> *And in my heart the strong and swelling evil*
> *Of my conception.*

> *Blood thou art blood.*

> *Why does my blood thus muster to my heart,*
> *Making both it unable for itself*
> *And dispossessing all my other parts*
> *Of necessary fitness?*

There is something profoundly sad about Angelo once he has fallen, as in the speech that begins "Ha! fie, these filthy vices!", which shows him in a complete despair about himself, fully conscious of the irony of his words which are deliberately spoken. It is a measure of how helpless a contemporary of Luther's might feel, once he had been struck by his own depravity, quite apart from whether he went on to capitulate or not. What follows between Angelo and Isabella as exchange is entirely in keeping with the despairing way the play itself is thinking out the problem of a libido that dictates to all. Does one have any other option but to impose judgment, since otherwise there could be *but* sexual license and the complete moral chaos that goes with that? The whole play is predicated on that situation. To run counter to the judgment of license, to be ready, that is, to indulge license, even if from a desire to save a life, must logically imply one's own readiness to countenance license. Angelo's further notion of Isabella's implication builds irrefutably on the logic of her own position, and it has been *inspired* by the sensual basis of the appeal she has made to him, which *has* compromised her. Angelo is only half or in small part aware of what has transpired between himself and Isabella or how it has happened, but he knows it enough to draw Isabella into a confession that by pleading on behalf of her brother, in spite of his transgression, she *has* compromised herself, and on a logical plane at least admitted to a readiness to the same disposition in herself. In the meantime, what has transpired between them is what is unconsciously driving Angelo to believe in the idea that she *could* and *may* be ready to indulge him, in order to redeem her brother's life.

It is a strange notion of redemption, of course, but we have to understand on what basis it is put forward:

> *Which had you rather—that the most just law*
> *Now took your brother's life; or, to redeem him,*
> *Give up your body to such sweet uncleanness*
> *As she that he hath stain'd!*
>
> *Might there not be a charity in sin*
> *To save this brother's life?*

A "charity in sin": it is automatically assumed that what they will share will *be* "sin", but it would only be inevitably "sin", only, that is, what human nature is already given to, being fundamentally and in every moment in any case already fallen. (This is to approach Angelo's offer from a perspective that *draws* on Luther, and I am far from saying that Angelo knows what he is saying or has suddenly become a Lutheran.) The act itself could not make things worse; it would be the same inevitable act Isabella is ready to condone in her brother, and in the meantime a life would be saved; hence the "charity" that would be reaped from it. A sensible! undertaking in spite of the intense! irony, and a *very* bold take on Luther (Angelo having in the meantime given up his Puritan position), but *not* (appallingly—I speak as a Catholic myself) incompatible with the premises of Luther's thought. That is, one *could* imagine Isabella going through with it very simply, without neurosis and without capitulating, and Angelo along with her, and the act would simply be the same "natural" act Luther himself could conceive of as taking place between himself and the nun *he* married, or between any man and any woman, even if also a monk and a nun: because the act itself, sin itself, was inevitable and simply the condition of life in the flesh. One could rise from the act, knowing that one was condemned in the flesh anyways and that it was on *other* grounds, quite irrespective of such sex or not, that one would have to seek the salvation of one's soul. Isabella has in the meantime brought *herself* to that position by the logic of her stance in seeking to extenuate her guilty brother.

It seems to me that Angelo (who is mediating Shakespeare's thinking) really has trapped Isabella here, and all of her efforts to justify herself in her position only go to show how she *has* compromised herself. As where she says:

> *O pardon me, my lord; it oft falls out,*
> *To have what we would have, we speak not what we mean:*
> *I something do excuse the thing I hate,*
> *For his advantage that I dearly love.*

This self-accommodating moral relativism, which could only be further dependent on the indulgences gained from prayer and which only Isabella's Catholicism allows her, is precisely what Luther was saying would never go over with God. Angelo's response to Isabella's unconvincing apology, this cavilling, is sublime in its despair of what is inevitable in human nature:

> *We are all frail.*

And he goes on to insist, in spite of Isabella's shifting:

> *Nay, women are frail too.*

This is fundamental Lutheranism, and irrefutable in its own terms, which is why it absorbed Shakespeare so terribly. For it is of course not Angelo but Shakespeare who is thinking this through Angelo; Angelo is not fully aware of where he is going with himself or why, and is himself (as his own character) inclined to plunge further in "sin" than Luther could allow him to go. In the meantime, the pressure on Isabella to accept Angelo's proposal is tremendous, as the further scene between Isabella and her brother emphasizes overwhelmingly. I don't have to bring out all that this scene is insisting on: that this is the still very young Claudio's life! that is at stake, that death *will* appear to be a very terrible thing to someone so young, and that he would be only too justified in wishing to put it off:

> *Ay, but to die, and go we know not where;*
> *To lie in cold obstruction and to rot;*
> ....
> ....*and the delighted spirit*
> *To bathe in fiery floods,* ......
> ....*or to be worse than worst*
> *Of those that lawless and incertain thought*
> *Imagine howling—'tis too horrible!*
> Etc ...

Isabella is outraged to think that her brother feels she should be ready to consider Angelo's proposal, but what I hear in the hysteria of her reaction is *also* her own disturbed suspicion, somewhere in herself, that perhaps she is wrong to refuse that proposal and to let her brother die. All very shocking and very challenging, to say the least.

What are we to make, then, of the *Duke's* way of coming to terms with all this? It is he, of course, who initially lets things go in the state as a whole, to the point where there is less and less regard for morality and religion. Leniency has been the order of the day—as if there could *only* be an application in mercy, since everyone will be guilty of sensual faults in one way or another. The law, which has regulated such practice in the past, has been set aside, but an uncontrollable situation has thereby been created, both morally and socially. We have here a picture of the ironic breakdown of the modern Christian state, to which will now be brought the uncompromising counter-action of the Puritan judgment in the figure of Angelo. The Duke sets this situation up, *knowing* that Angelo will come down on this society, and the question is already raised: how will Angelo appear in *his* application of justice?

Even to Escalus and the Provost it appears wrong: humanity has always been guilty of these vices. *But their position still begs the question.* From those who are most implicated in the sexual licence *also* comes the view that such justice is unnatural; sexual activity, even to the point of sexual indulgence, is inevitable, as natural even as eating and drinking; it is the general practice of humanity, and there has been, in any case, so much of it already! To make all pay for this now is absurd (for the most part this, Lucio's view). Yet some sort of control there must be, and the

Duke's purpose is clearly to find a way of exposing this general situation and bringing his society to task for it. He is given more of an opportunity to do so than he had anticipated, when Angelo compromises himself with Isabella. Now he can use that situation as a springboard for some kind of act of general condemnation of his society's mores and pretensions, can proceed to his own style of solution, which will consist in impressing his subjects with the terror of their being seen through where they thought they weren't perceived, and, on the basis of this form of imposed shame to be created in everyone, re-imposing law, most notably the conventional laws about marriage. In the meantime, the rival Puritan solution, which might have had its own severe way with the condition of the state, has been conclusively debunked. The hypocrisy that is associated with that solution has been exposed incontrovertibly.

The Duke is clearly a much wiser or more politic soul than the poor Angelo. His advantage *is* a politic use of retirement, secrecy, and espionage; he has, what is more, the traditional Catholic forms of subterfuge, of pre-Reformation Vienna, to hide behind. *His* solution to the additional imbroglio that develops around Angelo is to get Isabella to promise herself to Angelo as a pretext for supplying Mariana in her place [Mariana who was formerly betrothed to Angelo though he reneged]. In fact, Shakespeare brings us directly into the feeling of what the proposed tryst would be like. Isabella is drawn into the intrigue to the point where we appreciate intimately how Angelo thinks he will enjoy her.[3] In the meantime we are asked to accept that Mariana should deceitfully engage Angelo into making love with her while he thinks he is making love to Isabella, and all this in the name of justifying betrothal!

I see nothing comic in those developments, but rather a grotesque debunking of any idea of resolution that might be associated with this kind of subterfuge. The Duke is grotesquely writing his own moral laws. Also, the extent of his control over all those who now come into his power is appalling: he lets Isabella think her brother has died, and wilfully extends the exposure scene, going as far as to pretend to arrest her! Isabella, for her part, is so desperate, as to allow herself to be made into a pitiful pawn in this dramatic game. You may say that the scene in which she cries out for justice so extravagantly has a comic effect, but that is hardly how the scene comes across to me, when one considers that *for her* it is a very desperate cry for justice, for her abused self *and* a brother who is dead! And how is there any need *for her* to be put through such a gruelling moral lesson?!

The Duke wishes to take everyone's mind and soul into his power! The effect in the end is very impressive, especially when the Duke is unmuffled, and it is no comic effect. Except for two who are privy to the subterfuge[4], everyone else on stage goes through the experience of being seen through as by God! And it is no less impressive because *we* watch knowing all along that the Friar is the Duke.

The Duke's power at the end is dreadful; he could do anything he wants at this point, and no one could argue against him. His very elaborate manipulations have been the only way Shakespeare can conceive of really bringing a new kind of licentious society under control again. But the solution, now that we see it at work, is draconian, frightfully unreal, and all the more so when one considers all the marriages that are finally imposed. They are not so much grotesquely unbelievable as they are so badly based morally: the imposed consequence! of having indulged in an astonishing range of sexual deviancy very consciously pursued. I speak only of the situations of Angelo and of Lucio; in the case of the Duke and Isabella, we surely ask ourselves how and where anything has ever developed between them of any such kind as to motivate his assumption that *they* are meant for marriage?! unless one were to assume that the Duke, like Angelo, has *himself* fallen victim to the same sensual motions in his close dealings with Isabella. The collective eyebrows are surely raised over this coupling! which, as in the case of every coupling except one in this scene, grossly denies the whole idea of free choice in marriage. Claudio and Juliet are the only ones who put any kind of face on this scene of grotesque accommodation of human aberrancy, but they have become, in spite of the centrality of their story, by then a *minor* pairing in this assortment of couples, and have barely appeared in the play linked together. They are like the unthinking youthful Elizabethan couple of old, who in their own (unfree) extravagances, now appear as only *another* expression of sexual aberrancy, in this later, much more culturally "adult" take on the sexual scene.

Now, where is your comic decorum in all this? In comedy there is always at least one instance of significant believability among the couplings, and otherwise such a lightness in respect of the representation of human nature that we are indeed ready to countenance a general use of marriage as a way of bringing the action around to a final end of social harmony. But in this case, the range of fouled up virtue is so extensive and the depth of compromised behavior so disturbing, how could a proper sorting of couples come from amongst those who have been involved in this chaotic degradation of life?

An *illusion* of social control and decorum is finally asserted. But a mere *form* of morality, even a purely social morality for purposes of order, can no longer be so dictated. Authoritarianism, like Puritanism, is itself shown up (though it might still be possible for an extreme authoritarian like James to think himself well-reflected in the play's ending). But in any case, could authority like the Duke's continue indefinitely from here? He has created only a momentary illusion of God's implication in the scene and could hardly proceed in this way again. We would soon enough return to the same situation of disbelieved authority that we start from at the beginning of this play. No external solution can do any longer, because the problem of freedom, which involves a frighteningly chaotic open-endedness in human nature, will be ongoing. There *is* the option of legal imposition masquerading as religious authority, as practised for example by Rome, the fake solution of those whom Luther called "the Romanizing oppressors", with their high-handed notions of the "necessity" of marriage: which is just the sort of corrupted solution that is finally imposed in this play, and this Shakespeare was concerned in the long run in seeing out of the way. In the meantime, what transpires between Isabella and Angelo has taken the presentation to yet another even more problematic level; here the Lutheran notion of *a universal culpability* has shown its ugly head, and at this level there are, very simply, no mainstays and no solutions. (I refer you here to the other part of Luther's critical statement that "Nothing can cure libido, not even marriage"). At this level individuals are simply left to themselves and will be very much on their own with the issue of their redeemability.

*   *   *

But Shakespeare is only on his way with his tragic explorations at this level. His technique, from *Hamlet* through *Othello*, has been for the most part indirect, his explorations of the implication in human depravity pursued primarily at the level of subtext in the case of his good or generally decent characters. (And here I must send you back to how I present the case about Hamlet and Ophelia in *Otherworldly Hamlet*, and to the section on Desdemona in *Muse*, which I very consciously wrote to add to what I had said in *Otherworldly*.[5]) The indirection in Shakespeare's technique expresses the fact that he would have had much trouble, as we do, thinking evil of his good characters and especially of his best characters. It was, very simply, a way of thinking that was hard for him to learn. You speak of a careful sorting out of the "good" or "kind" and the "evil" or "ruthless" among Shakespeare's characters, but that is just the sort of distinction that, in Shakespeare, is slowly worn away at and finally *tragically* given up as pointless. What's more, what finally transpires in Othello is far more than about the "unkindness" that Desdemona superficially attributes to him; a far greater power of evil, or force of depravity, is at work, while "kindness", including her own "kindness", is *no* great power, or at least not good enough. Any "kindness" or "goodness" that is incapable of evolving *with* the "ruthless" or "evil" so that "good" can serve to redeem "evil", and triumph over it, is judged to be finally pointless. That does not mean that the kindness of Shakespeare's good characters is not still *our* choice, only that we recognize that in itself it does not lead anywhere.

Escalus and the Provost are kind or good characters in *Measure*, but what difference does that make when it comes to addressing the moral problem of human nature that is brought out in all the rest of the characters in that play? Kent in his kindness can persevere all he can to bring Lear back into Cordelia's company; he is there at least to protect Lear's person from a worse bodily harm, but what effect does his kindness have on Lear's mind, tormented as it is by the great evil of depravity that has been let loose? Lear is presented as another Ixion in hell. The limits of the value of Kent's kindness are drastically exposed most especially, of course, at the end of the play. In any case, even the so-called kind characters show themselves to be susceptible to something highly problematic in a deeper analysis. It is only a lack of character that keeps Albany from dealing with Goneril in her own kind (forgive the pun) by "dislocating and tearing her flesh and bones" (cf. Lear's "she'll flay thy wolvish visage", said of Regan and what she will do to Goneril). Edgar alone, as Poor Tom, has any sense of all that further implicates him in his subconscious nature (and there is something for everyone here):

> *false of heart, light of ear, bloody of hand; hog in sloth, fox in stealth, wolf in greediness, dog in madness, lion in prey.*

Edgar becomes consequently Shakespeare's greatest expression of self-confession among the good characters, and that makes him, potentially, the most evolved character amidst all of this old humanity. Yet Edgar himself can accomplish nothing, in the end, in the face of the effects of depravity, except to let his heart feel the whole hopeless tragedy that has in the meantime seen itself through inexorably.

As for Desdemona's love or kindness, what value can *it* still have *through all the horror of her death*? The appalling horror of that death overwhelms the scene. [I give an account of that effect in Chapter 9.] I speak here also of the way we are drawn into the excruciating physical horror of that death. What possible meaning can Desdemona's love for Othello have in the midst of that action, and once he has become her murderer? We live at the end with the finality of that situation, and any further expression of his love for her, which returns to him afterwards, only appears to us the more horrible as it is now rendered null. We feel the same about her commendations to him when she dies. They have been rendered null, can no longer have any application to him, no matter how hard we want to believe it. The effect of horror in *Othello* is intensified still further, one might almost say perfected, in *Lear*, in the death of Cordelia, which is even more insistently horrible. This is because we don't really anticipate that death, even if we know it's been ordered. We forget about Edmund's order for her death because we cannot believe it will happen, and we also cannot believe it when it *has* happened. When Lear walks onto the stage at the end with Cordelia in his arms, we are really overwhelmed, and the sight of her strangulated body is (as Johnson insisted) especially unendurable in its horror.

Once again love had been brought to bear on the tragic scene. We had been through the moment of Lear's recovery, unquestionably the scene in Shakespeare in which there is the greatest promise of amendment and hopeful resolution, and we have been engrossed in the idea that love, Cordelia's love, *has* come through to redeem. But we are later forced to give up that idea at the very point where we thought ourselves secure in it. We do not merely give it up; it is wiped out as an effective reality and as a power for dealing with the world's evil. That evil has prevailed monumentally, and it has denied all possible further life to that love. And that is all that Lear sees. There is nothing for him but his love of her, but now she is dead as earth, and so horribly dead, unendurably so. What sort of reality can what you call Lear's "absolute" love have in this picture? We do not look ahead to any compensating life in the otherworld, or to any otherworld at all in this insistently earthly view. "Absolute" where and how? Not in space and time. And only for *us* perhaps, in an unreal way, sentimentally, merely from our privileged position on the outside, where the reality has not reached us, even though Shakespeare's presentation draws us as powerfully as it can into that reality, calls on us, in fact, to enter into it.

If I speak of this scene as "the point of greatest devastation" in Shakespeare, "the farthest extremity of a stifled humanity" this is because here love is involved to the very utmost and it is crushed, pulverized, negated. In *Macbeth* love is not there. I made the point long ago (in *Sacrifice*, in a footnote) that "With *Macbeth* we have moved beyond that point where love is still being tragically affirmed". There isn't even a possibility of love in the *Macbeth*-world, which is what makes that world already a far less human world. If still great devastation, there is *less* devastation here in human terms, because love has quite retired from the scene. There is certainly "greatness of soul" in Macbeth, as you put it, on a scale that is unsurpassable in its own way, but this greatness has been radically divorced from love from the start. That is a deeper tragedy perhaps, but beyond where we could wish ourselves to be, and certainly beyond any power of recourse. Hence my relative account of *Lear* and of *Macbeth* in *Muse*.

Among other things Shakespeare can see very clearly in *Macbeth* how especially great violent expressions in "goodness", being merely human, naturally convert to "evil". I speak of the initially "good" Macbeth who must be fighting so fiercely for his king. We have in the rest of this play yet another range of so-called "good" characters, but what does "goodness" in *this* form avail? Banquo, who appears after the murder of Duncan bedraggled and barely dressed, might just as well be looking for a ghost as make any difference in his determination to stand against evil. Later, Macduff's family is simply wiped out, left unprotected; and as Lady Macduff puts it:

> to leave his wife, to leave his babes,
> His mansions and his titles, in a place
> From whence himself does fly?
> . . . .
> All is the fear and nothing is the love;

Malcolm [the heir to the throne, after Duncan's death] at some point expresses himself in a form of self-confession that compares with Edgar's in *Lear*, but the effect is ironic (we appreciate this all the more in comparison with Edgar's sincere account). He doesn't believe anything of the sort about himself! does not even suppose that he may have some significant smattering of a good number of the things he mentions somewhere in his make-up! He is the same old superficial Malcolm now as then. (And have you considered that to his pretensions to being hopelessly lustful Macduff actually says: "We have dames enough."?! Whatever these two may have in the way of virtues, the state will see no tremendous advance in moral vision, although at least there will not be tyranny like Macbeth's.)

As for the antithetical "virtues" of the English court, to what extent have Malcolm and Macduff partaken in them? The English king happily offers them military support, appalled as everyone else is with the reign of Macbeth's evil. But this English king's "holiness" is his own. His *exceptional* saintliness (like one of Luther's elect) only makes the rest of humanity appear all the more terribly abandoned to *its* hopelessness. Shakespeare radically undercuts the presentation about him (this in IV.iii) by bringing Ross in at that very point to relate the unspeakable horrors that in the meantime have been committed against Macduff's family. What compensation or consolation, in this context, in this highly privileged, distant king's power of "goodness"?

One *could* see in his virtues I suppose a forecast of what a power of "holiness" like his might accomplish in the state, but his kind of rule is a very distant prospect as far as the immediate *Macbeth*-humanity is concerned. It has the value in the end of a very disturbing, an almost imponderably *contrasting* scene. In relation to the evil Shakespeare is in process of presenting, that sort of goodness does not in fact concern him, because it hasn't met up with, does not meet up with, all the forces of evil in the world he has exposed. In the end the remote "grace" that Malcolm calls on to help his cause is a far cry from the power that is in possession of the saintly English king alone. Macduff, in the meantime, has prevailed by dint of another power that also has very little to do with those English virtues. *Their* ultimately *conventional* social powers, which prevail very simply from sheer brutishness, will always find a way of re-asserting themselves in the face of a greater evil that has manifested, but we are then only returned to the same point we were at when we started, to begin the whole cycle all over again (a point that has often been made in connection with *Macbeth*).

Otherwise a *general* implication in a universal evil has led humanity to the point of *its* tragic annulment. Trace this evil to the will to power or uncontrolled libido and its effects in those whom we recognize as ruthless, evil characters; there is nevertheless still the tragic implication in that evil also of the good, 'kind' characters. It is Shakespeare's tragic heroes (not his villains) who bring in the catastrophic turn towards annulment by their obvious implication. But *none* of Shakespeare's good characters are free of the evil in the final reckoning—not Isabella, not Desdemona, not even

Cordelia. There is indeed a great sacrifice of human potential here, and one might say that Shakespeare's development in the vision of evil, by the time it sees itself through, will have cost not less than everything. But even the best characters *share* in the evil as a result of their own perverse natures, which are not untouched by violence or ferocity. This is true even of Desdemona and of Cordelia. All are bound by the perversity in human sensuality itself, because that is the fundamental condition of life in the flesh, the condition precisely of earthly natural humanity.

I think the compromising effects of Desdemona's sensuality are clear enough, tragic as it is to think that *her* romantic sensuality would compromise her. But Cordelia is no less free of the ambiguous effects of *her* sensuality. This is how I put it *Impasse*⁶: "Of the perversely sensual basis of Lear's love of Cordelia there is no doubt, but to the extent that Cordelia is *involved* in this love, who can say that she does not *share* in that sensuality or express *herself* in it? As far as I know no commentary exists on what we may suppose Cordelia is experiencing through the extensive silence that marks her response to Lear's [ferocious] outburst [in the play's first scene]. But we can surely imagine that, among other feelings, Cordelia would be wondering about the basis of the love shared with him until now, and feeling some guiltiness about it. Not in the sense that she wonders how she could love this man, but that she wonders on what grounds she herself has been having this love, since it was love partaken of with him. When she and Lear meet again later in the play, after much suffering, both have by then been largely purged of the sensual basis of the love that they once shared."

This is not to deny that in the case of *Hamlet, Othello* and *Lear* love continues, in its various forms, right up to the end, *but there is no way through with it*, no possibility with it of overturning evil or of redeeming it. Love simply ends there, tragically. And that is the experience we should come away with after watching these plays. We come away from these plays with the one question Shakespeare finally wanted to leave with us: if evil *is* our lot, what *then* of good? where does *it* find itself finally in relation to evil? Or is *all* lost? From here Luther felt he had only one way to go, *upwards* through justification by faith alone. Shakespeare forges his own way *through* the evil. We might see it as his extraordinary destiny: taking *on* the evil in order somehow to turn it into good. But if Shakespeare finally does see his way through, it is only by imagining that what there is of human good *will* be sacrificed to evil. The power to undo evil can only lie through *that* experience. Goodness cannot just stand over and against the evil. It must somehow have gotten beyond it by assimilating it, *and this it does by being sacrificed to it.*

* * *

Beyond this point we have to begin to imagine the very elaborate process I try to describe in both *Sacrifice* and *Muse*, where I proceed to the late plays. What you keep insisting on as the "tragicomic" pattern in Shakespeare only properly fulfills itself in those plays because only in those plays has the whole human tragedy been addressed. Until then we are given only the roughest prognostication of any such eventuality: Shakespeare only *projecting* that outcome, quite abstractly, rather as Keats does in his "Endymion". In reality, it will turn out to be a very different matter (the process will turn out to be much harder than was thought).

Measure is for me, in any case, no tragicomedy, even in your accommodating sense, but definitely a problem play, as is *All's Well*. Shakespeare has reached a point very different from where he was, say, with *Much Ado* where the tragicomic pattern is first elaborated with some flourish. But *Measure* and *All's Well* stand on the near side of Shakespeare's greater development in the tragedies. He is addressing the fanciful human idea of bringing what (it is becoming more and more clear) is uncontrollable under control, and finding that effort grotesque. The range of human aberrancy and reprobacy has become too great, and is spilling out all over (especially so in *Measure*). He is well into the reality of it all by then but still not fully into it. As for *Much Ado* the conclusion that is reached is that "Man is giddy"; Shakespeare has no greater insight into the matter at that point, and we continue to be given up to the happy dream. Changeableness is suffered, and then there is the dream: the typical bipolar life that most of us live out to the end of our days, without searching ourselves any further. It is all very charming and very enviable in fact, all this human innocence, and we *are* tempted to go back to it and remain there! But there came a time when Shakespeare had begun to see his way through to some deeper accountability for what we are.

Not that there isn't still a place for "comedy" in Shakespeare's later serious development. You misread me also on this count. What I say is that after *Hamlet* he gives us no more "comedies", which is literally true, which is to say that he has given up (for himself) the happy dream. In the meantime his audience was, of course, in every position to re-play his "comedies" at will. In fact, there always would be a place for "comedy", simply because Shakespeare was gathering up to himself the whole human scene, and human beings *will* remain addicted to it. But the comedy as such is associated more and more with a baseness that he is in the process of judging. This goes beyond the critical perspective on his comic action that he is already giving us in his earlier comedies. This baseness we even laugh at (Lucio and Pompey are still very funny), but we are implicated only because of our own unreadiness (for the moment) to get more serious about ourselves (or because we revert to that condition). That we are not more ready may even lead to a whole other way of receiving Shakespeare's plays of that later period that I would argue has nothing to do with how they come across.

However, we are by then definitely with Shakespeare on the *far* side of comic action and definitely in the position of looking down on, or at least out at, it. The fact is that we *can* laugh and do continue to laugh, but this is because although we may, up to a point, have evolved with Shakespeare in *his* very serious development, we remain who we are in our general life, for the most part for now the same people we always were. All of *that* continues, so that we are in every position also to return to his "comedies" whenever we wish to, and still derive something of significant human value in them. I make a similar point in *Sacrifice* about where we stand in relation to all the beauty and the charm that continues all around us in life beyond the inward process Shakespeare is engaged in in his tragic development.

In the case of his tragedies and his late plays seen in combination, we are talking about a process of development that is taking place beyond our present lives, pursued in relation to all that more of what we are that we are only slowly coming to terms with. In the meantime, I am free to dip back into this play or the other, in order to glean from each some notion of what human nature is about and how Shakespeare has gone about shaping his understanding of how we stand in relation to it. Why would you assume, because I am intent on tracing the psycho-biographical development in his work, that I have not seen and appreciated, or cannot continue to appreciate, how each of his plays works? I can also be more or less satisfied with each, depending on where I know I am in relation to Shakespeare's whole development. There is indeed a great body of knowledge to be gained from all of his plays that precede *Hamlet*, but I happen to think this, for the most part though not altogether (there are some exceptions), a *formal* knowledge: the expression of a *general* development in the exercise of which Shakespeare remains more or less the same person in consciousness; only he is progressively maturing, having experienced more and more of the world as he goes along. I indicate in *Muse* what I think constitutes, in counterpoint with this, the line of *essential* development in the exercise of which Shakespeare is deepening in consciousness to the extreme point of *Lear*, beyond which point he breaks open (miraculously) altogether new forms of consciousness that are hardly known to us as yet. (You know my argument in *Sacrifice*.) This essential development does not keep Shakespeare from continuing to express himself massively *also* in his consciousness of old, the old heroic consciousness that has become perversity. This he is doing, beyond *Lear*, in *Antony, Coriolanus* and in *Timon*, and even in *Cymbeline* (though the essential development is to some extent also reflected in those middle three plays in the *judgment* of perversity, in the case of *Cymbeline* in its unfulfilled, or not quite fully realized, association with the other late plays of *its* period in which there *is* the essential development).

Your own mistake, if I may be so bold as to identify *it*, is in thinking that we will remain in consciousness always only what we were or, which is the same thing, that we are always, and will always be, only the same in consciousness. Thus for you Shakespeare is already from early on substantially what he will be later, and so your term "tragicomedy" is applied equally to the later plays as to the earlier. But the term is then stretched in a way that becomes meaningless, and it has for this reason been thought by many to be unsatisfactory. It begs the whole question of qualitative differences among the plays that would make us feel that a more significant set of energies is being addressed in some plays rather than in others, and also in rather *different* ways that would constitute separate genres, or that some resolutions are more satisfying than others etc . . . Thus I think *The Tempest* resolves successfully almost everything about the human condition in *its* form, while *Much Ado* resolves absolutely nothing, and does not pretend to, and that there we simply escape from our potentially disturbing changeableness back into the dream. That is a measure of the distance of one play (*The Tempest*), which is a result of the whole evolution in consciousness I attribute to Shakespeare from *Lear* onwards, from another play (*Ado*), in which he is not even deepening in consciousness in my terms but simply intelligently offering us a view of human nature that is fixed and predictable. But you deny beforehand any possible further *evolution* in consciousness that will make Shakespeare a very different being in consciousness by the time he is writing *The Tempest* than he was at the time he was writing *Much Ado* or *Measure for Measure*. Assuming that there has been such an evolution, however, what you call psychobiography becomes quite a necessary additional feature to our approach to Shakespeare.

What, shall we say, *is* the link through, then, from *Lear* to *Pericles* and the other late plays? Here I can only repeat what I have developed at length in my books: that it has everything to do finally with the 'death of the beloved', and so, at a certain stage, with how Desdemona and Cordelia are sacrificed to the evil that otherwise prevails with everyone. Something tremendous is happening at this time that I have tried to formulate in *Prospero's Powers* with the illuminating guidance of Rudolf Steiner's Anthroposophy: some great sacrificial 'death' of the Goddess *as* the Sophia that is being accomplished *through* the deaths of those tragic heroines and that brings about a further evolution even out of the extreme triumphing evil Shakespeare had finally isolated as the all-determining factor in this age. In the meantime clearly Shakespeare's Muse, to the extent that he is driven by Her, has transformed—from what She was, when Shakespeare was as yet unfree in his understanding of tragedy, into the reflected image now of his full understanding. In this latter guise She appears more properly as Herself, as it were in Her *own* being, in the process of developing *with* him. I know of no other way to explain what is happening. What is the import of such an evolution? Ultimately, the transformation of an earthly natural humanity which pretends to rely only on itself and which can, therefore, only be finally overwhelmed by evil, into a higher, transcendent spiritual humanity that has genuinely overcome evil, having passed beyond it for good. That transformation is not accomplished by one single leap out of our skin into an otherworldly Paradise (as Luther thought, and please note that I am not an apologist for Luther) but (as Shakespeare presents it) by a long, drastic process of self-overcoming that must take place in stages if *each* part of us and of our universe is to be rightfully accommodated back to the spirit, and that *must* go forward progressively out of where we happen to be at any given moment.

That is the long, drastic process in which I have argued Shakespeare is finally engaged, once he had broken out of a fixed way of seeing human nature, which he had inherited from his culture. How is transformation accomplished for you? From what I understand, only as a momentary phenomenon that is perpetually repeated from inside a condition in which we remain forever. Thus Freud explains for you what is down below, all that lies in the unconscious that is "dark and dangerous", while Plato explains what is above, "immortality and the good". But for you all is statically fixed beforehand and there can only be movement in one degree or other up and down, as it were barometrically. (Incidentally, this more or less agrees with Luther's worldview, except that for him it was all polarized and a matter, almost literally, of leaping out of sin into God's grace if that could be done. Sexuality, in the meantime, *was* sin.) Sexuality in *your* worldview constitutes potentially at least one way of working one's way up from below, so long as those dark energies of the unconscious are "acknowledged", at which point these dark forces become "sources of creativity and growth". Presumably in Platonic terms by then; that is, there will come a time when you experience a further sublimation of "sexual desires" into "higher desires" such as the desire for immortality and good. But in the end all this will only get you back repeatedly to the same place, where you will, precisely, be "forcing the pained impotent to smile." I am not saying that this is not how we also experience things right now, but what I would call the prophetic experience of Shakespeare should alert us to the idea that things will not remain where they are forever, as we perhaps might like to think.

I have also enclosed for your interest a text that was intended for another general commentary on Shakespeare's development that I started to write but that I'm not sure I'll ever complete. I include this fragment here by way of addressing your point that Othello should have known better what love is. As for your idea of how love between a couple comes to be seen after they have children, that seems pretty remote from the situation in *Othello*, doesn't it? Even so, I am not sure that love so conceived can possibly account for all that brings a couple together at first. Compassion, or what may simply be a form of dissipated or tired love, after one has had children, is not what drives a couple to *desire* each other, at any stage. And then, love as a case of being tricked, as it were, into sexual union so that a child might be born, surely that kind of love would not be a higher but a lower thing, all about the reproduction of the species. At the same time there *is* parental love, and that would be—for Freud certainly, wouldn't it?—*also* a sublimated love and so still involved, somewhere along the line, in libido. And so it was I think also for Shakespeare, certainly between Lear and Cordelia; this is, in spite of all our protestations, just what they must pass through the fire for, so they can reach through to another depth of love that is at least considerably more selfless. (Yes, they have learned, but again that still does not mean that they have fully properly overcome themselves in Shakespeare's all-demanding vision.) As for your basic idea that love is not reducible to libido, that just can't be true while Othello and Desdemona are in a sexual relationship. To what extent theirs is also a marriage of true minds is another matter, but that marriage is clearly overrun by the whole complication of their very complex sexual engagement. Yes that love between minds comes into it later, as where Desdemona says: "his unkindness [will] never taint my love." It is the idealized love Shakespeare brings back from the Sonnets. But that love is *also* finally negated, is shown to be itself not enough of a power to withstand an overriding evil. But what *does* see us through it all somehow eventually *is* a sacrificial love, a love accomplished *through* death, of which we have as yet little understanding and which does not work as simply as we would think (as you know from my books) . . .

In *each* of the three so-called "great" tragedies that follow *Hamlet*[7], we find a comparable phenomenon breaking through at the start that decisively alters everything for evil, a phenomenon that is equated with the human "will", which breaks out of its own sphere of "darkness" and predetermines from that point on the whole course of the action that follows. It is precisely what the Reformation theologians meant when they spoke of the fundamental "depravity" of the human will and the frightful effect associated with it of predetermination.[8] In *Othello* it is Desdemona who, in her sexual will, has that effect, though it takes some time before the full consequences of that effect begin to show. Very much is made at the beginning of the impact Desdemona's elopement with Othello has had. There is something so inexplicable about the way Desdemona has altered her father is utterly horrified. Setting aside his ugly prejudice about Othello, as well as his dreamed up (yet not illogical) idea that Desdemona has been worked upon by witchcraft, we *are* left wondering how Desdemona can have changed so very suddenly and so radically from the kind of woman that she "was" until then.

> Brabantio. *O thou foul thief, where hast thou stowed my daughter?*
> *Damned as thou art, thou hast enchanted her,*
> *For I'll refer me to all things of sense,*
> *If she in chains of magic were not bound,*
> *Whether a maid so tender, fair and happy,*
> *So opposite to marriage that she shunned*
> *The wealthy, curled darlings of our nation,*
> *Would ever have, t'incur a general mock,*
> *Run from her guardage to the sooty bosom*
> *Of such a thing as thou? to fear, not to delight.*
> *Judge me the world if 'tis not gross in sense*
> *That thou hast practised on her with foul charms,*
> *Abused her delicate youth with drugs or minerals*
> *That weakens motion: I'll have it disputed on,*
> *'Tis probable and palpable to thinking.*
>
> *A maiden never bold,*
> *Of spirit so still and quiet that her motion*
> *Blushed at herself; and, she, in spite of nature,*

Of years, of country, credit, everything,
To fall in love with what she feared to look on?
It is a judgment maimed and most imperfect
That will confess perfection so could err
Against all rules of nature, and must be driven
To find out practices of cunning hell
Why this should be.

There *is* something frightfully preternatural about the way Desdemona's sexual will so suddenly overcomes her, *if it is the case*, and it does seem to be, that *she has only just come into* this will. It is immediately absorbed into the overwhelming romantic ethos of the couple's way of engaging with each other; by this ethos we are at first distracted, but that does not alter our view of something almost alienly constituted as a force of will, when we look into it for itself, stripped of all the romantic investment that colours how we see it. Iago will come back to the impact Desdemona's alteration had, later in his temptation of Othello; what takes Othello over later and *clinches* Iago's effect on him (all this in III.iii) is not the thought that Cassio and Desdemona are engaged with each other so much as that her sexual will *has* that overwhelming character to it, and *is* that kind of driving force, that it is too easy to see how it *would* have taken her over and *of its own alien momentum* driven her elsewhere. Thus, the thought of the *intrinsic* "foulness" of such a preternaturally strange "will", with which is immediately associated Desdemona's impulse to reject the many who sued for her in marriage.

Iago. *Ay, there's the point: as, to be bold with you,*
Not to affect many proposed matches
Of her own clime, complexion and degree,
Whereto we see, in all things, nature tends—
Foh! one may smell in such a will most rank,
Foul disproportion, thoughts unnatural.
But pardon me, I do not in position
Distinctly speak of her, though I may fear
Her will, recoiling to her better judgement,
May fall to match you with her country forms,
And happily repent.

The picture of Desdemona presented here is the opposite of that which the father gives of her before her sudden "change". If *not* "the maiden never bold", then in fact one who already had her "will", which she would surely also have needed to satisfy, and did with Othello, though the need for "satisfaction" has now driven her elsewhere. Precisely *how* Desdemona engaged with Othello is thus accounted for, and it is *this* impressive demonstration (where there would otherwise be pure bafflement about this) that dominates Othello's thoughts later and lays the *basis* for the idea of the affair she is thought to be having. Desdemona's sexual will was *already* highly developed. One would otherwise have to suppose that an instantaneous and violent transformation had taken place in her that very much defies natural explanation. (And even the most accommodating theories of pubescence would have difficulty sounding plausible in this instance.) Interwoven with Iago's densely packed set of tendentious suggestions is the further insinuation that Othello could not for long favorably compare with Desdemona's own kind—which of course works additionally on Othello's sense of his very real difference and distance from *them*. To this picture is *also* added the thought of the power of deception Desdemona exercised in pretending *not* to be the creature of sexual will that she was, to the point where only an effect of witchcraft could explain her transformation for her father:

> Iago. *She did deceive her father, marrying you,*
> *And when she seemed to shake, and fear your looks,*
> *She loved them most.*
> Othello. *And so she did.*
> Iago. *Why, go to then:*
> *She that so young could give out such a seeming*
> *To seel her father's eyes up, close as oak—*
> *He thought 'twas witchcraft.*

Another ambiguous impression is seized upon where attention is brought to the way Desdemona was taken up with Othello in their days of courtship. Her "love" is brought up in association with the kind of anxious response about being overtaken that *can* register as "fear". The problematic nature of the libidinal response is again hinted at in passing, and perhaps Iago intends some suggestion of guilt in Desdemona *about* her "will". But the "fear" is here primarily appropriated to the idea of her giving a deceiving impression, which *is* how this kind of anxiety can manifest. On the *other* side of Iago's approach is the overwhelming concern he displays about Othello himself because of his "free and noble nature", which will easily be abused by a Venetian race that, Iago confirms, is given to deceiving ways:

> Iago. *I speak not yet of proof:*
> *Look to your wife, observe her well with Cassio.*
> *Wear your eyes thus, not jealous nor secure;*
> *I would not have your free and noble nature*
> *Out of self-bounty be abused: look to't.*
> *I know our country disposition well—*

Iago's point works on Othello's *cultural* vulnerability as an outsider to Venetian mores; it also works on his *characterological* vulnerability, since it is in his very nature, as an open-hearted man, *not* to understand deception. Iago impresses himself upon Othello in this same motion also as that very person of "love and honesty" everyone in the play takes Iago for and who confides himself to Othello out of that "love". It is a situation Iago fully exploits when "horrified" by what he pretends is actually happening. One cannot understate the impact Iago has on Othello initially, on assuming the horror of his thought that Othello is being deceived. What informs this projection of "horror" is Iago's fear of what he risks from Othello's wrath in proceeding to his temptation should Iago's stratagem fail. However, the "effect" of horror is identified by Iago, of course, with the "import" of Desdemona's deception—ultimately, and most crucially, with the horrid nature of her "will". From other references in the play, it is clear that Iago really is offended by that "will", which he actually believes of Desdemona, in spite of what he knows is her faithfulness. It is, at the same time, significant that, when Iago first approaches Othello in the temptation-scene, his language should directly echo Hamlet's when *he* approaches Ophelia in the nunnery-scene, as if the same horror of sexual deviancy were being voiced again here. This horror is registered at first in connection with Cassio but of course comes to be overwhelmingly associated with Desdemona, just as it was once expressed in relation to Ophelia.[9] We are thus in the position to measure a great deal of the impact Iago's approach has on Othello, though numerous other points of attack could be cited, for this is the scene into which Shakespeare put a greater number of characterological considerations perhaps than in any other he worked up.

Iago. *My noble lord—*
Othello. *What dost thou say, Iago?*
Iago. *Did Michael Cassio, when you wooed my lady,*
Know of your love?
Othello. *He did, from first to last.*
Why dost thou ask?
Iago. *But for a satisfaction of my thought,*
No further harm.
Othello. *Why of thy thought, Iago?*
Iago. *I did not think he had been acquainted with her.*
Othello. *O yes, and went between us very oft.*
Iago. *Indeed?*
Othello. *Indeed? Ay, indeed. Discern'st thou aught in that?*
Is he not honest?
Iago. *Honest, my lord?*
Othello. *Honest? Ay, honest.*
Iago. *My lord, for aught I know.*
Othello. *What dost thou think?*
Iago. *Think, my lord?*
Othello. *Think, my lord? By heaven, thou echo'st me*
As if there were some monster in thy thought
Too hideous to be shown. Thou dost mean something,
I heard thee say even now thou lik'st not that
When Cassio left my wife: what didst not like?
And when I told thee he was of my counsel
In my whole course of wooing, thou criedst 'Indeed?'
And didst contract and purse thy brow together
As if thou then hadst shut up in thy brain
Some horrible conceit. If thou dost love me
Show me thy thought.
Iago. *My lord, you know I love you.*
Othello. *I think thou dost.*
And for I know thou'rt full of love and honesty
And weigh'st thy words before thou giv'st them breath,
Therefore these stops of thine fright me the more.
For such things in a false disloyal knave
Are tricks of custom, but in a man that's just
They're close delations, working from the heart,

That passion cannot rule.
Iago. *For Michael Cassio,*
I dare be sworn, I think, that he is honest.
Othello. *I think so too.*
Iago. *Men should be what they seem,*
Or those that be not, would they might seem none.
Othello. *Certain, men should be what they seem.*
Iago. *Why then I think Cassio's an honest man.*
Othello. *Nay, yet there's more in this:*
I prithee speak to me, as to thy thinkings,
As thou dost ruminate, and give thy worst of thoughts
The worst of words . . .

Iago. *I am glad of this, for now I shall have reason*
To show the love and duty that I bear you
With franker spirit: therefore, as I am bound,
Receive it from me. I speak not yet of proof:
Look to your wife, observe her well with Cassio.
Wear your eyes thus, not jealous nor secure;
I would not have your free and noble nature
Out of self-bounty be abused: look to't.
I know our country disposition well—
In Venice they do let God see the pranks
They dare not show their husbands; their best conscience
Is not to leave't undone, but keep't unknown.
Othello. *Dost thou say so?*
Iago. *She did deceive her father, marrying you,*
And when she seemed to shake, and fear your looks,
She loved them most.
Othello. *And so she did.*
Iago. *Why, go to then:*
She that so young could give out such a seeming
To seel her father's eyes up, close as oak—
He thought 'twas witchcraft. But I am much to blame,
I humbly do beseech you of your pardon
For too much loving you.
Othello. *I am bound to thee forever.*
Iago. *I see this hath a little dashed your spirit.*
Othello. *Not a jot, not a jot.*

Iago. *I'faith I fear it has.*
I hope you will consider what is spoke
Comes from my love. But I do see you are moved;
I am to pray you not to strain my speech
To grosser issues nor to larger reach than to suspicion.
Othello. *I will not.*
Iago. *Should you do so, my lord,*
My speech should fall into such vile success
As my thoughts aimed not at. Cassio's my worthy friend.
My lord, I see you're moved.
Othello. *No, not much moved.*
I do not think but Desdemona's honest.
Iago. *Long live she so; and long live you to think so.*
Othello. *And yet how nature, erring from itself—*
Iago. *Ay, there's the point: as, to be bold with you,*
Not to affect so many proposed matches
Of her own clime, complexion and degree,
Whereto we see, in all things, nature tends—
Foh! one may smell in such a will most rank,
Foul disproportion, thoughts unnatural.
But pardon me, I do not in position
Distinctly speak of her, though I may fear
Her will, recoiling to her better judgement,
May fall to match you with her country forms,
And happily repent.

To come away from this scene simply with the idea that Iago is an out-and-out villain and Othello a gullible fool is truly to fail to read what Shakespeare is presenting. The whole effect of this temptation-scene depends on our grasping that the sexual will, especially in the preternatural form in which Desdemona expresses herself in it, *does* defy our notions of any possible integrity that can be claimed of it. In itself, which is to say as its own alien force as libido, it eludes *all* ennobling or romanticizing views that can be taken of it, and in this sense is *essentially* perverse, so that it can easily *be thought to be* the kind of force that can create the circumstances Iago "thinks" Desdemona into, along with Othello. In a certain sense *we* are being forced to think this through along with them, and this *in spite of* our "better" knowledge that nothing is actually happening. In respect of this necessary thought, which the play insists upon, Iago's work on Othello is but a strategic mechanism. It forces a condition of vision upon Othello, and upon us that, incidentally, corresponds extra-textually to the effect the Dark Lady has over our poet in the Sonnets [as described here in Chapter 2]. This same poet/playwright now feels compelled to think *through* the devastating reality of human perversity, in spite of every indication that he is going *against* his better sense and abandoning his vision of nobleness and of normality. To simplify these developments—nobleness has been set aside, and perversity (or the thought of it) is now the dominating fact. The conflict that is created by this extraordinary shift in ideological perspective is gigantic, *just because* the vision of nobleness is retained and, one might even say, is expanded (in the romantic direction). The conflict is the more disturbing because the vision of perversity breaks in upon a scene that otherwise gives a full impression of nobleness and of normality. In this case, unlike Ophelia, Desdemona will come to meet the thought of corruption head on, defending herself as fully and as openly as she can, but to no avail—for the tide of reality has turned, and it is the thought of corruption that is now *uppermost* in the active will of the playwright. All of the tragic despair over this thought as registered by Hamlet in the nunnery-scene as well as in the closet-scene, *both* of which are being echoed here, is brought into Shakespeare's presentation again in IV.ii, as if we were re-visiting the same situation, though on a scale more awful yet, because so much more in the way of the noble life is being sacrificed to it:

> Desdemona. *What is your pleasure?*
> Othello. *Let me see your eyes.*
> *Look in my face.*
> Desdemona. *What horrible fancy's this?*
> Othello. [To Emilia]
> *Some of your function, mistress,*
> *Leave procreants alone and shut the door;*
> *Cough, or cry hem, if anybody come.*
> *Your mystery, your mystery: nay, dispatch!*
>   [Exit Emilia.]
> Desdemona. *Upon my knees, what doth your speech import?*
> *I understand a fury in your words*
> *But not the words.*
> Othello. *Why, what art thou?*
> Desdemona. *Your wife, my lord, your true and loyal wife.*
> Othello. *Come, swear it, damn thyself,*

Lest, being like one of heaven, the devils themselves
Should fear to seize thee: therefore, be double-damned.
Swear thou art honest!
Desdemona. *Heaven doth truly know it.*
Othello. *Heaven truly knows that thou art false as hell.*
Desdemona. *To whom, my lord? with whom? how am I false?*
Othello. *Ah, Desdemona, away, away, away!*
Desdemona. *Alas, the heavy day, why do you weep?*
Am I the motive of these tears, my lord?
If haply you my father do suspect
An instrument to your calling back,
Lay not your blame on me: if you have lost him
Why, I have lost him too.
Othello. *Had it pleased heaven*
To try me with affliction, had they rained
All kinds of sores and shames on my bare head,
Steeped me in poverty to the very lips,
Given to captivity me and my utmost hopes,
I should have found in some place of my soul
A drop of patience; but, alas, to make me
The fixed figure for the time of scorn
To point his slow and moving finger at!
Yet could I bear that too, well, very well:
But there where I have garnered up my heart,
Where either I must live or bear no life,
The fountain from the which my current runs
Or else dries up—to be discarded thence!
Or keep it as a cistern for foul toads
To knot and gender in! Turn thy complexion there,
Patience, thou young and rose-lipped cherubin,
Ay, here look, grim as hell!
Desdemona. *I hope my noble lord esteems me honest.*[10]
Othello. *O, ay, as summer flies are in the shambles,*
That quicken even with blowing. O thou weed
Who art so lovely fair and smell'st so sweet
That the sense aches at thee, would thou hadst ne'er been born!
Desdemona. *Alas, what ignorant sin have I committed?*[11]
Othello. *Was this fair paper, this most goodly book*

Made to write 'whore' upon? What committed!
Committed? O thou public commoner!
I should make very forges of my cheeks
That would to cinders burn up modesty
Did I but speak thy deeds. What committed!
Heaven stops the nose at it, and the moon winks[12],
The bawdy wind that kisses all it meets
Is hushed within the hollow mine of earth
And will not hear't. What committed!
Impudent strumpet!
Desdemona. *By heaven, you do me wrong.*
Othello. *Are not you a strumpet?*
Desdemona. *No, as I am a Christian.*
If to preserve this vessel for my lord
From any hated foul unlawful touch
Be not to be a strumpet, I am none.
Othello. *What, not a whore?*
Desdemona. *No, as I shall be saved.*
Othello. *Is't possible?*
Desdemona. *O heaven, forgive us!*
Othello. *I cry you mercy, then,*
I took you for that cunning whore of Venice
Who married with Othello. You! Mistress!
         [Enter Emilia.]
That have the office opposite to Saint Peter
And keep the gates of hell—you, you, ay you!
We have done our course, there's money for your pains,
I pray you turn the key and keep our counsel.

In a master-stroke of tragic irony, which only Shakespeare could think of and which measures how far he was ready to go to challenge himself, it is Iago who now enters, to a Desdemona who, from this confrontation, has been reduced to a very awful kind of self-questioning. It is awful not simply because Desdemona in her actual condition is innocent of the charges laid against her, not being guilty of unfaithfulness. It is awful because we understand *along with the play* that, in spite of her actual condition, these charges *very likely are* in essence true, in their *oblique* application, beyond Othello's bitterness about unfaithfulness, as a perception about the nature of the sexual will itself:

Iago. *What is your pleasure, madam? How is't with you?*
Desdemona. *I cannot tell. Those that do teach young babes*
Do it with gentle means and easy tasks.
He might have chid me so, for, in good faith,
I am a child to chiding.
Iago. *What is the matter, lady?*
Emilia. *Alas, Iago, my lord hath so bewhored her,*
Thrown such despite and heavy terms upon her
That true hearts cannot bear it.
Desdemona. *Am I that name, Iago?*
Iago. *What name, fair lady?*
Desdemona. *Such as she said my lord did say I was.*
Emilia. *He called her whore. A beggar in his drink*
Could not have laid such terms upon his callat.
Iago. *Why did he so?*

Desdemona. *I do not know; I am sure I am none such.*

Iago. *Do not weep, do not weep: alas the day!*
Emilia. *Hath she forsook so many noble matches,*
Her father, and her country, and her friends,
To be called whore? would it not make one weep?

Desdemona. *It is my wretched fortune.*

Desdemona's two quiet comments, which I have isolated from the rest, are *intentionally* suggestive of her self-questioning in this regard—*Shakespeare* intending this suggestion, and one may well *wonder* at the direction into which he felt he now had to drive himself. It is as if nothing could offer any defense against the overwhelming thought of fundamental human perversity, once this thought was sown. We are then further appalled by the vast mess of chaotic human reaction that is opened up by the sudden incorporation of this thought into human society . . .

4

From *Othello's Sacrifice*:
Shakespeare's Progress Through Tragedy

The world of Shakespeare's tragedies marks the point in human evolution where a human consciousness—Shakespeare's own—is brought to bear on inherited forms of love and sensual engagement that, for reasons that cannot be grasped at that time, have now to be renounced. The renunciation itself is a profoundly tragic experience. A perversely hopeful notion continues to be entertained at this time as to what it is that can be had in the way of a 'life of the senses'.[1] Characteristically, a great power of 'faith' is now being applied to an experience of 'love' in sensual terms, and that is what has become unreal as experience. An element of absolute freedom from these terms would have first to be introduced, before a right relation to them could be restored. It is precisely Shakespeare's great achievement at this time that *he* embodies the standard of true consciousness by which the attitudes of his characters, in respect of faith and of love, are judged wanting. However, Shakespeare's role in this regard is far from being an indifferent one, as indicated in Owen Barfield's point that he was "only unconsciously the bearer of—consciousness".[2] It is as if Shakespeare could not himself accept the profound failure implied in the self's tragic dissociation from any sure basis in faith and in love, as these had been known up to that time. The extent of his identification with the situations of his characters is reflected dramatically in that characteristic impulse to provide a complete representation for his characters in their aims, even where these aims have become perverse. The attempt itself may appear to us perverse, though to see it that way would be wrongly to dissociate ourselves from the profound evolution in experience Shakespeare was himself living through at the time, if only as creative genius.

One main line of development in Shakespeare's 'tragic progress' traces the route that would have to be taken if an experience of faith and of love in this kind were pursued without regard to the further evolution now necessitated. From this point of view, Wilson Knight's comprehensive tracing of the abysmal hate-theme in Shakespeare remains of tremendous critical value.[3] 'Hate' is the name Knight gave to an extreme form of violent cynicism about 'love' that overtakes many of Shakespeare's heroes from the time their own deepest aspirations regarding love are confounded. As we have seen, they themselves are abandoned to their own depraved natures, and in the end all transmutes into the spectacle of violent death *via* the hero's hatred, itself the involuntary and bitter negation of faith in love. That hatred is also by implication—in the violence of its effect—negation of the heroic. In fact, any view which continues to espouse the nobility of the hero in the face of the spectacle of evil Shakespeare offers must eventually founder against his final emphasis on the violent death of a loved one—that of Desdemona and that of Cordelia—in which the hero has become (in a sense that is new in terms of the heroic) hopelessly implicated.

No idea of expression in heroic spirit can be finally reconciled to that aspect of the spectacle. Before these deaths Shakespeare's heroes stand, whether consciously or unconsciously, at an absolute loss. They are, moreover, in a substantial sense that is pointless to deny, guilty of them. Nor can they make amends. It is no more possible to reserve from this aspect of the spectacle the further idea of some greater Life that remains intact from the debacle. To the additional, ongoing idealization of "Nature" as the "given body of experience and substance sustaining and supporting human life"[4]—which is thought to remain free of the tragedy—we may oppose the following emphasis from the ending of *King Lear*:

> *I know when one is dead, and when one lives;*
> *She's dead as earth.*

> *No, no, no Life . . .*

By the time we get to the ending of *King Lear*, the process of *life itself* is being re-valued, in the face of a more absorbing concern with the all-levelling power a cumulative evil could have, in Shakespeare's imagination. The overriding focus which I am saying finally crystallizes the essence of tragedy for Shakespeare is not brought to complete expression until the ending of *King Lear*. It is already, however, anticipated in the ending of *Othello*, which suggests that Shakespeare was working his way progressively towards that later point. Othello, unlike, Lear, cannot find words to express it, but his own fate comes around to the same obsessive focus:

> *O Desdemon! Dead, Desdemon! Dead!*
> *O, O!*

Ever since Johnson first declared the ending of *King Lear* itself a scene not to be 'endured', echoing with this comment his similar comment on the ending of *Othello*, critics have striven, in every manner and form, to circumvent the impression of all-levelling hopelessness on which the

Lear-ending especially appears to insist.[5] Only Nicholas Brooke in our time has sought strenuously to keep us to the way Shakespeare insists on our seeing it:

> *We are driven to see, not only the very human pain of Lear's*
> *end with Cordelia in his arms, but also the absolute negation*
> *of all forms of hope . . .*
>
> *Her death kills all life.*[6]

There is no getting around, or away from, the final import of these tragedies. Shakespeare may have had to continue to trace the course of the hero's hatred through, as Wilson Knight proposed, if only to ensure that the hatred would be finally purged. He would have had to take us, that is to say, as far as *Timon of Athens*, taking up again a play he had already commenced. And along with *Timon* he would have also had to give us *Antony and Cleopatra* and *Coriolanus*, simply because an attachment to heroic faith would not die so easily. This is apart from the fact that Shakespeare, as a member of his age, was more or less bound to continue working in the 'heroic idiom', as least for a time longer.[7] It would take much to break the illusion of the value of heroic spirit. But with the ending of *King Lear*, there is no further way to go. Either there *is* no further hope, as the ending suggests, and we *remain* deluded about the surviving value of love, faith, and all systems of life in the familiar forms we have known—we remain deluded also about the value of the heroic—or it may be that there is a further purpose to an enforced renunciation of these forms. In fact, the renunciation of all systems of life to which Shakespeare's tragedies bear witness as a whole has its justification finally in the *higher* life that miraculously emerges from that renunciation, corresponding to the experience as given in Shakespeare's last plays. An idea of 'tragic progress', in this context, necessarily assumes a *further* evolutionary relation to a triumphing evil, even in the overwhelmingly final form we get in the ending of *King Lear*. The *key* lies in the transition from *King Lear* to *Pericles*. Crucial to our understanding of this transition is an implied shift in focus away from the experience of the tragic hero to the transfigured mind of Shakespeare himself. A new life has already appeared, and the process by which it has come about is now to be outlined for us in a new form of 'allegorical' representation richly suggestive of the experience that lies behind, that is Shakespeare's own.[8]

The distinguishing characteristic of Shakespeare's representation in the tragedies may be said to lie in his progressive accentuation of the literal status of the tragedy, culminating in the ending of *King Lear*. It would be grossly to misconceive of the very different approach taken to the representation of action in *Pericles* to suppose that the characters of Thaisa or Pericles, or Marina, or the tragedy that befalls them, are invested with anything like the same literal status. We have, with *Pericles*, in fact moved far beyond an art which holds the mirror up to nature, where evil and death literally prevail. We are on firm ground with the action of *Pericles* when we see it rather as mirroring allegorically what evil and death have finally made and are still making of themselves in Shakespeare's own mind. This would seem to be already evident from the obituary Pericles pronounces over Thaisa who is dead before we have known her:

> *Most wretched queen!*
> *A terrible child-bed hast thou had, my dear,*
> *No light, no fire. Th' unfriendly elements*
> *Forgot thee utterly, nor have I time*
> *To give thee hallowed to thy grave, but straight*
> *Must cast thee, scarcely coffined, in [the ooze],*
> *Where, for a monument upon thy bones,*
> *The [e'er]-remaining lamps, the belching whale,*
> *And humming water must o'erwhelm thy corpse,*
> *Lying with simple shells.*

'Lying with simple shells' reflects back to us a kind of assimilation of a loved one's death that is inconceivable to one who has just been through the tragedy. Already we are alerted to the fact that Pericles cannot be viewed as a character who is literally undergoing tragedy here, any more than we have a conception of Thaisa herself as a character. I do not want to claim that the literal death is not still Shakespeare's focus, but we are on firm ground with Pericles's speech only when we see it as representing the effect which the death of a loved one has had *over time*. The death percolates down, as it were, to the bottom of the mind (represented here as the sea-floor) to become *there* the simple event it could never have been when it actually happened. It is from that point *in* the mind—Shakespeare's own—that Thaisa is then 'returned' from death, by no means as a literal personage.

Approached in this way, Pericles is nothing in himself. He is everything when seen as echoing in himself the Shakespearean tragic hero's experience as this continues to reverberate in Shakespeare's own mind in the extreme and final form to which it had come. Addressing himself to the death that has occurred, Pericles remarks of his loved one, with a truth that fits the case literally: "Th' unfriendly elements/Forgot thee *utterly*." Earlier he had said: "I do not fear the flaw,/It hath done to me the *worst*". Awareness of the extremity of evil undergone is also reflected in the words Pericles pronounces over the 'child' that is born with, and of, destruction and death:

> *A more blusterous birth had never babe.*
> *Thou art the rudeliest welcome to this world*
> *That ever was prince's child.*

Focus is on *the death that ends all life*, and all corresponding attachments to life. It cannot, therefore, appear how any new or ongoing life can contain anything within itself to compensate for the destruction:

> *Even at the first*
> *Thy loss is more than can thy portage quit.*

And yet, already a new life has appeared, though Pericles does not himself as yet bear any consciousness of this. That he does *not* testifies to the lingering power of the tragic experience in Shakespeare's mind even at this point, though the circumstances in which Pericles finds himself, with the birth of his daughter, already imply an evolution out of that experience.

Who is this 'daughter', as she reveals herself in time, but the image of Pericles's own suffering—Shakespeare's own suffering—somehow miraculously bearing fruit in the form of a power that now lifts the tragic psyche beyond itself? She is the image of *the psyche's* own suffering that is now made good:

> *she speaks,*
> *My lord, that, may be, hath endured a grief*
> *Might equal yours, if both were justly weighed.*

How else shall we characterize this 'daughter' but as the enduring self *become* the higher self through which transcendence has come? The tragic self in Pericles, which in enduring transcends itself, has made itself worthy of uniting with a now *higher* aspect of itself in Marina. This kind of experience, as constituted by Shakespeare's extreme form of tragedy, is precisely what Rudolf Steiner had in mind when he spoke of the 'Consciousness-Soul experience' and of how out of this experience progressively comes the 'Imaginative Soul'. This 'Imaginative Soul', in its first full-fledged, *historical* manifestation, is none other than what Coleridge and other Romantics would identify as the 'Imagination'—that new, expansive Soul-power, proceeding from a *further* development of self-consciousness, which, for Owen Barfield, represented *a new form* of human consciousness.[9] A first objectification of the Imaginative Soul in Shakespeare, which for him arises *out of* the Consciousness-Soul experience, coincides with his presentation of the birth of Marina, although not until Marina's 'coming of age', and Pericles's later 'recognition' of her, is the vision of this Soul-power brought to full expression. Rudolf Steiner speaks of the Imaginative Soul in association also with the Spirit Self or Higher Ego, this last term reminding us that the evolution in question emerges fundamentally as a further development of *Ego*-consciousness. In the structure of this evolution, Marina objectifies that new, *higher* power in the Ego, expressing itself *in* the Imaginative Soul. This power is then shown slowly lifting the Ego in its suffering aspect, as represented by Pericles, out of its experience of death in the Consciousness Soul.

It is by this extraordinary route that we come, then, to the famous 'recognition'-scene between Pericles and Marina. At this stage of the 'progress', the suffering Ego has recognized, and is uniting with, a higher aspect in itself that is itself perfectly sensitive to suffering yet insusceptible to despair. Pericles himself notes of Marina:

> *Yet thou dost look*
> *Like Patience gazing on kings' graves, and smiling*
> *Extremity out of act.*

What union with a higher power of Ego now opens up for Shakespeare is the prospect of a new 'life' in which the Ego can be *fully reconciled to tragedy*. Accordingly, Shakespeare's symbol of an extreme, destructive evil (the sea) converts in this context into the symbol of new joy:

> Pericles. *O Helicanus, strike me honored sir,*
> *Give me a gash, put me to present pain,*
> *Lest this great sea of joys rushing upon me*
> *O'erbear the shores of my mortality,*

And drown me with their sweetness.
[to Marina]
O, come hither,
Thou that beget'st him that did thee beget . . .

Fourteen years have gone by, a symbolic period of spiritual gestation, before re-integration could begin, during which time the human psyche would seem to be adapting to the tragedy still further, a time in which there is a further, one might say a complete, absorption of the tragedy. Finally the support comes through again. A daughter had sprung in the meantime between the hero and his beloved, and what had been lost is again recovered. Pericles and Thaisa had been separated from the normal sensual life they would have led. The reunion of all three now takes place in a sphere where the engrossment in sensuality has been virtually abandoned. The process of separation has been drastic and complete. And now there is the return to an experience of mutual support on every hand, with no tragedy subverting: indeed the tragedy has been fully taken up into the new experience.

Only *after* the union of elements within the Ego (at the meeting between Pericles and Marina) does the inspirational dream come to Pericles that exhorts him to visit Diana's temple, a dream in which the Goddess Herself appears to him. At this temple he is to rehearse the tragic story he has been through, as if to say that *that* has been the only way to come to this point and is to continue to be borne in mind.[10] Only thus is Pericles further re-united with his beloved 'Thaisa', we can only imagine in *what* sphere of higher life together. Thaisa is herself an other-than-literal personage. She is not the loved one who has been lost to death, but rather, allegorically, all that was lost as a consequence of that death: a 'lost connection to the world' following on 'lost faith' in *all* systems of life. A new connection and a new faith are what are now bestowed upon the Ego, the consequence of acts of preservation as well as of guidance (as in the case of the vision of Diana) that open out on still other mysteries that involved Shakespeare at this time. For the allegorical implications of the action in Shakespeare's romances are extensive, indeed vast.[11]

The Ego's re-connection to the world, in faith and in love as well as to the senses, represents at this stage, an altogether different experience from what connection to the world was before. The whole experience takes place now on a higher plane. Shakespeare's experience in this regard is only partially reflected to us in that additional, ethereal Soul-quality in the verse which every commentator on the romances recognizes is new and is first sighted in this play. We understand Shakespeare's experience primarily through an allegorical structure that he has built into the qualitative representation, from which we gather the greater development or progress that now engages him far beyond the confines of this (or any other) single play. The development or progress in question extends over both *Pericles* and *The Winter's Tale*. Thus we find the same fundamental experience at the basis of the action in the later play, with Leontes substituting for Pericles, Perdita for Marina, and Hermione for Thaisa. But with this new addition: that the whole is approached, in this instance, from the point of view of the Ego's guilt or direct responsibility for tragedy.

Thus *Pericles* gives us the experience from the point of view of the Ego's innocence in tragedy, *The Winter's Tale* from the point of view of the Ego's guilt. And only in the combined effect of *both* plays, as the expression of what is taking place in Shakespeare's own mind, do we find the evolution that corresponds fully to Shakespeare's experience of the whole tragedy as this relates to the tragic hero who is himself both innocent *and* guilty. In light of what has been said, we will not be surprised to find *The Tempest* extending representation of Shakespeare's experience still further. Here, however, we have a momentous return to the literal level and well-rounded characterization of the tragedies, reflected in a dramatic foregrounding of the principal characters, Prospero and Miranda.[12] Here, again, there is the case of a loved 'wife' who is lost to death, coinciding with the birth of a 'daughter'. Miranda, we are told, is "not/Out three years old" when she and Prospero are put out to sea. The mother is, thus, only recently dead, and not so long before that we cannot see her death as coinciding with Prospero's renunciation of state and devotion to study, or, for that matter, with Miranda's birth. The whole action is an integrated one. Prospero's decision to "neglect" all "worldly ends, all dedicated/To closeness and the bettering of my mind" may be directly referred to Shakespeare's own commitment, since the 'death' of a loved one became *for him*, his one, essential tragic preoccupation.

Prospero incurs further consequences for his commitment to his experience, being, along with Miranda, ambushed and driven out to 'sea' in what presents itself as yet another marvellous transfiguration of the essential tragic sorrow:

> *There they hoist us,*
> *To cry to th' sea, that roared to us; to sigh*
> *To th' winds, whose pity, sighing back again,*

Did us but loving wrong.
Miranda. *Alack what trouble*
Was I then to you!
Prospero. *O, a cherubin*
Thou wast that did preserve me. Thou didst smile,
Infusèd with a fortitude from heaven,
When I have decked the sea with drops full salt,
Under my burthen groaned, which raised in me
An undergoing stomach, to bear up
Against what should ensue.

It is the 'whole' sorrow that comes to expression once again here, the death of a loved one being at the center of it. But the supporting power is, likewise, bestowed, by Miranda as higher power, according to the pattern already described. We may take it as an implicit understanding that the whole evolution Shakespeare has reflected to us in his last plays is here climactically embodied—insofar as literature can embody this—in Prospero and Miranda as literal inheritors of that evolution [there is also, as we shall see, Ferdinand who works his own way into this evolution]. That we have returned to the literal level in this play will also explain why in this instance Prospero's wife is *not* restored, for there can be no question of restoration at this level.[13]

Other aspects of the extraordinary experience that underlies these plays may be observed, notably the fact that in *Pericles* and *The Winter's Tale* the loved one is 'kept' alive. In the latter play especially this gambit intensifies comparison between the order or level of representation as given in the end of the play and our imagination of what a literal restoration of the loved one might be like. But the comparison works in a way opposite to what we might think. The purpose, it would appear, is to suggest that the experience of being restored to the world has *the same value as* a literal restoration of the loved one, though it may even be that we are being directed to speculate on some further meeting with the loved one beyond death. The Hermione who speaks at the end, in any case, speaks in the tones of one who is dead, like a revenant. Certainly the idea that the loved one would have kept alive and silent over sixteen years is not to be literally credited. In fact, Shakespeare arbitrarily 'kept' Hermione alive, in order to get us to speculate on a whole number of effects *other* than a literal restoration of the loved one.

With each new play, a new element or aspect of Shakespeare's experience is revealed. Concentration in *Pericles* lies with the emergence and recognition of a higher power of Ego (Marina) expressing itself freely in the Imagination, beyond tragedy. On the plane of innocence, a higher power of Ego is clearly in itself sufficient to lift the Ego out of its experience of tragedy. Hence, that peculiar limitation to the quality of the representation in *Pericles*, as if the whole drama were taking place inside the Mind, with no further substantial connection to Nature. The case is different with *The Winter's Tale*. Here the greater problem of tragic guilt is addressed, the different concern corresponding to a significant extension of focus beyond the Ego *into* the realm of Nature. In keeping with the evolution I have been tracing, the saving power in this instance depends crucially on a relation to Nature established in the higher Ego (through Perdita). Concentration here, however, is not on the higher Ego itself so much as on a still greater ordering Power in Nature outside the Ego which the higher Ego yet mediates.

Beyond an experience in the Consciousness Soul, Rudolf Steiner speaks of an experience of Imagination, of Inspiration and of Intuition, one experience leading progressively into the other. Conforming with that evolution, we notice, with new developments in *The Winter's Tale*, a corresponding *extension of the operation of the Imaginative Soul* to a point *inside* "great creating Nature" (see IV.iv) where a great *Inspirational* order is now revealed. Here we reach the realm of *systematic* Imagination, of regenerative, evolutionary creation—where a higher life is constantly being re-created out of death. It is Perdita who expresses this (it is Florizel who signals her value to us in these terms):

> *What you do*
> ***Still betters*** *what is done. When you speak, sweet,*
> *I'd have you do it ever; when you sing,*
> *I'd have you buy and sell so; so give alms;*
> *Pray so; and for the ord'ring your affairs,*
> *To sing them too. When you dance, I wish you*
> *A wave o' th' sea, that you might ever do*
> *Nothing but that; **move still, still so**—*
> *And own no other function. Each your doing*
> *(So singular in each particular)*
> *Crowns what you are doing in the present deeds,*
> *That all your acts are queens.*

We remark about this representation, especially, its powerful suggestion of a greater order or system, in progressive motion, *behind* the re-creative power attributed to Perdita as higher Ego. And it is only on being taken up into this order, active from a realm deep within Nature, that the suffering Ego (represented by Leontes) can hope to find again the integration that, insofar as it is guilty and hopeless, the Ego cannot itself bring about.

On the other hand, the Ego reserves, over time, a direct link and claim to that order's saving power, by virtue of a constant devotion to the memory of the harm that was done, as represented in Leontes:

> *Whilst I remember*
> *Her and her virtues, I cannot forget*
> *My blemishes in them, and so still think of*
> *The wrong I did myself . . .*

That a higher power of Ego can still be positively active here might be taken as an indication that the Ego, in spite of its guilt, still retains a measure of innocence at some level. In a sense this must be true since, from the point of view Shakespeare has established on approaching this play, it is really a matter of a complementary division of the Ego's functions, in innocence and in guilt, enacted *between Pericles* and *The Winter's Tale*. And so in going from one play to the other, we imagine what the Ego has already achieved: in its innocence it links up, beyond tragedy, to a higher power in itself. This achievement is *now* brought to bear on the Ego's guilty part. The Ego in its higher power has in the meantime tapped into a still greater Power in Nature, which is the principal saving agent here.

By the time we reach the end of *The Winter's Tale*, we may confidently assume, in fact, a pattern of experience which points to a complete re-integration of the Ego beyond tragedy. That re-integration is the consequence of the activity of a higher power of Ego as well as of Nature, corresponding to an extension of the Consciousness Soul in Imagination and in Inspiration. In *The Tempest* the pattern is brought to fruition in an experience of Intuition. The whole evolution in Imagination and in Inspiration finds a final focus here *literally* in Prospero's own person who is in some sense Shakespeare himself, since it is *his* experience that is reflected to us in the progression of these plays. As Steiner reminds us, Intuition means "dwelling in God".[14] Hence the focus here on a concentration of power in the individual 'I' insofar as it finally comes to dwell within the 'I' of God. Consider Prospero's words to Miranda early in the play:

> *who*
> *Art ignorant of what thou art, nought knowing*
> *Of whence **I am**, nor **that I am** more better*
> *Than Prospero . . .*

They mediate the words in which God declares Himself (in *Exodus*):

> *I am that I am . . .*

We thus reach the point where the individual 'I', beyond the higher relation it has found within itself and within Nature, finally consummates its identity in the God Who dwells within it all. To understand how Prospero has reached this degree of self-development, we should have to inquire further as to what all those 'secret studies' of his have been about. In doing so, we shall be getting closer still (or as close as we *can* get) to *identifying* the kind of initiation-process Shakespeare was passing through in his time.

5

Prospero's Powers:
Shakespeare's Last Phase

I

THE RELATION TO *PERICLES* AND *THE WINTER'S TALE*

Prospero's 'secret studies' are not just another, independent part of the story that ranges from his wife's death through his later abduction. These 'studies' constitute, in fact, an altogether intrinsic part of the same story. Beginning with Miranda who, when the abduction takes place, is "not/Out three years old", we are reminded of the mother who in this period has died. We then hear of Prospero's reputation in the liberal arts, which now become "*all* [his] study", to the point of a temporary renunciation of state. From here Prospero grows all the "stranger" to his state, as he finds himself further "transported/And rapt in secret studies". It is all too easy to overlook, in this fast-concatenating story, the role that Prospero's intensifying 'studies' have played *as a direct response to the mother's death*. It is the very effort from which Prospero is dissociated when Antonio casts him out to 'sea' where Prospero must again live out the great sorrow of loss and dispossession that, over a great many years, had continued to engage Shakespeare himself, up to this point:

> *There they hoist us*
> **To cry to the sea that roared to us**, *to sigh*
> *To th' winds, whose pity, sighing back again,*
> *Did us but loving wrong.*
> Miranda. *Alack, what trouble*
> *Was I then to you!*
> Prospero. *O, a cherubin*
> *Thou wast that didst preserve me. Thou didst smile,*
> *Infusèd with a fortitude from heaven,*
> **When I have decked the sea with drops full salt,**
> **Under my burden groaned,**

Prospero's experience, in this climactic 'sea'-passage, has the effect of some great tunnicular vision. For one last time, we look back down the dark tunnel of Shakespeare's harrowing emergence through the tragedies, as Prospero is forced to live out again the great 'sea-sorrow' of *that* momentous progression. Here Prospero gives no overt sign of effective power over that 'sorrow', although Shakespeare himself had passed through a great transformation over that entire time. At a certain point, all had come to a head for him in a great symbolic end-point in which the very worst of tragedy finds representation as the death of the mother of all faith, love, and life.[1] This is what Shakespeare's repeated representations of the death of a loved one had come to mean for him. It is how we are asked to see the deaths of Thaisa and Hermione that follow (respectively in *Pericles* and *The Winter's Tale*): as a great ongoing symbolic event of that extraordinary magnitude working itself out further in Shakespeare's own mind. On one level, the death of Prospero's wife clearly repeats and adds to this event. It distinguishes itself from these representations in being also a literal action now projected outside Shakespeare's own mental preoccupations—which is to say fully dramatized anew. Like Shakespeare's great tragic heroes before him (Hamlet, Othello, Lear), Prospero undergoes the death of a loved one literally, although unlike them he is not guilty of this death. Nor, unimaginably great as this death is, is he unprepared for it. Standing there as the dramatized reflection of Shakespeare, Prospero has the advantage of having, in the meantime, passed through all that Shakespeare himself passed through, in living out the consequences of the many earlier deaths as the expression of the great symbolic event of the death of the mother. [2]

For one thing, by now, that death has come to be linked further with the symbolic birth of the daughter—in this case, Miranda, who has her own extraordinary lineage in the anterior figures of Marina and Perdita, both likewise born of the death of the mother (respectively in *Pericles* and *The Winter's Tale*). Miranda, in the 'sea'-passage I quoted above is, indeed, the very power that bears Prospero up from within the dire maelstrom of the symbolic event:

> *a cherubin*
> *Thou wast that didst preserve me. Thou didst smile,*
> *Infusèd with a fortitude from heaven,*
> *When I have decked the sea with drops full salt,*
> *Under my burden groaned,* **which raised in me**
> *An undergoing stomach to bear up,*
> *Against what should ensue.*

Out of the tragic Ego's experience as borne by Shakespeare himself across his last plays, there emerges over time, precisely through the death of the mother, a saving power of higher Ego of new, indefatigable quality, represented in the birth of the daughter. This new power Shakespeare extracts from his own psychological experience, allegorically dramatized between *Pericles* and *The Winter's Tale*. From there, he will go on to bestow his own experience dramatically upon Prospero. This is to suggest that Prospero contains in himself the entire drama that precedes him: not only those newly allegorized abstractions of the tragic Ego as given to us in Pericles and Leontes—respectively the tragic Ego in its aspects of innocence and guilt—but also the power of the suffering mother in her own correspondingly different aspects as Thaisa and Hermione; likewise, the new power of higher Ego that emerges *from* the death of the mother, which undergoes its own further evolution as saving power.

Prospero and Miranda together take the whole previous experience still further. Miranda, as higher power, represents yet another, still more evolved aspect of Prospero's now all-encompassing Ego. She is herself a literal embodiment of this higher power, who 'profits' in turn from an education at Prospero's hands, is 'given' to Ferdinand—the panorama is endless. From these structural developments, it follows also that Prospero's wife—as the mother—is likewise both a power that he incorporates and herself (more remarkably still) a literal embodiment of this power. *Her death is the actual sacrifice without which the rest of power would not follow.*

Clearly Prospero is not alone in facing this death. However, it is precisely what gives Prospero's fate its sublime pathos that he must (in extended form) undergo this representative death again. On the other hand, he is borne up by powers of which we can barely have an idea unless we make ourselves fully acquainted first with the more recent lives/dramas that Prospero interiorizes. These are given to us in the action of both *Pericles* and *The Winter's Tale*. This is another way of saying that we first approach Prospero, in fact, coming away from those earlier plays, in relation to which Prospero assumes the function of Presenter as his very first role.[3] Prospero's 'studies', as we shall see, coincide directly with the development of those powers that lie dormant in him from his association with his previous 'lives' in *Pericles* and *The Winter's Tale*. Prospero does not come into full possession of these powers, however, until the full significance of his wife's 'death' comes 'home' to him—that is, not until he is cast out to 'sea', where his whole 'sorrow' awakens and is consciously given full scope, and he *now* experiences his wife's death *as* the 'death of the mother'. Then it is that there revives within him all that has lain dormant from his *past* 'experiences' of this 'death' in his earlier 'lives' (in *Pericles* and *The Winter's Tale*). In relation to this decisive 'experience' Prospero's 'studies' have been a *preparation*, and they now bear fruit as a direct experience of those higher powers reserved for Prospero from his 'past'/the very powers he has unconsciously been cultivating in himself in the course of his 'studies' (the two developments are one).

II

STUDY OF THE LIBERAL ARTS

To get to the bottom of these developments, we shall have to assume quite another attitude than the purely external one taken by the most recent Oxford editor of the play, for whom there is nothing "inherently mysterious about the[se] studies themselves (they were, after all, the 'liberal arts')."[4] On the contrary, these studies were hedged round with very great 'mysteries', as we learn from more authoritative sources. Rene Querido[5] has shown that in the School of Chartres, study of the liberal arts served as the basis for the accomplishment of a very grand goal:

> *On the cathedral* [at Chartres] *they placed the seven liberal arts around the Virgin Mother and Christ Child to indicate the goal of their striving:* **the virgin-like soul and the birth of the higher self** ...

Querido explains further that:

> *This inner birth occurs through man's own efforts ... [by] working on his soul with the seven liberal arts.*[6]

A fuller account follows:

> *For the masters and their pupils, the seven liberal arts were more than disciplines; they were beings. The study of an art was an approach to a being. The mastery of an art was a connection with a being who, belonging to the spiritual hierarchies, would then inspire one as the priestess or guardian of that particular art. Each of the seven guardians*

had her 'place' in the spiritual world, which was one of the planetary spheres . . .[7]

The main steps of the process are in this way opened out to us:

[1] Man's soul, they taught, was influenced by the activities of the seven planets . . .
[2] Thus, following the path of the liberal arts was bringing one's soul into the right relationship with the planetary system . . .
[3] . . . reformation, or purification, would result in the virginity of the soul, which could then bear the child of the true self, or divine ego . . .[8]

As I have argued, it is Prospero who, as the hero who represents Shakespeare, incorporates this entire development in the higher Ego. Prospero incorporates all the powers separately represented by Marina, Perdita and Miranda, after himself experiencing purification through death, or the worst of tragedy (in Shakespeare's sense), and along a route on which *he* was at one time a master of the liberal arts ("in the liberal arts without a parallel"). What Shakespeare, through Prospero, consciously *recovers* in his own time are powers that were largely *given* within the possibility that the Masters of Chartres conceived of. In connection with the latter, Rudolf Steiner speaks of "a true inspiration of ideas", though the "old teachings . . . were well-nigh shadowed-down to concepts and ideas"[9]. However, Steiner also gives us a full account of what "until the 7th or 8th century"—"in the last relics of the ancient Mysteries"—it was still possible for some to attain *as direct experience*:

above all there appeared to them as a living Being . . . the Goddess Natura . . . the ever-creating Goddess with whom he who would seek for knowledge must in a certain way unite himself . . . And when the seeker after knowledge had been sufficiently instructed by the Goddess . . . the teachers saw to it that their disciples should gain a feeling, an idea of this living intercourse with Nature . . . Then . . . they were introduced to the planetary system. They learnt how with the knowledge of the planetary system there arises at the same time the knowledge of the human soul. 'Learn to know

> *how the wandering stars hold sway in the heavens, and*
> *thou shalt know how thine own soul works and weaves and*
> *lives within thee.' This was placed before the pupils. And at*
> *length they were led to approach what was called 'The Great*
> *Ocean'—but it was the Cosmic Ocean, which leads from the*
> *planets, from the wandering stars, to the fixed stars. Thus*
> *at length they penetrated into the secrets of the I, by learning*
> *the secrets of the universe of the fixed stars.*[10]

Steiner speaks also of the extraordinary experience to be reserved for Brunetto Latini in the age that immediately follows that of Chartres, Latini's experience being among the very last of this kind:

> *Then he saw what man could see **under the influence of***
> ***the living principle of knowledge:** He saw a mountain*
> *mightily arising with all that lived and sprang forth from*
> *it, minerals, plants, and animals, and there appeared to*
> *him the Goddess Natura, there appeared the Elements, there*
> *appeared the Planets, there appeared the Goddesses of the*
> *Seven Liberal Arts, and at length Ovid as his guide and*
> *teacher. Here once again there stood before a human soul the*
> *mighty vision that had stood before the souls of men so often*
> *in the first centuries of Christianity.*[11]

Shakespeare's own extraordinary transformation, as reflected in his last plays, would appear to represent another crystallization of this fundamental experience, in a later and rather different age. In *The Winter's Tale*, it is Perdita who reflects (in the power of Inspiration) this newly found, higher relationship to Nature as well as to the still greater planetary world that Nature mediates. In *The Tempest*, it is Miranda who reflects (in the power of Intuition) that supreme relationship to the secrets of the fixed stars (the secrets of the I). [12] Both relationships are present, as we have seen, in Prospero himself. Behind the entire development is the birth of the higher Ego first represented (as Imagination) by Marina in *Pericles* and continuously *extended* in the figures of Perdita and Miranda. This birth of the higher Ego—as we learn from Steiner[13]—takes place itself out of that sphere where the planetary world opens out on the world of the fixed stars—the sphere of the 'Great Ocean' in Steiner's present account[14], the higher Ego coming to fuller and fuller expression first through a development of the relationship to Nature, to the planetary world and so on.[15]

Rudolf Steiner also testifies that, among those who carried the knowledge forward from the Masters of Chartres, the Rosicrucians too could claim:

> 'We have been among the stars and among the Spirits
> of the stars, and have found the old teachers of the occult
> knowledge'.[16]

But the route of the Rosicrucians to 'Star Knowledge' would come, rather, by the *suppression* of the Intelligence which had by then already become too gross for Revelation of this kind, not having as yet undergone purification. The Rosicrucians would have had to heed the momentous words of their Master, who was Christian Rosenkreutz himself—as Steiner dramatizes these:

> 'I am come to reveal to you that the inner being of man
> remains unchanged, that the inner being of man, if it
> bears itself aright, can yet find the way to divine-spiritual
> existence. For a certain period of time, however, the human
> intellect and understanding will be so constituted that they
> will have to be suppressed in order for that which is of the
> Spirit to be able to speak to the human soul.'[17]

Indeed the full recovery of such Revelation, through the faculty of the human Intelligence, would have to wait for Steiner himself. For the moment, the Rosicrucians would have to *give up* their 'Star Knowledge', in the form of a rite. So, the Rosicrucians could tell themselves:

> 'in order that man ... may be able to find for himself of his
> own free will what in earlier times the Gods have tried to
> find for and with him, let now the higher knowledge be
> offered up for a season ...'[18]

What Shakespeare comes by somewhat later, in his own degree, represents in fact a *return* of such 'Star Knowledge', sometime after the act of Sacrifice is accomplished by the Rosicrucians:

> *Whatever in the years that followed, showed itself to be of*
> *a truly spiritual nature, was a kind of echo sounding on of*
> *this creative working from out of unknown spiritual worlds.*
> *Side by side with the external materialism that developed*
> *in the succeeding centuries, we can always find here and*
> *there individuals who are living under the influence of*
> *that renunciation of higher knowledge . . . /[K]nowledge*
> *was communicated . . . we cannot quite say, without words,*
> *but without ideas, although not on that account without*
> *content.*[19]

III

THE FREEING OF ARIEL

The great repository of such higher knowledge *today* are the works of Rudolf Steiner, who has put the task of understanding for our time in the following terms: "in what natural science gives us we must find something which stimulates us inwardly *toward* Imagination, Inspiration, and Intuition. In this way we acquire", Steiner informs us, "the help of Christ within"[20], and through this help we find once again that "*inner astronomy* that will show us the universe proceeding from and working out of the spirit . . . the rediscovered power of Isis, which is now the power of the divine Sophia . . ."[21]. The Sophia appears in this advanced period of time thus as the *new* form the Goddess takes from the midst and on the other side of the purifying process that engages one who, like Shakespeare, has been able to embrace that process. In Her medieval and Renaissance manifestations, the Goddess appears typically in the form of a Virgin, reflecting the purifying process with which She is *also* connected—Diana, especially as Diana of Ephesus, being in this respect Her classical prototype (see above **43, 123**)[22]. Thus we may speak of the purifying or refining power of the Goddess as She progressively assumes a higher and higher function as Sophia. Contrastingly, for one *not* properly engaged, if otherwise quite fully engaged with Her, in moral and imaginative terms, as we shall see in the case of Coleridge (in Chapter 6), She reverts to being the chaotic Goddess of the Underworld in which She also has Her beginnings.[23] Contrasting further with *this* spectrum of full Imaginative manifestation is the strictly *ambiguous* condition She assumes as Graves experiences this in *his* morally *neutral* condition—Graves not being so fully engaged with Her, either in Her higher or Her lower functions, as he might otherwise be (as above, **41, 43**). One needs to consider, at the same time, the further complications inherent in the historical developments that follow Shakespeare's age. As we shall see (in Chapter 6) there is the further, interposing influence over the centuries of an attitude that is generally *not* as engaged with the challenge of human depravity as the process of developing vision demands this.[24]

Rudolf Steiner's experience carries on from the refining process as first lived out in Shakespeare's age. Significantly, Steiner bases his own great power of development in supersensible vision on the very achievement that Valentin Andreae depicted in *The Chymical Wedding of Christian Rosenkreutz*, the famous text which first appeared in Shakespeare's own time.[25] Commenting on this text, Steiner points out that:

> *For his contemporaries Andreae wishes to portray the*
> *foremost spiritual investigator of a declining epoch, one who*
> *perceives in the spiritual world the death of that epoch and*
> *the birth of a new one . . . Andreae wished to say to [his*
> *contemporaries]: Your path is fruitless; the greatest who has*
> *most recently followed it, has seen how useless it is: realize*
> *what he has perceived and you will develop a feeling for*
> *a new path . . .* **The present-day scientist of the spirit**,
> *if he understands the signs of the times,* **still** *finds himself*
> *continuing the effort that originated with Johann Valentin*
> *Andreae.*[26]

One way of having 'Star-Knowledge' (i.e., one form of the higher wisdom) had necessarily to give way to another, and Rudolf Steiner has accounted for that difference: in lieu of a "spiritual *instinctive* understanding rooted in man's heart and mind"—in what Steiner generally refers to as the 'Intellectual or Mind Soul', there now arose spiritual knowledge based on "understanding which, *liberated* from the instinctive forces, worked in the light of full consciousness of self"—in the 'Consciousness Soul'.[27] Christian Rosenkreutz was to be the one who would bear the *new* form of knowledge into the modern age. Steiner, in another context, refers to this great event as "the passage of the Sophia through man".[28] *Shakespeare himself reflects that event* to us in his great theme of the 'death' of the mother of all faith, love and life *in those now outdated forms that had come down to him in his day.*[28]

Prospero's tremendous experience of this 'death', as the prototypic experience of Shakespeare's last phase, further awakens *in him*, as I have argued, altogether new powers of Imagination, Inspiration, as well as Intuition in nascent form, as reflected in the three-year-old Miranda. On the *other* side of this 'death'—when Prospero reaches the island—lies *the freeing of Ariel*, in which these now newly activated powers find their first expression. The 'island' is, of course, a literal feature of Prospero's story but is itself allegorically significant, standing as it were for some final 'resting-place' of power in the Ego to which Prospero has come along with Miranda, the only two who can properly inhabit this ultimate 'region'.[30] One must not overlook in this allegorical context, as well, the use that is made of the 'boat' to get to the 'island', or, indeed, the 'books' with which, we are told, Prospero was at this time supplied, though it would be naïve of us to suppose (along with Caliban) that Prospero's powers continue to depend directly on his books, for they are powers that derive by this point from within his very Ego (symbolically reflected to us in the 'staff' which he later bears.)

Ariel, we learn, was confined to a tree for over twelve years by the witch Sycorax "in her most unmitigable rage", Sycorax being unable to undo her act. In the tremendous dramatization of this "rage"[31] we have the *supersensible* extension of all that Shakespeare had had to contend with *from the time he started out* on his momentous progress in tragedy, going back at least as far as *Hamlet*.[32] Along this way comes *also* the more rapid *emergence* from tragedy that begins with *Pericles* and continues for another three years, to the time when Prospero is made to re-live that whole progress through tragedy, when he is violently thrown out to 'sea'. Miranda literally marks that emergence, being about three at the time.

'Crying to the sea', which sympathetically 'roars' back to him, Prospero at this point unconsciously unites *with Ariel's own 'groaning' of twelve years* while the latter is confined to the tree. Prospero and Ariel are in this way *identified* in their role as 'sacrificial' victims, and, uniting himself with Ariel's suffering, Prospero now finds the further power *to free* this great Spirit. He does so by a power of 'compassion' that he has learned from his own comparable suffering—at the other extreme from the 'rage' that has caused it. What Prospero then frees, with the compassionate freeing of Ariel, *is his own power of supersensible vision*. Ranging suddenly through powers of Imagination, Inspiration, and Intuition, he comes into a power of magical action that derives *from* his progression through supersensible worlds. Presumably, then, such power of action (simultaneously a power of compassion) becomes available in what one might call an *early* Intuitive phase, when the secrets of the fixed stars—the secrets of the I—are first plumbed. This condition is symbolically reflected to us in the three year old Miranda. From here Prospero will develop his capacity for Intuition still further, to the point that characterizes his powers when we first encounter him in the play, by which time Miranda, now fifteen, has 'come of age'.[33]

IV

'RAPT IN SECRET STUDIES'

In Rudolf Steiner's account, the momentous change that takes place in the Renaissance is from an experience in the 'Intellectual or Mind Soul' *as well as* remnants of the 'Sentient-Soul' experience ('spiritual instinctive understanding' formerly rooted in the senses)—respectively, an older "faith", and "love in sensual terms", as described above (see **117**)—to experience in the 'Consciousness Soul'. This great change, reflected in Shakespeare himself over the course of his tragic progress, would be the occasion for a new experience of an old wisdom, which has since become a possible experience for us. Steiner elsewhere gives a further account of what Christian Rosenkreutz was the first to achieve fully:

> *Man has learnt to relate to the Sophia through his*
> *consciousness soul, to associate her directly with human*
> *beings. This happened during the consciousness soul age. The*
> *Sophia has therefore become the Being that elucidates man.*
> *Once having entered into humanity, she has to take up this*
> *human nature and set it objectively before mankind. She*
> *detaches herself again but takes with her what man is and*
> *places herself outside him, **no longer merely as Sophia but***
> ***as Anthroposophia** as that Sophia who has passed through*
> *the soul of man, through man's being, and henceforth bears*
> *this being of man within herself.*[34]

Steiner also speaks of a *counter*-tendency at that time, arising out of an older Goddess-based knowledge now become anachronistic—for man would now have to go through a refining process, in order to see his own proper being through. Steiner cites a "power" at this time which

> *wants to keep [man], with his consciousness, in spiritual*
> *realms that were adapted for him in ancient times. It*
> *wants to prevent pure thinking, directed towards the*
> *understanding of physical existence, from flowing into his*
> *dream-like, imaginative conception of the world. It is able*
> *to hold back, in the wrong way, man's power of perception*
> *from the physical world. It is not, however, able to maintain*
> *in the right way the experience of the old Imaginations. And*
> *so it makes man reflect imaginatively, and yet, at the same*
> *time he is not able to transplant his soul completely into the*
> *world in which the Imaginations have their true value.*[35]

The transition from one epochal knowledge-base to another is directly reflected in the new effort of will that Christian Rosenkreutz accomplishes, as portrayed in *The Chymical Wedding*, setting him apart from the other rival aspirants to higher knowledge at this time. When, on the second day, those who are given to the older form of seeking enter the Castle, *he* remains behind in the hall, allowing himself to be fettered. There follows, on the third day, the "weighing of the souls", as Steiner describes it, "to ascertain whether to their own weight *as man* [purified, that is, of their old sensual tendencies] they [the aspirants] have added what corresponds to the seven other weights."[36] The "weight of the (seven liberal) arts" has had to become [in this sense] "weight of soul" in accordance with the "true world content" of the new age[37], and on this basis, the illegitimate intruders are now expelled, while Rosenkreutz himself is allowed to proceed. This momentous development from the *Wedding* corresponds in Shakespeare's presentation to that fateful moment when Prospero evolves from his position in the liberal arts "without a parallel" to that further climactic point where he becomes finally "*rapt* in secret studies" and is further "*transported*". From here he is given up more fully to the great epochal 'death' of that time and the passage that follows from this into a fresh experience of the old powers.

It is at this very point that the candidate for higher knowledge stands poised for that *further* progress in the faculties of Imagination, Inspiration and Intuition, which Steiner's own productive life fully illustrates in *our* time. Steiner would himself be able to speak from direct experience not only of the further faculties of Imagination, Inspiration and Intuition, but also of more far-reaching experiences still—the whole proceeding from a *first* stage of 'study' corresponding to a full grasp and exercise of what it is now in our power to do as inheritors of these new developments. Such 'study' would involve *for us*, initially, a consideration of Steiner's extensive 'science of the spirit', and so the seven steps of *modern* Rosicrucian spiritual training or initiation, as Steiner elaborated on these[38]:

1. *Studium—the study of the science of spirit*
2. *Imagination*
3. *Inspiration*
4. *Intuition*
5. *Correspondence between Microcosm and Macrocosm*
6. *Living into the Macrocosm*
7. *Divine Bliss*

Shakespeare's Prospero, as we shall see, goes a similar route, from his own starting-point in a study of the liberal arts, which he then takes further. His participation in the more far-reaching stages beyond Intuition we glean by reflection, in his further 'initiation' of Ferdinand culminating in his 'marriage' to Miranda. Shakespeare, writing out of his own time, was, however, building on the course of *alchemical* initiation as re-established by Christian Rosenkreutz through his Chemical Wedding. The further progression of events, from the time *The Tempest* opens, repeats the structure of that *earlier* form of initiation quite literally (I follow the account of that initiation as given by Paul Allen Marshall whose further elucidations I quote below[39]; the applications to *The Tempest* are my own).

1. The prima materia massa confusa
This characterizes the state of things at the beginning of the process of Transmutation.
. . . Prospero's subjection to tragedy and to treachery up to the tempest he raises (the death of his wife, his abduction and further exiling, his dispossession from state) . . .

2. The sevaratio, divisio
This separation or clarification of the Elements concerns the factors at work in the process.

... Initially, Miranda's 'saving' action at sea: Prospero's story (of initiation) as narrated by him: his 'studies' and successive transformations of consciousness through Imagination, Inspiration and Intuition: the separate presentation of Ariel, Caliban, Ferdinand . . .

3. The conjunctio
A uniting of 'male and female', that is the active and passive natures of the Elements involved.
... Ariel's music, Ferdinand's first sight of Miranda (Imagination) and his inspired words about her (Inspiration), including his effusions about her in III.i . . .

4. The mortificatio calcinatio
This is the 'mystical death' of the substance, the central point in the series.
... Ferdinand's 'trial': his separation from Miranda; the parallel judgment of Prospero's enemies; Ferdinand's purifying 'death' (Intuition), corresponding to Prospero's own development (in Imagination, Inspiration and Intuition) up to that point . . . [40]

5. The ablutio, baptisma
This 'washing' or 'whitening' leads to the re-uniting of the soul of the element to its dead body.
... Ferdinand's release: Miranda *given* to Ferdinand by Prospero, *reflecting Prospero's further progression in initiation* . . .

6. The albedo, tinctura alba, resurrectum
This bursting out of the 'reborn' or 'purified' element into many colors is imaged in the peacock's tail.
. . . The masque played out before Ferdinand and Miranda, cosmically blessing their marriage to come . . .

7. The rubedo
This denotes the appearance of the King (Red) and the Queen (White), who celebrate their 'Chemical Wedding', thus completing the process.
... The projected wedding of Ferdinand and Miranda (as purified Ego and Higher Ego, respectively). Ferdinand and Miranda are (in this respect) finally *the image of the new couple that has displaced the old*: this, however, only *after* the whole drastic process of self-overcoming we have been tracing. Until then, they will continue to represent all that we may suppose

will progressively unfold as a concomitant of this process as humankind involves itself in this process more and more. (And so the value, culturally speaking, of continually re-playing Shakespeare's dramas as an incentive to such engagement.)

*   *   *

In the end, Andreae's *Chymical Wedding* is more obviously devoted to the inner processes of initiation than is *The Tempest* which from its opening assumes these processes as a given and builds on them in covert structural form (only those who have kept their eye on the inner development will be able to follow Shakespeare up to this point). Perhaps Shakespeare did not feel he could say how these processes operated exactly; perhaps he did but assumed that a more open account of them to a dramatic audience would fail to go over as intended. Whatever the case, a significant link can be traced between the two works that establishes *The Tempest* as profoundly rooted in the same tradition of inner progress through spiritual worlds.

Thus in Andreae's *Wedding* we find the same link-up to the sphere of the 'Great Ocean' of which Steiner speaks in connection with the vision of the Masters of Chartres and their heirs. (It seems one can assume from Andreae's work a continuous tradition dating back to the time of that earlier cultural era.) Thus on the fifth day of Rosenkreutz' initiation, we hear of a journey that he takes by ship (along with the few other aspirants who are successful) across a "Sea" to an "Island" on which the seven-tiered "Tower of Olympus" is erected [41] where the great "chymical" process is to be accomplished. This point in the structure of the action of *The Chymical Wedding*—as in *The Tempest*—corresponds to progress into the sphere of Intuition. It is part of a whole *sequence* of successive transformations that begins in the *Wedding* when the seven "weights", which stand for the seven liberal arts, are borne on the third day by the seven virgins who appear in the Wedding's opening ceremony led by the Queen Virgin who stands for Theology; her own "greatest" weight is borne symbolically by the Virgin Alchemy with whom she seems to be united and who has accompanied the candidates for initiation from the outset.[42]

This *first* great transformational passage has its direct counterpart in the structure of the progress among the Masters and their heirs where, building on the study of the liberal arts, one brought one's soul into the right relationship with the planetary system, passing on into the sphere of Inspiration. In the *Wedding*, this stage in the progress is transcended through a further "hanging up", or sacrifice, of the weights to the "Honour of God". Beyond this action comes the further procession to the "House of the Sun" whence the journey proceeds across the "Sea" to the "Tower" on the "Island"—into the sphere of Intuition. At this point Christian Rosenkreutz, along with the others, attends, through an intensive process of concentrated alchemy, on the re-birth of young King and young Queen.

The alchemical basis of Rosenkreutz' initiation, by which it is distinguished from the progress, into spiritual worlds, of the Chartres Masters, is especially pronounced in this section. The different basis is finally expressive of the possibility of a new concentrated self-consciousness in the midst of the vast expansion in vision and in power to be found in both cases.[43] Surrounding the amazing re-birth of young King and Queen in the *Wedding* is the dramatic resurrection of a "Bird" from the "dissolved" substance of the dead bodies of the "Kings" whose solemn "be-heading" initially launches the new process. The correspondence in this case is with the series that extends from the 'mortificatio calcinatio' through to the 'resurrectum'. (In the *Wedding*, the Bird is itself be-headed and its blood used to feed the "Images" that are created out of the Bird's ashes and that are finally given life as the re-born young King and Queen.) Among other congruent points of structure, one should note also the appearance, towards the end of the *Wedding*, of the young King and Queen at a game of Chess, *vide* Ferdinand and Miranda, "only it had other laws; for it was the Vertues and Vices one against another, where it might be ingeniously observed with what Plots the Vices lay in wait for the Virtues, and how to re-encounter them again."

There seems no doubt that with *The Tempest* Shakespeare was referring his own tremendous progress in spiritual vision, which he had conducted over the course of many years, to a long tradition of progress through spiritual worlds running from the medieval Masters of Chartres (in the twelfth century) right through to Andreae's *Chymical Wedding* (in the early seventeenth). We note, what's more, the uncanny structural congruencies in Shakespeare's later work with what Frances Yates has called the 'Rosicrucian Enlightenment' covering those extraordinary European developments, beginning in Shakespeare's own time, that seemed to offer hope in a new social order *based on* Rosicrucian principles of spirit-knowledge.[44] Shakespeare's primary focus on Ferdinand and Miranda in *The Tempest* could certainly be, and was, made to serve the hopes that were being placed in contemporary terms in the new order promised specifically around the projected Wedding of Princess Elizabeth to the Elector Palatine. These great social hopes came to nought, were violently squelched, but Rudolf Steiner draws the following moral from the eventual outcome:

> *But progress in human evolution is possible only when*
> *personalities of an attitude similar to that of Johann*
> *Valentin Andreae oppose the retarding forces of certain*
> *world-currents by others of a truly constructive nature.*[45]

It is, of course, easy in hindsight to second-guess the outcome of history, and any superiority about this, in any sense, would be contemptible, but it may be that we should indeed be searching out some other, long-term moral to Shakespeare's association with the Rosicrucian incision into history at this time (as in Steiner's focus on a greater "progress in human evolution" extending beyond the particulars of that time). Shakespeare's relation to the Rosicrucian Enlightenment, as we understand this in strict historical terms, I take to be peripheral. His very long course of development, running through his extended series of many tragedies into the later romances, was, I believe, in the end his own; it testifies *independently* to the new possibility that Rosenkreutz' initiation brings in, with the passage from the older Intellectual-Soul age, in which Shakespeare begins—there are strong remnants in his time also from the Sentient-Soul age—into the new, modern Consciousness-Soul age into which we ourselves are born.[46] Behind this greater historical development, as I have indicated, lies the transmutation (taking the form of a sacrificial death *into* human consciousness) of the traditional Sophia into the Anthropos-Sophia of our time. The moral to be drawn from Shakespeare's production finally is this: he was among the first to break into supersensible realms on the basis of a new development of self-conscious knowledge of the kind that belongs to our own epoch to this day.

V

THE ALCHEMICAL EXTENSION AND THE NEW LIFE

Also in the *alchemical* experience we detect that same background of expansive progression into spiritual worlds that I have emphasized is the one that principally concerns us in understanding Shakespeare's evolution through his last plays. For the alchemist, concentration on the material transformations that were brought about before his eyes was an occasion for the far more significant, corresponding transformations that were taking place in his soul, and it is in this context that we recognize that same progression into the sphere of the Great Ocean, associated with an extraordinary development of the faculty of Intuition, *behind* the stage of the process that has been described as the *mortificatio calcinatio*:

> *All is changed by a total destruction of life which will yet flower again . . . The glowing ash is . . . **placed on a ship to sail the dark seas** to an unknown destination . . . **In this long voyage in the vessel over the dark waters** (the purified materia prima is passing through sessions of slow heating in a vessel . . .), the planets surround the sufferer, and each one, being also a metal, beams influences which balance up to a new life, compounded of all life . . .* [47]

Shakespeare would have recognized in the alchemical progress not only another confirmation of the extraordinary experience through which he had ranged, but also a model as to where that experience might take one *further*. He could look back upon his immersion in tragedy as another form of engagement with the *prima materia massa confusa* taken right up, through the many extraordinary transformations that follow, into the *sevaratio* of Miranda's astounding emergence from that process. Ferdinand's appearance onto the scene is itself part of a series—Miranda, Ariel, Caliban, Ferdinand—representing a continuation of the *sevaratio*. In this *sevaratio* "the elements that had separated were also opposites"[48], and so alongside Prospero and Miranda on the one hand, we find Sycorax and Caliban on the other. Ted Hughes has described the significance of Caliban well where he speaks of a residual deposit of the whole tragic process, now separated out from the higher development on the other side: "in stunned, half-animal form . . . [and, for the first time, as tragic evil] baffled . . ."[49] For his part, Ferdinand has already been through a process of higher development, evolving from the anterior figures of Lysimachus and Florizel in whom he originates, having in some sense then already attended on the previous events of purification and redemption of the Ego in *Pericles* and *The Winter's Tale.* The further inter-association among Miranda, Caliban and Ferdinand at this point reflects a stage of the alchemical experience in which all the substances are still combining, even as they are in the process of separating out through the additional influence of the *conjunctio* that now firmly binds Ferdinand to Miranda.

In the alchemical development the transformation among the substances is a graphically pictorial one, involving red and white as well as pigments of green-blue and brown descending into black. They stand respectively for the individual Ego (red) about to be reformed in the Higher Ego (white) on emerging from the tragic process (black). Miranda as Higher Ego might be imagined in white. Ferdinand, as the individual Ego about to be reformed, from his first appearance would be in red. Caliban and the company he attracts—Stephano, Trinculo—embody on the other side the baser residuum of the tragic process, and so might appear in any number of combinations of dark-green/brown, or black. The whole of *The Tempest* might be seen as a drama involving these pictorial forces, beginning with the opening scene during which all the characters might be imagined in black or in associated colours of dark brown and green. The court party emerges on shore later, however, conceivably in various forms of a new combination of black, white and red, open as they are by then to the influences of reforming action on the island. There is also a general darkening at a certain point, as all the substances and forces at work seem to vanish into a concentration of black mass, the process of the *nigredo*, or blackening[50], leading to the central point of the *mortificatio calcinatio.* The corresponding moment in Shakespeare's play coincides with the deepest point of Ferdinand's trial, which interestingly is not directly represented in the play. Combining the play's contrasting, developing scenes into one continuous experience, we thus arrive at a full picture of the alchemical processing of substances as the adept might be imagined working on them as part of the long process of his own development in spiritual powers.

When Ferdinand appears in IV.i, *re*-emerging from the process of his *mortificatio*, one imagines him suddenly in a more sensationally luminous red, reflecting the great 'washing' or 'whitening' through which he has passed and is still passing (Miranda herself one imagines in a more sensationally luminous white). This is the fifth stage of *the ablutio* or 'new life', associated expressly in the alchemical development with the image of the re-birth of the Phoenix from its ashes (the emergent "Bird" of Andreae's *Chymical Wedding*).[51] Prospero's evolution now takes him *beyond* the Intuition in which he has worked right through the *mortificatio*, into the next stage described, in modern Rosicrucianism, as the Correspondence between Microcosm and Macrocosm. We are given an intimation of what this involves when Prospero 'gives' Miranda away. His voice is for the first time in the play altered, suddenly more open and confiding of his extraordinary strengths and purposes; he has found in Ferdinand another in whom some understanding of the reaches of human evolution can now be assumed:

> *If I have too austerely punished you,*
> *Your compensation makes amends; for I*
> *Have given you here a third* [52] *of my own life,*
> *Or that for which I live . . . .*
>
> *   . . . O Ferdinand*
> *Do not smile at me that I do boast her off,*
> *For thou shalt find she will outstrip all praise*
> *And make it halt behind her.*
> Ferdinand. *I do believe it,*
> *Against an oracle.*

Accompanying this first eruption of 'the new life' is a sequel involving the joy and celebration of the masque, which highlights, among other things, Iris's rainbow presence and the colorful peacocks that draw Juno's chariot. As we have it in the alchemical development, at this point:

> *The white became red, then golden, then it burst into a*
> *coruscation of colour, the Peacock's Tail . . .* [53]

Corresponding to this account is the bursting out of highly coloristic speech and song in this section of Shakespeare's play, bringing together and harmonizing, through the figures of Ceres and Juno, Earth and Heaven.

But the evolution cannot stop here: there must be a further impulse to extend the fruits of this accomplishment beyond the limits of the present, and so we reach the *resurrectum*. We pass on from the 'Paradise'[54] that Ferdinand recognizes of his perfected state of being with Miranda (being the "heaven" and "earth" of his previous solemn vow of allegiance to her) to the further 'passion' that now drives Prospero to break up the masque, looking ahead towards a still greater goal. In the alchemical development,

> *This is the end of the Paradise Garden . . . . [and] [i]t is*
> *a problem to move into another state, for this beautiful*
> *dreamland is not the answer to the mysteries, it is simply*
> *the beauty of the universe in its ineffable orderliness. So*
> *mankind has to go on the journey into timelessness . . . and it*
> *is then that the soul who truly understands that the **materia***
> ***prima**, the matter of the universe, is somehow within him is*
> *faced by illumination.*[55]

This supreme moment would seem to coincide with the moment of Prospero's disturbed 'passion', as a further quote suggests:

> *The expected light was something utterly beyond the*
> *imagination. It was something in which the adept was*
> *engulfed and altered. The experience was not to be described*
> *in terms which we can fully understand. We hear of the*
> *terror as well as the beauty, and note that the adept was*
> *often a changed personality after the experience. The ecstatic*
> *experience was the crown of the alchemist's life, but it was*
> *not always comforting. We have two Christian parallels,*
> *in St. Paul who was waylaid and shattered with the Light*
> *on the Damascus road, and ever afterwards went on his*
> *way towards martyrdom; and in St. Francis of Assisi who*
> *suffered the vision which implanted most painful stigmata*
> *to add to his virtues and complete absorption as well as his*
> *physical breakdown . . .*[56]

*   *   *

Lecturing long before the account of latter-day historians of alchemy, Rudolf Steiner explicitly identified true alchemy as an early form of Rosicrucian practice. Ultimately, it was designed to bring the practitioner-devotee into a climactic condition in which he could share in Rosenkreutz' fundamental experience, which Steiner tells us *was* an experience "of the event of Damascus", "a repetition of the vision of Paul on the road to Damascus."[57] The Higher Ego, which has been in process of developing in Imagination, Inspiration and Intuition, is at this point taken over by what modern Rosicrucian Anthroposophy has described as the True Ego in which alone the resurrected Christ Himself is revealed, through the mediation of His greatest servant on earth, who, since the thirteenth century, has been Christian Rosenkreutz.[58] In Prospero's case the moment of transfiguration shows all the marks of a disturbance that comes from bearing the intensity of a progressive expansion that seems to know no bounds, which seems to anticipate prophetically the dissolution of the world (there would seem to be a further structural link with the process of Christ's Ascension):

> *And like the baseless fabric of this vision,*
> *The cloud-capped towers, the gorgeous palaces,*
> *The solemn temples, the great globe itself,*
> *Yea, all which it inherit, shall dissolve,*
> *And, like this insubstantial pageant faded,*
> *Leave not a rack behind.*

In Prospero's fulfilled relationship to Ferdinand, there has been a turning back, as it were, *into* the creation out of the sphere of Intuition, thus effecting the Correspondence between Microcosm and Macrocosm, and this sublime accomplishment crystallizes now in the idea of bringing that creation forward, a bringing forward that is clearly a matter of Living *back* into the Macrocosm. Profoundly upsetting, in this context of progressive creation, must seem the intractable perversity of a Caliban or for that matter the whole group of those who have conspired against Prospero, to whom his attention must now turn. No doubt another part of the disturbance that characterizes Prospero's ecstatic breakthrough comes from this necessary further diversion of consciousness away from creative expansion back to the grating perversity that continues to try him immediately.

An infinite loneliness comes upon Prospero from his consciousness of the vast disparity between the powers he now wields and the grotesque offensiveness of a human nature that continues to *insist* on its own perversity. The loneliness is intensified the more by the temptation Prospero has sensed to meet such perversity with severest judgment. It seems, consequently, inevitable that Prospero should feel the paradoxical compulsion in such circumstances to 'give up' his powers, as if he understood that, from this 'deed' of renunciation, these powers would have to return (at a later date) with still greater force, if there is to be a chance of dealing with the powers of resistance that remain, which he also sees at work in himself.[59] Be that as it may, there follows a choice of virtue *over* vengeance, as all are presently accommodated and everything moves on towards the moment at which Prospero will draw back the curtain to reveal Ferdinand and Miranda to the chastised Alonzo and court party. It is the moment that anticipates the final stage of the *rubedo* or the Wedding proper, projected for the return to Naples.

Already one is given in the present scene an intense intimation of what this Wedding will be like, which modern Rosicrucianism has characterised in relation to the prospect of Divine Bliss. All is in the mode of intensest religious awe, and for a moment one has some understanding of what world dissolution would feel like, as even Antonio—who will finally balk at enlightenment—is irresistibly drawn into an infinite wonder. All is centred in Miranda's miraculous Higher influence and the tremendous effect her introduction now has on the whole of the real world. At this moment we have reached the point of the greatest possible enlightenment *for* the world, given its present circumstances, and we must wonder at the great sacrifice Prospero's act of bestowal entails, though it is the point to which Shakespeare *had to* come to test the value of all that he had gained from his experience.

* * *

Elsewhere[60] I have described the profound extension of terms implied in the transition from *Pericles* to *The Winter's Tale*, corresponding to a progress in the power of Higher Ego out of the more limited sphere of influence in the Mind, in which it originates, into the still greater sphere that unites the Mind with Nature and the further world of the 'wandering stars': the greater world of Inspiration, as I describe this above. Beyond *The Winter's Tale* lies the further embodiment of the Higher Ego in the power of Intuition, as we have seen. Shakespeare has worked his way *forward* to this point by first working his way *through* the new Age of the Consciousness Soul. Unconsciously, Shakespeare was following the lead of Christian Rosenkreutz. That Shakespeare should then revert in *The*

Tempest to what had become outmoded forms of alchemical-Rosicrucian expression, which his own evolution transcends, is merely an indication that no new language or appropriate ideas for that evolution had yet been supplied. That evolution for Shakespeare, as for Rosenkreutz, extends *beyond* the older terms and rather underlies them in a form that only *later* modern Rosicrucian Anthroposophy accounts for. Hence the necessity at a certain point of throwing ourselves beyond the immediate terms of Shakespeare's presentation onto the further elucidations Anthroposophy provides. The coming of those elucidations in our time would have to wait on the necessary *further* development, over the course of those centuries, of the Anthroposophia Being through which the new age is brought in at the time of the Renaissance.[61]

Modern Rosicrucian Anthroposophy informs us that the Higher Ego or Spirit Self will come fully into its own centuries from now, when the Age of the Consciousness Soul has run its course. There will then be a further Age of Imagination equal in length to the Age of the Consciousness Soul, and another Age of Inspiration after that, until we reach the boundaries of Intuition etc ...[62] Still more lies beyond that, as we have seen, corresponding to a still further time in which the True Ego will manifest further, from which spring in turn the still greater (almost unimaginable) faculties that evolve from Intuition. Of *these* sublime faculties we only have a concrete idea today in relation to the Life of Christ out of which they spring, and here, only an Anthroposophical Christology can begin to shed light on that relation. Suffice it to say that the fifth stage of the Rosicrucian initiation (the Correspondence between Microcosm and Macrocosm) mediates the influence of the Life of Christ Jesus before His Passion, from the time of His first miracle to His last. At one end of this Life is the miracle at Cana, when Christ Jesus learns to find a relation with His mother as "the woman who had become virgin again"[63]. This condition is progressively added to right through to His last miracle, when He initiates Lazarus, raising him back to life from death. From here He is then ready to pass on, through His Passion and Death, to the Resurrection. The analogy at this point is with Prospero passing on from his initiation of Ferdinand who has himself claimed a relation to the virgin force expressed through Miranda (the mediated force of the mother herself). In the sixth stage (the Living into the Macrocosm), there is the further reflection in Prospero of Christ's influence in the Resurrection, which has continued since the Event at Palestine and is later channelled by Christian Rosenkreutz. It was in Christian Rosenkreutz' power to mediate that influence up to a certain point and in one way in an earlier age, and to another point and in another way, as we have seen, from the time of the Wedding to this very day. For it is a matter of a continuous development over time, a progressively greater and greater prophetic intimation of the evolving powers as we proceed from age to age.

A FURTHER NOTE ON THE HIGHER EGO IN SHAKESPEARE

Re-emerging from the vortex of tragic time is for Shakespeare (along with Prospero, who inherits this whole process in the end) a matter first of coming through into the Imaginative Soul-world apart, a result of the extraordinary birth of a Higher Ego out of the tragic existence in which Shakespeare's mind is at one point seemingly irreversibly submerged. This is the extraordinary, unanticipated moment of Marina's birth and further life, from which we gather those sublime qualities in which the Higher Ego first manifests itself. Marina is, as Lysimachus notes, 'a [master-] piece of virtue', a phrase that Prospero will echo later in speaking of Miranda's mother, and Marina is indeed born of the self-sacrificing action of this very same mother, who bears the whole burden of tragedy, at this earliest stage of her intercession as Thaisa.

This Higher Ego comes forth in fact as the inviolable counter-force to tragedy, at once connected to it and yet beyond its reach. There can be consequently no possibility of degrading or desecrating this Ego's existence, as Marina so simply insists to the Bawd:

> Bawd . . . . *and you shall live in pleasure.*
> Marina. *No.*

Also, having a transcendent existence, this Ego can bear no relation to the import of depraved suggestion:

> *I understand you not.*

The Higher Ego is, however, no less connected to the whole burden of tragedy than is the tragic Ego, as Marina's words to Pericles imply:

> *She speaks,*
> *My lord, that, may be, hath endured a grief*
> *Might equal yours, if both were justly weighed.*

The Higher Ego has, in fact, separated out as an entity beyond tragedy's downward pull, and it is just the strength of this Higher Ego that it does float about inviolable in its own Imaginative Soul-world apart, from which heights it lifts up the other side of itself, the Ego in its tragic, downtrodden state. One need not labour the relation that these terms have to the later Romantic Imagination. Indeed one has here nothing less than a short view of how and in what form the world of the Imagination comes forth—namely as part and parcel of a Higher Ego which manifests itself in it. Penetrating that world in the case of Shakespeare's experience is to encounter also the presence of many other powers that crystallize around the Higher Ego, notably Cerimon, e.g., who stands in a tremendous relation to the mother, on whose 'revival' he attends. And what are we to make of the mysterious 'maid' who is Marina's constant companion and must appear alongside her in the recovery of Pericles? Or Helicanus who faithfully attends on the overridden Pericles? Or Lysimachus, a further power who comes to 'court' Marina and will eventually 'marry' her? These same figures appear again in the representation of *The Winter's Tale*, respectively as Paulina (Cerimon), Camillo (Helicanus) and Florizel (Lysimachus). We notice also the greater and greater prominence given to the suitor-figure, as we go along: Lysimachus, Florizel and, finally, Ferdinand. An Imaginative allegory on an altogether grand scale is thus contained in the progressive representation of this expanding world across Shakespeare's last plays.

There is in Shakespeare's case, in fact, a continual outgrowth as we have seen, taking us ultimately far beyond the terms of the Romantic Imagination. For, although there is something of the Higher Ego among the Romantics and something of its further union with Nature—something of Imagination and something of Inspiration—the Higher Ego is not yet fully channelled, is not yet directly perceived, and so as yet is only partially if magnificently productive. And it is in this respect that Shakespeare's account of the Higher Ego in his last plays, as illuminated by Steiner's science of the spirit, takes the further lead into a future inheritance of which we have had but the first intimations thus far.

6

From

The New School of the Imagination:
Rudolf Steiner's Mystery Plays
in Literary Tradition

I begin here from the impasse into which Western literature has fallen, indeed fell as long ago as the twenties of the last century. A continuous line of historical change up to that point (and it is thought, by some, beyond that point) will make it difficult to see that a special leap in evolution is involved, unlike anything before in tradition. It is the leap we have been unable to make, and the consequence has been what I would call the modern stasis: a period that has run its course for almost a hundred years now, marked by a mere repetition of the same modes of progressively worldly consciousness, falling away into manifestations of severe dissociation.[1]

Samuel Beckett took the dramatization of the process of dissociation about as far as it could go. In plays like *Godot* and *Endgame*, he is the anti-Shakespeare of late Western tradition, pursuing the further bottomless route down from tragedy, not the route back up as Shakespeare did in his late plays. Ionesco, in *The Chairs*, brings the process of dissociation to the point of the apocalyptic end of veritable human civilization and of veritable human consciousness. Only a virtual universe remains, in the midst of which Ionesco's protagonists take their final plunge into the annihilation of human consciousness. Both authors knew (as did many others) that the modern and postmodern age could only be seen in the most frightening of terms.

In the meantime a mainstream worldly consciousness carries on to this day in the expression of an effete stoicism, straining after a platitudinous moral propriety. This is the end result of an attitude that cuts itself off from the living tradition of the Romantic Imagination. It begins, in a more vital artistic form, with Hemingway in the late twenties. Characteristically, in "A Clean, Well-Lighted Place", the hero's whole effort is aimed at sustaining the self-created dignity of his own separate existence artificially maintained in the face of what has become an inchoate universe. The power of Imaginative thinking cannot be extended further, cannot be given further form and content, and the result is that it continually haunts Hemingway's hero from the unconscious and must be severely repressed. In later times, literature declines drastically with this slow, systematic killing off of the Imaginative power in this deeper sense.

This profound creative failure of our time is connected with the tragedy of the Romantic Movement. Brave spirits sought to press forward into an otherworldly sphere that beckons with knowledge of the sources of the world's creative forces and its evolutionary life. They sought to do so building on that extraordinary, expansive Soul-power that Wordsworth and Coleridge once defined immemorially as the Imagination.[2] Soon, however, Wordsworth would associate this power with "days gone by", an indication that he brings this power with him into life unconsciously—all authors of this and subsequent periods, who are possessed of it, do; it was a *new* evolutionary possession that had in the meantime defied their control, and one would have to acquire a better understanding of it in the future.[3] Characteristic of these first Romantic spirits, indeed, is a poignant combination of tragic perplexity and resigned faith in the face of what would appear to have been inevitable failure:

> *The days gone by*
> *Return upon me almost from the dawn*
> *Of life: the hiding-places of man's power*
> *Open; I would approach them, but they close.*
> *I see by glimpses now; when age comes on,*
> *May scarcely see at all; and I would give,*
> *While yet we may, as far as words can give,*
> *Substance and life to what I feel, enshrining,*
> *Such is my hope, the spirit of the Past*
> *For future restoration.*

Wordsworth was not alone in this supreme bafflement. We may claim it also of Coleridge and of Goethe as well as of Yeats and of T.S. Eliot, among many other authors that could be named. I mention these authors here because I am returned to them over the course of my treatment of Rudolf Steiner's Mystery Plays, on account of the tradition of reading from which I emerge. No doubt, other readers will be able to link up with many other authors from their own traditions. In other work I have presented[4], I have already brought forward the profoundly integral connections that can be claimed, in their attempts to comprehend the Imagination, among Steiner, Goethe, Coleridge, Emerson and Novalis. What was lacking in Romantic tradition, until Steiner makes his appearance in the late nineteenth-century, was a systematically grounded *theory* of the Imagination. *On* this basis Steiner would go on to build *his* overwhelmingly successful venture into the otherworld conducted over many years until his death in 1925. He would become the founder of a new Society among whose membership since then the task has arisen of carrying on with the production of a full-scale culture of the Imagination. To a large extent we are offered a first image of what that Society constitutes among the many characters presented in Steiner's Plays produced between 1910 and 1913.[5] They comprise among themselves a picture of the first great School of the Imagination in our time. While the modern age was about to take its plunge into a fearful hopelessness, and while the tradition of the Imagination was sputtering to its tragic foreclosure, Steiner was taking us back *through* that tradition to the point at which the Imagination *ought* to have emerged triumphantly, had the right approach to its further evolution been manifested at the time.

We recall the despair with which Wordsworth, in Bk. XI of *The Prelude*, addresses his lost hopes to Coleridge while the latter was himself convalescing in Malta. The year is 1804; Wordsworth had just produced the "Intimations Ode", his great tragic elegy on the passing away of the Imagination in the primal form he had known. Coinciding with Wordsworth's acknowledgement of his tragic alienation in these terms is Napoleon's self-proclamation as Emperor, in which Wordsworth sees a grotesque correlative of the general "catastrophe" of the time. In the *Prelude*, Wordsworth further invokes the partnership of Coleridge's sad self while the latter was convalescing:

> *To me the grief confined, that thou art gone*
> . . . .
> *A lonely wanderer . . . by pain*
> *Compelled and sickness, at this latter day,*
> *This sorrowful reverse for all mankind.*

At this time Coleridge was suffering from the tragic hopelessness of his love for Sara Hutchinson; he is confounded as well by the depth of his own power of Imagination which (unbeknownst to Wordsworth, ironically) Wordsworth had overbearingly repressed in him. In this repressed form, Coleridge's own deep link to the Imagination returns to haunt him in horridly fearful ways, to the point where he feels compelled to flee from that Power forever.[6] It is the end of English Romanticism in its pure, original phase.

Over in Germany Goethe too had failed, in spite of the grand optimism in which he is expressing himself at this time. Later Goethe, whom we know as the great Sage of Nature, elaborating on a highly penetrating understanding of the universal link between Nature and the Mind, and evolving through a progressively greater and greater *expansion* in poetic consciousness, emerges through what is finally an evasion of the great tragedy of that time, into which he otherwise peers so intensely. Years earlier (in 1775) Goethe's Faust had stood himself for a moment before the Spirit of his Imagination, only to find that, caught up in his reductive, sensual nature, he could not sustain the sudden moment of breakthrough (in the scene "Night. Faust's Study"):

Faust. (turning away) *O fearful form!*

Spirit. *At length*
You have compelled me here. Your strength
Has wrestled long about my sphere,
              And now—

Faust. *I tremble: come not near.*

Spirit. *With bated breath you laboured to behold me,*
To hear my voice, to see me face to face.
You prayed with might, with depth that has controlled me,
And here I am—What horror now can chase
The colour from your lips, my superman?
Where the soul's cry? The courage that began
To shape a world, and bear and foster it?
The heart that glowed, with lofty ardour lit,
To claim ethereal spirits as your peers?
Are you that Faust whose challenge smote my ears,
Who beat his way to me, proclaimed his hour,
And trembles now in presence of my power,
Writhes from the breath of it, a frightened worm?
. . . .
You match the spirit that you comprehend,
Not me. (He vanishes)

Faust goes on to draw an agreement with Mephistopheles on the basis that, having failed to penetrate properly to the otherworldly sources of his Imagination, he can only give himself now to all that drives a human soul in its perpetual restlessness—the sphere of merely sensual existence (however grand in spirit) to which Mephistopheles freely opens the door.[7] Goethe does not seem to have grasped Faust's condition in these terms until he sat down to write the agreement-scene over twenty-two years later in 1797. He was building, on the other hand, on a view of his hero's sensual nature that he had already grasped well in 1786 when he paints a Faust who knows precisely what he stands for in the comparison with Margaret:

> *Do I not know myself to be her doom?*
> *I, the uprooted, I the homeless jade,*
> *The monster I, whose only aim is this:*
> *To scour the rocks like any blind cascade*
> *Racing and eager for the dark abyss.*
> . . . .
> *And I, the curse of God upon my brow,*
> *I, not content*
> *To grip the rocks and make them bow*
> *And leave them rent,*
> *Must undermine her innocence as well,*
> *And make of her a sacrifice for Hell!*

In spite of the threat he poses, Faust *will* make a sacrifice of Margaret, unable to endure his dilemma, and Goethe will take us through what is perhaps the most distressing tragedy in late Western European tradition. In the last scene of Part One, Faust will penetrate Margaret's prison cell unable to entice her away from her certain death and ultimate social opprobrium, which he has brought upon her.

At only one other point (besides the early *Faust*) does Goethe return to the issue, though with a success on which he could not have counted, since he remained only half-conscious of his venture and would not pursue the matter further. He returns to it in his great *Tale of the Green Snake and the Beautiful Lily*, written around 1795. Here Goethe suddenly, and almost haphazardly, invests the Youth with precisely the capacity that had eluded Faust up to that point—the capacity of properly "dying into" otherworldly Powers that further the Imagination in its being. It is the moment in Western European tradition to which Steiner returns in his

Plays, to carry on with the task of helping with the further emergence of the Imagination in our time. Steiner's Johannes—the main hero to whom we are introduced in the first play—is based directly on Goethe's Youth, his extraordinary course of growth in the Imagination moving along the very same lines. It is not an easy growth, as Goethe himself knew well, for it proceeds through a profound assumption of guilt, of the sort that Goethe's *Faust* evades. Challenged to direct spirit-knowledge by the initiate leader of this School—who bears the name of Benedictus—Johannes finds himself abandoning the value of his temporal being (as an artist among other things) and, consequently, experiences an appalling emptiness through which the voice of one he has betrayed returns to haunt him as her murderer. This voice could well be that of Margaret from Goethe's *Faust* (the echo appears to be intentional):

> *"He brought me bitter need.*
> *I gave him all my trust.*
> *He left me in my misery alone.*
> *He robbed me of the warmth of life*
> *and drove me into the cold earth."*

The act of self-emptying leaves a void in Johannes in which at first nothing else is experienced *except for* the voice that proclaims his guilt to him. Beyond this experience, Johannes is confronted further exclusively with the essence of his lust and greed, which now appears to him, out of the abyss of his being, in the form of a revolting dragon:

> *Knowledge chains me to you, you destroying monster.*

Faust also comes as far as to see the monster in himself (as reflected back to him by the Spirit of his Imagination), but *he* is otherwise unable to confront himself any further, as we have seen. Post-Romantic experience is emphatically defined by an inability to confront this deep guilt in the self in the pure form and to the extreme extent that was required. The consequence of this avoidance, paradoxically, would be the great ravagement by *uncomprehended* guilt that subsequently pervades the course of the nineteenth and early twentieth centuries, leaving at some point nothing but terror and waste in its wake.

English literary experience points the historical impasse rather sharply. The Protestant *angst* of being fallen in the self, which at a certain point overtakes all the major authors of post-Reformation England, from Marlowe and Shakespeare right through to Milton, strangely enough has disappeared by the time we reach Wordsworth's efforts to link the self directly to Nature and to the Imagination. New forces of Nature and of the Imagination have spontaneously emerged in their own right, but there would be no successful attempt to relate these emergent forces back to the question of inalienable guilt that had so occupied an earlier age. Milton's whole endeavour consisted in the faith that he had come, in the epic grandeur of his Republican cause, to offer an historical solution to human depravity, which, like everyone else in the post-Reformation age, he took to be the first condition of human nature. Milton, as we know, was dramatically defeated in this attempt and in defeat strikes a figure that compares poignantly with the figure of the ailing Coleridge that Wordsworth invokes as an image of their common condition by 1804. Indeed, between the age of Shakespeare and of Milton, on the one hand, and that of Wordsworth, on the other, lies an abiding abyss, and it is tragic but fitting that Coleridge and Wordsworth both should be returned to that abyss by 1804 when Wordsworth is himself dramatically admitting defeat in his relation to the Imagination.

In the meantime, in a strong tradition of moral engagement—between the towering figures of Swift on the one hand and Blake on the other, the fact that the abyss was *not* being plumbed is just what human society was being excoriated for. "How morally and imaginatively small humanity is!", we seem to hear them saying. Swift would never cease to call his readers' attention to the intolerable smallness of their moral natures, the hopeless incapacity humanity showed for experiencing moral shame, while at the other end of the scale, Blake would for years bewail, unheard, the pathetically small use humanity was making of its Imaginative potential, incapable as he supposed humanity to be of any shame over the smallness of its imaginative ideas. Lacking was any proper understanding of the necessary intercorrespondence between the two orders that would link the further emergence of the Imagination with a full encounter with the depravity in human nature that remained.

One recalls that for Shakespeare it always was a matter of his assuming a direct responsibility for all the human tragedy he could imagine, a matter, that is to say, of bearing the full burden of human depravity himself. Only *on this basis* was the possibility then given to *him* of passing onwards into a new Imaginative life. Johannes in the opening of *The Portal of Initiation* confronts his own share in human depravity with a degree of exclusiveness and a completeness that, in European literature, is likewise unique. A further progress in Imagination becomes uniquely available to him precisely as a result of the extreme nature and degree of his engagement with that depravity. Significantly, Johannes undergoes his experience in the company of a fully emergent and well-founded School. Hence the figure of Maria, who comes to meet Johannes in the depths of his terror, bearing the faith that there is a purpose to his suffering:

> *You must experience every terror*
> *to which illusion can give birth*
> *before the truth reveals itself to you:*
> *thus speaks your star.*

Benedictus, as the Leader of this School, explains how at one point he had to help with the ensoulment of

> *.... that Spirit*
> *who should be given power to work*
> *now through our human world.*

Steiner's research as a whole identifies this Spirit as *Anthropos-Sophia*—the traditional Sophia who, since the Renaissance, now works directly in and through Man.[8] Benedictus's choice for the ensoulment of this Spirit is Maria, who, consequently, mediates the Power by which one emerges into an otherworldly Imagination in a way that is fully certain. Working, as she does, *purely* in this way, Maria must first convert those who become involved with her from all that continues to bind their interest to the temporal world, all of which must now appear as perversion. Thus Johannes has had to confront, in the purest and most direct terms, the full extent of *his* share in human perversion, in the form of the dragon of lust and greed that confronts him early on as the essence of his nature. Benedictus acknowledges the extraordinary self-preservation Johannes has shown when faced with the forces of destruction that have sought to overcome him:

> *My son, you have preserved your self,*
> *when . . . .*
> *. . . . wrapped in terror . . . ;*
> *Your self has strongly battled through*

The parallel with Shakespeare's extraordinary breakthrough should be noted here, and this raises the further (for now unresearchable) question as to what his own experience might have been at this level. Benedictus lets Johannes know that, from the time he had shown a power of engaging the abyss, himself as an Initiate was there to offer Johannes a further strength to hold himself together:

> *Truly you have been my pupil since that hour*
> *when you were near despair about yourself,*
> *and took yourself for lost,*
> *and yet the strength within you still held firm.*
> *I was allowed to give from wisdom's treasures*
> *what brought you strength to hold yourself*
> *though you believed no longer in yourself.*

And from Benedictus, Johannes now discovers that he must seek Maria in the Spirit-regions to which she has momentarily ascended. But the circumstances of this ascent have been frightful. Johannes must witness Maria's spiritual separation from the temporal part of her that remains behind, in Johannes's full view, demonically possessed:

> *But who is speaking?*
> *I do not see Maria,*
> *I see a ghastly being.*

Having preserved himself in the abyss, Johannes is now given the privilege "to look on spirit-being consciously", even if this be, at first, but another harsh trial, since Johannes gazes only upon the demonic counterpart to Maria's higher self:

> *and you, my son, have seen the temporal part*
> *of her to whom your love streams out entire,*
> *drop into darkness.*
> *Since often through her mouth*
> *the spirits spoke to you,*
> *world Karma has not spared you*
> *from hearing through her too*
> *the prince of hell.*[9]

In the presentation of Geraldine in Coleridge's "Christabel", one likewise finds the psychic reflection of an activity illuminating the demonic concomitant of the inner quest. On the verge of his own spirit-breakthrough, Coleridge broke down and withdrew: apart from Coleridge's own doubts in the face of demonic manifestation, Wordsworth made sure his literary associate and friend considered nothing more of the sort.[10] However, advancement in spirit-knowledge would seem to *presuppose* some such direct encounter with those demonic powers in the world that seek to pervert or distract from spirit-growth, especially through terror of them in their primal manifestations.[11] In a certain portion of itself, though in a way that is unpremeditated, the individual spirit finds the further "strength" that sees it through "to look on spirit-being consciously". Johannes's success in this respect grows out of his longstanding experience (of ten years) in the School and is inconceivable outside that experience. All that follows depends strictly on Johannes finding this primordial "strength" of which Steiner's Plays speak. Elsewhere in Steiner's work, in his actual preparation of the School his plays allude to, we find a detailed account of the process by which Johannes comes to this point of unfolding "strength"[12].

At issue is the kind of "strength" to which Coleridge himself aspired and which he distinguished from the mere prophetic "power" he possessed, an impressive faculty in its own right but one he knew was insufficient to allow for the kind of breakthrough into spirit-worlds he could anticipate.[13] Johannes has been tested further and found ready to be "released out of the world of sense". Unflinchingly he looks upon horrible spirit-representations of obstructive perversion in himself, and thereby comes to distinguish between the mere temporal part of his existence by which he is misled (the consequence of his devoting himself so entirely to Maria in the flesh) and his actual, genuine spiritual direction, which Maria now represents to him purely, out of the "spirit-heights" to which her soul retires. Into these heights Johannes himself now ventures, very largely because of the direction Benedictus feels justified in offering him:

> *Now it is right that you should seek her*
> *and learn to know her innermost being.*
> *And she shall represent for you*
> *that higher human being*
> *toward which **you** shall raise yourself.*
> *Her soul is hovering in the spirit heights*
> *where men can find their being's archetype,*

which is sustained within itself.
Follow her now into the spirit region,
. . . .
My son, since you have held yourself so far,
you will reach further.

II

The deeper challenge facing Johannes comes from the situation in which he is placed when his hidden lust for Maria is revealed to him. In "Christabel", Coleridge also grasped the lust in his love for Sara Hutchinson (frustrated as this love was by his marriage to another Sara), which he too saw as a grotesquely violent attack on what was most holy.[14] Coleridge also understood that great forces of self-knowledge lay hidden in such a revelation, and that it devolved upon him to *confront* this secret aspect of his nature, but he would be unable to explore the matter any further. Self-knowledge is given to Johannes through the dreadful appearance of the demon of his Double in whom this lust continues to be morbidly dramatized. Johannes's Double thus continues to drive him, in spite of his resistance, into deeper and deeper spheres of the knowledge of himself. Even in his perverse spirit, Johannes recognizes what his Double is capable of doing for him:

> *O likeness of my being, you have shown*
> *yourself till now before me with the purpose*
> *of making me appalled at my own self.*
> *I understand about you still but little;*
> *and yet I recognize that it is you*
> *who guides my soul. You are the hindrance*
> *against my free existence, and the reason*
> *I do not comprehend my own true being.*

The perversity in Johannes consists in pretending that his sensual dependency on Maria is inevitable and that he remains free to express himself in this nature even in the inner quest. He is even led fallaciously to suppose that such sensuality must serve as the basis for that quest. Likewise later Yeats will make as much of the subjection to the sensual self (and its "bitterness" and "violence") as the need for creation is felt. Implied in this development, however, is the acceptance of atavism, and it is a measure of the psychological risk involved in the turn inwards, which is otherwise inevitable.

To Ted Hughes it seemed clear that while Coleridge was in possession of the deeper turn inwards, he stood poised, exceptionally among the English Romantics, to tap into a comprehensive, "holistic"[15] basis for Imagination. This basis, Hughes speculates, has to do with what he calls "the deity of the blood-stream"[16], which is how Coleridge himself expressly represents it. In this way, Coleridge is thought to have been another D.H. Lawrence before his time, for whom "the Serpent Power" behind his figure of the "Serpent Woman", or the awakening of Kundalini, was his true subject, though he fled from it in dismay.[17] Whatever we may think of this as a final reading of Coleridge, the question remains how this "Serpent Power" in the blood is to be tapped into, for it would appear to involve at every turn a struggle of great moment, with a way through that is far from being assured, or for that matter, very straightforward at all.

That which Hughes suggests Coleridge ought to have *celebrated*, as "the river of life" represented *in* the "blood stream", in Lawrence presupposes a tremendous struggle first with what *he* called "the river of dissolution", from which there was no great assurance of coming free.[18] Coleridge is himself much embroiled in this "river of dissolution", as Hughes's account of him superabundantly makes clear (I invoke one case of this below). What we might describe as Lawrence's emphatic, first (or primordial) "river" signifies, in fact, all those dangerous ensnarements of sensual passion in the "blood" that *he* was very clear have always stood in wait upon the inward journey, and which would have to be very wisely circumvented before one could even *begin* to transcend and come free. We are returned in this way to the immoveable problem of lust and greed with which Johannes is found grappling from the beginning. Not that there is another way to come *fully* "to the light" than by means of such an in-depth inward engagement with one's sensual nature, or one would have to forego all human warmth in the process. Only it will be seen that the "blood" is bound, in the nature of the case, continually to confound, short of a greater perfecting of our nature. Hence, there *must* be the further help of a gratuitous dispensation that allows one to be "brought to the light" *in the midst of one's sensual nature.* Such illumination takes place even as one ensures that no encroachments of that nature are allowed to interfere with the purity or truthfulness of the illuminating process.[19]

The very great gift of the Anthroposophical School of Initiation in our time consists precisely in its act of support and bestowal of gratuitous illumination even while the further struggle with our sensual natures continues. It is the lesson that Johannes himself derives from the long course of instruction in which he is directed by the powers that have taken his initiation in hand:

> *Spirit–pupilship*
> *has granted me a Self which can be strong*
> *and can unfold its own creative work*
> *although its bearer has to know himself*
> *far from the highest purposes of souls.*
> *In this condition, when he has the duty*
> *to devote this second man awakened in him*
> *to earthly evolution—always must he*
> *let shine as his most earnest rule of life*
> *before his spirit's sight, that **he must never***
> ***let anything that comes from his own self***
> ***enter disturbingly the work** done not by him*
> *but by his second self.* [20]

The consequence of any such illicit act of identification must be the further breakdown into sensual degradation that drastically clogs the nature of those who partake in the Imaginative ideal without having first carefully separated themselves out. That ideal is simultaneously curtailed in its expression, dispossessed at that point of any further potential for opening outwardly to revelation. The effects of that degradation are now themselves projected in place of the outer reality that has thus failed to fully manifest. To reach this point of deeper self-understanding, Johannes must depend on the process of Initiation itself to set him right. Even his Double is confounded for a time by the strength of Johannes's illusions about himself which he has projected onto his Double. Then the Guardian of the Threshold finally intervenes to expose the basis of Johannes's sensual drive in his subversive love of himself.

III

As we have seen, of crucial significance is the challenge posed by the problem of holding *together* in "strength" in that extraordinary moment when the action of spirit-growth first makes itself felt. In Johannes's case, the problem is highlighted in the form of the overwhelming terror of being destroyed in his ego, from his helpless participation in the vision of his demonic nature. Capesius, another character with whom Johannes is linked, undergoes a significantly different experience, in *The Soul's Probation. His* terror is of losing himself to a sudden expansiveness in the spirit, without the support of *any* knowledge of his ego, which he has hitherto exclusively identified with his historical-cultural practice as a scholar. This compounded predicament—highlighting the spiritual anguish of the artist/poet, on the one hand, and the cultural-historical scholar, on the other—T.S. Eliot would fix upon, ten-to-fifteen-years later, in the transition from *The Waste Land* to *Ash-Wednesday*. Like Eliot the scholar, infusing his despairing consciousness into the poetic fabric of *The Waste Land,* Capesius tormentedly acknowledges the illusory nature of *his* intellectual-cultural constructs, which, for all their success in worldly cultural terms, leave him imprisoned in a condition of spiritual ignorance:

> *Through my whole life, I only wove in pictures*
> *that form as shadows in the dreaming soul*
> *as, in its prison of illusion,*
> *it mirrors nature and the works of spirit,*
> *trying to solve the riddles of the world*
> *in spectral fashion with its web of dreams.*[21]

Trying to respond to the exhortation he receives from Benedictus, to know himself in spiritual terms, Capesius can fathom only the collapse of his former world, with something of that suggestion of being left both spiritually airless and in terror that is a strong effect in Eliot's poem:

> *It is as if breath leaves me,*
> *when I attempt to grasp[his] words.*
> *Before I feel what I should think, appalling fear takes hold of me.*
> *It seems as if all the surroundings*

I had in life till now, were crashing round me,
destroying me among their ruins.[22]

Ironically, Capesius, as the type of the humanistic scholar, turns out to be a victim of his own hopefulness, disposed to *over*credit the value of man's accomplishments in the world, in relation to the spirit. He can only see the possibilities of cultural achievement *for man*, must compulsively refer any possible language of the spirit to man's language, since for him this is the all-in-all. This disposition of humanistic hopefulness must fail Capesius when he finally plunges into the actual realities of spirit, which demand a purer, less self-concerned and so less vulnerable sense of identity. His position compares directly with that of Eliot who, in the beginning of *Ash Wednesday*, looks upon the renunciation of his cultural-poetical self as his only hope if he is to progress further in the spirit. The effort to preserve himself, after renouncing every attachment to the world both scholarly and poetic, will lead Eliot to those tremendous involutions of self-searching that characterize his progression through the many parts of *Ash-Wednesday*, where he lays claim to his own understanding and experience of supportive worlds.

Capesius's weakness stems from fear. Remaining bound to his cultural-intellectual identity, he continues in fear of what the spirit-world has to reveal about the self-transformation he must undergo. Capesius fears what the spirit-world has to think out with him, because it points to purposes other than those supposed by the idle projections men *take* for cultural-intellectual thinking, which he now perceives as mere "weightless dreams":

> *Fear and bewilderment would come upon them*
> *if they could learn how spirits guide the course*
> *of being, as they will.*

But as in Johannes's case, Maria is sent to help Capesius. She makes him see what is another side to the spirit-reality with which a spirit-life must contend. She shows him that his fear derives from an excess of thinking involved in the form of cultural-intellectual thinking he has always practised, which in an interfering way translates the expectation of the revelation of spirit-purposes into fear. Because Capesius cannot dissociate himself from this familiar form of thinking, he is unable to progress further in spirit-purposes; he remains stuck in a form of spirit-vision that merely "sees", intellectually, without further power to affect or to take forward, unable to begin to transform himself. Until, from the gratuitous influence of Maria and Benedictus both, having been deemed inwardly worthy of this help, Capesius is led a little further along. He is brought to the point of perceiving how he can at least begin to effect a breakthrough, beyond the arresting fear that is holding up his development for now. Freedom from fear lies in the power to see that fear outside oneself, as the projection of an intellectual power in oneself that is not who one really is, and with that revelation a more promising prospect lies ahead for Capesius:

> *And since you could behold yourself,*
> *what you have dreamt as your own being—*
> *now find yourself; do not draw back in fear*

With the advantage of these advanced insights from Steiner's Plays, we begin to fathom the struggle Coleridge himself went through, who found himself likewise overwhelmed by his own self-concern, to the point of a terrible distortion in himself of the Goddess-influence that Ted Hughes shows was also at work in him. Coleridge's dreams bear witness to a powerful connection to the Goddess, but distorted and disturbed, on the one hand by the self-love in which Coleridge remains fixed, the combined result of his frustrated love of Sara Hutchinson and Wordsworth's pitiless rejection, and on the other by the cultural-intellectual identity Coleridge re-assumes in the face of his humiliation, which, seeking to appropriate the experience to itself, falsifies and introduces fear into the spectacle. In Coleridge's dreams, as Hughes points out, the Goddess "seems wholly negative, utterly horrifying. As in:

> *. . . a most frightful dream of a Woman whose features were*
> *blended with darkness catching hold of my right eye and*
> *attempting to pull it out—I caught hold of her arm fast—a*
> *horrid feel—Wordsworth cried aloud to me hearing my*
> *scream—heard his cry and thought it cruel he did not come/*
> *but did not wake till his cry was repeated a third time—the*
> *woman's name Ebon Ebon Thalud . . ."*[23]

In her name this 'Serpent-Woman' reveals much of the essential nature of the Goddess "in her rejected (vengeful) phase"[24], as she reverts to her original chaotic powers as Goddess of the Underworld. In that function she is what the world was originally formed from, "the creative womb of the inchoate waters, gradually refining herself into human form, and everywhere tending to be fish-tailed"[25]. She is fully present in this primordial function in the "deep romantic chasm" of Coleridge's "Kubla Khan", as Hughes points out:

> *Here again are the serpents, the giant slimy things that crawl*
> *with legs, bottomless springs, underworld seas, eruptive*
> *fountains, etc.—flowing into a river who* [sic] *is also a*
> *woman with a musical instrument in one hand and snakes in*
> *her crown (as in Apuleius' vision of Egyptian Isis).*[26]

In the poem ("Kubla Khan") the vision of the Goddess's world is more carefully balanced out, and Coleridge himself still fundamentally centred, but that hopeful sense of himself, out of which he begins his poetic quest, would soon crumble, under the weight of tragic circumstances which he could not set right.

But in any case it needed the Anthroposophical dispensation to make the Goddess's world more genuinely comprehensible, and in Steiner's Plays it is Maria who reflects the true Spirit of the Goddess in Her *now breakthrough* influence, which takes place in our time.[27] In her we see how and why, today, one is *not* to fear in the encounter with oneself as one engages with the Goddess. This is not to gainsay the depths of the moral self-confrontation that is still required of us, but no longer need the crushing influence of our disadvantaged condition, in the face of a developing Imagination, be what it was or can still be. Coleridge *retreated* before his own disadvantage into his superintellectualized abstraction (to become, by default, the greatest theorist of the Imagination in English tradition), but in his repressed passionate life all converted to inner nightmare. He lingers out his life in the midst of these intense complications as the most profoundly haunted of English poets. Eliot, for his part, was ready to do more than merely suspend *his* material cultural-intellectual thinking. In *Ash-Wednesday* he struggles to renounce such thinking altogether, just as he also works at abandoning self-love. These are the twin conditions (corresponding to the shared struggle between Capesius and Johannes) Eliot knew he *had* to transcend, to achieve any further authentic progress in spirit-vision. His struggle with himself in the meantime compares directly with the liberating effort Capesius makes, at a different level, to envision the fearful effects of continued temptation outside himself, as in the third section of Eliot's poem:

> *At the first turning of the second stair*
> *I turned and saw below*
> *The same shape twisted on the banister*
> *Under the vapour in the fetid air*
> *Struggling with the devil of the stairs who wears*
> *The deceitful face of hope and of despair.*[28]

Eliot was not operating with the advantage of the Anthroposophical revelation, and consequently his effort is not transposed directly to the sphere of spirit-vision, but in his spiritual disposition—struggling against the idealizations of self-love and of cultural-intellectual thinking both—he is clearly moving in that direction. Thus Eliot strenuously directs himself in the new centring influence of his poem's "Lady" who, mediating the refining power of the Goddess as "Mother", gathers to herself the "white light" of grace out of which Eliot's spiritual progress is shaped. This "white light" re-appears in full splendor in the second section of "Burnt Norton", where it takes on more openly the significance of the Word of which it bears witness. The same central, supporting significance is assigned to the Christ in Steiner's Anthroposophy but on the basis of a full reckoning with the Christian-Rosicrucian stream which finally brings forth a direct vision of the spiritual worlds. The Plays themselves bear this out to a very significant extent.[29] Steiner's unfolding powers of vision, in the meantime, would offer those around him a tremendous vantage point on the progressive variety of higher forces that now lie open to the human spirit, with the inevitable demands such access must bring for clearer insight into the moral tasks that lie ahead.

It is easy to see how resistance to these demands could be great, and Steiner's Plays themselves acknowledge the many forms of resistance that are bound to be put up from the tremendous complexity of the venture, which requires much self-searching and culminates indeed in an extreme form of self-confrontation.[30] Thus Johannes can still pretend to turn away from the imminent prospect even with the immense progress he has made up to this point:

> *Johannes will **not** know how spirit*
> *can answer riddles in dark depths of soul.*

He will create, will do an artist's work.
Let that be hidden from him, that in him
would look on cosmic heights with conscious vision.

Denying all that he has gained from his further evolution, Johannes pretends to revert to that form of artistic commitment that would go on working simply with the sensual forms of the sensory world, in a merely individual relation to them. On the other side, Capesius—as the one who should "be proclaiming/ the *knowledge* of the spirit unto others"—denies being able to translate the content of experience of the spirit-world into concepts that would lay the ground for a more general cultural approach to such an experience:

Much more than in creating outer things
the power of the spirit has to lose
itself in words. The words compel one
*to **understand** the thing perceived; and concepts*
oppose the power of the seer.

The process by which the otherworldly creation forces are engaged can be (but need not be in the Anthroposophical dispensation) a terrible one, accompanied by much shifting about and anguished self-questioning—until the breakthrough comes. There does not, in any case, appear to be any other choice in the long term. The alternative to this further, necessary effort to rise up again with the Imagination, it would appear, is a humanity that will only self-dissociate further and further, given up to greater and greater depths of a purely ironic existence, until we shall reach a world such as the one presented in Beckett's *Endgame.* Here the light of Nature's creation has been virtually extinguished, the Goddess appearing in this play as Mother Pegg who could not find what exchange of light with Man She needed, to recover Her creation:

Clov. *When old Mother Pegg asked you for oil for her lamp*
and you told her to get out to hell, you knew what was
happening, then, no?
You know what she died of Mother Pegg? of darkness.
Hamm. *I hadn't any.*
Clov. *Yes you did.*

In Beckett, humankind is already falling away with the creation, the devolution forces having here fully taken over; they express themselves through a physical creation that has now been left to itself, to erode away. How humankind will appear and what it will be left with, when thus dissociated from Nature's creation, determines the whole extent of Beckett's presentation, but one will find even in it, an implied exhortation to us to find ourselves again. There is nothing but despair, that this can be achieved at all, but what impresses about Beckett's presentation is the way despair *continues*, as itself a form of resistance to ultimate negation.

II

7

Visionary Miraculism in Shakespeare and Contemporaries: Its Origins, Import, and Tragic Fortunes

I

THE PSYCHOLOGICAL AND LITERARY BACKGROUND

In the poetic drama of Shakespeare's own time one notes, from its outset, a far more intense involvement in an otherworldly reality than we are today accustomed to allow. In the language of these early poets and dramatists we find, in fact, initially a fully *literal* absorption in an otherworldly dimension—'vision' in that very strict sense. Poet and dramatist, and even the contemporary psychologist, insisted on otherworldly terms as if these were real because for them, as I shall show, *they were real,* and it is only to us, in our own distance from the recorded evidence, that this appears to be merely a rhetorical insistence. One is indeed overwhelmed by how radically engaged with an otherworldly experience this literature was from its outset. *At the same time,* mind and language seemed then to be undergoing an extraordinary transition-process, a process that was felt to be extraordinary just because, for the contemporaries of this time, mind and language do originate in an otherworldly experience. Poet and dramatist are at first unaware of having fallen out of that experience. Then, awakening to that fact, 'consciousness' becomes for them a matter of their 'distance' from that otherworldly experience, as they are left in tragic 'conflict' with themselves. In fact, these poets and dramatists are at a certain point appalled to discover that language is *not* creating in the otherworldly dimension as they had supposed, and this because *for a while it really seemed to them that it had been.*

Most dramatic of all is the strenuous effort that immediately follows to *recover* literal vision in order to reverse the debacle. Here we must speak of more than an admirably proactive use of rhetorical language that is only flirting again with the otherworldly. Absorption in the visionary or miraculous has *literally* a retrospective function; it is itself the reliquary reflection of a previous *achievement,* and it therefore becomes a radically urgent matter to be working language up for all it might once again yield by way of a realization of vision. This is featured in an especially astounding way in the case of Shakespeare's Richard II, on whom I concentrate a great deal in the following essay. Significant attention is also given, however, to Shakespeare's Hamlet and to Thomas Kyd's Hieronimo, as well as to

Marlowe's Faustus. As it happens, this subsequent effort would be to no avail and but the prelude historically to a long period of tragic alienation from which we have yet even to begin to recover[1]. But in the meantime the resources of language were necessarily stretched to their uttermost, with all that that truly extraordinary effort has to teach us about what language was at least once *thought* capable of achieving—a disposition of thought to which, as we shall see, many poets and critics have wished to return in the modern age.

Perhaps the best way of proceeding in accounting for the full scope and import of the visionary experience in Shakespeare, as he inherits this at the outset of his career, would be to develop the implications of a statement by Hardin Craig which points some relevant terms. For the Elizabethans, Craig once remarked:

> *The distinction between the material and the spiritual*
> *was largely a distinction between the perceptible and the*
> *imperceptible, or between ordinary matter and a more finely*
> *attenuated substance thought of as spiritual. To make this*
> *distinction was the utmost reach that philosophy was then*
> *capable of making. One effect of this form of thinking was to*
> *make the unseen and the imperceptible a real thing, so that*
> *the supernatural seemed ready at any time to pass over the*
> *margin and assume a perceptible form.*[2]

I am concerned here with what Craig describes significantly as a unique historical "form of thinking", in elaborating on which I shall not assume any greatly in-depth familiarity with the "philosophy" that is said to have given rise to it. Rather, I shall operate from representative citations picked out at random from various Elizabethan texts where I believe such a "philosophy" is at work. One will note that this is philosophy at its "utmost reach", where a marvellous transformation is projected, according to which the imperceptible seems ready "at any time" to assume a perceptible form. One will note, too, that the projected transformation is accompanied crucially by an absorption in the imperceptible as a "real thing".

I shall begin by tracing the projection of inward reality in Elizabethan psychological texts on the innermost level of what may be called the structure of the individual self. This effort represents what we may define as the *physiological* approach to the relation between body and soul, in which we can trace precisely the distinction Craig refers to between "ordinary matter and a more finely attenuated substance thought of as spiritual". As Herschel Baker once remarked:

> *Not everyone had Bacon's candor in defining the soul as*
> *a "corporeal substance, attenuated and made invisible by*
> *heat", clothed in the body, and "refreshed and repaired by*
> *the spirituous blood of the arteries"; but virtually everyone*
> *accepted the naturalistic assumption of a very intimate*
> *correlation between the state of the body and the state of the*
> *soul. Without the four elements and the corresponding four*
> *humors, the Renaissance physiologist and moralist would*
> *have had a hard time.*[3]

In spite of this and other such assertions of this Elizabethan commonplace, as far as I know little attempt has been made to account very closely for the process of radical imagination such a postulation of the correlation set loose. That postulation did not serve only to elaborate an essential truism about man's condition; it expressed, in fact, the wishful effort to circumvent a fundamental deficiency in knowledge in order to recover "the whole man"—to return to a pre-lapsarian state of full metaphysical knowledge of the kind Godfrey Goodman invokes in *The Fall of Man*. Speaking of "Man", Goodman remarks:

> *as he is Lord of his outward action; so he should have the full*
> *power and command of himselfe, **and of the most inward***
> ***and secret operations of his owne body** . . . But, see, see,*
> *whole man is corrupted, and therefore body neither with*
> *soule nor soule with her faculties can together consist; . . .*
> *The soule and the body, though parts of one man, and*
> *mutually subsisting together; yet are they strangers one to*
> *another, nor any **way acquainted with the counsels and***
> ***secrecies of each other**. Whatsoever is proper and peculiar*
> *to the soule (for her faculties, her nature, and powers) she*
> *doth not any way impart it to the whole man but only by*
> *way of reflection: looking upon the action we judge of the*
> ***substance** . . . Againe, whatsoever is proper to the body, as*
> *forme, figure, the use and disposition of the inward parts,*
> *notwithstanding that the soul first squared out the body, and*
> *fashioned the members for her owne use and service . . . yet*

> **she knows them not**, *and therefore* **must learn them againe**
> *by inspection, and dissection of man's body.*[4]

One should like to know to what extent the physiology on which Bacon grounded his own definition of the soul could be said to have been informed by the motive ideal that Goodman expounds on here—i.e., attainment to that immediate, metaphysical identity in knowledge between body and soul that Goodman posits for himself in his projection of "the whole man". The case of Bacon is ambiguous, as D.G. James once reported:

> *It was one thing to remove the thought of final causes from*
> *the action of the mind engaged in investigating the natural*
> *world . . . but, Bacon goes on, "when a man passeth on*
> *further, and seeth the dependence of causes, and the works*
> *of Providence, then, according to the allegory of the poets,*
> *he will easily believe that the highest link of nature's chains*
> *must needs be tied to the foot of Jupiter's chair".*[5]

What this last quotation from Bacon implicitly describes is an activity of natural investigation that is ultimately based in the very identity in knowledge of body and soul of Goodman's projection. On the basis of the "inspection and dissection of man's body", Bacon has himself pretended in his definition to a knowledge of the soul that strongly suggests the ultimate formal identity of Goodman's projection.[6] For Goodman in the passage cited, the process of inward identification takes place in the most generalized form, as my bold print indicates. Even so, this is made significantly "real" to us by the pressure of feeling one senses Goodman generating about this. Bacon himself has the further advantage of working from the definite and detailed physiological explanation. Working thus through a concrete form of "philosophy" at its "utmost reach", Bacon himself proceeds through an absorption in the imperceptible as a "real thing". To quote again from Craig,

> *the distinction between the material and the spiritual is*
> *largely [here] a distinction between the perceptible and the*
> *imperceptible, or between ordinary matter and a more finely*
> *attenuated substance thought of as spiritual . . . which makes*
> *the unseen and the imperceptible a real thing.*

Much inspiration would seem to hang on Bacon's definition of the soul as a "corporeal substance, attenuated and made invisible by heat", with its idea of something fully there, only unseen. One suspects, too, that much inspiration has also been taken from an idea involved in this definition which suggests a direct pathway of subtlization through the body's tangible "heat" to the soul. The suggestion is made more strongly perhaps in the idea of the "spirituous blood" making its way inwardly directly to the soul that is to be "repaired".

I shall have more to say in a while about the total physiological basis that gives Bacon's definition its power and inspiration. First, I should like to call our attention to another passage from Thomas Bright, where the processes at work in Bacon are presented from a more generalized perspective. At this point, I shall return for a moment to what Herschel Baker pointed out as the *basis* of the contemporary correlation between body and soul—the doctrine of the four elements and the corresponding four 'humours'. I shall assume that an account of the full theory is unnecessary since it is familiar knowledge to students of the Elizabethans. I will merely remind us of the fact that the 'humours' were sometimes subjected to excessive natural heat, in which case there resulted an "unnatural" humour called "melancholy adust", and that from the "adustion" or burning of a humour, an "unkindly" passion might arise. It is the action of this passion that Thomas Bright traces in the following passage, where again one can detect, in the inward identification involved in tracing such action, the twin aspects I have remarked in Bacon of subtlization and inward movement. One will note here, however, that the specific psychology traceable in Bacon's definition has given way (though Bright was speaking from immediate experience as a doctor) to generalized rhetorical description:

> *Thus the passion whereof the humour ministreth occasion by this unkindly heat advaunceth it selfe **into greater extremities**. For becoming **more subtile** by heate, both in substance and spirit, it passeth **more deeply** into all the parts of the instrument it selfe, and is a conveyance also of the humour of the same kind: making way for naturall melancholie, wherewith it is mixed, **into the verie inward secrets** of those instruments, whereof passions are affected, even hart and braine.*[7]

Inward projection in Bright is meant to take us as far as we can go—"into the inward secrets" of heart and brain. It is difficult to imagine actually being taken there, but, as we shall see, that is more or less what happens in a passage from Pierre Charron. Bright himself merely provides us with a description of the inward progress of the passions. But as L.B. Campbell once pointed out, "the effect of the passions on the spirits was all-important, because the spirits were the medium or go-between between body and soul."[8] As she elaborates:

> *It is because the passions have their seat in the heart and*
> *affect the spirits which are there refined, and because the*
> *spirits are the natural conveyors of heat, maintaining the*
> *humours at their proper balance by maintaining the proper*
> *heat in the blood, that we find, then, the passions having a*
> *direct effect on the humours. And it is also through this same*
> *channel of the spirits that the humours move the passions*
> *directly.*[9]

The direct influence of the "spirits" on the body "heat" will help to fill out the physiological basis of Bacon's definition of the soul as "a corporeal substance, attenuated and made invisible by heat". So, too, the association of the "spirits" with the blood, also implied in the Campbell passage, with the *other* part of Bacon's definition: "refreshed and repaired by the spirituous blood of the arteries"—the spirits being, in fact, regarded as "a substance subtill and aerious of our bodie bredde of the part most pure and thinne of the blood"[10] To this we may now add a closer account of the function of the arteries, which Pierre Charron makes the basis of a truly extraordinary description of the progress of the spirits "into the verie inward secrets" of the brain. Through an awareness of the process of subtlization and a transference of visual function from the arteries to the spirits, Charron has left us with a description of the progress of the spirits truly rich in inward identification, the value of such identification lying precisely in the evidence it provides of a mind at its utmost reach where it is shown pressing against the sensible world for a manifestation in it of the *supersensible* reality projected. Thus,

> *The vital spirits are raised by the arteries to the brain, where*
> *they are concocted and re-concocted, elaborated **and made***
> ***subtile** by the help of the multiplicity of small arteries, as*

*fillets diversely woven and interlaced, by many turnings
and windings, like a labyrinth or double net.*[11]

*   *   *

So far I have been tracing inward identification on the innermost,
physiological level of the individual self. As a process illustrating absorption
in the imperceptible, this involves at some point, as we have seen, the
projection of inward reality in sensible form. A similar phenomenon can be
traced as one moves not inwards but, still on the level of the self, outwards
towards the external appearance and behavior of the body, where an *inverse*
projection takes place. Here it is not the soul that seeks to be "clothed in the
body", but inversely the body that is to be informed with the soul. Indeed,
it was felt that the powers and gifts of the soul could be communicated
directly between one mind and another; but, as Lemnius puts it:

> *Not only in the inward mynd do these ornaments and
> gifts of nature appeare and expressly shew out themselves
> but even in the outward shew, shape and behaviour of
> the body . . .* **the countenance, which is the image of the
> mynd . . . the eyes,** *which are the bewrayers and tokentellers
> of the inward conceipts:* **in the colour, lineamentes,
> proportion and feacture of the body.**[12]

I shall be concerned here with inward identification in another direction,
one paradoxically interchangeable with a general process of externalization.
On closer view, however, the difference between inward identification on
this level and that on the first is not, strictly speaking, one of kind but
focus; for whether the projection takes place inwardly or outwardly, it is
the same material body in whose sensible processes inward reality is being
projected.

Having made use of Bacon as the chief representative of such projection
on one level (without any suggestion that Bacon is the only, or necessarily
the best, choice but merely a convenient one), I should now like to turn
(with the same qualifications) to Lemnius as the chief representative on
another level. I shall proceed now to a consideration of several other, mainly
post-Elizabethan, texts which will help to fill out Lemnius's statement,
as the texts from Bright and Charron helped to fill out the statement
by Bacon. We will notice that Lemnius singled out for attention, in the

general context of the body, the countenance, the face and the eyes, one suspects as areas where the revelation of the inner man might be especially clear and direct. In a kindred passage from La Primaudaye, the focus of attention is entirely on the face:

> *the heart doeth so enlarge it selfe, that it is represented in*
> *the face, as it were in a glasse, or **in an image** framed to*
> *expresse the joy and gladnes which it hath.*[13]

Here we may note (it operates through the flow of blood implied in the word "enlarge") more evidence of the *physiological* basis that permits La Primaudaye to identify face and inward state (here joy or gladness) through the medium of the heart, itself ambiguously material and spiritual. In a while, I shall have more to say about the kind of faith that the material-spiritual identification expresses. My first concern is with the recurring view in La Primaudaye of the face as the "image" of the heart, and of its joy, which echoes Lemnius's view of the countenance as the "image" of the mind. The use of "image" would appear to suggest the residual sense of derivation or of correspondence, or at most the sense of correlation. I shall not attempt to deny that this is so, but it ends, nevertheless, in a relation of full *identity*. It isn't that the face is merely an "image" of the inner state, that on its own level it reflects or correlates to the inner state that belongs on another level; it is rather that the inner state finds in the face its full manifestation in sensible form, its full "image" in that sense. One cannot say that all this is immediately clear in La Primaudaye or Lemnius. But it is there. That the relation described is ultimately one of identity and not merely correlation is brought out fully when one places Lemnius and La Primaudaye in the context of a sequence of passages from Andreas Laurentius who concentrates himself on the other of Lemnius's two major areas of inner revelation—the eyes.

The advantage of the Laurentius texts is that they begin precisely from the limited effect to which one might confine Lemnius and La Primaudaye until, gradually, the full, radical character of the statement is filled out for us:

> *And as the face doth shadow out unto us the lively and*
> *true image of the minde, so the eyes doe lay open unto us*
> *all the perturbations of the same ... To be short, they be*
> *wholly given to follow the motions of the minde, they doe*

change themselves in a moment, they do alter and conforme
themselves unto it in such manner, as that Blemor the
Arabian, and Syrenus the Phisition of Cypres, thought it no
absurditie to affirme that the soul dwelt in the eyes ...

Here Laurentius would seem to hold out no more than what Lemnius or La Primaudaye might seem to: a vivid statement of the intimate correlation between mind and body; except for that last line, which suddenly lifts Laurentius's statement onto another level. That this is undoubtedly an extraordinary level is already suggested by Laurentius's need to deny the impression of absurdity; Laurentius's statement, in fact, finally works through some very bold embracing of absurdity. This is brought out fully in the second part of his statement, which deserves to be quoted in some fullness if only for the suggestion of a position that might be amusing were Laurentius himself not dead serious:

See here thy selfe condemned, O shameless findfault Momus,
and utter-terly [sic] overthrowne in thine action, and delay
not but come and make condigne satisfaction, by honourably
recompensing of na-ture, whom thou hast so maliciously and
falsely accused of follie in the framing of mans bodie, for that
she did not set two windowes, next neighbours to the heart,
through them to spie all the passions of the same. Canst thou
wish more goodly windowes then these of the eyes? Doest
*thou not see therein **as in a glasse** the most hidden things*
of the mind? ... It grieveth me that ever I should find so
vaine a discourse, as should containe the eger desire of any
man to have the breast framed of christalline cleereness, to
the end he might see what is within the heart, seeing we are
***alreadie possessed of this** round christalline **humour** within*
the eyes ... [14]

This is an extraordinary statement. What makes it extraordinary is the way Laurentius finally allows his mind to be absorbed by the metaphor that Momus himself presents as literal fact. That the unfortunate Momus should have thought that the "passions" of the heart or "the most hidden things of the mind" might let themselves be fully seen if the "breast" were "framed of christalline cleereness", as with windows, is already an unthinkable absurdity. It is even more of an absurdity for Laurentius to suggest that an equivalent for this already exists in the eyes, the more so if, as would seem, Momus's absurd suggestion arose itself from a consideration (in "two windowes") of the inadequacy of the eyes for the kind of extreme revelation Momus had in mind. Here indeed is a measure of the value of inward projection in Laurentius, as I will suggest in La Primaudaye and Lemnius. When these speak of the eyes or the face or the body in general as an "image" of the mind, all *imply* finally the visionary transparency that Laurentius develops astonishingly from Momus. To look into the eyes (or the face) for a revelation of the passions of the heart or the hidden things of the mind was to see *directly* into heart and mind, as through a window, "as in a glasse", in a phrase whose final value has by now been established. More accurately, it was to see heart and mind *in* the eyes: eyes and heart or mind being thus one, standing in a relation of full identity.

Unfortunately, such a magnificent claim obscures its basis in absurdity. For to say that one might actually see the heart or mind in the eyes would not of course follow any more than it would follow that by peering fantastically at the heart (the physical organ) through imagined windows in the breast, Momus would have managed to see all that is "within the heart". It is a measure of the projection at work. The claim of full identity necessarily assumes at bottom a marvellous transformation, a transformation that, from one point of view, would seem to be at best a magnificent projection. What is assumed is the material-spiritual transformation I remarked upon in La Primaudaye, which finally makes the heart *at once* material and spiritual, a transformation and identification transferable, amongst Elizabethan psychologists, to the face and the eyes, indeed to the body in general.

Of this complex phenomenon of transformation literary criticism has given us an account. It is what John Crowe Ransom illustrates, using a passage from Cowley's "The Change":

> *Oh, take my Heart, and by that means you'll prove*
> *Within, too stor'd enough of love:*
> *Give me yours, I'll by that change so thrive*
> *That love in all my parts shall live.*
> *So powerful is this my change, it render can*
> *My outside Woman, and your inside Man.*

As Ransom comments:

> *In Cowley's passage above, the lover is saying not for the*
> *first time in this literature: "She and I have exchanged our*
> *hearts". What has actually been exchanged is affections, and*
> *affections are only in a limited sense the same as hearts.*
> *Hearts are unlike affections in being engines that pump*
> *blood and form body and it is a miracle if the poet represents*
> *the lady's affection as rendering her inside into man . . .*

We may interpose that it is equally a miracle if the poet represents his own affection as rendering his outside into woman. Yet both transformations are made possible by assuming that hearts are affections; moreover, in the case of transformation in the man, there is the added assumption that faces are affections. In what follows, I will be concerned with the exploration in dramatic poetry of just such transformational thinking as I have been outlining here, ultimately with a view to illuminating the very complex metaphysical *activity* to which such an exploration bears witness. As Ransom continues:

> *We may consult the dictionary, and discover that there is a*
> *miraculism or supernaturalism in a metaphorical assertion*
> *if we are ready to mean what we say, or believe what we*
> *hear . . .*
>
> *A conceit originates in a metaphor; and in fact the conceit*
> *is but a metaphor if the metaphor is meant or predicated so*
> *baldly that nothing else can be meant . . .*
>
> *Specifically, the miraculism arises when the poet discovers by*
> *analogy an identity between objects which is partial, though*
> *it should be considerable, and proceeds to an identification*
> *which is complete. It is to be contrasted with the simile,*
> *which says "as if" or "like" and is scrupulous to keep the*
> *identification partial.*[15]

Such for Ransom is "'Metaphysics', or miraculism", from which it will be clear that by "metaphysical" in these pages I mean finally what Ransom means:

> *the meaning of metaphysical which was common in Dryden's*
> *time, having come down from the Middle Ages through*
> *Shakespeare, was simply supernatural; miraculous.*[16]

Ransom is generally discreet in his view of the process as an "illusion" of reality, as merely the "extension of a rhetorical device". But in settling into that position, Ransom finally reduces his own view, if one can gather this from his expression of it in my extended quotation above. For what emerges of value in his account is the understanding shown of a *completeness* in the metaphysical process which arises when we are ready to mean what we say or believe what we hear. As we have seen, the pattern of inner reality-making assumes the mind penetrating the sensible world for an identification between it and a supersensible "reality" projected onto it by a marvellous transformation. In the end, all depends on the belief that that "reality" is fully there. In fact, the psychology involved takes its character from the projecting rhetoric in which it is expressed. However, to say that it is merely rhetoric would be to reduce the matter, for the point is that an intense psychology emerges because the rhetoric *grows out into* reality.

As Thomas Wright puts it, from a text that I shall use to recapitulate the implications of the second level: "An action as a whole is an external *image* of an internal mind". In another passage, having reduced the internal mind to the specific influence of passion, Wright brings this view to its fullest possible statement, in doing so providing us with a usefully complete account of the scope and impact of self-revelation in its transformational aspect:

> *the passion in the persuader seemeth to me to resemble the*
> *wind a trumpeter bloweth in at one end of the trumpet, and*
> *in what manner it proceedeth from him, so it issueth forth*
> *at the other end, and cometh to our ears; even so, the passion*
> *proceedeth from the heart, and is blown about* **the body,**
> **face, eyes, hands, voice, and so by** *gestures* **passeth into our**
> **eyes, and by sound into our ears.**[17]

Here again, we can follow the characteristic pressure of insight building up, through implicit transformation, climactically to the full identification of mind and body, at the point I have emphasized by a use of bold print. The act of self-revelation so described has been traced here to its furthest possible point—to its full *reception* through the eyes and ears of the spectators. We are thus left with a significant part of the view that *Hamlet* elaborates when, re-assuming for a moment "the motive and the cue for passion", Hamlet turns from his experience of the Player's passion in II.ii. to project an act of self-revelation that would "amaze the very faculties of eyes and ears". What *Hamlet* presents in this moment is the conception of an act of self-revelation that would involve a full visionary transparency in Laurentius's sense. His idea of self-revelation is specifically motivated, in fact, by the transformational energies of miraculism, with all that this elaborates of a mind radically absorbed in the supersensible as a "real thing".

The complex process of inner reality-making which I have been tracing here would not, as the focus of these psychological texts suggests, necessarily have been assumed to stop at the level of the structure of the self. An individual had his place in the world, and in *Hamlet*'s climactic moments, the structure of the world is itself involved in the same transformational psychology I have been tracing in the Elizabethan psychological texts at the level of the self. In the action that immediately accompanies the disappearance of the Ghost in *Hamlet*, one finds the broadest and most abstract effort by the hero to project onto the larger world those radical identifications intrinsic to a full accommodation of his involvement in vision:

> *O all you host of heaven! O earth! What else?*
> *And shall I couple hell? O, fie!* **Hold, Hold, my heart**;
> *And you, my sinews, grow not instant old,*
> *But bear me stiffly up. Remember thee!*
> *Ay, thou poor ghost, whiles memory holds a seat*
> **In this distracted globe***. Remember thee!*
> *Yea, from* **the table of my memory**
> *I'll wipe away all trivial fond records,*
> *All saws of books, all forms, all pressures past,*
> . . . .
> *And thy commandment all alone shall live*
> . . . . [Writing]
> *Now to my word:*
> *It is 'Adieu, adieu! Remember me!'*
> *(I.v.92ff)*[18]

Here the focus lies with what are presented as the sensible-material forms of the world—Hamlet's "heart" and "tablebook"—upon which Hamlet proceeds to project a value of visionary reality. That is, Hamlet takes his "heart" (Momus' physical organ) and (like Momus) proceeds to identify this with all that is "within the heart"—at this point with what survives in Hamlet's consciousness of his vision of the Ghost. In the same way, Hamlet proceeds to identify his "tables", as well as the scribblings which he inscribes in them, with his literal memory of this vision, which he hopes thereby to perpetuate. The full value of this radical identification hangs on the phrase Hamlet notes down in his book, by which Hamlet finalizes the impression of his vision—"Remember me"—a phrase emphasized by Hamlet in a manner intended to clinch the identification in question by specifying the radical act of memory involved.

It is thus that one can speak of a direct and full correlation between self and world being implied, even if the philosophical exploration is left radically undeveloped, suggesting abstract treatment. The very same intimate correlation between self and world is posited in the phrase by which Hamlet projects similar radical identifications between (simultaneously) his head, and the world, and the broader, universal implications of his distracted state:

> *Remember thee!*
> *Ay, thou poor ghost, whiles memory holds a seat*
> *In this distracted **globe**.*

It is clear from such developments in *Hamlet* that the belief in vision goes hand in hand with an involvement in reality that, in spite of the abstract element, runs far beyond the projection of the Elizabethan psychologists. It is the difference between a treatment in the play that *frankly* assumes its full metaphysical subject, that is to say, that is metaphysical in the first place,[19] and a self-circumscribing naturalism, among the psychologists, that would seem to be being subverted by latent metaphysical motives.

The assumption of full metaphysical development is what accounts finally for an integral relation at *all* levels—not only between self and world as here in these developments from *Hamlet*, but, comprehensively also between these *and the otherworld*. Thus, in a very bold development, the Ghost takes on, at a very early point in *Hamlet*, a precise significance as the direct outgrowth of Hamlet's emotional perception of his father in his "mind's eye" (I.ii.185). Familiarity with the idiom of miraculism will put us in mind of the value of the phrase as expressing the language of vision. The suggestion of a perception of visionary 'reality' in Hamlet at the level of the self finds its direct expression in the Ghost—a visionary manifestation from the supernatural world. That is, as the projection of Hamlet's mind, the manifestation of the Ghost illustrates strikingly that unique form of thinking which Craig ascribes to the Elizabethans that made "the unseen and the imperceptible a real thing so that the supernatural seemed ready at any time to pass over the margin and assume a perceptible form".

However, what Craig's description leaves unexpounded, when one applies it to *Hamlet*, is the full *continuity* between levels implied in the act of vision—the whole integrated, what's more, at the level of the real world. Thus the remarkable thing about the representation of the Ghost is the way, while being presented all the while as a sensible manifestation from the supernatural world, it is attributed with the impression of possessing *bodily* actuality, suggesting that it is at the same time a transformed being *of* the natural world. In fact, when Hamlet first confronts it, the Ghost gives Hamlet the ambiguous impression of being his father resurrected from the grave. This is an emphasis which takes on all the more resonance when referred to Hamlet "*seeking*" earlier with "vailed lids" for his "noble father *in the dust*" (I.ii.70-71). One can only look upon this series of integral relations as the boldest form of metaphysical projection, such projection presenting itself in Hamlet's "seeking", as an extreme kind of metaphorical development, one that assumes a form of thinking in which metaphor is meant, where metaphorical "seeking in the dust" grows out, boldly and comprehensively, into reality.

What is absent from Shakespeare's presentation at this point is an analysis of the informing *psychology*, some closer hint of those developments that would trace the realization of vision in the figure of the Ghost to the transformational energies of a mind radically absorbed in the value of its own projection as reality. This omission is in striking contrast to the analysis presented of the *reality* of vision in this same part of the play. Noteworthy on this point is the complex, final value of reality ascribed to the Ghost as Hamlet's psychological projection, as a representation, simultaneously, of the natural and the supernatural worlds.

The status of the Ghost as a figure of the grave is also of crucial value in illuminating another aspect of the structure of the vision in *Hamlet*. This focus on the dead as the *locus* of vision has its immediate origin in the tradition of narrative tragedy, in the poet's vision of the speaking Ghost. In *The Spanish Tragedy* this figure takes on a very complex function, thus setting the pattern for the representation of the Ghost in *Hamlet*. As someone who, in Kyd's play, is attributed, for the first time in this literature, with a power of vision *himself,* the figure of the speaking Ghost calls attention to the power of full vision of otherworldly Judgment made available in death. However, this is accompanied paradoxically by a dramatic emphasis on the pathetic *reduction* of power associated with the Ghost's revelations, evident in both plays in the enforced incompleteness of the account of the otherworld the Ghost gives us. This is something that, especially in Kyd, is presented as a dramatic reduction of *speech*—suddenly the Ghost aborts his account; in *Hamlet*, it is immediately expressed through the complex muted suggestiveness of the Ghost's reference to the "eternal blazon".

In *Richard II*, too, the projection is of an order of otherworldly Judgment brought to near realization and this is presented more barely as a development of metaphorical thinking. In this case, more remarkably, it is spoken by someone who is still alive. Hence the implications that emerge from the speech Richard addresses to Aumerle upon landing in England with news of Bolingbroke's insurrection, which ultimately projects the returning King in the function of Christ the Judge at the Second Coming, ("rising in [His] throne"):

> *Discomfortable cousin! know'st thou not*
> *That when the searching eye of heaven is hid,*
> *Behind the globe, that lights the lower world,*
> *Then thieves and robbers range abroad unseen*
> *In murders and in outrage boldly here:*
> *But when from under this terrestrial ball*
> *He fires the proud tops of the eastern pines*
> *And darts his light through every guilty hole,*
> *Then murders, treasons, and detested sins,*
> *The cloak of night being pluck'd from off their backs,*
> *Stand bare and naked, trembling at themselves?*
> *So when this thief, this traitor, Bolingbroke,*
> *Who all this while hath revell'd in the night,*
> *Whilst we were wand'ring with the Antipodes,*
> *Shall see us **rising in our throne**, the east,*
> *His treasons will sit blushing in his face,*
> *Not able to endure the sight of day,*
> *But self-affrighted tremble at his sin.*
>
> *(III.ii.36–53)*

The radical force of the projection in this speech depends ultimately on the subtle, *transformational* relation to the projection made possible here by Richard's extraordinary position as King. It is this position that allows, in the first place, for Richard's radical identification of himself as King with the Sun, itself treated, via another radical identification, as Divine Judgment. What's more, the basis of these identifications—what to all intents and purposes, is a single identification—in the analogical correspondences of contemporary microcosmography extends the area of reference in the speech to include Richard's identification with his Heart. For the microcosmographical correspondence between the Heart and the Sun in the Elizabethan world-view (which is being treated there, ultimately as an identity), there is Helkiah Crooke, to quote for evidence:

> *For as that celestiall part, the Sun is predominant, by whose motion, beames and light, all things have brightnesse, lustre and beauty; so in the middest of the chest, the heart resideth, whose likeness and proportion to the Sun, is such and so great,* **as the ancient writers have been so bolde as** *to calle the Sun the heart of the world, and the heart the Sunne of man's bodie . . .* [20]

There is also Robert Burton:

> *the heart is the seat and fountain of life, of heat, of spirits, of pulse and respiration; the Sun of our body, the King and sole commander of it; the seat and organ of all passions and affections; . . .* [21]

It is clear from the Burton citation that the correspondence between the Heart and the Sun could be extended to include as well, on the human or political level, the King; and it is therefore probable that the Divine Judgment is being viewed in Richard's speech as the fourth and highest term in the analogical progression, representative of the supernatural or cosmic level, though I have not seen this final correspondence made among the Elizabethan psychologists. Yet, in his book *The Shape of Things Known*, Forrest Robinson quotes Roger Bacon, the medieval Franciscan: "God is to the soul as the sun is to the eyes . . .", of which Robinson remarks "Bacon and many of his peers invested the comparison with far more than figurative significance."[22] Assuming such a world-picture, then, the invocation of this final divine term seems inevitable: Richard is here claiming a power of emotion as God's deputy that involves him ultimately in an identification with God's control over the human and natural worlds.

The basis of Richard's position in the microcosmography of the age is precisely what lends added force to a metaphorical development of these identifications in the speech that is already quite powerful in itself. In fact, it is a question, in Ransom's terms, of metaphor that is meant. The metaphorical development, that is, takes on radical force from the awareness lent to it from an inherited, cosmographical view of the basis of the projected identifications in reality. Thus, the overwhelming immediacy with which the Sun is looked upon as Divine Judgment; also, the natural inevitability with which the kingship is united to this identification at the climax of the speech, which is also the moment at which Richard projects himself as Christ the Judge. This last apocalyptic detail, seen in the context of Richard's speech as a whole, shows in what comprehensive visionary sense Richard's projection, as in *Hamlet*, is a projection of Judgment.

The crucial feature of the projection, thus, is the way Richard experiences this as reality. Here is another expression of a mind absorbed in the supersensible as a real thing. The energies of the speech are rooted, precisely, in this visionary bent of mind, in this subtle *transformational* relation of Richard as King to the projection. In this case, the focus of vision resides in the "eye" of Judgment in Richard himself: it is the visionary transparency of the Elizabethan psychologists: Richard embodying his heart. In Richard's next speech, this experience is traced to its physiological basis, as Richard says of himself; "But now the *blood* . . . /Did triumph in my face . . ." (III.ii.76-77). From the very beginning, there is the jump from this focus in Richard to identifications with the Sun and Divine Judgment, and finally, as we have seen, to Christ the Judge. What seem like metaphorical accretions to this focus are no 'mere' accretions at all but parts of a comprehensive development of visionary power. To focus the development, Richard's assumption of the reality of a universal identity as King is what allows him his own radical identification with his multi-levelled projection. This development is based on a view of the full *continuity* between levels, projecting, finally, a prospect of complete integration at the level of the real world, in Richard himself. It is not, to point a crucial distinction, a question of visionary power experienced merely in the mind.

And we do well to remember that this power, insofar as it is seen as an embodiment of Richard's heart, is, as in Hamlet's case, power that is based in an emotional-imaginative development. That is, in embodying in himself, through the power of his kingly emotion, the Sun and the Divine Judgment, Richard is seen as embodying his own emotion, the claim and aspiration to identification with Divine Judgment being implicitly presented as a portentous act of emotional self-embodiment.

Conspicuous in the initial action in *Richard II* and *Hamlet*, thus, is the striking evidence presented of metaphorical development pursued as literal fact, accounting for an extraordinary, portentous development of metaphysical vision. In that most suggestive book, *Induction to Tragedy*[23], Howard Baker speaks of a process of forming figurative language, in which Thomas Kyd "reduced" the traditional material of the marvellous journey into hell into "figures of speech which could convey the personal emotions of a Hieronimo": "[e]ach of the speeches in which Hieronimo swears that he will go down into hell in search of justice and revenge develops an intensity which mounts from line to line". It was thus that "Kyd provided the imagery necessary for a metaphorical journey of the troubled spirit." The problem with Baker's account, so suggestive as it is, is that it does not go far enough in explaining the extreme kind of metaphorical development one finds actually taking place in Hieronimo's speeches, which throws further light on developments in *Richard II* and *Hamlet*.

In one scene, for example, two "Portingales" appear to Hieronimo to ask the way to Lorenzo's dwelling: Hieronimo's reply begins, according to expectation, as a physical direction, but it soon takes a strangely metaphorical turn. It does so at first in a startling and impressive way but then becomes uncomfortably humorous under the burden of Hieronimo's persistence with it until, at a certain point, the humor quite fades out of the account as the metaphorical direction proceeds further to a frankly *literal* plane:

> *But if you be importunate to know*
> *The way to him, and where to find him out,*
> *Then list to me, and I'll resolve your doubt,*
> *There is a path upon your left-hand side,*
> *That leadeth from a guilty conscience*
> *Unto a forest of distrust and fear,*
> *A darksome place and dangerous to pass:*
> *There shall you meet with melancholy thoughts,*

> *Whose baleful humours if you but uphold,*
> *It will conduct you to despair and death:*
> *Whose rocky cliffs when you have once beheld,*
> *Within a hugy dale of lasting night,*
> *That, kindled with the world's iniquities,*
> *Doth cast up filthy and detested fumes—*
> *Not far from thence, where murderers have built*
> *A habitation for their cursed souls,*
> **There**, *in a brazen cauldron fix'd by Jove*
> *In his fell wrath upon a sulphur flame,*
> *Yourselves shall find Lorenzo bathing him*
> *In boiling lead and blood of innocents.*[24]
>
> (III.xi.10–29)

To speak in connection with these lines of a "metaphorical journey of the troubled spirit" is indeed to speak of a reduction of material; for, at a certain point in this speech one is made aware of metaphorical development being pursued as literal fact, the metaphorical identification with a literal valuation of the material accounting for a more portentous intensification than the kind Baker calls attention to about the figurative process at work, indeed dramatizing the rhetorical-visionary development to far greater effect than one might suppose.

Such a development assumes a view of metaphysical significancy the inverse of that put forward by Rosemund Tuve, in her *Elizabethan and Metaphysical Imagery*, as for example, in her consideration of Greene's lines from *Menaphon* (1589):

> *Whiter than be the flocks that straggling feed*
> **When washed by Arethusa faint they lie**
> *Is fair Semela.*

or her account of Herrick's "Upon Julia's Voice":

> *So smooth, so sweet, so silv'ry is thy voice*
> **As, could they hear, the Damn'd would make no noise;**
> **But listen to thee,** *(walking in thy chamber)*
> *Melting melodious words to Lutes of Amber.*

of which latter piece Tuve remarks, "we give our belief to the significance conveyed, while disbelieving, the 'facts' used in its conveyance—disbelieving, for instance, Julia's power to silence the lamenting damned".[25] But it is precisely in the ambiguous revelation of the reality of such "facts" as Tuve would banish to unreality that the metaphysical process absorbs us even in what appear to be its most scrupulously self-limiting uses.

Tuve's view is determined by her assumption that with Metaphysical, as well as Elizabethan, poetry "It is the concept which the metaphor helps to make manifest which has the vastness and the metaphysical reach . . ."[26] My own purpose in these pages is to provide evidence of metaphysical development in which clearly it is rather the metaphor that has the metaphysical reach. I would refer this view further to what Hiram Haydn, in his great book, *The Counter-Renaissance*, judged to be "the exultant expression . . . of man's metaphysical ache" representative of Counter-Renaissance spirit; such spirit is immediately dramatized for Haydn in "the general Elizabethan susceptibility to the denial of limit", as witnessed in its "bold metaphysical imagery, hyperbole and exaggeration . . ."[27] It is in the nature of my commitment here that I am seeking to recover status for a radical functioning of metaphor in areas where such a functioning seems slighted, as in Tuve's examples from Herrick and Greene, where it does not appear at all obvious that the poetic effect is not rather to give metaphor itself the metaphysical reach. If this is true of such minor efforts as these, it must be the more true of the major poetry of this age (both narrative and dramatic) whose subject and realized effect is boldly and explicitly metaphysical or miraculous (as, e.g., *Paradise Lost*). As it happens, it is just this radical view of metaphysical development through metaphor that Tuve goes on to consider herself in her chapter "Significancy, Ancient and Modern"—finally pronouncing against it.[28] In that chapter, Tuve addresses herself centrally to Eliot's encapsulating formulation (showing a penetration that goes beyond even Ransom) that in metaphysical poetry "the idea and the simile become one". As Tuve elucidates, "especially as modern ideas[29] have come to be developed, something further seems to be in question: in that what is praiseworthy is a relation between percept and "felt thought" which is nothing less than identity, and in that what is especially interesting [significant?] about a thought is that it was experienced (cf. "is true") . . ."[30]

Indeed, we may refer the visionary development in Kyd further to what Eliot has to say about the employment of:

*a device which is sometimes considered characteristically
'metaphysical'; the elaboration (contrasted with the
condensation) of a figure of speech to the furthest stage to
which ingenuity can carry it . . . In one of the finest poems
of this age . . . , the "Exequy" of Bishop King, the extended
comparison is used with perfect success: **the idea and the
simile become one** in the passage in which the Bishop
illustrates his impatience to see his dead wife, under the
figure of a journey:*

> *Stay for me there; I will not faile*
> *To meet thee in that hollow Vale.*
> *And think not much of my delay;*
> *I am already on the way,*
> *And follow thee with all the speed*
> *Desire can make, or sorrows breed.*
> *Each minute is a short degree,*
> *And ev'ry houre a step towards thee.*
> *At night when I betake me to rest,*
> *Next morn I rise nearer my West*
> *Of life, . . .*

One needs to recognize of this bent of mind a subtle transformational
rhetoric that proceeds, in Kyd's case, from the effect, in a dramatic context,
of a frankly literal appropriation of narrative material. This is rhetoric that
serves to build up the view of an extreme kind of metaphorical thinking,
straining, as in developments from *Richard II* and *Hamlet*, towards
something literally embodied and seen. If what I am claiming about
Hieronimo's speeches is right, one ought to be able to find elsewhere in
Kyd's play evidence of a dramatic re-constitution of traditional visionary
material. And that is what we do find. Moreover, in this Kyd had a
forerunner.

* * *

When Kyd preceded the play's events in *The Spanish Tragedy* with
the Ghost of Andrea giving an account of his descent into hell, he was
building on an innovation that Thomas Sackville had introduced years
before in his contribution to the *Mirror for Magistrates*.[31] When Sackville's

Induction was first presented to the *Mirror*'s curiously sensitive body of distinguished compilers, the poem had roused them to wonder and consternation at the audacity of its invention.[32] Radically unlike the other stories in the *Mirror*, the *Induction* was being made room for as a "preface" to Sackville's less anomalous contribution of the story of Buckingham. As an artistic cadre for that story, Sackville's *Induction* was unusual, for both its elaborate sophistication and its audacious use of the vision-structure that all of the Mirror-poets had been applying to their stories, in the tradition of Boccacio and Lydgate. Each story in the *Mirror* was narrated by the Ghost of its subject who was to be imagined appearing to the poets in a vision. With only one exception (the ghost of Richard of Gloucester was pictured "howlinge" from the deep pit of hell), the ghosts had been imagined by the *Mirror*-poets as speaking either freshly dead or on the point of death (and thus as an "Image of death"), or else "newly crept out of the grave". Sackville's *Induction* had disturbed this pattern by setting its speaking ghost among thousands of others in the depths of hell, after claiming to have been led there on a journey by the Goddess Sorrow.

The fear of the Mirror-poets was that Sackville's procedure was likely to be ill-taken, since the hell-setting implied a judgment on the statesmen-ghosts, whereas it had been until then the general procedure to refrain cautiously from some judgments. Even worse, in its sympathetic qualities Sackville's judgment "savoured" of Purgatory, thus catering to the papist misrepresentation of the otherworld. The fretfulness was allayed by the intervention of the *Mirror*'s less excitable voices. Their conclusions are revealing. Falling back on Renaissance syncretic method, they concluded that Sackville's Hell was really no Hell at all, but in fact a symbol for the grave; and so it was that Sackville's subversive *Induction* was re-appropriated to *Mirror*-procedure: even then, the syncretic solution was unnecessary since Sackville's Hell was seen as "a Poesie", relevant "adornment" merely.

The decision of the *Mirror*-poets to restrict their visions to the moment of death was not to be traced merely to their determination to eschew political and theological controversy. The extraordinary complacency with which some of the *Mirror*-poets treat of the topical implications of the *Induction* show that. The procedure said a great deal rather about their basically rationalist assumptions about the nature and function of the creative imagination. In refraining (with the exception of Richard of Gloucester, whose damnableness was obvious to all) from taking their ghosts beyond the brink of the grave, the *Mirror*-poets were acting on their limited belief as to how far the creative imagination could go in developing a conceit that had in any case been adopted more from deference to tradition than from any real insight into its poetic function. Nor is this implication of *Mirror*-procedure contradicted by one or two spectacular exceptions to the rule, most notably in the Ghosts of York and Colingbourne who are imagined speaking one out of a headless trunk, the other with his heart in his hand "smoking forth the lively spirit". In these cases, the *Mirror*-poets were merely employing a sensationalistic rhetoric guided by an idea of the miraculous reality one might effectively project onto death for compulsive reading; for which the conceit, that is, served merely as conceit without any suggestion of a projection of literal reality. Not only were the ghosts kept scrupulously close to the grave, it was clearly established that they were to be regarded as the creations of story-telling: at most, they could receive a sensationalistic representation from the influence of a fantastic ardor always avowedly rhetorical in purpose.

The basic procedure for telling stories thus finally rationalized the appearance of the ghosts. But, in proceeding along the lines it did, the practice of the *Mirror*-poets stood out in sharp contrast against the claim to visionary organization that even the *Mirror*-poets themselves acknowledged respectfully of their models, Boccaccio and Lydgate. This isn't to say, of course, that the *Mirror*-poets did not believe in the power of creative imagination; the effectiveness of their stories depended on it. Thus it is correct to say, with Alwin Thaler, that "the *Mirror*-group believed in true feigning, true imagining by poet and audience".[33] It is an account, however, that finally obscures the actual position of the *Mirror*-group, for whom "true feigning" consisted in seeing that "imagining" was merely an effective means for conveying what was true and not actually true in itself.

It was inevitable, therefore, that the *Mirror*-poets should fail utterly to appreciate the extraordinary status of Sackville's *Induction* as vision. Significantly, the obvious function of Sackville's poem as vision led them to associate it rather with the extraordinary creations of Lydgate and Boccaccio than with the more sensible fictions of the *Mirror*-group. Yet far from representing an effort at real understanding, this gesture merely served to highlight the group's spectacular incomprehension, for the syncretic-rhetorical reduction showed how Sackville's visionary journey was finally to be taken. Sackville's vision was to be reduced to symbolic "thought" or to "fiction": what the *Mirror*-group had failed to see was that the journey Sackville described took reality precisely from the extraordinary developments by which mere "thought" had transformed itself into vision. The Goddess Sorrow, who serves as Sackville's guide for the journey into Hell, could not have put the import of Sackville's experience more unambiguously:

> *behold the thing that thou erewhile*
> *Saw only in thought . . .*
>
> *(ll. 530-531)*

Thus, Sackville's *Induction* stands out from the other, more modestly-shaped stories in the *Mirror* by virtue of its active belief in the transformational powers of the imagination. From that belief, it followed that any account of the mind's workings where the "fiction" appeared to be an outer shell for "thought" was to be taken as literal "vision".[34] This would seem to make Thomas Sackville the first prominent writer of the English Renaissance to build on the view which, running through Sidney, would find its consummate realization in the work of Milton, whose *Comus*, for instance, provides the most overt exposition of the view of literary reality at issue:

> *I'll tell ye 'tis not vain or fabulous*
> *(Though so esteemed by shallow ignorance)*
> *What the sage poets, taught by th' heavenly Muse,*
> *Storied of old in High immortal verse*
> *Of dire Chimeras and enchanted Isles,*
> *And rifted rocks whose entrance leads to Hell*
> *For such there be but unbelief is blind.*
>
> *(ll. 513-519)*[35]

In the Elizabethan Renaissance, Sidney had broached the same view:

> *Neither let this be jestingly conceived, because the works*
> *of one [nature] be essential the other [man] in imitation*
> *or fiction; for any understanding knoweth the skill of the*
> *artificer standeth in that Idea or fore-conceit of the work,*
> *and not in the work itself. And that the poet hath that Idea*
> *is manifest by delivering them forth in such excellency as he*
> *hath imagined them.* **Which delivering forth** *also is not*
> *wholly imaginative, as we are wont to say by them that*
> *build castles in the air, but . . .* **substantially it worketh** *. . . .*
> *for the poet . . . , lifted up with the vigor of his own*

> *invention, doth grow in effect another nature, in making*
> *things either better than nature bringeth forth, or quite*
> *anew, forms such as never were in nature, as the Heroes,*
> *Demi-gods, Cyclops, Chimeras, Furies, and such like . . .* [36]

Here we touch on the mythical extension of visionary development, the aim of such development being (among many other of Sidney's descriptions) "to satisfy [man's] inward conceits with being witness to itself of a lively true knowledge"—compare Tuve on the view of what "is true".[37] Forrest G. Robinson's association of terms at one point in his book, *The Shape of Things Known*, is further telling of the *modern* affinity with this development:

> *When poetry is described in terms of an "objective*
> *correlative" [in Eliot], there is indeed nothing very striking*
> *about the "speaking picture" of poetry [in Sidney].*[38]

As a comment by Robinson on the currency and too easy familiarity with which such terms tend to be greeted, this text only highlights the more what should be taken as his point: that such terms express a penetrating perception of art's literal, metaphysical idiom, its visionary structure and basis.

In presenting its vision, Sackville's poem drew on the conventional medieval form of the marvellous journey. In doing so, it had taken on the narrative form as literal fact. The power that had made possible the journey was the Goddess-guide, Sorrow, who according to the pattern may be taken to be more than merely a personification. She is the spiritual objectification of the poet's own grief, round whom the expanded vision of Hell now takes place: the visionary product of a "busie minde" lost to its metaphorical "musings" (1.64, 1.156). In beginning *The Spanish Tragedy* with a descent into Hell himself, Kyd could not have been unaware of Sackville's use of the marvellous journey as vision. Whether or not the intensity of the narrative actually justified the claim to vision is not at issue, neither here nor in Sackville; both accounts, unlike the *Mirror*, acted on the assumption of the literal function of narrative, thus projecting, in contrast to the *Mirror*, an unlimited belief as to how far the imagination could develop the traditional conceit inherited from Boccaccio and Lydgate. In *all* cases the conceit of the speaking ghost had been adopted to intensify the impact of the tragic events treated. That much is clear from the use made of the conceit by the *Mirror*-poets. The capacity of the audience to imagine a speaking ghost, to lose themselves, as it were, to the "fiction", accounted for the intensity with which the stories would be received. By filling out the fiction, the imagination of the audience thus built on the intensity that the poets likewise had brought to their story-telling by projecting themselves into the situation of the speaking ghosts. However, the fact that the narrative could also serve, as in Boccaccio, to express a claim to literal vision ("As hym thoughte in the inward si[g]ht")[39] could only have added to the psychological value of the narrative for both poet and audience. That value was likely to be intensified the more extraordinary and expansive the vision, so that Sackville and Kyd had everything to gain from linking a vision of the speaking ghost with an evocation of the otherworld, a larger vision of the descent into Hell.

The full metaphysical significance of this linkage in Kyd is best appreciated by first tracing what Sackville had done to Boccaccio. Boccaccio's vision had operated within the tradition of an artistic framework for the narrative of falls, which set the pattern for the later narrative tragedy of the *Mirror*. As Howard Baker points out, in his *Induction to Tragedy*:

> the ordinary procedure was to have the ghosts of the fallen
> Worthies appear successively as in a vision, before the poet . . .
> The ghost . . . was sometimes conducted from the infernal
> regions to the poet's chamber to the "stage" by a guide . . . [40]

It was Sackville's daring innovation, building on a profound intuition of the possibilities of literal development in sorrowful imagination, to develop these possibilities of the journey in Boccaccio's vision. The appearance of the ghost before the poet already assumed a journey from the infernal regions to the poet's chamber. In that journey, the ghost had been led by a guide. In his own development of the vision, Sackville had used the guide, inversely, to carry the poet from his chamber on a journey into the infernal regions where ghosts awaited him.

In a further development, Kyd had brought both models together. The drama of the Ghost's appearance in the Prologue ultimately emphasizes his immediate presence in the world: that is where the Ghost finds himself quite unexpectedly after the process of judgment in the underworld is mysteriously interrupted. There Andrea performs the function of the Ghost in Boccaccio, appearing before the audience on the "stage" as the ghosts had appeared to the poet on his own "stage" in the poet's chamber. This is a presence, however, that, unlike in Boccaccio, recreates as immediate background the marvellous journey into hell following Sackville. Once again, it is necessary to insist that Kyd's narrative, like Sackville's, functions as literal vision. Though the narrative itself may be far from totally convincing as embodied vision, it is more than merely a fiction: there is no basis, that is, for allegorizing the narrative or reducing it to something else, for not taking it exactly as it appears as itself.

Moreover, the function of the ghost and his narrative as vision would have been immeasurably *enhanced* when the transposition from one "stage" to the other had been fully grasped. For the whole power of the Prologue depends on seeing it as a dramatic development of narrative procedure. What this meant was that the total vision which we see and hear on the "stage", in the form of the Ghost and his narrative, was to be taken as the direct transposition of the vision acted out before the poet on his own "stage" when writing the play out in his chamber. The transposition implied an analogy between the audience watching and listening to the Ghost on stage and the poet watching and listening to it in his chamber; indeed, on the analogy of the poet in his chamber, the audience was being compelled to respond to what was taking place before it as a vision of their own, in a final extraordinary merging of the poet's vision with the vision of the audience. Something of this complex, metaphysical relation, one assumes, survives in the presentation of the Ghost in *Hamlet*, and it may indeed explain the portentous intensity that unites us with the Ghost in his account. But one wonders if it is not also there in Richard's visionary address to Aumerle—that is, in a view of metaphorical assertion that involves the writer and ourselves in the belief that what is said is meant and what we hear believed.

One can see from developments in narrative tragedy that a perception of visionary development was intimately associated in this literature with the immediate inspiration of the chamber or the study, the concentrated solitude of which it is easy to imagine offering the poet precisely that marvellous setting for dynamic thinking that he would have been seeking, to realize the possibility of vision. Nowhere is the sensitivity to the inspiration of this setting reflected in more dramatic terms than in that great inward achievement in drama of the Elizabethan Renaissance, *Dr. Faustus*. As Helen Gardner has noted, "The play begins and ends with the hero in his study."[41] Moreover, in a central scene from (one version of) that great play, the devious power of supersensible manifestation which Faustus brings with him to the court of the Emperor Carolus is explicitly projected by the Emperor as fulfilling that insistent identification with the sensible realization of metaphorical thought brought into dynamic focus in the concentrated solitude of the study—that intimate yearning preoccupation with supernatural vision—that one ought to look upon as a typical experience for the Renaissance:

> *Then, Dr. Faustus, mark what I shall say.*
> **As I was sometime solitary set**
> **Within my closet**, *sundry thoughts arose*
> *About the honour of mine ancestors,*
> *How they had won by prowess such exploits,*
> *Got such riches, subdued so many kingdoms,*
> *As we that do succeed, or they that shall*
> *Hereafter possess our throne, shall,*
> *I fear me never attain to that degree*
> *Of high renown and great authority;*
> *Amongst which kings is Alexander the Great,*
> *Chief spectacle of the world's pre-eminence,*
> *The bright shining of whose glorious acts*
> *Lightens the world with his reflecting beams,*
> *As when I hear but motion made of him*
> **It grieves my soul I never saw the man**.
> *If, therefore, thou, by cunning of thine art,*
> *Canst raise this man from hollow vaults below,*
> *Where lies entomb'd this famous conqueror,*
> *And bring with him his beauteous paramour,*
> *Both in their right shapes, gesture and attire*
> *They us'd to wear during their time of life,*
> *Thou shalt both satisfy my just desire*
> *And give me cause to praise thee whilst I live.*[42]

The treacherously self-destructive process by which Faustus comes by the "cunning" of his art of supernatural command (it is achieved through a bargain with the 'devil') is ominous of the disastrous condition into which a precipitation in visionary power might drive the hero where an idea of such power is acted on without restraint. We do better, to put ourselves in touch with the fundamental inspiration of *Richard II* and *Hamlet*, to refer them, rather than to *Faustus*, initially to a work of *positive* implication, such as the *Burial of the Count Orgaz*, which El Greco painted several years before these plays in 1587. El Greco's preoccupation with vision is notorious: one day a friend found him in his artificially darkened studio neither working nor asleep, preferring the light of his own inner vision to the spring sunshine.[43] And this painting of El Greco's in particular offers the most suggestive possibilities of comparison with the scope and tenor of visionary imagination in Shakespeare's plays—what is in fact an expression of that denial of limit, "the exalted or exultant expression of man's longing, vertical aspiration, autonomous free will, his metaphysical ache", characteristic of the Counter-Renaissance.[44]

II

ANALOGUES FROM RENAISSANCE PAINTING

AND MODERN POETRY

El Greco's painting has a special appropriateness to the nature of visionary imagination in Shakespeare's plays ultimately for the way it projects vision, in the foreground priest, as a direct outgrowth of the belief that thinking is seeing, but also, to bring back an earlier emphasis, for its view of the full continuity between levels implied by the act of vision, integrated at the level of the real world. The metaphysical intensity of El Greco's painting can be pinpointed to the crucial use he makes of the clouds as the intermediary link between the real world of the Spanish court below and the visionary world above. It is this richly ambiguous status of the clouds as visionary atmosphere that lends intensity of reality to some of the dead figures in the top right of the frame (who include John the Baptist), who, incidentally, wait on Christ in postures of utter obeisance, in a projection strongly suggesting the impact Richard might have wished to have on Bolingbroke on his return. These dead figures seem to rise up from the real world quite naturally on this visionary buttress that the clouds provide: possessing in this respect the same fully 'real' visionary status as the Ghost in *Hamlet*. What's more, the intensity I speak of accounts specifically for the power of vision in the foreground priest who, from a pictorial view, rides the wave-length of this intensity, which is to be explained as the result of an extreme valuation of psychological projection as reality, resulting in a portentous effect of immediate revelation.

The spectacular visionary intensity of the priest's attitude contrasts sharply with the attitude of the other courtiers, some of whom stare upwards towards events in the otherworld in a more conventional if intense piety (it is still unrealized vision), while others, such as the upturned head in the back row, seem to look up as if spectators to El Greco's painting. These secondary attitudes are not irrelevant to El Greco's theme, for the distance between the intense piety of the courtiers and the spectacular visionary intensity of the priest lies precisely in a fuller involvement in the latter case in the root awareness that the upturned head would seem to register in looking upon El Greco's painting as compelling evidence of a belief in the supersensible as a real thing. Indeed, one might proffer the case that the difficult, complexly conceived process of visionary realization to which El Greco's painting bears witness concerns El Greco more immediately than the miracle that is the painting's explicit subject—that is to say, the miraculous appearance on earth of St. Stephen and St. Augustine, who are reported to have themselves buried the Count. This miracle, as one can infer from the attitude and postures of the courtiers, is significantly not itself depicted as miracle in El Greco's painting, but seems rather to represent a force of inherited authority in the Church that is seen as developing alongside the prospect of a direct visionary perception of the otherworld.

The function of the seemingly wayward figure of the upturned head in this picture is further significant for the reason that, as a spectator to El Greco's painting, he reflects us to ourselves: his effect, indeed, is to draw us as audience directly into the 'space' of the painting, so that in taking our own 'place' among the other courtiers, we become involved in El Greco's representation of the other world as that marvellous embodiment of reality it constitutes for the priest: reality that in this partial effect we experience directly as our own. The effect is an indication of the advantages to be gained from the added baroque treatment of a metaphysical development in the painting that is nevertheless portentous on its own account. As Ransom says of miraculism as a whole, "It leaves us looking, marvelling, and revelling in the thick *dinglich* substance that has just received its strange representation."[45]

The understanding of the visionary process I am pursuing, and especially the analysis of that process's *reality*, including reality as a representational process, all three major aspects of my theme are brought to magnificently full expression in Yeats's poem *Byzantium*, a work that I should like to offer as extending the framework of comparison further. That we can trace so developed a manifestation of visionary realization to a modern poet is some indication that we are dealing here with a universal function of the metaphysical imagination. (And here one might adduce as further evidence the introduction onto the modern scene of Hopkins—another poet whose imagination was of the metaphysical bent—see, e.g., "The Lantern Out of Doors".) Apart from illustrating the process of vision in an especially vital and successful way, Yeats's poem has its value also in helping to fill out the crucial middle ground between Shakespeare and El Greco, by bringing out more closely the kind of *thinking* we are asked to imagine as necessary in bringing about a successful development in vision.

Consider this passage[46] from the Yeats poem:

> *Miracle, bird or golden handiwork,*
> *More miracle than bird or handiwork,*
> *Planted on the star-lit golden bough,*
> *Can like the cocks of Hades crow,*

The kind of miracle Ransom shows Cowley projecting onto the lovers' hearts is *mutatis mutandi* the same kind of miracle Yeats himself projects onto the bird. In both cases, the poets have projected a situation in which inanimate matter takes on living animate function through an interchange postulated between sensible and spiritual worlds. Thus, in the Cowley passage, the assumption of an identity between hearts and affections leads the poet to project a miraculous movement of hearts between lovers. This is on the level of art, and similarly in Yeats's passage, the close interaction of handiwork and feeling in the poet leads him to project the handiwork as coming miraculously to life. That Yeats can permit himself such a projection is due, to begin with, to a given potency in the handiwork. It is because golden handiwork already suggests so strongly living bird that the poet can act on his emotional response to it as if the bird were coming to life indeed.

What is more, as the bird 'comes' to life, it assumes the function of the cock in Hades: that is, a *double* process of transformation is suggested by which the manifestation of the spiritual in the sensible is associated with the supersensible in a supernatural sense. The miracle of living handiwork operates in its own representational context—Byzantium; and the crowing of the cock in another—Hades. Yet, the miracle itself is an identification of the two contexts and thus a complex metaphysical fusion of representation and reality, to which the poem itself approximates.

Indeed, the conceit of bird coming to life is more than conceit—metaphor, what's more, metaphor that is meant: it is a miracle inasmuch as the poet means what he says, and we in turn forced to believe what we hear. That is not to say, of course, that the bird actually comes to life in Yeats's representation: the whole tension of the passage depends, in fact, on our viewing the miracle as a projection of the mind of the poet. The ambiguous reality of the poem's miracle suggests that the miracle exists entirely as a projection of the poet's mind, though I shall insist that this is not the same as to say that it exists only in the mind of the poet. This tension is upheld in the poem by a fundamental ambiguity: the miracle does and does not occur. This complex fact throws a proportionately complex function onto the simile which is made to carry the poem's transformations. Thus, if we assume the poem's identification between Byzantine bird and Hadean cock, the simile shows that the poet is, in Ransom's terms, "scrupulous to keep the identification partial": the miracle does not occur. Yet, on another level it does, and not merely in the mind of the poet. In spite of the simile, the poet "proceeds to an identification which is complete". The double phenomenon calls for an important modification of Ransom's account. Even the simile can come within the compass of miraculism. The complete identification of terms that one associates with miraculism can occur *despite* appearances of a scrupulous effort to keep the identification partial. This will be a crucial point, as we shall see, in considering the transformations Richard II projects for himself through a similar use of analogical forms like 'as thus' and 'as if'.

The previous stanza from Yeats's poem, itself more elaborate in filling out the Hadean link in the transformation, analyzes more fully the specific psychology involved:

> *Before me floats an image, man or shade,*
> *Shade more than man, more image than a shade;*
> *For Hades' bobbin bound in mummy-cloth*
> *May unwind the winding path;*
> *A mouth that has no moisture and no breath*
> *Breathless mouths may summon;*
> *I hail the superhuman;*
> *I call it death-in life and life-in-death.*

What the poet does to the bird in the later passage he does here to a stray walker who appears before him in the charged significance of nightly solitude. Once again, it is because the man already occupies an intermediate existence of some potency that he is transformed by the poet into an "image" of the supernatural. The transformation is made possible by the ambiguous existence that associates "shade" with 'shadow', "shade" being at once the 'shadow' of the man as well as the Hadean "shade" of which he is the "image", here the point of miracle in which both contexts unite. What's more, the process of 'seeing' thus enacted is directly traced to a certain kind of 'thinking'. In his transformational function, the man is associated with a mummy, a midpoint between life and death. In his mummy-function, the man offers a way out of life's labyrinth (unwinds the winding path) by drawing out of the poet the mental operations that can trace life back to its transformational source and point of origin. In fact by contemplating man as mummy, and by thinking on mummy-cloth as the very stuff that winds life's pattern round a man's corpse, we can look upon corpse and mummy-cloth, or man, as the point of death where the reality of life is fully defined, being here also the point of the afterlife. Corpse and mummy-cloth or man are in actual fact "Hades' bobbin", not just in the sense that, its reality being fully defined, life is here brought to the point of Hades, but that all of Hades crystallizes round this point: in fact, that is the point of death from which by a supreme act of transformation one looks out on Hades as the full pattern of life—afterlife and pattern of life being thus one.

The very complex process of thought illustrated is offered as a metaphysical structure for vision. It helps us to interpret the "Hades'bobbin" of the man's "shade", here at once an uttermost point of *physical* vision in the poet (the man's 'shadow') and *in that very process*, through the kind of thinking *implicit* in the metaphorical development of "Hades' bobbin", the spiritual vision of the Hadean shade of which the man's "shade" is the "image". Nor is the process thus outlined offered as mere speculation: the metaphor of "Hades' bobbin" is meant, and I offer it to provide some indication of the basis of that forbidding process of otherworldly vision that engages not only Yeats, or El Greco (as in the "Hades' bobbin" of *his* visionary atmosphere), but, also, I am claiming, Shakespeare (in the development of the "eye of heaven" and the "eternal blazon", respectively in *Richard II* and *Hamlet*[47]). I shall claim that it is the chief characteristic of the pattern governing the *initial* development of vision in *Richard II* and

Hamlet—marking Shakespeare's effort off significantly from the positive religious faith of El Greco on the one hand, and the bold, ambiguous faith of Yeats on the other—that the plays proceed on the basis that only an ambiguous faith is finally possible, even though the *motivation* behind the quest for vision in these cases is, and I believe always remains, a positive faith that compares with that of El Greco. That is, like El Greco, the plays are motivated by the belief that vision is real, although they seem to recognize in projecting on this belief, at the same time, that vision is finally real and unreal, that vision does and does not occur, to state the case as one finds it elaborated not only in Yeats but also in Kyd.

For the truly significant development in Kyd's Prologue was the final placing of the vision. The immediate vision of the Ghost, as in Boccaccio, remained 'real' enough, but the vision of hell had shifted, from being the immediate vision of the poet himself, as in Sackville, to being the remote vision of the Ghost. The literal function of narrative already ensured that even a vision presented at second-hand would be experienced by the audience as literal vision, even as immediate vision; but when it finally becomes clear that the Ghost has actually been narrating his vision from *this* side of the world, the vision undergoes an extraordinary deflation. What had been experienced by the audience at first as immediate vision becomes a vision suddenly placed in time and space beyond the world: indeed, in the bafflement we re-enact with the Ghost in finding ourselves with him on this side of the world, it is as if the vision had never taken place, having vanished "in the twinkling of an eye" (I.i.85), as quickly as the Ghost had been transported back to the world. Our initial experience of vision has convinced us that the vision has been real, but it is no longer immediate, and there is a sense in which it has even become unreal.

This ambiguity in the status of the vision is clinched when Kyd has the Ghost remark that in being transported from one place to the other, he has passed "through the gates of horn" (I.i.82). G.K. Hunter has seen Andrea's return through the gates "as dramatic equivalents to the introductory sequences of medieval dream allegory"; from this, he concludes that "the play may be viewed as what Andrea dreams".[48] But the use of the gates surely works the other way around: they finally confer the status of dream on Andrea's vision of the otherworld, not on the world to which he returns, which is the reality the dream-vision throws into relief. That Andrea's dream is associated with the gates of horn suggests that Andrea's vision has been real, but once relegated to dream it becomes something less than itself, indeed the memory of what has taken place on another plane. Nevertheless, we might add that Kyd's use of the dream-vision contrasts sharply with the mundane use made of it in the *Mirror*, as in Baldwin's dream of the Ghost of the Duke of York, which, though it puts the dream-vision into its traditional setting, presents something quite unlike the potently ambiguous reality of the dream-vision,[49] since here the dream-vision amounts merely to "fantasy" (I.59; p.181). By contrast in his Prologue, Kyd relies on a more subtle use of the vision-structure for the creation of 'real' perspective. Thus the abstraction of the Ghost is given its own forceful 'reality' in the play through the theatrical transposition by which the poet's vision merges into the vision of the audience. The problem of abstraction posed by the descent into hell is likewise obviated through recourse to a literal appropriation of narrative: thus the Ghost's vision of the otherworld is to be experienced for itself; in fact, as elaborated, it draws on the sense of immediate wonder one can easily imagine being associated with the marvellous journey into hell.

The significance of the placing of the vision in the Prologue can be fully grasped, however, only within the context of the Ghost's re-appearance as a whole. Here we will note that the dramatic placing of the vision corresponds with the limits placed on the Ghost's vision just where Pluto's judgment is anticipated—the climax of the journey being reached at the point where Andrea stands before Pluto and Proserpine anticipating judgment. At that point our sense of wonder is involved in the idea of an action made final in the knowledge of reward and punishment. That Andrea's vision in the underworld should suddenly undergo deflation at this point is all the more extraordinary considering the pains Kyd has taken in the Prologue for the creation of perspective. But the deflation would seem to be crucial to Kyd's theme: the ultimate elusiveness of a final action is associated with a re-adjustment in perspective in which we are finally made aware of our psychological *distance* from the vision.

In the initial pattern of Shakespeare's plays, we will note what appear to be two distinct stages, though I shall suggest that they are to be taken as twin aspects of the one, ambiguous experience: an *initial* stage, as I have shown, involving us in a belief in the reality of vision, followed subsequently by a dramatic fall from vision experienced as a failure of reality, by analogy with developments in Kyd's Prologue. The same breakdown into unreality, with its new, paradoxical awareness of limitation-*in*-reality, could be demonstrated in the progression of Hieronimo's speeches, making Kyd,

I believe, the first among Elizabethan dramatists to embody, to his own limited degree of realization, what I shall call the Counter-Renaissance "conflict of *consciousness*":

> Hier. *And art thou come, Horatio, from the depth,*
> *To ask for justice …*
> . . . .
> *But let me look on my Horatio:*
>
> Senex. *Ha my good lord, I am not your young son.*
>
> Hier. *What, not my son? Thou, then, a fury art,*
> *Sent from the empty kingdom of black night*
> *To summon me to make appearance*
> *Before grim Minos and just Rhadamanth,*
> *To plague Hieronimo that is remiss*
> *And seeks not vengeance for Horatio's death.*
>
> Senex. *I am a grieved man, and not a Ghost,*
> *That came for justice for my murder'd son.*
> Hier. *Ay, now I know thee, now thou nam'st thy son,*
> *Thou art the lively image of my grief:*
> . . . .
> *And all this sorrow riseth for thy son:*
> *And selfsame sorrow feel I for my son.*
>
> *(III.xiii.133ff.)*

The ambiguous characteristic I am claiming of the presentation of vision in this literature is demonstrated in a fully integrated way in Richard's speech to Aumerle, in the gap that survives between a real or positive experience of vision and the ambiguous reality of Richard's projection. Richard's complex effort in this speech really builds on an ambiguous faith such as Yeats's, but it is very significant that Richard should become subsequently overwhelmingly disillusioned about his projection, unlike, for example, the attitude to the projection maintained in Yeats, one can see because Richard approaches his projection as if the ambiguous relation between projection and reality were a positive one.

The case I am making for the ambiguous reality of vision is demonstrated in a more dissociated way in *Hamlet* since the Ghost is clearly presented there as substantial grounds for a belief in the reality of vision, not being 'merely' the ambiguous projection of Hamlet's mind. This certainly states a case for positive vision more squarely, reflecting in this respect an ideal established more strongly in *Hamlet*, although as we have seen only by posing the taxing problem of a projection of vision of the otherworld that is problematically incomplete and unreal to that extent, also leaving the psychological basis for this development unelaborated. But in any case, like Andrea's experience of vision in Kyd's Prologue, when Andrea is returned to the world, Hamlet's vision *becomes* unreal as soon as the Ghost disappears. Indeed, the problem of the unreal vision is raised immediately as Hamlet is shown struggling in the aftermath with the gap between his recent experience of the reality of the Ghost and his radical, ambiguous projection of memory.[50] The failure of reality I am claiming of the initial development of vision in *Richard II* and *Hamlet* is immediately expressed in those qualities of fragmentation and strangeness that especially mark the creative projections of the hero in this stage of the action. However, such qualities are paradoxically part of a desperate redressive manoeuvring leading to the third and most complex stage of the pattern—the effort in consequence of the fall, to *recover* to a point of vision in actual fact. One would have to turn to Faustus's magnificent last speech where he is trying to make up in a positive direction for the failure of his borrowed supernatural command—building on the structure of real, metaphysical assumption in the background—for a difficult (because morally contrasting) analogy in Elizabethan tragedy:

> *See, see, where Christ's blood streams in the firmament!*
> *(XIX, l.146)*

It is the most dramatic evidence we have that where the metaphysics is not frankly assumed in this literature it is being penetrated. The intensity of the metaphysical effect *depends*, in fact, on this tension between the assumption and the penetration of reality: and it is with *this* evolving dialectic, as it comes to be crystallized in the hero's creation, that we find the metaphysics beginning to express, in an ever-deepening sense, the Counter-Renaissance 'conflict of consciousness'.

In *Hamlet* the effort of recovery is in the very terms of the injunction to revenge. It is the problem ultimately of psychological correlation, of proportionate intensity: the process of retribution that concerns Hamlet presents itself as the need to build on the psychological energy of Claudius's crime—in the play's terms, to take the full horror of Claudius's murder as Hamlet experiences that in himself, and in the act of revenge against the murder, to *invert* that into horrid judgment. As such Hamlet's revenge seeks to build implicitly on his basic identification with the rhetorical inspiration of the Ghost's reference to the "eternal blazon", the term the Ghost uses to indicate the full tenor of the horror. There is the suggestion in "blazon" of a power of speech opening out on reality, a suggestion that finds further elaboration in Hamlet's theoretical formulation of the power of "horrid speech" reserved to him in his revenge. To appreciate the force of this extraordinary view of rhetorical reality that the play builds on, it is necessary to bear in mind the initial value of the Ghost as Hamlet's psychological projection of himself: he stands there as evidence of a state of mind in full possession of the horror, requiring judgment as inevitable to the possession. The figure of the Ghost points, that is, to the extraordinary integrity of experience possible to Hamlet in revenge by uniting, through the complex idiom of his speech, the conflict of moral and emotional nature revenge would seem to pose, as well as the problem of the distance such a conception of revenge brings into focus between nature and supernature.

Richard II is not itself formally concerned with revenge, yet the action Richard would bring against Bolingbroke for what Richard pronounces as rebellion has the same visionary-judgmental significance as the action Hamlet would bring against Claudius for murder. As such, it too builds, like Hamlet's action, on the basic inspiration of rhetorical reality—on Richard's fundamental identification with himself as the "eye of heaven". Moreover, the absence of an explicit revenge theme in *Richard* will serve to bring out the value of visionary judgment as revenge-action. It is not so much in *Hamlet* a matter of revenge simply, as of revenge seen as mediating and standing primarily for the realization of an order.

III

WHAT BECOMES OF VISION

What then, we may ask, *becomes* of this visionary thinking that these plays conceive and build on, this metaphorical development turning into literal fact that accounts for a development of visionary reality? The complex answer lies in a third stage of thematic development, where one finds not only a development of thinking that is a development of vision, but inevitably, in the uncertainty of that development, thinking of or about vision. In this further development also one finds evidence of an implied valuation of projection as reality, a pursuit of metaphorical development as if it were fact, expressing a direct development of vision. I have already called attention to the transformational value of Hamlet's effort, in the aftermath of his experience of the Ghost, to project a visionary status onto heart and tablebooks. In the deposition-scene, Richard attempts a similar kind of effort with his face, reflected to him in a mirror. To make his face express by a radical identification the sorrow Richard feels over the failure of vision I have described, Richard unexpectedly and dramatically dashes the mirror to the ground, having this to add about his face:

> *For there it is, crack'd in a hundred shivers.*
> *Mark, silent king, the moral of this sport—*
> *How soon my sorrow hath destroy'd my face.*
>
> *(IV.i.289-291)*

Comparable with Hamlet's effort, Richard's here expresses a mind radically absorbed in the supersensible as a real thing. "For there it is" expresses a use of language that forces upon us an extreme valuation of the projection as reality. By his stunning gesture, Richard forces all for a moment to believe that the mirror *is* his face, and that his sorrow *has* been radically expressed by its dramatic destruction and shattered form on the ground, lying there as paradoxical evidence of Richard's frustrated expectation of visionary manifestation. In Richard's case, there is the complex element of playacting that is added to this, making everything also explicitly unreal.

The complex transformational effect of Richard's gesture is the more significant here because belonging to a pattern implicitly linking Richard's sorrow/grief with a penetration of psychological depth. Thus, in his "seize the crown" speech Richard associates himself in his grief with a bucket lying underground in the deeper part of a well where (we are to understand) Richard's psychological energy is concentrated:

> *Give me the crown. Here, cousin, seize the crown.*
> *Here cousin.*
> *On this side my hand, and on that side thine.*
> *Now is this golden crown like a deep well*
> *That owes two buckets, filling one another;*
> *The emptier ever dancing in the air,*

> *The other down, unseen, and full of water.*
> *That bucket down and full of tears am I,*
> *Drinking my griefs, whilst you mount up on high.*
>   *(IV.i.181–189)*

The well is at once the grave and the well of the mind. It is also linked, by a strong analogy—through the symbolism of the "golden crown"—with the visionary power projected as lying inherent in the kingship. Here indeed is a stunning representation of the visionary power of mind that it is assumed Richard reserves to himself as King in his psychological confrontation with death.

The significant thing, however, is the way this confrontation is accompanied by projections of transformational effect showing a complex consciousness of *failure*, reflecting, only in a peculiarly limited and unreal form, the full visionary power expected. I have considered the limitations of the effect of Richard's projection with face and mirror. In the passage I have just quoted, the representation of visionary power latent in death is defined by an extremely complex attempt to project this value onto the real crown that Richard and Bolingbroke hold between them. As in Yeats in whom one can trace a similar effort with bird, the projection here is propelled by an intensity far more involved in a full actualization of the case than would appear to be suggested by the scrupulous recognition of limitation implied by the use of "like". This is in spite of the fact that the limitation is itself *emphatic*, involving us explicitly in the unreality of Richard's projection.[51] Furthermore, the pattern of subterranean consciousness implicit in Richard's projections, which constitutes further analysis of the visionary process, expresses a general 'downward' metaphysical movement in the play first brought to dramatic climax in the visionary splendor of Richard's identification of himself with Phaeton in his fall. To appreciate the 'real' force of this identification as a development of vision, it is necessary to bear in mind that, like Richard's action with mirror and crown, this action is also built directly into the immediate physical property of the stage. In context, Richard's projection of himself as the falling Phaeton is shouted eerily during Richard's action of descending from the balcony where he stands to the lower stage where he is to meet with Bolingbroke.

Richard's realization of himself *in Phaeton* implies, within the falling subterranean pattern, the pattern of death, an initial form of definition in Richard's thinking *about* vision, presenting the visionary process as something finally co-terminous with the energy of falling to death. This is set up to contrast with the implications for the definition of the theme of Richard's other, major realization of himself in his fall *in Christ*, in whom the visionary process comes to be seen, by analogy with Richard's frustrated power, as a power emerging through and beyond death. We may look upon this contrast as expressing the difference between what may be called a *sceptical* and a *transcendental* view of the visionary process, reflecting Richard's complex ambivalence about a crucial relationship newly posited in this stage between vision and death.

Of the transcendental assumption, too, there is no lack of forceful development. Here I might quote the example of the ironic effect Richard rings on the traditional shout of allegiance to the King in the deposition scene, by way of insinuating that he *remains* King in spite of Bolingbroke's insidious assumption of the role:

> *God save the King! Will no man say amen?*
> *Am I both priest and clerk? Well then, amen.*
> *God save the King! Although I be not he;*
> *And yet, amen, if heaven do think him me.*
>
> *(IV.i.172–175)*

This dramatic projection of usurpation onto the scene of the action has an obviously startling character. However, its *full* effect is lost on us unless we recognize that it draws on an implied identification between the startling impression thus momentarily wrung from the real world and the 'real' visionary-judgmental state of events as these appear to "the eye of heaven". The basis for this identification lies in Richard's literal status as the figure of God's majesty, the assumption put forward in the speech to Aumerle. Richard being God's representative on earth, it follows that violence against Richard is in an immediate sense violence against God. Thus, what gives the impression of being merely a startling insistence on Bolingbroke's usurpation reflects a view of the state of events in the world seen in relation to their immediate visionary implications, as action in which Bolingbroke stands in immediate judgment for the immediate violence done to God.

Significantly, this view actually falls short of conceiving of the immediate possibility of a visionary revelation. The limitation is enforced, of course, by the knowledge of the immediate absence of God from the real world. Yet, paradoxically, this absence merely serves Richard as an occasion for a more pointed insistence on Bolingbroke's usurpation, since if the King takes his authority from God, only God could authorize Bolingbroke's action against Richard, something that is logically out of the question in God's absence. What needs insisting on here is the extraordinary visionary significance of the action. Missing is the literal presence of God as a real thing.

A climactic expression of this complex import comes in the deposition scene where the Bishop of Carlyle is stirred to violent denunciation of Bolingbroke's treason just as he moves to ascend the throne. It is another startling reversal of impression. Carlyle speaks "Stirr'd up by God" (IV.i.133), but his central appeal is rather a stunning representation of the implications for Bolingbroke's action of God's *absence* from the world, one that paradoxically evokes strongly the presence that is missing: the effect is brought about by the ambiguous reference finally dictated by Richard's status as the figure of God's majesty, so that in speaking of Richard's absence from the scene Carlyle inevitably invokes *God's* absence:

> And shall the figure of God's majesty
> His captain, steward, deputy elect,
> Anointed, crowned, planted many years,
> Be judg'd by subject and inferior breath,
> And **he himself not present**?
>
> *(IV.i.125–129)*

The imposing element of the central action in *Richard II* is thus the evidence it provides of a forceful development of reality intricately involved in failure (and indeed confounding). However, what remains is a motivating *intention* of creating reality that combines at a certain point at least with an *idea* of the full extent of the viability of that intention in Richard.

The dramatic climax to this insistent intention of forceful creation in Richard comes when Bolingbroke, responding to the imputation that Richard attaches to his mirror-smashing gesture, brings the latter face to face with its *un*reality:

> The shadow of your sorrow hath destroy'd
> The shadow of your face.
>
> *(IV.i.292–293*

To which Richard's reply, so far from reflecting an attitude that courts despair, is rather a reinforced sense of his basic metaphysical view:

Say that again.
The shadow of my sorrow? Ha! Let's see.
'Tis very true: my grief lies all within;
And these external manner of laments
Are merely shadows to the unseen grief
That swells with silence in the tortur'd soul.
There lies the substance; *and I thank thee, king,*
For thy great bounty, that not only giv'st
Me cause to wail, but teachest me the way
How to lament the cause.

(IV.i.293–302)

The confidence expressed here may be cited in support of a treatment that would look sympathetically upon the intention of forceful creation in Richard. For dramatically unreal as Richard's gestures may be on one level, they are convincingly seen here as but shadows of the intensity of the real thing, the extraordinary "substance", as he puts it, at which all of Richard's actions have aimed. In fact, Richard's speech is merely another way of pointing the essential question Ransom posits as *basic* to the undertaking of metaphysical poetry:

Where is the body and solid substance of the world?

The answer, as I have suggested, lies in the very terms of the exploration, in Richard's case in a grief which, in his very consciousness of it as defiantly *im*material, presents itself as a tortured answering to the possibility of that extreme transformation of the immaterial into the material that has its basis in the psychology of miraculism, as we have seen in an extreme development of metaphorical thinking that we are to imagine at some point producing the transformational energy necessary for a successful development of vision.

The immediate emphasis in Richard's speech to Bolingbroke is on his grief in its aspect of pure force or essential energy of emotional-imaginative being—the "unseen grief/That swells with silence"—with its suggestion of a *reserve* of psychological-metaphysical energy to be brought to full development. To present it in such abstract terms is to suggest that the thinking of vision exists for Richard first as a metaphysical *donnée*, as an energy or 'force' of assumption that precedes the full thematic development it holds in conception. However, it does not as such become fully known to us *as thinking* except as the thematic development that emerges from this given emotional-imaginative absorption of the hero at the level of vision. Moreover, it is only in *keeping* the visionary level before us that we can allow ourselves to *follow* the complex development of thinking that we find actually going on in these characters, which along the way opens out on the further relation to death.

Thus, when Richard's initial expectation of visionary power with Aumerle fails to find any confirmation in reality, Richard is immediately plummeted into a consciousness of death as ironic, mocking emptiness—in the "Let's talk of graves" speech. There is something in this reaction that is not understood at first: the thinking is instantaneous and extreme. But on reflection we are made to understand that a metaphysical projection of the kind in Richard's speech to Aumerle, which takes its reality as it does for Richard from its immediate embodiment in the Kingship, cannot well be assumed to *have* reality after the kind of complete failure he experiences. If the Kingship does not after all embody the Judgment of an Eternity assumed beyond the world, then it can be felt that death, as life, holds no such reality, a view of the matter made poignantly conscious in the sense of being finally made for death rather than for visionary life, the note that is also struck throughout the whole of the last part of *Hamlet*.

It is clear, to draw the major comparison here, that for El Greco, as for Yeats, the experience of death is crucial for the full vision of the otherworld it makes available, in El Greco not only to the dead but to those too in life capable of losing themselves to the dramatic 'reality' of the experience. In Yeats this is an act of pure imagination. Shakespeare's plays share *something* of El Greco's view of the experience of death; at least the deaths of Richard and Hamlet are accompanied by a curious *activation* of the visionary faith that underlies these plays. Richard II dies alone, in an undignified and disrespectful solitude, but his end is a splendid, complex posture of visionary self-projection:

> *Mount, mount, my soul! Thy seat is up on high;*
> (V.v.111)

In the same way, Hamlet's death is, in statelier circumstances, the occasion of a visionary panegyric from Horatio that also suggests the world of El Greco's painting:

> *Good night, sweet prince,*
> *And flights of angels sing thee to thy rest!*
>
> *(V.ii.352–352)*

The terminal emphasis, for all its power, is nevertheless curiously incidental and secondary in any complete analysis. Not that these Shakespeare heroes are any less committed than is El Greco to a belief in the continuity between worlds, even at the end. However, they only show signs for this of having become more and more painfully absorbed in the experience of separation and duality that inevitably attends on such an ideal projection. That experience receives further representation in both plays as an underlying despair that perhaps death might yield no such triumphant knowledge as these heroes anticipate. It is the eventual result of a growing perception of the confounding influence of tragic limitation in their complex attempt to forcefully develop what is real.

However, it is a long process by which the plays come to that point, for the initial failure in Richard immediately becomes itself the paradoxical occasion for a dramatic re-orientation in the pursuit of vision. Though death may be supposed to have no such reality as described, the psychological need for reality remains, and it is out of this complex motivation that Richard finds himself acting on the view that sees in the psychological confrontation with death, in the subjection of the knowledge of death to the positive projection of the creative mind, the only 'real' formula for visionary success incorporating Richard's projected ideal of himself as King. In the "Let's talk of graves" speech this process has already begun in the thought of death and decay as grounds for a development of visionary self-projection, culminating in the projected figure of Death. The crucial view of the basis of vision in a psychological confrontation with death is assumed in *Hamlet* from the beginning as we have seen, which on this account would seem to be spared the charge of naivety. This view is in the very terms of Hamlet's vision of the Ghost—"seeking in the dust"—and it is subsequently *reinforced* with Hamlet's experience of an elusive significance in death as conveyed through the incompleteness in the Ghost's account, which frustrates a full development of vision. However, it is in the survival of this significant death-relation in this problematic form that we become aware in the later stage of a more strenuously 'real' penetration of the visionary possibility than the one sketched out for us initially, which though portentous enough in the figure of the Ghost nevertheless fails to provide a full analysis of the *psychological* process that has led up to this vision.[52]

One does not get the very fullest sense of the death-vision complex that absorbs Richard until that complex syncopation of developments pitting the transfigured figure of Phaeton against that of Christ which I have traced in Richard's central action at Court, which indeed expresses the fullest evidence we have of Richard's thinking in the matter. It is a very admirable "body" of projected thinking (to borrow Ransom's term), standing up well to the evidence of projected thinking that Hamlet gives us, which by comparison seems by moments crude, sometimes radically uncertain of its intention and its validity, even though paradoxically there is in its elaboration a more complex sense of its reality. This is to point a relative strength in Richard, who is too likely to suffer from the comparison with Hamlet more than he should, having been too often treated as displaying much the weaker and more febrile imagination, which is not at all true. Certainly it is not as deep or penetrating an imagination, but it does not 'show' less well for that, in fact much the better for it.

The salient characteristic of Richard's projected thinking, apart from the evidence it provides of a valuation of projection as reality, is, as I have said, the complex *ambivalence* it expresses, which reflects Richard's own uncertainty in the matter—Richard's thinking being in this characteristic of ambivalence a logical extrapolation from the particularities of his experience. Thus what I have called Richard's *transcendental* view (associated with the figure of Christ), focusing a power of judgmental vision inherited in death, is presented as evolving naturally from Richard's faith in the existence of a moral-imaginative reality that Bolingbroke is assumed to have flouted by returning to England in rebellion against Richard. What, in a rival development, I have called, by reference to the projected fate of Phaeton, Richard's *sceptical* view of vision, building on the assumption of death as a radically confounding force, stems from the despair Richard is simultaneously forced to feel over the unresisted success and confident ease with which Bolingbroke actually achieves his aims in rebellion, which make a mockery of the reality Richard had thought unquestionable.

Richard's "grief" defines itself precisely by the complex tension obtaining when both developments of thinking, the transcendental and the sceptical, are set against that pre-existing, assumed *ideal* of visionary-judgmental thinking to which he has answered inwardly as metaphysical *donnée*—the ideal given climactic expression in the speech to Bolingbroke. Richard's grief is all in the immediate urgency for him of this ideal, in relation to which his ambivalence merely serves as added *pressure*. The urgency is reflected in the case of the Christ identification as a tortured grief over having to wait upon death for a full inheritance of vision; it is further reflected in the case of the Phaeton identification, as an equally desperate grief over the conflicting view of death as empty catastrophe, whose outgrowth, paradoxically, is Richard's spectacular visionary realization of himself as the falling Phaeton that builds so vitally on the energy of falling to death. This is as much an outline of the matter as the play affords us, except for Richard's forcefully stated intention at the climax of the Court action to reinforce his answering to the basic ideal. Subsequent action in *Richard* merely brings home the severe limitations besetting Richard in his implied resolution with Bolingbroke to arrive at a further development of success. For when Richard appears to us again in prison, it is clear, from the simplified, laboured build-up of a point-for-point analogical correspondence between his thoughts and the people of the world, that what we have here is a radical *breakdown* of metaphorical thinking, when one compares this to the extraordinary developments Richard had given us earlier at Court. The significance of this failure can be inferred from the terms in which Richard presents his intention to Bolingbroke. The failure may be described as a failure of emotional-imaginative knowledge. But it is to be characterized at the same time as a failure of psychological depth, for by the time we encounter Richard in prison it is clear that the reserve of inner life has all but gone out of him, from character being unequal to its isolation.

In *Hamlet* likewise our sense of the theme's full definition depends on the final *accumulation* of detail. In this way we are put in possession, as in the case of *Richard*, of a complex "body" of projected thinking stemming from Hamlet's absorption at the level of vision. Moreover, Hamlet's "grief" defines itself in the same way by the extraordinary distance such thinking is seen to hold from the pre-existing, assumed *ideal* of visionary-judgmental thinking in which Hamlet is likewise assumed to be absorbed—this ideal being the complex "substance" of *his* experience. Yet these plays define themselves in the end precisely by the extent to which they continue strenuously to deny the force of the tragic that is dictating to them precisely where the identification with positive vision *seems* real. It is a definition of the matter *already implicit in the pattern of the fall from vision*, in the experience of an act of vision suddenly presented and perceived as unreal. The force of tragedy is immediately reflected in these plays in that general experience of duality that is all that is finally thrown into relief in the development of reality, in the dramatic metaphysical 'gap' separating the hero in his inward identification with what is 'real' from the strange, ambiguous impression actually made by the interplay between his own action and the action of others in the real world. There is the further experience of inconsequence and final disjunction, which is all there is to show for result from the hero's identification with what is 'real', of which it can be safely assumed that to act on such an experience would certainly be psychologically chaotic: there is the occasional reduction to rant and shouting or mere rhetoric in both heroes to show for that.

If we ask ourselves whence then springs this denial in the heroes that the identification with vision is not a realistic projection of reality, the answer lies in the overwhelming motivation to which the initial development in these plays bears witness, in the received evidence of a strength of assumption and influence implicit in the traditional metaphysical material to which this development gives expression, material which, in the specific development of Christian judgment, moreover, bore authority that one imagines could not easily be denied, if indeed it could be denied at all. For a religious visionary like El Greco, the belief in positive vision may well have built upon a specific Christian tradition of meditation that Louis Martz has shown inspired a whole poetry of meditation from the period of Shakespeare onwards.[53] I am thinking here of the practice of imagining oneself as if one were really present at the event one meditated. Of closer relevance, I believe, is the basis of such imagination in a process of miraculism, that is, in a *projection* of presence springing from an extreme development of metaphorical thinking. For the crucial relation is all in that 'as if', that is, in a projection of rhetorical thinking the complex forceful development of which as reality is in no obvious sense to be judged a matter of certain knowledge.

It is on this basis that in his *Divine Poems* John Donne would submit the reality of meditational practice to some profoundly undermining scepticism. Donne would show, as in Sonnet IV[54], that the reality to which meditational practice supposed the visionary aspirant should identify himself was in fact no reality at all, since, once this reality had been imagined, the initiate was always left free to *remove* himself from it, in the end by way of making the "petition" to which the whole meditational practice was intended to lead. The dramatization of this freedom is given all the more impact in Donne's poem from the extreme forcefulness of Donne's rhetorical effort, in the poem's first part, to break through into the reality of Judgment Day. It is an awesome function, which Donne boldly assumes for himself out of the Faustus-like notion of countering the inevitability of his destruction by sin through a power of identification with its judgment, a power that Donne has calculated assumes first the realization of his urgently sought-after redemption from sin. With the dramatic failure of this effort (a failure paralleling Faustus's) Donne is then left free to fall back on his petition in a way that emphasizes it as the inevitable weak ground of advantage to retreat to for the moment (for Faustus, failure spells immediate damnation). At the same time, when Donne considers what it would be like really to look upon reality—Christ's death for instance—as in "Goodfriday 1613 Riding Westward", it is with the challenging irony (challenging identification with the power of redemption) of an assumed horror at the prospect of being confounded by the ultimate brutal reality of any such vision.

Might there not, then, as the difficulty in Donne's fate suggests, as conceivably be horrible danger in living out rhetoric as if it were reality, in supposing that one ought to be able to reach *out* to reality, as if one could assume a power of *determining* reality like God? For, as Hiram Haydn declares

> the old Elizabethan Jack Donne, the insatiable seeker after
> certainty and yet an unanswerable skeptic, never wholly
> disappears in the Dean of Saint Paul's. His pursuit is of
> God—"But though I have found thee, and thou my thirst
> hast fed,/A holy thirsty dropsy melts me yett" ... The boldness
> of Donne's assertion ... The almost drunken ardor of Donne's
> search extends **beyond** God, and so can have no goal, no final
> satisfaction ... it has much of the quality of aspiration to
> be found ... in the vertical imagery of Faustus' defiant cry,
> "O Ile leap up to my God." ... The aspiration expressed in
> these passages articulates a **metaphysical** ache ... the denial
> of limit ..., and an excessive insatiate emphasis upon ...
> value ... that constitutes quite literally a revolt of the ego.[55]

And yet for a consummate poet like Shakespeare engaged early, as Donne was engaged later, as we have every reason to believe, in the complete possibilities of realization through speech, it must have seemed that what was being determined in the forceful development of rhetorical thinking was the whole *fate* of metaphysical poetry and the very basis of substantial life. At least in the heroes of Shakespeare's two dramas, in whom the determination of reality was being decided, the experience of an impulse already fulfilled that absorbs them, which is indeed the measure of their hubris, is still being pursued, in spite of the suggestion of its basis in a revolt of wilful being, as a *positive* identification with reality. That pursuit reflects on the stubborn hold of an initial ideal in the literature of this period. Indeed, in the insistent motivation to which *Richard II* and *Hamlet* bear such tense witness, in spite of deepening evidence of the determination of the tragic at work in reality, a unique counter-projection is expressed that contrasts poignantly with that growing sense of the tragic in the visionary development of reality to which Shakespeare would give free rein in *Othello*, *Lear*, and *Macbeth*. In these dramas Shakespeare's heroes embrace *their* rhetorically motivated visions (as romantic adventure, the family bond, valor) in a manner that is finally wanting in Richard and Hamlet (as royal authority, and filial devotion) only to expose themselves, by such an act of revolt, to tragic disaster of the most acute kind, falling prey to the complete violent *unreality* of their visions. A more far-reaching perception of the dark depths of human nature is now being brought to bear by Shakespeare on the pretensions of the visionary life as this had been inherited from a former time.[56] On the other hand, the possibility of losing oneself to one's own purely mental projection in this horrifying way is precisely what Hamlet unconsciously anticipates; Shakespeare allows Hamlet the power finally to *reserve* himself from a tragic determination of fate of the acutely horrible psychological kind as those later dramas enact. It is a singular difference—one that significantly measures the abiding strength of the basic identification in *Hamlet* with a positive outcome for reality, in spite of a disturbed sense of the tragedy that looms ahead. In the meantime, it is just the unique value of *Richard* and *Hamlet* that they allow us to live out the full marvellous power of the positive visionary assumption before a further evolution in understanding breaks this process down decisively, as indeed beyond these plays it has broken down for good.

8

Shakespeare's Richard II,
God, and Language

I

UNDERMINED

Richard II's climactic attempt, in the play's later scenes, to justify himself in direct relation to God represents his own spectacular share in a complex hubris that also involves, and can be said to begin with, Bolingbroke. Bolingbroke himself claims that he returns to England merely to recover his lands which have been brutally seized from him by the King at Gaunt's death. Indeed, it is Richard's seizure of these lands that makes possible or gives some justification to Bolingbroke's invasion. This is so even if one chooses to believe, what is not entirely clear, that Bolingbroke had been planning on an invasion anyways. However, the seizure is not altogether a gratuitous act; it is a direct development of Richard's highly-strained relationship with his kindred, with Bolingbroke and with Gaunt most notably. The strained nature of that relationship is given explicit recognition after Gaunt's attack on Richard from his death-bed, in II.i:

> *Right, you say true: as Hereford's love, so his;*
> *As theirs, so mine; and all be as it is.*
>   *(II.i.145–146)*[1]

Nor is this tension a matter merely of personal antagonism. The antagonism works through and involves a dangerous and far-reaching challenge to the kingship.

Gaunt's attack on Richard from his death-bed in II.i. brings this challenge to an obvious climax. Of course, there is no reason to believe that Gaunt's full condemnation of Richard as King is itself gratuitous, that it is not based on a process of degradation in the kingdom that is actually going on. However, that degradation is not made entirely obvious to us. It is centered primarily in Richard's action of farming out the kingdom: and this is only very barely sketched out for us very suddenly just before Gaunt's attack, leaving us significantly confused about the facts. Indeed, the force of Gaunt's attack depends almost entirely on an exposition of abuses elaborated as the attack is being built up, without any more direct confirmation. However, there is no need to fall back on *Woodstock*[2] for an explanation of the economic-political situation: we have no reason to assume that the sketchiness was not part of Shakespeare's plan. In fact, the obscurity in the exposition is deliberate. It creates a state of confusion that *adds* to the status of Gaunt's condemnation as presumption. For, whatever the exact basis and justification may be for Gaunt's condemnation of Richard as Landlord of England, Gaunt is definitely expressing hubris in presuming to answer the question of the King's integrity initially (and in the end primarily) centered in the controversy over Gloucester's death:

> *That blood already, like the pelican,*
> *Hast thou tapp'd out, and drunkenly carous'd.*
> *My brother Gloucester, plain well-meaning soul—*
> . . . .
> *May be a precedent and witness good*
> *That thou respect'st not spilling Edward's blood.*
>
> *(II.i.126–131)*

Gaunt's general condemnation of Richard on this point is expressed in deliberate defiance of the mystery about the King's integrity posed earlier by Gaunt himself, before the reality of Bolingbroke's banishment breaks Gaunt down. Then the King's integrity was a question concerning which Gaunt had quite properly suspended judgment, for as he himself points out, only God could say whether in Gloucester's death, His deputy, the King, had been right or wrong, so that the question of redress finally *remains* with God:

> *God's is the quarrel, for God's substitute,*
> *His deputy anointed in His sight,*
> *Hath caus'd his death; the which if wrongfully,*
> *Let heaven revenge;*
>
> *(II.ii.37–40)*

Gaunt's hubris in finally attacking Richard consists in taking upon himself a judgment that rests with God. Richard may indeed have been wrong in having Gloucester killed; but he may also have been right: only God could say. Despite this, Gaunt is finally moved to commit himself on the mystery posed, thus presuming in his action to a capacity for full knowledge of reality like God. Set against the obscure basis of his other charges at this point, Gaunt's condemnation is thus given the full impact of presumption. As such it merely extends the presumption that Richard had tried to control in Bolingbroke himself in his quarrel with Mowbray (see I.i.102-108).

There Bolingbroke's near-hysterical championing of Gloucester's cause represented an ill-disguised attack on the kingship and an implicit challenge to the King's integrity. The impingement on the kingship becomes more obvious when, having balked with Gaunt at the King's decision to have Bolingbroke banished (a decision taken in council with Gaunt's approval), Bolingbroke rides out of London acting as if he were King indeed.

> *Ourself, and Bushy, Bagot here, and Green,*
> *Observ'd his courtship to the common people;*
> *How he did seem*
> *As 'twere to banish their affects with him.*
> . . . .
> *As were our England in reversion his,*
>
> *(I.iv.23ff)*

In acting this way, Bolingbroke makes of his fortune in having been banished the occasion for an impingement on the King's authority. He takes an action designed to vindicate the King's power, and building on the ambiguity about the King's integrity, turns that action round so that it becomes an emblem rather of the King's tyranny, making the true King rather of Bolingbroke the challenger. In relation to this development, Bolingbroke's later ascent to the throne is thus merely the outward realization of an inward impulse that is already fulfilled, of which one can say that it is self-fulfilling.[3]

Bolingbroke's later action is indeed regarded structurally as a product of "the rage of Bolingbroke" (III.ii.109-110), and thus as an outgrowth of the "high rage" that initially involves him over Mowbray in an indirect challenge to the kingship. In the meantime, grief over Bolingbroke's banishment is what breaks down Gaunt's initial loyalty to the King. Thus Gaunt takes up where Bolingbroke leaves off—one can say, in consequence of the latter's frustrated challenge. And it is as a result of this pattern of presumption and power re-asserted in Richard this time to the point of outright tyranny, when he is driven to seize the lands and rights left to Bolingbroke on Gaunt's death, that Bolingbroke returns, bringing the challenge to the kingship into even sharper focus.

The antagonism that involves Richard, Bolingbroke and Gaunt begins, then, when Gaunt and Bolingbroke balk at the decision to have the latter banished. It is subsequently reinforced by the strange hubris Bolingbroke displays on leaving London. Significantly it is at this point (I.iii.35ff) that the play pounces upon us the obscure facts of Richard's irresponsibility as King. It is as if a direct connection were being made between Richard's careless irresponsibility as King and his resentment of presumption in his kindred. Then follows Gaunt's overt attack, the effect of which as presumption is strengthened by the obscure basis of his more general condemnation of the King's irresponsibility implied in the charge "Landlord of England art thou now, not King." (II.i.113). We are never sufficiently in possession of the facts that we do not share, despite a growing *awareness* of abuses, in the King's judgment that Gaunt *is* here "presuming upon an ague's privilege" (II.i.116) and speaking merely from the "sullens" (139).

It is when York subsequently apologizes for Gaunt's behavior and that of the absent Bolingbroke (141-144) that Richard himself points to the strain in their relationship as a justification for resentment and carelessness in him in the lines already quoted. Thus not until Richard's outright seizure of Gaunt's lands is there any *unmistakable* basis for bringing the King's integrity into question, and then this is meant to be seen in part as a reaction to presumptuous tensions in Richard's kindred. Significantly, it is at that point that the full spectrum of the King's action since Gloucester's death is brought to Richard's attention, as evidence suggesting an abuse of power, by a less partial voice, by York, who is himself, however, tortuously *apologetic* about the presumption of his remarks (163-185).

It is also just after York's outburst that Richard's abuses in the kingdom at large are filled out more fully for us, though not without leaving us with an uneasy sense of an account at second-hand, provided by nobles that one feels are already committed against the King—by Northumberland, Willoughby and Ross in conspiracy. (II.i.224ff). Through all of this the integrity of the King is by no means a closed question. Thus when Northumberland concludes, from such unstable evidence, that "the King is not himself" (241), the value of that statement as a judgment of political instability is undermined by the ambiguity in the King's position that makes Richard's putative abuse of kingship the immediate reaction to presumption in his kindred. This seems clear enough where Richard's abuses touch on matters that affect his kindred directly. But it is *also* true of

Richard's abuses in the kingdom at large, which are immediately presented as the product of careless desperation in a King who already sees his integrity being presumptuously undermined. These abuses, moreover, always remain significantly obscure, reinforcing as presumption the disposition in others to treat these abuses as though they predetermined the issue of integrity.

The significance of Northumberland's judgment is that it presumes, as in the case of Gaunt and Bolingbroke, to answer the unanswerable question brought into focus by their common challenge to Richard. The hubris of these men consists in taking the judgment of the reality of the kingship upon themselves, or more accurately still, in predetermining judgment: the challenge to the King's integrity carries within itself the judgment that the King is *already* dispossessed of integrity. In this sense, all three men are presuming to determine the reality of kingship's fortune: they take what is an irreducibly *ambiguous* fortune and decide in favor of the view of fortune anticipated; their position indeed presumes to a God-like capacity for determining the reality of kingship's fortune, which lies out of reach. The idea of that fortune subsequently acted on is in fact a *view* of what that fortune really is: a judgment on kingship despite the fact that a proper view of kingship escapes judgment and remains with God.

It is because Bolingbroke's invasion assumes of necessity a capacity like God to decide the status of the King's integrity that Richard, on returning from Ireland, is driven in his turn to call on God, for direct confirmation of his actual integrity as King. He anticipates a power of divine revelation that would serve as an immediate judgment on Bolingbroke's rebellion. That is a measure of the extraordinary hubris in Richard that rules out the possibility of a practical and more sober-minded reconciliation with Bolingbroke. It is hubris made inevitable by a corresponding hubris in Bolingbroke. Richard's subsequent failure to mediate an immediate divine judgment on Bolingbroke, as we shall see, Richard is inclined to take at first as an actual rejection by God. But as a final measure of the baffling reality of kingship, such failure merely extends to an extreme point that fundamental ambiguity in the King's position that leaves the issue of the King's integrity finally undecided. It is this surviving ambiguity that leaves Richard, despite failure, the scope to continue to act out the belief in his integrity as King, much as he is profoundly undermined at the same time by the failure that has played directly into the position of the rebels.

Thence follows Richard's deeper inward exploration of kingship, intent on tracing the kingship to its ultimate basis. With that development, the reality of the kingship takes on a more penetratingly radical character. By making that reality the object of a more complete, radical inward exploration, Richard's actions have, as we shall see, the effect first of emphasizing the questionableness of Bolingbroke's own position. Thus what appears in Bolingbroke to be a fully-considered position is exposed as a case of deliberate scepticism, unresponsive to that aspect of the kingship's reality that always leaves open the possibility that Bolingbroke is actually guilty of rebellion. At the same time, Bolingbroke's position suggests a viewpoint of brute naturalism—a fundamental indifference to the moral-metaphysical implications of action that blinds him to another aspect of the reality of the kingship, one that leaves all kings open, whatever their claim to integrity, to the real judgment that awaits them in death, a fact that has as much application to the aspiring Bolingbroke as to the down-trodden Richard. What makes this dramatic revision of Bolingbroke's position finally possible is a fresh sense of the value of inwardness as a means of grasping more fully, and ideally managing, kingship's reality. As we shall see, it is a value that Richard develops at great length: indeed, his inward exploration will become the motivating force behind an extraordinary psychological-representational impingement on the supersensible world.

II

FIRST RESPONSES

Of special concern to us, then, are (or should be) the metaphysical implications of Richard's rhetorical effort from III.ii onwards to externalize the full reality of his inward experience of kingship. Centrally, this takes the form of an attempt to externalize his experience of the hidden implications of Bolingbroke's return to England. In a literal reading of the action, there is indeed insufficient evidence to prove that Bolingbroke through his actions actually eyes the throne: Peter Ure is perfectly right in arguing that we cannot "conclude with Hazlitt that we are to see him as plotting for supreme power from the first."[4] Yet, as Brents Stirling has noted, Bolingbroke's ambiguity *is* the mark of the "opportunist", "vaguely aware of the ends to which his means commit him".[5] It is precisely because Bolingbroke's motives are deliberately withheld and unformed and (in this specially profound sense) unexposably inward that Richard is so consistently challenged and frustrated by Bolingbroke's actions: they cannot be proved to be what they are potentially. It is the problem that haunts Richard centrally from the moment he touches upon the outermost coasts of his kingdom, one that is made almost spectacularly emblematic in his initial confrontation with an obeisant Bolingbroke:

> *Fair cousin, you debase your princely knee*
> *To make the base earth proud with kissing it.*
> *Me rather had my heart might feel your love*
> *Than my unpleas'd eye see your courtesy.*
> *Up, cousin, up; your heart is up, I know,*
> [Touching his head]
> *Thus high at least, although your knee be low.*
>   *(III.iii.190–195)*

The inward challenge to Richard not only consists in endeavoring to make plain Bolingbroke's unformed intentions, or in externalizing the grief associated with Richard's 'knowledge' of what these consist in; Richard's grief is itself part of a larger emotional dilemma that is more personally his, whose expression is more forbidding. To understand this dilemma properly, it is necessary to set aside altogether those conventional attitudes that have been brought to the play that have only served to obscure the deeper metaphysical issues so far as these concern Richard. The tendency to see in Richard's reactions to what befall him an essential weakness of character (whatever the variety and range of meanings that have attached to this judgment) is the one, single feature of *Richard II* criticism that has positively forestalled a fair assessment of the nature and significance of Richard's predicament; it is what has blinded critics to the extensiveness with which this predicament actually *determines* Richard's actions and behavior. The tendency, as far as I can see, remains a strong one, and it has been misleading not because Richard does not in many moments show weakness of character, but because his weakness has been stressed in ignorance of the special difficulty in his position, which this weakness is largely designed to reflect.

One central line in this view of Richard is that in which animadversions have been brought to bear against him for his reversion to a fanciful dreaming and verbalizing instead of his taking positive action against Bolingbroke.[6] Since this judgment was made, it has become increasingly apparent to critics that part of the special nature of Richard's predicament is that, once stripped of military power, he is backed into a corner from which it is impossible for him to take action of any kind; that his is the "paradox", as it has been put, "of the rightful king who is without power to substantiate his right"[7], and that in the sequence of his fall "we are never given to feel that anything can be done: the result is foretold, and as inevitable as night following day".[8] Still weakness has been seen, and indisputably so, in his variableness and in his hysteria, as he proceeds to confront a fate that, though inevitable, he is unable to accept. But rather than seeing this as a serious flaw in his character variously conceived as womanishness[9], emotional exaggeration[10], or even a lack of personal courage[11], this weakness can be more profitably viewed as a reflection again of the special difficulty in his predicament.

Strictures such as Coleridge's to the effect that Richard's feelings are "misplaced in a man and altogether unfit for a king"[12] or Brents Stirling's criticism of Richard's "sentimental role"[13] become, on one level, irrelevant when it is considered that Richard's feelings serve to express his legitimate desire—since he *is*, after all, the 'rightful king'—to *retain* his kingship; ultimately, they serve to express his understandable dismay before the prospect of reconciling this continued attachment to *inevitable* loss and a debunked meaning. And that is the larger dilemma: it consists in being, on the one hand, inevitably bound to the kingship as, on the other, Richard is inexorably severed from it; and severed not only by Bolingbroke's actions but especially by what is instilled in Richard as a result of them: the disillusionment that he comes to feel towards the meaning of kingship when the prospect of losing it is first suggested to him, which plays the largest part in his acquiescence in, and precipitation of, his deposition.

It is necessary to stress that, apart from two or three other highpoints of strength known to him once his fate is scaled, Richard is hardly shown to be weak initially. When he arrives in England again after being away in Ireland, his mind, as it has been put[14], is "tense and large" with the knowledge of Bolingbroke's invasion. It is a masterful psychological touch, achieved simply by withholding immediate comment by Richard on the situation, and by virtue of it, Shakespeare lends added emotional power and intensity to Richard's first two great speeches of defiant majesty. These are speeches, it is true, whose truth as a representation of Richard's power as king the play eventually debunks. Nonetheless, in the moment they are spoken, they are extraordinarily effective speeches, speeches whose metaphysical significance is never lost or forgotten to us: their significance is dramatically taken up later on by Richard at several points.

The first of these speeches—"Feed not thy sovereign's foe, my gentle earth" (III.ii.12-26)—enacts what has been called "the sacred, animistic bond between king and land—the *corpus mysticum*"[15]. This may appear to be useless nonsense to the more practically—and realistically-minded onlookers like Aumerle and even (ironically) Carlisle, but in fact it is a brilliant expression of imaginative faith, building on the presumed certainty of a literal connection between the King's inward emotion and the forces of Nature by which Nature, as the servant of God, serves His deputy the King as emotional agent—earth, stones and creatures being presumed to possess a power to rise to life to avenge Bolingbroke's rebellion in mystical response to the King. In the second of Richard's two speeches, this connection is emphasized as a universal *identity*, as the King's emotion, the force of Nature, and the Divine Power unite in the symbol of the Sun-King who is Richard:

> *Discomfortable cousin! Know'st thou not*
> *That when the searching eye of heaven is hid*
> *Behind the globe, that lights the lower world,*
> *Then thieves and robbers range abroad unseen*
> *In murders and in outrage boldly here;*
> *But when from under this terrestrial ball*
> *He fires the proud tops of the eastern pines*
> *And darts his light through every guilty hole,*
> *Then murders, treasons, and detested sins,*
> *The cloak of night being pluck'd from off their backs,*
> *Stand bare and naked, trembling at themselves?*
> *So when this thief, this traitor, Bolingbroke,*
> *Who all this while hath revell'd in the night,*
> *Whilst we were wand'ring with the Antipodes,*
> *Shall see us rising in our throne, the east,*
> *His treasons will sit blushing in his face,*
> *Not able to endure the sight of day,*
> *But self-affrighted tremble at his sin.*
>
> *(III.ii.36-53)*

As the speech represents him here, Richard as King is projected as embodying in himself not just the Sun (and, by extension, the force of Nature) but, even more, Divine Judgment working on the spirits of the wicked, action that was traditionally associated with the day. Moreover, as the embodiment of the Sun and the Divine Power in a world-view assuming the identity of these and the Heart, Richard is projected as embodying simultaneously his own emotion. The structure of this speech is very grand: the symbolism of the Sun-King is drawn on by Richard, in the face of the challenge to his authority represented by Bolingbroke's return, to serve a supreme *act* of visionary authority, one that would constitute at once an act of emotional self-embodiment and an embodiment of the whole universe, suggesting the possibility of a power of emotion so complete in its authority as to constitute a power of opening up the world to the visible operations of the Divine Judgment behind it.

We remark that all that Richard is saying on the plainest level is that he is confident that his return to England will bring Bolingbroke to a consciousness of the moral implications of his actions, that immediate sight of the symbolism of the King will make Bolingbroke and all those involved in the political crisis of the kingdom once again aware of the moral order of the universe that categorically pronounces Bolingbroke's return a moral violation. However, we note how deeply Richard's speeches are shaped, at the same time, by the possibility that Bolingbroke shall choose in his arrogance to flout this order altogether, confirmed as the latter is for the moment in the immediate security of worldly power and the flattering evidence of political actuality. A large part of the effect of Bolingbroke's action on returning to England is to suggest in the face of imputations of treason and rebellion that he is secure both in the evidence of facts and the opinion of the world, which confirm him as being neither technically a usurper nor even necessarily wrong in taking into his own hands the redress of injustices committed against himself and the kingdom. I would wish to insist that it is a major part of the purpose and effect of Richard's speeches to address just such a set of conditions, which they *anticipate*, opposing to the evidence of worldly actuality belief in an eternal actuality beyond it treated as *no less real* or immediate. To the evidence of worldly actuality, Richard's speeches oppose the traditional religious-imaginative belief that the evidence of the world is not all, that there lies behind it as a real and living actuality, *immediately* accessible to intense imaginative faith, the whole moral order of reality linking conscience to Divine Judgment, what's more, that the King as the living embodiment of this order, reserves potentially the imaginative power of laying this whole order of reality immediately visible to the world by a supreme imaginative act of visionary command. Richard's initial speeches, taken together, assume that there exists behind the ordinary world of sensible phenomena a sphere of visionary realities—fighting angels, and a natural world in anthropomorphic commotion—ready by an act of visionary power to be set loose in the world to confirm and preserve, should this be necessary, the moral order of reality thus literally embodied in the King.

So far as Richard's imaginative effort mediates the possibility of an immediate revelation in these terms, in the hope thereby of securing an immediate resolution of events, it is undertaken in the face of opposition showing such a literal development to be inevitable as the only means of effectively counteracting that rigid adherence to the evidence of the world that keeps Bolingbroke out of the reach of moral exposure. However, such an effort becomes more and more frantically urgent the more obvious it becomes that no such development will take place and that the moral-imaginative reality that it assumes is more likely than not simply a wishful faith. In fact, no sooner are Richard's speeches spoken than they are immediately reduced to what Shakespeare suspects they may be—pieces of emotional symbolism with no imaginative basis in fact.

It has been said that the basis that is being undermined here is the "expectation of a miracle".[16] On one level, this is misleading, for divine right does not *necessarily* carry with it for Richard the direct intervention of heaven (or a visitation in the Elizabethan sense of the word) but, on the immediate level, simply the support of men, in whom the moral universe (or a sort of *synderesis*) he assumes will operate, at once weakening Bolingbroke's resolution and rallying all men round the King. Neither of these things happens, and the skepticism that the play thus expresses on this level would seem to be that imaginative constructs of the kind that are built up in Richard's speeches may be invalid outside the social imagination without whose endorsement and support they are as good as being dead myths.

At another level, however, the remark about the expectation of a miracle is utterly revealing, for it properly acknowledges the deeper import to Richard's speeches. On a deeper level, Richard's speeches expound an imaginative world view treated not simply as a projection of social belief, but as unquestionable doctrine, what's more as literal fact; it is on this basis that Richard permits himself the expectation of a miraculous act of visionary self-revelation confirming him in the reality of his divine authority as King. Thus, when it becomes clear that events will fail to support Richard, what is emphasized is not just the failure of social faith, but the failure of what was formerly regarded as moral-imaginative reality—specifically, the failure of a visionary development directly linking the King's experience to Divine Judgment.

As it is, Richard is left alone with himself, thrown back upon a purely isolated grief over what appears to him to be inevitable defeat before Rebellion. Richard suddenly finds himself in an isolation that brings to his awareness his actual emotional limitations. These are measured at first by the spectacular shift from the cosmic grandiosity of the speeches of defiance to a purely physiological emotional self-representation:

> *But now the blood of twenty thousand men*
> *Did triumph in my face, and they are fled;*
> *And, till so much blood thither come again,*
> *Have I not reason to look pale and dead?*
>
> *(III.ii.76-79)*

Accompanying Richard's realization of his limitations, moreover, are the first signs of an emotional fragmentation that is to plague him to the very end of the play:

> *Awake, thou coward majesty! thou sleepest.*
> *Is not the King's name twenty thousand names?*
> *Arm, arm, my name! a puny subject strikes*
> *At thy great glory.*
>
> *(III.ii.84-87)*

Most will see this is as an obviously strained attempt on Richard's part to stir himself up again, after a relapse, to the earlier defiant manner. But what most have interpreted as weakness of character is more profitably seen as the first manifestation of an incipient consciousness of conflicting implications, the consciousness of Death and Kingship's empty symbolism, which Richard eventually elaborates and explores later on in the scene's central speech, the "Let's talk of graves" speech. This consciousness of Death strikes Richard like a bolt the moment he first hears of revolt:

> *All souls that will be safe, fly from my side;*
> *For time hath set a blot upon my pride.*
>
> *(III.ii.80-81)*

and he first grasps it, at least conceptually, in the second speech following:

> *Cry woe, destruction, ruin, and decay—*
> *The worst is death, and death will have his day.*[17]
>
> *(III.ii.102-103)*

From this point of view, Richard's efforts to affect kingliness can be seen to reflect less a show of weakness than his understandable dismay before the emotional implications of a terrible, newly acquired consciousness.

When he *first* proceeds to represent himself in this consciousness—after Scroope's self-introduction dashes his shakily-reared hopes—it is clear from the *tone* of Richard's sudden renunciation of the kingship that he still remains deeply attached to what he claims to renounce:

> *Say, is my kingdom lost? Why 'twas my care;*
> *And what loss is it to be rid of care?*
> *Strives Bolingbroke to be as great as we?*
> *Greater he shall not be; if he serve God,*
> *We'll serve him too, and be his fellow so.*
>
> *(III.ii.95-99)*

Judging from Scroope's reaction to Richard's speeches, however:

> *Glad am I that your Highness is so arm'd*
> *To bear the tidings of calamity.*
>
> *(III.ii.104-105)*

and Richard's reaction to Scroope's

> *too well, too well thou tell'st a tale so ill*
> *(III.ii.121)*

it is clear that Richard's representation of his bitterness over the imminent loss of kingship has not come through—to Scroope at any rate, who uses Richard's apparent renunciation to justify, to Richard's understandable disturbance, a vividly complete account of the rebellion. Partly to re-adjust the point of view, but partly too out of initial frustration with the emotional task demanded of him, Richard for the moment endeavors once again to resume his kingliness:

Where is the Earl of Wiltshire? Where is Bagot?
What is become of Bushy? Where is Green?
That they have let the dangerous enemy
Measure our confines with such peaceful steps?
If we prevail, their heads shall pay for it.
I warrant they have made peace with Bolingbroke.
(III.ii.122–127)

But, as with the first attempt, this too is unconvincing. Richard's language (consider "the dangerous enemy", "measure our confines") is clearly strained, and besides, as the last line of the speech reveals and as his reaction to Scroope's reply confirms, under the appearance of kingly wrath really lies anxiety over the feared treachery of his favorites. When it is said that they "have made peace", Richard reacts excessively and hysterically, execrating them at once. Instantly he loses himself to the single vengeful passion as a temporary but futile escape from the larger emotional challenge. When, to his obvious shock and shame, it is then disclosed that his favorites have been killed, Richard knows he can no longer evade the issues: shamed and beaten, he is now forced to really confront his imminent loss of power as King.

Richard's "Let's talk of graves" speech provides us, in this connection, with a complete *reversal* of those metaphysical assumptions about the kingship that underlie his initial speeches of defiant majesty. The speech brings to a climax the dramatic deterioration that Richard's initial idealization of the kingship undergoes as a result of the encroachment made on his faith by his failure to crystallize in himself the moral-imaginative reality he assumes is intrinsic to the kingship. In Richard's initial speeches, the role of kingship was viewed from the point of view of the King as divine representative. As man's immediate link with Eternity, the King was projected as the divine guardian and living embodiment of the moral-imaginative order of the universe, a status that was seen to confer upon him, ideally, miraculous powers of spiritual revelation and political resolution. In contrast with this extraordinary idealization of the kingship (fully symbolized in the image of the "golden crown") Richard's "Let's talk of graves" speech now projects (through the opposing image of the "hollow crown") a kingship emptied of all metaphysical meaning whatever. It is a reversal that follows from Richard's failure to experience in himself, either in literal fact *or* by symbolical reflection in the reverence of men, any of the moral-miraculous powers ideally associated with the kingship. This failure leads him to see behind the King's grandiose claims to majesty and power simply the bluster of empty pomp and vain conceit, and in place of the assurances of Eternity once thought to be immediately embodied in the kingship the empty finality of Death.

That Richard owes his displacement as King immediately to Bolingbroke's blasphemous violation of the moral-imaginative order that has always been associated with the kingship is an intuition and a claim that from the beginning Richard does not permit to escape either his own consciousness or Bolingbroke's for very long. All the same, the implications of his displacement are such that they engender in Richard simultaneously a profound scepticism, one questioning the very basis of that order; and it is between these two extreme positions, between faith in the inalienable sanctity of the kingship on the one hand and scepticism from unchecked degradation on the other, that Richard remains suspended through the greater part of the play. It is his scepticism over the kingship that leads him to feel that the kingship ought to be renounced as empty pomp; it is his faith in the kingship that keeps him, despite this, deeply committed to the kingship; his scepticism that compels him to acquiesce in and precipitate his own deposition, his faith that leads him to complicate this action to the point of denying it altogether. If Richard watches helplessly as the kingship is subjected to a ruthless process of degradation, this may be, as his scepticism leads him to suspect, because the kingship really possesses none of that special sanctity he is originally inclined to give to it. Nevertheless, Richard's faith always remains strong enough to keep him from actually adhering to this position; and it is an indication of the predominance of Richard's faith that he is *ultimately* inclined to lay the blame for his grief over the degradation of the kingship, despite the deep scepticism, on Bolingbroke's blasphemy. Richard, in other words, continues, despite everything, to believe in the final sanctity of the kingship, although it is his fate to have to suffer, to the point of his own death, the complete degradation of the kingship, from the initiative of the scepticism of others and his own.

That scepticism derives jointly from an experience of the gap separating the kingship in its ideal significance from the King's highly limited embodiment of that significance in the world, a gap that originally discredits Richard in the eyes of men, and then the kingship in the eyes of Richard. Ultimately, Richard's fate expresses the gap separating the King in his actual impotence as a man from the kingship's ideal potentiality. This is as much as to say that for a man there is no potentiality in the kingship at all, the burden in fact of Richard's scepticism and the play's.[18] Yet if there is anything that *would* have settled the question of the sanctity of the kingship and the moral-political ambiguities surrounding Bolingbroke's return, it is the power of visionary revelation Richard originally assumes ought to have been his as King despite everything, and the recovery of which, as I shall argue, through all, he continues to expect and to seek to secure.

III

DEVELOPMENT

Richard's profound vulnerability in his situation is linked from the beginning with the idea of an *individual* creative power that would fill the void created by the collapse of the moral-imaginative order ideally associated with the kingship. Richard's "Let's talk of graves" speech possesses in this connection a profoundly creative character; what it represents is his immediate exploration of the challenge Death suddenly poses to him as a King. What makes this exploration especially significant representationally is that it integrates, as most of his speeches do later, Richard's essential ambivalence, already including in its form his grief over being violated as King as well as a newly enforced scepticism about the kingship, which the speech is designed expressly to elaborate. Far from simply *recording* the perception of Death, moreover (a function largely confined to ll.149-154), the speech seeks to *externalize* Death as inward emotional experience, partly as reflected in the nature of social relationships (ll. 171-173), partly as reflected in Richard's idea of himself (ll.175-177). But these manifestations of the experience come at the tail end of a more extensive and profounder consideration of the possibilities of the creative projection of experience. Central to the speech is a ritual action that Richard proposes as a means of controlling creatively the terror of imminent death, which serves as a symbol and model of his creative effort throughout the play.

It is to be remarked in this connection how seriously Richard's speech is shaped by the thought of decay. The reference to "worms" at the beginning of the speech has the effect of interpolation, too glib perhaps to compel seriously our imagination; but there can be no doubt about the disturbing effect of Richard's reference to the body as "paste and cover to our bones" (l.154), which has a strong suggestion of corruptible flesh. In fact, the whole speech is structured immediately around the thought of Richard's favorites in the grave; it is a direct echo of Scroope's account of them as "grav'd in the hollow ground" (l.140). Thus when Richard proposes as a ritual action that they all "sit upon the ground" (l.155), the gesture is neither sentimental nor frivolous but seriously connected with the thought of death and decay. As an action set upon the "ground", Richard's ritual addresses itself directly to the experience of death "in the hollow ground". But this ritual also addresses itself to the experience of creative emptiness, to the "ground" as barren earth, of which the decayed body in the "ground" is model and microcosm. A direct connection, in other words, is established between the individual death and an empty relationship with the earth, no doubt because the prospect of death is intimately bound up for Richard with the failure of the *corpus mysticum*, the failure of that visionary power, among other things over the earth, that he originally associates with triumph over rebellion.

In fact, it would seem that this ritual action as a creative confrontation with Death is designed to counteract specifically this failure of power. One finds a direct parallel for this ritual action in Hamlet "seeking for his father in the dust"—in the emphatic rhetorical thought of death and decay that prodigiously contains that visionary power of thinking that is seeing, as Richard illustrates at the climax to this action:

> *—for within the hollow crown*
> *That rounds the mortal temples of a king*
> *Keeps death his court; **and there** the antic sits,*
> *Scoffing his state and grinning at his pomp;*
> *Allowing him a breath, a little scene,*
> *To monarchize, be fear'd, and kill with looks;*
> *Infusing him with self and vain conceit,*
> *As if this flesh which walls about our life*
> *Were brass impregnable; and, humour'd thus,*
> *Comes at the last, and with a little pin*
> *Bores through his castle wall, and farewell, king!*
> *(III.ii.160–170)*

The personification of Death in this passage is externalized with all the crystallizing force and vividness that an active miraculism[19] fully expressive of rhetorical reality could bring to the elaboration of a conceit: the effect indeed is a projection of the immediate *presence* of Death in the ritual. Just how the passage could be made to achieve such an effect in the theater is a question that seems answered by the possibilities inherent in the personification of Death as King, which would seem to call at this point for Richard to embody Death in himself.

Of the final status of this personification in Richard's eyes, something can be gleaned from what he explicitly says about his effort later, when he curses Aumerle for having enticed him out of his resolved despair:

> *Beshrew thee, cousin, which didst lead me forth*
> *Of that sweet **way** I was in to despair!*
> *(III.ii.204-205)*

which appears to stress the *relative* significance of the development. However, once Richard has allowed himself to be shaken from his resolution (beguiled by the hope that he might still be able to retain his kingship), he finds himself again comfortlessly alienated from his innermost experience, and as if in despair of recovering the emotional-metaphysical 'reality' worked towards in the "Let's talk of graves" speech, for the moment he resumes the bitter, rhetorical manner of his initial 'renunciation' before Scroope:

> *A king, woe's slave, shall kingly woe obey.*
> *(III.ii.210)*

*   *   *

In my discussion of III.ii, I have tried to suggest that the judgment of Richard as weak is on one level irrelevant to the appreciation of his predicament. The question posed in III.ii is not how strong or weak Richard is as a king in a crisis, but rather what he can do both as king and as a man when he is stripped entirely of the power of action. In fact, we do well (despite his blatantly simplistic misconception of Richard generally as "wise, patient and pious" in his distress) to adopt the viewpoint of Johnson on the status of the attitudes represented in this scene by Carlisle and Aumerle:

> *Nothing is more offensive to a mind convinced that his distress*
> *is without remedy, and preparing to submit to **irresistible***
> ***calamity** than these petty and conjectured comforts which*
> *unskillful officiousness thinks it virtue to administer.*[20]

In his response to his fate, Richard progresses from an expression of visionary power through a recognition of his actual limitations to a condition of disjunction or alienation that impresses upon him his need for imaginative self-exploration. This, as we have seen, ultimately takes the form, in the "Let's talk of graves" speech, of an extraordinary effort at rhetorical self-projection. The structural pattern of III.iii would appear likewise to point to creative action of this complex kind as the natural resolution of Richard's dilemma. In that scene, we are presented with three possible responses available to Richard in his predicament, the point of whose representation, however, is to show how inadequate any of these is to someone in his position.

The first two responses are implied in Richard's first two, dramatically contrasting speeches to Northumberland when initially approached by him under Flint Castle. The first of these speeches is of undoubtedly majestic power, re-invoking in its challenging confidence the cosmic faith of the initial speeches of defiance in III.ii:

> *show us the hand of God*
> *That hath dismiss'd us from our stewardship;*
> *(III.iii.77–78)*

The speech is magnificent in its sublime contempt, which, in the visionary context, is not far-fetched at all. Yet Richard's subsequent charges are no sooner denied by Northumberland, and dutiful submission unexpectedly pledged, than Richard submits himself, contemptibly, to Bolingbroke's presence and demands. He is motivated by the sudden hope of avoiding the fate he had thought till now inevitable, a sudden twist of emotion whose shamefulness, it should be noted, he immediately recognizes:

> *We do debase ourselves, cousin, do we not,*
> *To look so poorly and to speak so fair?*
> *(III.iii.127–128)*

It is a reaction for which he eventually loathes himself:

> *O God, O God! that e'er this tongue of mine*
> *That laid the sentence of dread banishment*
> *On yon proud man should take it off again*
> *With words of sooth!*
> *(III.iii.133–136)*

But this second response is no more inadequate than the first. Submission is obviously contemptible, but defiance is equally contemptibly ineffectual and would only be foolish. Richard's highly dignified, heroically-sustained charges of rebellion are simply diverted by Northumberland's insolent denials, and there is a suggestion in Richard's lines, when he contemplates defiance again after his initial indulgence of the rebels, that defiance would achieve nothing more heroic or grandiose than simply death for Richard:

> *Shall we call back Northumberland, and send*
> *Defiance to the traitor, and so die?*
>
> > *(III.iii.129-130)*

The inadequacy in one way or another of these responses impresses upon one the special difficulty in Richard's predicament. His royal power being insolently and rebelliously denied, Richard is yet too kingly to remain a king in submitting to Bolingbroke's demands. At the same time, being rightful King, he remains inevitably attached to the kingship, a point poignantly brought out when, deprived of any course of action, Richard contemplates, as a third possibility, worldly renunciation, in his "What must the king do now?" speech. The inadequacy of *this* response is soon signaled at the point in the speech at which Richard suddenly lingers on the thought of the grave, thence going on to fresh, strangely intense emblematic projections of his grief (see III.iii.154). But it is also observable as an emotional disjunction in the speech implied by the speech's serial form, which reflects a strained attempt to work himself up to a belief in renunciation.[21]

Renunciation, like defiance and submission, proves equally inadequate for Richard's emotional needs, and it is with these and these alone that he is left, failing all possible courses of action. It is these that, at the same time, he is desperately impelled to *externalize*, as if in an attempt (for want of any other outlet) to raise the power of self-projection to the level of action. In fact, it would appear that the solution to Richard's dilemma over the inadequacy of action would consist in seeking to give to the creative projection of his experience the direct function and effect of action. Ultimately, as I shall show, this takes the form of an attempt to project the ambivalent aspects of his experience directly onto the structure of the outer world, through a rhetorical transformation of the prevailing import of the external impressions created by the language and gestures of men in society, both his own and that of others.

* * *

The significance for this purpose of the first and third emblematic images from the "What must the King do now?" speech is that they provide us with further forms of the realization of death:

> *Or I'll be buried in the king's high way,*
> *Some way of common trade, where subjects' feet*
> *May hourly trample on their sovereign's head;*
> *For on my heart they tread now whilst I live,*
> *And buried once, why not upon my head?*
> . . . .
> *Or shall we play the wantons with our woes*
> *And make some pretty match with shedding tears?*
> *As thus: to drop them still upon one place*
> *Till they have fretted us a pair of graves*
> *Within the earth; and therein laid—there lies*
> *Two kinsmen digg'd their graves with weeping eyes.*
>   *(III.iii.155-169)*

What makes *these* forms of expression peculiarly significant is that Richard momentarily projects his emblems as representations that might be actually embodied, in real life. As representations of his fate, the emblems derive their full significance from Richard's impulse to confer upon them the status and power of literal action. Moreover, in the second case, Richard projects an emblem that depicts a *miraculous* action, projects this *as if* it could actually be realized: "As thus". This is not to say that he finally assumes that his emblem *can* be realized, for it is part of the pathos of his response to events that he knows it cannot ("Well, well, I see I talk but idly, and you laugh at me", 170-171). However, Richard *is* drawing here on the suggestive power of a complete identification between speech and reality in which speech is being pushed to its extreme limits, where it merges with a magical feeling for the final realization of the emblems it projects. There is an intensely dramatic instance of this level of suggestion in his "mockery king of snow" emblem: "O that I were a mockery king of snow", where the emblem caters to his momentary relapse from his imaginative assault on the 'rebels':

> *O that I were a mockery king of snow,*
> *Standing before the sun of Bolingbroke,*
> *To melt myself away in water-drops!*
>
> (IV.i.260-262)

Here the emblematic projection is even more immediately identified with the reality it represents, through a radical use of the wishing structure we see Richard indulging elsewhere, the final determination of this projection promising him the escape into the simplified death he requires to be free of the complex, metaphysical demands of his dilemma.

The second of Richard's emblematic representations in the "What must the king do now?" speech directly echoes the visionary power projected in his original speeches of defiance:

> *Aumerle, thou weep'st, my tender-hearted cousin!*
> *We'll make foul weather with despised tears;*
> *Our sighs and they shall lodge the summer corn*
> *And make a dearth in this revolting land.*
>
> *(III.iii.160-163)*

Richard's image here invokes the same kind of retributive visionary power invoked in the original symbolical speeches. By comparison with these, this suffers considerably; the difference, to invoke the Romantic distinction, is one between imagination and fancy, reflecting Richard's faded strength at this point, his emotional desolation and lost faith. Still, the difference measures dramatically the drastic nature of Richard's task: in the context of a discredited imaginative world-view in which rebellion goes unrevenged, what imaginative power is left to him? The emblematic effort *here* possesses a reduced, remotely symbolical significance, but by no means does this individual instance exhaust the expressive significance of Richard's emblematic projections generally. It contains, moreover, the germ of a more immediate self-projectional 'plan' that Richard goes on to execute with considerable power and conviction in the deposition-scene, from which the emblematic efforts themselves take on great power.

Attached to the words "foul" and "despised", that is, are specific tactical implications: Richard appears to conceive of his grief as in some way undesirable to his enemy, indeed as a personal weapon. Implied is the strategy he goes on to indulge with great moral and imaginative power against Bolingbroke from the end of III.iii and throughout the whole of the second half of IV.i—viz., the systematic projection onto the external impressions created by Richard's deposition of that extraordinary ambivalent grief over the kingship that alone constitutes the full significance of his deposition as King.

*   *   *

Before we turn to Richard's strategy in IV.i, and the great variety of expressive forms whose adequacy as projectional self-representation that scene explores, it is necessary to point out that III.iii puts forth two other isolated attempts at creative self-projection that help to fill out the fundamental ambivalence in Richard's experience. The first attempt, showing Shakespeare's personal hand in the representational design, takes place between the set of descriptions of Richard made alternately by Bolingbroke and York when Richard first appears on the walls of Flint Castle:

> Bol. *See, see, King Richard doth himself appear,*
> *As doth the blushing discontented sun*
> *From out the fiery portal of the east,*
> *When he perceives the envious clouds are bent*
> *To dim his glory and to stain the track*
> *Of his bright passage to the occident.*
>
> York. *Yet looks he like a king. Behold his eye,*
> *As bright as is the eagles', lightens forth*
> *Controlling majesty. Alack, alack, for woe,*
> *That any harm should stain so fair a show!*
> (*III.iii.62–71*)

The juxtaposition of impressions here would, at first sight, appear to be designed as a commentary on the ethical situation, on the adequacy and particularly the validity of Richard as King, with Bolingbroke (assuming York's account to be equally valid) somewhat over-anxious to show Richard acknowledging his guilt and fear in his appearance. By "envious clouds" with a 'staining' action, one can suppose that Bolingbroke has in mind Richard's irresponsible actions as King, of the kind Northumberland presses

Richard to confess to in the deposition-scene (see IV.i.222ff), and which Bolingbroke's presence and action here, it is assumed, implicitly confront Richard with. Coherent as this reading may be, however, it must be held to be rather awkward, for as the speech stands, it would be hard not to feel that the "envious clouds" were associated with Bolingbroke himself, something that would certainly be inconceivable if Bolingbroke were speaking the passage in character. In fact, it is far more likely that Bolingbroke's speech here is *out* of character, that it possesses a psychological-representational design focusing, through the emphasis on Richard's eyes, on the character of Richard and *his* response to events.

The speeches taken together provide us, in fact, with the first objective presentation of Richard's experience since his crisis. Between them the speeches seek to emphasize in Richard's outward appearance, which suggests ambivalently "blushing discontent" and "controlling majesty", the dual aspects of his experience at this stage: on the one hand, his sense of fear, guilt and disillusionment attaching to the deposed fate he expects and his consciousness of Death; and on the other hand, his continuing sense of himself as King. We are to imagine an expression of anger conducive simultaneously to a dual impression of fearful disillusionment and angry majesty (an anger masking fear and disillusionment being a normal phenomenon of the emotional life). And it is through this anger as portrayed by the actor, and while postulating an ultimate identification of passion and appearance, that Richard is shown once again externalizing his inner experience, which is here more firmly grounded in the ambivalence I am claiming of his position as a whole.

The second attempt at creative self-projection in this scene takes place at the point in his dealings with Bolingbroke at which Northumberland returns to the Duke with the King's greetings, when Richard, after denouncing himself for the gesture, acknowledges by implication the profound difficulty of his position:

> *O that I were as great*
> *As is my grief, or lesser than my name!*
> *Or that I could forget what I have been!*
> *Or not remember what I must be now!*
>
> *(III.iii.136-139)*

On the surface the lines appear to repeat the single point of the great extremity of Richard's grief before which he feels painfully and shamefully limited. Richard implies that if he had the power to endure so great a grief, he would not have been given to contemptible submission. Inevitably, however, because of the extremity of his grief, he has, the extremity of grief arising, as he elaborates this in ll.138-139, out of a consciousness of the extraordinary, psychologically unbridgeable gap between what he has been, namely King, and what he appears to be fated to become. However, ambiguities in the words "great" and "must be" deepen the burden of Richard's lines. The lines "O that I were as great/As is my grief" can also mean that he wishes he had the power to make good his grief, that he had the power to express it, to project it upon his world, and particularly upon the usurpers who have manipulated appearances to their advantage, an idea that emerges into explicit consciousness in ll.140-141:

> *Swell'st thou, proud heart? I'll give thee scope to beat,*
> *Since foes have scope to beat both thee and me.*

The line "Or not remember what I must be now!", at the same time, can also mean, apart from what Richard feels he is being forced to become, what he feels he should become on the basis of his continuing realization (presently emphasized by the very fact of having to submit contemptibly to usurpers to remain King) that the power of the kingship is illusory—an idea that attaches itself more clearly to the word "must", in addition to the first meaning of the word, in Richard's following speech:

> *What must the King do now? Must he submit?*
> *The King shall do it. Must he be depos'd?*
> *The King shall be contented. Must he lose*
> *The name of king? A God's name, let it go.*
> *(III.iii.143-146)*

It is not sufficiently stressed in commentary on the play that the crisis to which he is submitted leaves Richard deeply disillusioned about the meaning of the kingship, that the failure of any actual power as King, in confronting him with the prospect and inevitability of Death, leaves him, because of a stubbornly persistent attachment to the kingship, with a crushing sense of the kingship's essential mockery, and that it is this consciousness that impels him, eventually, to renounce the kingship, as the truer, if not in itself alone the most fully self-representative, action. This is the basis, specifically, of his self-deposition, as Richard explicitly informs us later:

> *For I have given here my soul's consent*
> *T'undeck the pompous body of a king;*
>
> *(IV.i.249-250)*

Now it is just this impulse that is entailed in the second meaning of the word "must", and as a result of this, Richard's expression of desperation in ll.136-139 acquires a bewildering complexity. An ambiguity in the word "great" in l.136 should already have us following two simultaneous meanings corresponding to Richard's ambivalence about his experience. Richard is saying simultaneously that he wishes he could endure patiently, and yet strike back for, the grief that, because of his peculiarly difficult situation, is too strong for him to bear. And it is because we follow both meanings *simultaneously* that the second ambiguity, in the word "must" in l.139, not only provides us with the appropriate corresponding reason for each of these strands of meaning but at the same time forces the strands to intersect, with a bewildering complexity. So that by the passage we are to understand:

a) I wish I could endure my grief because it is what should be
b) I wish I could strike back because I am being forced to become what I do not want to become, nor feel I should become

but because we follow both strands of the first ambiguity simultaneously:

c) I wish I could endure my grief because it is unavoidable
d) I wish I could strike back because of the pain of disillusionment entailed in knowing what should be

and so compositely:

e) I wish I could endure my grief because it is unavoidable and because I now know that this is what should be

and at the same time:

f) I wish I could strike back because I am being forced to become what I do not want to become or feel I should become, and because I have been forced to know what I should never have wanted to know—nor should I have known it.

So understood, Richard's utterance, as a crystallization of his emotions, is quite extraordinary. On the one hand, there is the simple obtrusive form recalling the earliest antithetical verse-style of the period, and on the other Richard's dilemma, of singular complexity, which he is unconsciously attempting to condense into it. It is thus a complex attitude indeed that Richard brings to bear on the determination of reality he expresses the wish for here, across the use of a construction—"O that I were"—that, as I have pointed out about his language generally, shows him far more involved in a full realization of his idea than mere wishfulness would imply.

Richard's overt desire for some kind of self-projectional power as indicated in the lines "O that I were as great/As is my grief" confirms, I believe, what I pointed out earlier about Richard's emotional-psychological tactical intentions towards the rebels. Although Richard's desire entails in some sense the desire for physical or military power, the real issue is rather the creative search for an alternative projectional power in the absence of this. The power considered does not simply serve Richard's grief over the loss of kingship, among other things his grief over rebellion and the blasphemous disregard of the imaginative order that has made the loss of kingship inevitable. This is or should be an obvious feature of his predicament, and in this connection, Hazlitt's remark that Richard is submitted to insults and injuries "which he has not courage or manliness to resent"[22] could not be further from the truth. The question, less obviously, also serves Richard's grief over the lost meaning of kingship, his irreversible disillusionment (with its attendant feelings of fear, guilt, and dismay) connected with having seen beyond the empty pomp of kingship to Death and another forbiddingly unfamiliar reality stripped of all the assurances of Eternity.

Both aspects of Richard's grief taken together constitute the full metaphysical significance of his deposition as King, and it is this extraordinary ambivalent significance that, at the play's climax, Richard aims to project in the face of the apparent righteousness of Bolingbroke and his party entailed by Richard's deposition of himself. His self-deposition is motivated by and expresses his recognition of a new imaginative truth connected with the failure of Kingship and his vision of Death. At the same time, it is undertaken, insofar as it ignores the crime of Rebellion, in conscious violation of the imaginative order to which Richard, with the greatest demands on his integrity, remains simultaneously attached:

> *Nay, if I turn mine eyes upon myself*
> *I find myself a traitor with the rest;*
> *For I have given here my soul's consent*
> *T'undeck the pompous body of a king;*
>
> > *(IV.i.247–250)*

* * *

Richard's impulse to externalize the double significance of his deposition constitutes essentially a religious-political strategy undertaken to expose the unseen, metaphysical implications of Bolingbroke's violence to the crown. Richard's determination to confront Bolingbroke to this end leads him in the deposition-scene into an effort that is extensive and extraordinarily variegated, but it can be reduced to a series of different kinds of efforts ranging from the least to the most ingeniously formal and integrated, depending on how Richard manages his grief. Moreover, these ultimately converge in a broader tension between language and action by which Richard, as I shall show, syncopates resistance *against* compliance with his deposition. In III.iii, towards the end of the scene, as Richard descends to the court, the action of compliance is presented only very obscurely. But in IV.i, the action is specifically his self-deposing action, which dominates the whole of the second half of the scene, and which is first reported to the court by York sometime before Richard himself appears on the stage.

Paradoxically, Richard's emotional-projectional strategy in IV.i can be said to start here, with Carlisle's fiery speech of condemnation as provoked by Bolingbroke's determination to ascend the throne immediately following York's announcement. It is no small piece of political acumen that Bolingbroke demonstrates in recognizing the political controversy Richard has sought to arouse by absenting himself from a transfer of power:

> *Fetch hither Richard, that in common view*
> *He may surrender; so we shall proceed*
> *Without suspicion.*
>
> > *(IV.i.155–157)*

Moreover, when Richard does appear onto the scene, he continues to express in sundry ways his resistance to the action he has had officially announced, and which in fact he very shortly carries out, though as we shall see largely as travesty. His resistance takes, most straightforwardly, the form of verbal emphasis on the fact that rather than deposing himself he is actually being deposed, and that all are traitors to heaven and the crown. From the very moment he appears he assumes a trenchantly insinuating manner, calling attention to himself as the rightful King who cannot be but who he is, in himself and in the eyes of heaven:

> *God save the King! Will no man say amen?*
> *Am I both priest and clerk? Well, then, amen.*
> *God save the King! although I be not he;*
> *And yet, amen, if heaven do think him me.*
> *(IV.i.172–175)*

In fact, for a moment it is made to appear as if the business that he is now being asked to conduct is of the Court's determination and not his own:

> *To do what service am I sent for hither?*
> York. *To do that office of thine own good will*
> *Which tired majesty did make thee offer—*
> *The resignation of thy state and crown*
> *To Henry Bolingbroke.*
> *(IV.i.176–180)*

The terms in which Richard subsequently frames his acquiescence in this proclaimed purpose are rendered intensely paradoxical by the evidence of royal command he everywhere exercises in disposing of the matter, command that is only highlighted the more by his daringly drawing Bolingbroke into an action that explicitly defines the latter's assumption of power as a blasphemous violence done to the crown:

> *Give me the crown. Here, cousin, seize the crown.*
> *(IV.i181)*

Nevertheless, in spite of this very heavy conditioning of the matter, it is quite another view of the Kingship's reality that finally comes to absorb Richard as he proceeds to develop this exceedingly complex action:

> *Here, cousin,*
> *On this side my hand, and on that side thine.*

> *Now is this golden crown like a deep well*
> *That owes two buckets, filling one another;*
> *The emptier ever dancing in the air.*
> *The other down, unseen, and full of water.*
> *That bucket down and full of tears am I*
> *Drinking my griefs, whilst you mount up on high.*
> (IV.i.182-189)

W.H. Clemen, writing of this passage and the emblem it projects, remarks:

> *This image marks the climax of the scene, but at the same*
> *time it sums up the whole substance of the play: the tragedy*
> *of kingship which demands that the parting king must wane*
> *in the same proportion as the new king waxes . . .* [23]

But Richard's representation actually runs far deeper than this, and altogether in another vein. The image of kingship it projects, for one thing, is not nearly so splendid. Richard is not, as Clemen appears to believe, dispassionately generalizing the grand symbolism of kingship; he is projecting his profound sense of kingship's essential mockery and futility, a meaning poignantly conveyed by the endlessly mechanical process by which one bucket displaces the other at a well, one too that, though it hardly says much for one or the other, says less, in fact, for the waxing king. Richard's representation expresses a further element: accompanying this projection of the mockery of kingship is the striking emphasis on his subterranean griefs as waning king—griefs, we can be sure, over having been pushed down by the rising Bolingbroke as one bucket is pushed down by the other in Richard's analogy, but griefs too, surely, over the travesty to which kingship is reduced when it is seen in the light of a process of this kind.

Of further striking relevance is Richard's complex development of the descent idiom, which points the direction to the whole "substance" of the play, but by a more complex and precise formulation of the matter than Clemen appears to suggest by his own use of the phrase. The descent idiom expresses Richard's subtle representation of that complex understanding of his fate that he identifies with the determination of death and the unfathomable grief associated with that fate. "Was ever grief like mine?"

Herbert would have Christ say in his powerful re-creation of the *O vos omnes* lament drama, and we shall see how Richard's identification with Christ in his Passion and Death projects *one* tortured idea of the determined conclusion, with its assumed assurance of a power of visionary judgment to be got at only *in* death. At the same time, Richard gives us his dramatic emblematic identification with the falling Phaeton, which Richard projects in the most spectacular terms as he descends dishonorably from Flint Castle at Bolingbroke's command, to signal the initial realization of the pattern of descent, the pattern of death:

> *Down, down, I come, like glist'ring Phaeton,*
> *Wanting the manage of unruly jades.*
> *In the base court? Base court, where kings grow base,*
> *To come at traitors' calls, and do them grace.*
> *In the base court? Come down? Down, court! down, king!*
> *For night-owls shriek where mounting larks should sing.*
>   *(III.iii.178-183)*

Once again, Richard's use of language supports a fuller realization of the matter than is suggested by the recognition of limitation implied by the simile (cf. "like"), and as such, the speech goes to show again that characteristic, far-reaching aspect of his language, breaking through metaphorical limitations, that serves to *embody* forms of the realization of death, as in his earlier projection: "for *there* the antic sits . . ."

In the play's central emblematic development of the visionary realization of death—"Now is this golden crown like a deep well"—Richard again resorts to an emphatically metaphorical process, but only, in the end, to break through metaphorical barriers, momentarily transforming and reconstituting a real action into an emblem projected as its inner reality. That process expresses, in the strange intensity with which it builds its emblematic reality out of a real action, as in Richard's action of descending from Flint Castle, an extraordinary impulse to visionary realization. In this it extends to great sophistication Richard's general effort, more basic instances of which can be cited in his manipulation of the language and action of Northumberland and Bolingbroke throughout the central scenes, to bend the external world to literally reflect his inner, imaginative vision. Richard's manipulation of language and action in these scenes—his own and that of Bolingbroke and Northumberland, constitutes his imaginative effort to bend *all* outward manifestations to reflect, represent, and ultimately materialize as vision the imaginative reality of deposition with which he, Richard, has identified inwardly.[24]

One example of this is what he does with Northumberland's curtsey to him in III.iii when Northumberland returns from Bolingbroke after delivering Richard's salutations to the Duke, a gesture that Richard uses to confirm, by a pointed wrenching of Northumberland's action to suit the context of Richard's own address, his insinuation that it is Bolingbroke who is now effectively King:

> *What says King Bolingbroke? Will his Majesty*
> *Give Richard leave to live till Richard die?*
> *You make a leg, and Bolingbroke says "ay".*
> *(III.iii.173-175)*

Later, when Bolingbroke presents himself on his knees after Richard has descended from Flint Castle, the latter uses the opportunity to turn Bolingbroke's action dramatically against him, by an undeniably powerful accusation of hypocrisy in a passage that strikes a key-note in the interpretation of the action:

> *Fair cousin, you debase your princely knee*
> *To make the base earth proud with kissing it.*
> *Me rather had my heart might feel your love*
> *Than my unpleas'd eye see your courtesy.*
> *Up, cousin, up; your heart is up, I know,*
> [Touches his head.]
> *Thus high at least, although your knee be low.*
> *(III.iii.190-195)*

In Richard's manipulation of Bolingbroke's gesture, the duality between inward and outward reality is a fact explicitly invoked to stress the inward reality that belies the outward manifestation. Yet, though the duality may be powerfully pressed and though the inward reality is made as dramatically present by Richard's projection as could be, we are only left the more aware of that duality's essential intractability for the singular forcefulness of the effort to resolve it. In spite of this, Richard's efforts to bridge the inner and the outer worlds show, as a rule, a deliberate insistence on breaking through this barrier. Indeed, as here, Richard tries on the whole to squeeze the inward reality into visible existence, attempting to project his inward knowledge directly onto the structure of the external action, onto those words and gestures—the rebels' and his own—that present themselves immediately to his imagination. In Richard's manipulation of Northumberland's curtsey as presented above, Northumberland's action is so ingeniously and forcefully twisted, for a moment it is through Richard's mind and imagination that we view and interpret it, and so essentially with Richard's twisting of the *language* of the rebels, with its consequent transformational effect on the visible state of events in the world: of Bolingbroke's "mine own" and "deserve" in III.iii (ll.196-201), of his "fair cousin" and "convey" in IV.i (ll.304-318), and of Northumberland's "base court" and "come down" in III.iii (ll.176-183).

Richard's manipulation particularly of Northumberland's words—"base court" and "come down"—which issues in his "Down, down I come, like glist'ring Phaeton" passage, and his manipulation also of Bolingbroke's "convey" (IV.i.316)—"O good! Convey! Conveyers are you all"—bear further singling out for the peculiarly clamorous manner with which Richard projects his imaginative view of reality, a feature that connects these instances with his ironically-spoken, vociferous declamation of "God save the King" on appearing to depose himself in IV.i. This complex effort ought to be referred to a tendency of Richard's, in the opening moments of the deposition-scene, to build up key words by carefully controlled repetition so that the single word is ultimately pressed to stand for the full reality it boldly projects:

> *Drinking my griefs, whilst you mount up on high.*
>
> Bol. *I thought you had been willing to resign.*
>
> Richard. *My crown I am; but still my griefs are mine.*
> *You may my glories and my state depose,*
> *But not my griefs; still am I king of those.*
>
> *(IV.i.189-193)*

The power of such forceful repetition depends on the projection of a complete identification of speech and reality, so that when Richard speaks of his "griefs" he literally represents them, just as when he cries "God save the King" and "amen", it is in a literal sense that the state of affairs he speaks of is confirmed and sealed. And so with Richard's effort with "down".

In these instances, one may feel that Richard's effort to shape the external action in accordance with his imaginative view of reality has degenerated into plain verbal violence and emerged as a kind of emotional shouting. But does what is in fact an effect of desperation demonstrate Richard's essential attitudinizing and thinness of inward experience? I do no think so. Richard's blurring of aural and emotional intensity, like his partially distorting imaginative re-structuring and re-interpretation of the visible action in general, expresses nothing less than his frustrated impulse to compel the visionary materialization of his experience. This impulse is motivated, as I have suggested, by a real need in the face of a deliberately skeptical and materialistic court, for whom metaphysical realities no longer hold credit, to amaze, with a full materialization, the very faculties of eyes and ears—the blurring in Richard's effort to this end only going to show the difficult basis of a projection of rhetoric in reality.

We may also consider Richard's extremely elaborate talk of "cares" in this scene, which returns us to his complex, ambivalent perspective on Kingship's reality, to the whole "substance" of his experience, which is his complex struggle with the determination of reality:

> Bol. *Part of your cares you give me with the crown.*
>
> Rich. *Your cares set up do not pluck my cares down.*
> *My care is loss of care, by old care done;*
> *Your care is gain of care, by new care won.*
> *The cares I give I have, though given away;*
> *They tend the crown, yet still with me they stay.*
>
> *(IV.i.194-199)*

A paraphrase of this extremely suggestive speech will serve as a convenient reference point for a summary of Richard's position: '*My* care or grief is the loss of the office of kingship by the care I have caused through my irresponsibility as a king, understanding that the violence with which I have lost the kingship has been grossly disproportionate to and largely unconnected with the nature of my crimes and is rather the doing of your rebellion. On the other hand, *your* care or grief is and shall be the gain of such an office as you have been burdened with as a result of your rebellion against a rightful king who is deeply grieved and resentful because of it, and whose grief and resentment reflect the gravity of your crimes. Thus the cares I give you, the cares I am compelled to give you but whose mockery at the same time I am glad to curse you with, and which consist of the office of kingship that entails for you the consequences of my action as king but above all the consequences of your rebellion—these cares I give I have, first in the form of regret and remorse for my own actions as a king, which I am the more crushingly aware of now that I see beyond the mockery power of being a king to the full reality of my kingship, which I must comprehend by going to my death. But hear of what I also know: that all this has entailed my violent separation from the kingship as the result of your blasphemy and rebellion, which ought never to have been. And therefore these cares "tend the crown"—they have all to do with the office of kingship that you now inherit; "yet still with me they stay"—they "stay" because, whatever power you may wield for now as a result of your rebellion, my descent into death puts me, and not you, in touch with what my kingship and your rebellion have really signified, though I go with an utter grief that I cannot prove these matters to you now but must first embrace my death in order to prove them.'

The essential, ambivalent perspective Richard brings to bear on the determination of kingship's reality is further reflected in his climactic action of self-deposition. That Richard intends his audience to attend closely to the manner and form of his self-deposition is evident from the solicitation with which he precedes his action:

> *Nay, mark me how I will undo myself.*
> *(IV.i.203)*

Ever since Pater first called attention to this matter, the invertedness of Richard's rite has been repeatedly dwelt upon in commentaries on the speech, and there can be no doubt that it is to this that Richard wishes to direct the rebels' attention. There can be doubt, too, that what emerges from this inversion is a spectacle of pure degradation, one further reinforced by the explicitly adverse image of the kingship Richard projects immediately before the actual deposition, where he dramatically juxtaposes the unmanageable burden and unreliable power of kingship with the false (and deluded) sense of pride with which it infects those holding sway:

> *I give this heavy weight from off my head,*
> *And this unwieldy sceptre from my hand,*
> *The pride of kingly sway from out my heart;*
> *With mine own tears I wash away my balm,*

> *With mine own hands I give away my crown,*
> *With mine own tongue deny my sacred state,*
> *With mine own breath release all duteous oaths;*
> *All pomp and majesty I do forswear;*
> *My manors, rents, revenues I forgo;*
> *My acts, decrees, and statutes, I deny.*
> *God pardon all oaths that are broke to me!*
> *God keep all vows unbroke are made to thee!*
>
> (IV.i.204-215)

But the degradation is not, as Pater seems to have assumed, principally self-directed; it is, in essence, ironic, a travesty and mockery (whatever the personal overtones and implications for Richard may be) of the office of kingship itself, expressing Richard's personally-tested sense and vision of its limits and lost meaning. Yet to note this is still to note only half of the gesture's complex irony. As inverted rite, Richard's self-deposition, his renunciation of the office of king, exists as a violent denial of the whole concept and meaning of kingship. But, taken *as* inverted rite, this self-deposition is strictly-speaking no rite at all, and thus no genuine self-deposition: the denial of state and the releasing of oaths are proclaimed by a king speaking out of office, whether actually deposed or ironically denying deposition is left (seemingly purposefully) ambiguous. The point is that in the very moment he is making his iconoclastic gesture, Richard is elaborately preserving his status as King by securing for himself the continued allegiance of his subjects.

What Richard thus manages to achieve through the invertedness of his rite is a gesture of unprecedentedly concentrated ambiguity, expressing simultaneously both aspects of his essential ambivalence—his disillusionment over kingship's lost meaning, and his grief over its loss manifested here as a continuing attachment to the office. Significantly, it is at this point that Richard's emphasis gives way, at the point at which Northumberland presses him to confess to his crimes, to a perfectly unveiled, intensely passionate accusation of treachery and rebellion, the justness of which would appear to be undeniable:

> *Gentle Northumberland*
> *If thy offenses were upon record,*
> *Would it not shame thee in so fair a troop*
> *To read a lecture of them? If thou wouldst,*

> *There shouldst thou find one heinous article,*
> *Containing the deposing of a king*
> *And cracking the strong warrant of an oath,*
> *Mark'd with a blot, damn'd in the book of heaven.*
> *Nay, all of you that stand and look upon me*
> *Whilst that my wretchedness doth bait myself,*
> *Though some of you, with Pilate, wash your hands,*
> *Showing an outward pity—yet you Pilates*
> *Have here deliver'd me to my sour cross,*
> *And water cannot wash away your sin.*
>
> *(IV.i.229-242)*

It is at this point in the play that Richard's creative drive as I have outlined it is referred back to the imaginative order from which it ultimately takes its inspiration. It is here that the conflicting claims of outrageous Rebellion and necessary Death meet: in Richard's Passion, seen here as an aspect of the Passion of Christ, Who, like Richard, though in an even more immediate sense, embodied in Himself the whole order of Eternity, that order that has once again been flouted in Richard's England, and which stands ultimately to be re-asserted, but whose Judgment must wait, as it did with Christ, upon Richard's immediate confrontation with Death. The allusion to Christ brings to Richard's imaginative claims, in fact, the full authority of the *O vos omnes* lament, but with this significant difference, that whereas Judgment was within Christ's immediate vision as God and actually within His power to command—a power that Christ did not use—the implication is that Richard would not shrink from acting on this vision himself were it within his own grasp—hence his wretchedness in all *its* terrible poignancy.[25]

Richard's insistence on his identification with Christ brings to what seems like its determined conclusion the full metaphysical significance of his status as God's majesty in whom the hand of God is at work: the power of vision must wait on death; that is what seems like the reality. However, the effect of Richard's insistence in context is to bring out a more immediate aspect of the reality. For, imaginatively transparent as his Passion may be here, it may still be felt to draw on metaphysical implications difficult to grasp, implications for the moment obscured, even contradicted by the evidence of the real world. The further irony of the matter is that neither Northumberland nor Bolingbroke is prepared to believe a word of what Richard claims for himself: as with Richard's earlier speech of defiant condemnation from the walls of Flint Castle, this one too is quite pathetically ignored and diverted by Northumberland:

> *My lord, dispatch; read o'er these articles.*
>
> *(IV.i.243)*

And it is in consequence of such an attitude pressing on him, pointing to conclusions other than those he has projected, that Richard is further driven to an intensely suggestive, rhetorical manipulation of language and action, not (as commentators have claimed) from a futile sentimentalism, but from the complex visionary need, the more complex for being felt as immediate pressure, to reconcile his inward experience of imaginative reality with the outward evidence of the real world.

A further result is Richard's complexly ambiguous, rhetorical manipulation of gesture in the mirror-smashing episode that follows only a little later. In the immediate context of the passage, Richard's gesture expresses primarily his sense of the duality between inner and outer reality, a gap with which, as we have seen, he is concerned all along, and which he now explicitly associates with the experience of an inward grief that fails deceptively to be recorded in his outward appearance:

> *No deeper wrinkles yet? Hath sorrow struck*
> *So many blows upon this face of mine*
> *And made no deeper wounds? O flatt'ring glass,*
> *Like to my followers in prosperity,*
> *Thou dost beguile me!*
>
> *(IV.i.277-281)*

The concern with duality expressed in the first part of this speech is emphatic; and it is in this context that we are asked to view Richard's subsequent self-dramatization, which functions explicitly as the projection of a complex act of inward realization:

> *A brittle glory shineth in this face;*
> *As brittle as the glory is the face;*

[Dashes the glass against the ground.]

> **For there it is**, *crack'd in a hundred shivers.*
> *Mark, silent king, the moral of this sport—*
> *How soon my sorrow hath destroy'd my face.*
>
> *(IV.i.287–291)*

There is no need to belabor further an interpretive scheme that has become obvious—that Richard's destruction of the royal face emblematizes his compulsive disillusionment over the lost meaning of kingship. Richard's action has also been seen, however, to emblematize the destruction of the self. E.H. Kantorowicz, for example, has interpreted the gesture to mean that Richard is now reduced "to the banal face and insignificant *physis* of a miserable man, a *physis* now void of any *metaphysis* whatsoever".[26] Peter Ure, taking a quite different view about the meaning of the face (it is for him the royal face that flatters Richard about his actual condition), has argued that the gesture means that Richard is left without a sense of self because he had formerly identified himself exclusively with the title of kingship that he has now given away.[27] Both views overlook the crucial fact that Richard's moral is but "sport", or, as Kenneth Muir has put it somewhat bluntly, "that Richard is putting on an act".[28] This is not to say that the "sport" is not without a 'moral', that Richard's gesture is not to some degree genuine. But it does cast a decidedly ambiguous light on his intentions. The gesture, it appears, is meant to be taken seriously; at the same time, it is qualified to the point of denying itself altogether. What Shakespeare intended by giving Richard this gesture can only be understood in the light of the inner ambivalence the latter has demonstrated throughout the period of his crisis. Richard, that is, does positively will his destruction as king, because of the flattering deception and meaninglessness that he has now come to see the office of kingship to be. But his insistent grief over its loss and continuing attachment to the ideal of kingship will not allow him to surrender himself whole-heartedly to this standpoint: hence the quality of pretense and self-consciousness about the gesture.

After Richard's marvelously ambiguous smashing of the looking-glass and of the royal face reflected in it, Bolingbroke is moved to the telling remark that Richard's symbolic gesture is unreal, that what Richard takes to be his sorrow and his face are in fact only shadows or reflections of the real things, and that therefore the visionary experience they are presumed to represent between them has not been demonstrated and is without actual substance:

> *The shadow of your sorrow hath destroy'd*
> *The shadow of your face.*
>
> (IV.i.292-293)

Cryptic as it may appear, Bolingbroke's remark is yet revealing of the nature of his world-view, because, although his remark implies the existence of a real 'substance' that these "shadows" only reflect (and it is on this feature of the remark that Richard will promptly seize, to twist Bolingbroke's actual meaning), Bolingbroke's focus falls entirely on the *un*reality of Richard's insinuation, implying that as the outward gesture is only derivative, the visionary experience it is said to represent should also be said to be unreal. This is not to say that Bolingbroke denies the existence of sorrow, any more than he is prepared to deny the existence of a face. But his denial of the ideal, metaphysical implications Richard claims to be attached to his sorrow makes clear that, as with Northumberland with Richard before the walls of Flint Castle and elsewhere in the deposition-scene, Bolingbroke assumes and acts upon an essentially naturalistic world-view. In this view the only reality that can command immediate and unconditional assent is the actual evidence of the world, which cannot support the implications Richard claims.

Richard responds to this position by bypassing Bolingbroke's meaning, using the implicit quibble in the word "shadow" to counteract the imposed naturalism with a triumphant insistence on the reality of the inner "substance" which the "shadows" of Richard's gestures have so far only reflected:

> *The shadow of my sorrow? Ha! let's see.*
> *'Tis very true: my grief lies all within;*
> *And these external manner of laments*
> *Are merely shadows to the unseen grief*
> *That swells with silence in the tortur'd soul.*
> *There lies the substance; and I thank thee, king,*
> *For thy great bounty, that not only giv'st*
> *Me cause to wail, but teachest me the way*
> *How to lament the cause.*
>
> (IV.i.293-302)

Richard's triumph in this passage consists not only in convincingly insisting that his inner experience is a substantial one, but in emphasizing that all the outward manifestations of his sorrow with which he has beleaguered Bolingbroke since they have met are only shadows of the intensity of the real thing, which is "the unseen grief", the ambivalent grief over the loss and lost meaning of kingship that are intrinsically linked to the implications of Death and Judgment in Eternity. All along during these scenes, it has been Richard's strategy to deprive Bolingbroke of the easy political victory he seeks by confronting him with his (Richard's) grief as a reflection of the enormity and the vanity of Bolingbroke's crime; and here Richard concludes the strategy by hinting at even larger and greater reserves of metaphysical violence waiting upon Bolingbroke's crime than what Richard's outward gestures have managed to reflect. In doing so, Richard formally abandons the creative drive that has shown him, until now, absorbed in the revealing powers of rhetorical projection. We are told now of another imaginative course of action as immediately obscure as the faith placed in it seems theoretical and uncertain. What it is isn't made clear until Richard's talk of "winning" "a new world's crown" (V.i.24) in the next scene, when it becomes clear that he has now placed his faith in the Judgment of the next world, and that as an expression of that faith, future efforts will lie in an imaginative absorption in that world. It is "there", it is assumed, that Rebellion will finally be avenged and Death overcome, through a faith that sees in Death the restoration of Richard as King.

Richard's triumph, in other words, is not simply political in the sense that he has consistently held his own against Bolingbroke's effort to secure an unsuspicious transfer of power, but above all a triumph of faith in which the political battle is ultimately subsumed, and on which level Richard believes himself to be the final victor. But attached to this double triumph of Richard's is a striking pathos, for implied in this triumphant insistence on the reality and final validity of his imaginative existence is the open confession that all his outward manifestations of sorrow throughout his confrontation with Bolingbroke *have* been inadequate. As a climactic expression of Richard's self-representational concerns, the speech concludes with the pathetic recognition that all his efforts towards an absolute manifestation of his inward grief have fallen short of their effect and that this has been so because of that immoveable condition of duality that finally keeps the sensible and the supersensible worlds firmly distinct.

Reviewing the whole range of Richard's self-representational efforts in these scenes, it is not surprising that he should be led to this conclusion, for although many of these show considerable scope and forcefulness and constitute all-in-all an admirably heroic stab at the problem, there runs persistently throughout these efforts an underlying stress (often explicitly acknowledged) on the pathetic folly associated with the very attempt at a visionary materialization of imaginative experience. This is reflected in the curious aberrations into which Richard is led as a result of trying to achieve what appears to be strictly-speaking simply unachievable. I have in mind, for example, his effort in the speech to Scroope in III.ii to arrive at an imaginative experience strictly through the tensions of aural form, or the gross deficiency of his efforts, observable throughout the confrontation with Bolingbroke and Northumberland, though most memorable as Richard descends from the walls of Flint Castle, to project an aural for an emotional intensity, a variant of which can be noted in the obscuring of emotional by physical intensity when Richard dashes the looking-glass to the ground in the deposition-scene.

Apart from this, the underlying stress on the pathos of Richard's effort is reflected on those several occasions in these scenes in which he is simply forced to stop short of the metaphysical barrier separating sensible actuality from imaginative reality, notably when he is first met by Bolingbroke under Flint Castle where Richard is pressed to establish the inward purpose and imaginative implications of Bolingbroke's return to England, to be checked and foiled by the gap between these and the outward evidence of allegiance; or again, when Richard peers into the looking-glass on the verge of his farewell gesture to Bolingbroke, towards the end of the deposition-scene, to contemplate the gap between the evidence of the royal face in the glass and the actual content and implications of his inner experience. But it is notable too in between these points, even while Richard is engaged in his most elaborate imaginative efforts to bridge the gap, as in the "seize the crown" emblem, where it is reflected in the form of a highly suggestive emphasis on the "unseen" griefs which continue to rankle in him beyond his ability to bring them to full expression; or finally, in the "cares I give I have" wordplay, in that trenchantly unaccepting tone that suggests positive bitterness about the limitations placed upon him in being unable to make his grief more evident ("yet still with me they stay").

Yet pathetic as Richard's efforts may be, never (not even in the "unseen grief" speech where he appears to be confessing defeat) is the urgency of his imaginative impulse for a moment seen to abate, or the imaginative quest that it serves ever assumed to be futile or other than simply necessary. The need to achieve the unachievable remains, and the result in the end are some extraordinary self-representational efforts, the most impressive of these being the four major efforts in the deposition-scene: the "cares I give I have" wordplay, the "seize the crown" emblem, and the self-deposing and mirror-smashing gestures. These four, as the product and consequence of an expressive imperative that Richard never ceases to feel, and to which he clings with a kind of imaginative perversity, emerge eventually by sheer dint of imaginative ingenuity; and what makes them extraordinary is not simply the scope of their reference or the forcefulness of their conviction but especially their status and power as efforts at the visionary concentration of Richard's unseen grief as this bears on the metaphysical implications of Death and Judgment. It is as perversions from this final end, and not as hollow eccentricities that we are ultimately asked to view the imaginative aberrations that I have noted among Richard's other efforts. It is on the basis, moreover, of the imaginative output that these major efforts represent towards this end, and not, simply, on the pathos explicitly associated in the play with an end of this kind, that we must ultimately assess the merits of Richard's imaginative intentions.

Moreover, I have said that this effort is an ongoing one. Thus, despite the confession about the inadequacy of his previous efforts at an absolute manifestation of his inward grief, Richard continues to feel the impulse to bridge sensible and imaginative worlds even when he leaves the court at the end of the deposition-scene. Indeed, his very last gesture in the scene spoken after this confession—"O good! Convey! Conveyors are you all"—is yet another piece of emotional shouting by which he endeavors to project onto the visible structure of the action the imputation that Bolingbroke and his party are nothing but thieves. It would appear in fact that Richard's determination to surrender himself to his "unseen grief" and to his faith in the unseen Judgment of the next world which he assumes this represents, implies not passive expectation but an active process of discovery, a determination to unite himself actively with the Judgment of the next world. And it may be that the assumption on which Richard plans to act in the future involves devoting himself exclusively to deepening his imaginative experience, quite apart from the additional need to refer this to the world. Yet in the light of his actions up to this point (and in the light of those to come), it seems likely that we are dealing with a more immediate imaginative aim: a desire to unite himself to the Judgment of the next world immediately—in himself, and in the present moment. One thing, at any rate, can be said with some assurance: that Richard's determination to evolve and deepen his imaginative grasp on his suffering as he leaves the court is as genuinely expectant as the nature of the grasp he expects is uncertain. Once this is admitted, it will be seen that the conclusion put forward by Virgil Whitaker that Richard is no tragic hero because he fails to "develop", or "respond to his suffering in any fundamental way"[29], pales before a far subtler and profounder dramatic point of view.

IV

CONCLUSION

However, when we encounter Richard again in Pomfret Castle several scenes later, to find that he is almost literally brooding over his isolation, it is evident that his resolution has bred poor results. From the claim to imaginative reality that he had made on leaving Bolingbroke in the deposition-scene, from the faith he had so triumphantly expressed in himself and in the finality of his imaginative existence, we would expect to find Richard in future in an attitude of intense *inward* exploration. Instead we find that for some time now he has been preoccupied rather with his inveterate need to refer himself *back* to the external world, betraying in this an impulse intimately connected with the experience of imaginative waste that his isolation has come to mean for him. By Richard's account his imaginative failure stems from the issuelessness of faith, from the fruitlessness of penury, and human powerlessness in "thoughts of things divine" (V.v.34;11-17). As the considerations of futile defiance and subjection had led him, at the outset of his crisis, to the fruitless thought of renunciation, so here the fruitlessness of a renunciation more fully grasped yet impossibly conceived brings Richard back again to the idea that defiance is sterile (ll.18-22), likewise to the unshakeable knowledge of shame in subjection (ll.23-30), and also now to a condition of final despair presented as the upshot of a fundamental failure in the nature of reality itself (ll.32-41):

> *Sometimes am I king*
> *Then treasons make me wish myself a beggar,*
> *And so I am. Then crushing penury*

Persuades me I was better when a king;
Then am I king'd again; and by and by
Think that I am unking'd by Bolingbroke,
And straight am nothing. But whate'er I be,
Nor I, nor any man that but man is,
With nothing shall be pleas'd till he be eas'd
With being nothing.

(*V.v.32–41*)

It is at this point that one must challenge Michael Quinn's seminal remarks concerning the perversity of Richard's emotional designs, which, in his view, demonstrate "Richard's increasing isolation from the social foundations on which true personality must apparently be built":

And this inclination to believe that ideas carry more weight than actions, that imagination has the power to change the nature of reality, expresses itself in a submergence in the passion of grief and derives from his isolation from his social context.[30]

Quinn's account of the implications of Richard's *aims* in the play seems to me just, but his viewpoint on the facts finally inadequate, and it raises a further issue regarding Shakespeare's presentation. It would be foolish to pretend from Richard's critical account of his designs in his monologue, and from the restoration of his personality in the end once he determines to have done with these designs and to address himself again to the world, that on one level Richard has not displayed imaginative hubris in pursuing his aims and beliefs in the extreme form in which he has conceived of them; that on one level, it should have been clear to him that for any man that is *but man*, to aspire, as Richard has done, to experiencing an imaginative resolution of events immediately, in his own person, is to confound the nature of a Power that operates rather through time and the interaction of character and destiny, precisely of the kind Richard and Exton themselves act out at the end of this scene. Still, Shakespeare's presentation of this Power is viewed on another level, and *has been viewed for the most part*, in the light of an impulse deemed *more fully* worthy of Richard, one that, so far from being seen as an imaginative distortion following from social isolation, is conveyed as a proper idealization of the imaginative power a man might have expected of himself *as King*. To the question posed by the play throughout the course of Richard's crisis—what imaginative powers adhere to the King as a man?—it is to this that we are led: what the ongoing expectation of an immediate Judgment brings Richard to is not so much a sense of the perversity of his designs as the drastic consciousness of visionary impasse, presented in the context of a profound insight into a fundamental failure in the nature of reality itself.

What follows after the monologue possesses thus a pathetic rather than a strictly moral significance. The pattern of will and fate that between them Richard and Exton enact at the end of the scene, by which the events of the play are finally resolved, exists and is presented fundamentally as a substitute for a more direct manifestation of Judgment. Ironically, surrounding Richard's gradual awakening into shame and rebellious anger over the futility of his designs is his imminent murder by Exton. Bolingbroke has expressed his irresistible need for this murder. Thus contrary to Richard's assumption in his monologue that his recourse to imaginative faith has had no effect on things, this shows the direct, imaginative influence on Bolingbroke that Richard's self-withdrawal in fact has had. Richard's eventual resistance to the way of faith, which itself arises out of his sense of an imaginative impotence that has turned the way of faith into the way of folly and spiritual waste, and which thus represents for him an imaginative failure on the level of character, coincides ironically with the imaginative effectiveness on *another* level of Richard's strategic surrender to faith, which now brings on his murder. What Richard and Exton act out is now projected by Richard as being precisely the resolution of the political situation he had anticipated from the first, but the realization of which he had inevitably wished to control by means of his own visionary power as God's deputy. It is a form of resolution that serves here as a *lesser* victory. It is the projected resolution of Richard's experience at least in this sense: that the murder of Richard, by spilling the King's blood, sets the seal on the damnableness of Bolingbroke's rebellion, at the same time as it constitutes for Richard the anticipation of his full and final validation as King in the otherworld:

> *That hand shall burn in never-quenching fire*
> *That staggers thus my person. Exton, thy fierce hand*
> *Hath with the King's blood stain'd the King's own land.*
>
> *Mount, mount, my soul! thy seat is up on high;*
> *Whilst my gross flesh sinks downward, here to die.*
>
> *(V.v.108–112)*

III

9

Othello's "Sacrifice" as Dialectic of Faith

*It is great to give up what one wishes, but greater to hold
fast to it after having given it up.*

*Should one perhaps not dare to speak about Abraham? I
think one should. If I myself were to talk about him, I would
first depict the pain of the trial.*

What is left out of the Abraham story is the anguish.

*Let us now have the knight make his appearance . . . he
infinitely renounces the claim to the love which is the
content of his life; he is reconciled in pain; but then comes the
marvel, he makes one more movement, more wonderful than
anything else, for he says, "I nevertheless believe that I shall
get her, namely on the strength of the absurd".*
Kierkegaard, Fear and Trembling[1]

The whole thrust and direction of the speech by Othello that opens
the fatal bedchamber scene from Act V brings Othello by degrees into a
relation to Desdemona diametrically opposite to that envisaged of him in
the following comment on the scene:

*She has become the symbol of the irrationality that corrupts
the world of his ideal . . .*[2]

Expressed in this comment is the view of Desdemona which Othello
elaborates rather in the second scene of Act IV, where, Othello, in
terms strikingly reminiscent of Hamlet with Gertrude, carries on about
Desdemona as a "strumpet". That view accounts, no doubt, for Othello's
ultimate decision to kill Desdemona, but it is now directly contradicted by
the whole spirit and thrust of Othello's approach in the later scene, where
it is precisely the case that Desdemona revives for him in all her ideality:

It is the cause, it is the cause, my soul.
Let me not name it to you, you chaste stars:
It is the cause. Yet I'll not shed her blood,
Nor scar that whiter skin of hers than snow
And smooth, as monumental alabaster.
Yet she must die, else she'll betray more men.
Put out the light, and then put out the light!
If I quench thee, thou flaming minister,
I can again thy former light restore,
Should I repent me. But once put out thy light,   [10]
Thou cunning'st pattern of excelling nature,
I know not where is that Promethean heat
That can thy light relume: when I have plucked the rose,
I cannot give it vital growth again,
It needs must wither. I'll smell thee on the tree;
O balmy breath, that doth almost persuade
Justice to break her sword! Once more, once more: [He kisses her.]
Be thus, when thou art dead, and I will kill thee,
And love thee after. Once more, and that's the last,
So sweet was ne'er so fatal. I must weep,
But they are cruel tears; this sorrow's heavenly,
It strikes where it does love. She wakes.

It would appear, indeed, that just *because* his decision to kill Desdemona has become irreversible and absolute, Othello cannot now stop himself from again valuing her with that characteristic total immediacy and completeness with which he had always valued her, before he began to see her differently. In fact, it would appear that any view of Othello's role which sees him in his resolution to kill Desdemona as ultimately separate from her in any sense, however favorably we may conceive of that relationship, is bound to distort the dreadful pathos of the tragedy—whether we think of Othello in "the role of a god who chastises where he loves," or "of a priest who must present a perfect victim".[3] We must rather think of Othello as disposed to killing Desdemona, paradoxically, in tragically sublime identification with her life. *That* identification, reinforced as it is by his sensuous kissing of Desdemona three times, involves Othello ultimately in an absolutely tremendous intensification of anguish that, in the philosophical sense, we must term absurd, since it has no reasonable limit whatsoever. For at a certain point, Othello goes so far as to say, or desire to say, right *through* the resolution to kill Desdemona, which remains unshakeable, "I nevertheless believe that I shall get her":

> *Be thus, when thou art dead, and I will kill thee,*
> *And love thee after.*

We may well feel that all Othello is expressing here is an intense form of wish-fulfilment, basing his desire on the familiar conceit, suddenly given a spectacular poignancy and relevance in context, of sleep as the counterfeit of death, that he is not really thinking this thought through and could not begin to believe what he says. Othello is, of course, only too aware in this speech of the absolute finality of death, and thus of the incommensurability of death and sleep. But to say that he is only aware of this truth, or that it is something he simply accepts, is to fail to enter into the drama, to see what it must mean for Othello to have to deal death to Desdemona as he has known her. The intention attributed to Othello of seeking Desdemona's death "to save her from herself, to restore meaning to her beauty"[4] grossly ignores the fact that, for Othello, Desdemona dead is meaningless. Othello's anguish is the more insufferable, especially now that his love for Desdemona has once again been freed, just because the resolution to put her to death *settles* the problem of her "guilt". Condemned to death, Desdemona has now ceased to be guilty, and the further issue arises: 'how is Desdemona's death to be reconciled with that characteristically complete and immediate love that is now once again freed in Othello, a love by nature entirely bound up with Desdemona's life?' It is from this more evolved and transformed point of view that we finally enter, in imagination, into the dreadfulness of what Othello 'must' do, suddenly struck by the likeness of Othello's case to that of the sublime-pathetic figure of Abraham, especially as Kierkegaard interprets him for us:

> *If one hasn't the courage to think this thought through, to*
> *say that Abraham was a murderer, then surely it is better*
> *to acquire that courage than to waste time on undeserved*
> *speeches in his praise . . . We let Isaac actually be sacrificed.*
> *Abraham had faith. His faith was not that he should be*
> *happy sometime in the hereafter, but that he should find*
> *blessed happiness here in this world. God could give him a*
> *new Isaac, bring the sacrificial offer back to life. He believed*
> *on the strength of the absurd, for all calculation had long*
> *since been suspended. That sorrow can make one demented*

> *may be granted and is hard enough; that there is a strength*
> *of will that hauls close enough to the wind to save the*
> *understanding, even if the strain turns one slightly odd, that*
> *too may be granted. I don't mean to decry that. But to be*
> *able to lose one's understanding and with it the whole of the*
> *finite world whose stockbroker it is, and then on the strength*
> *of the absurd get exactly the same finitude back again, that*
> *leaves me aghast. But I don't say on that account that it is of*
> *little worth; on the contrary it is the one and only marvel. It*
> *is commonly supposed that what faith produces is no work of*
> *art but a crude and vulgar effort only for clumsier natures,*
> *yet the truth is quite otherwise. The dialectic of faith is the*
> *most refined and most remarkable of all dialectics, it has an*
> *elevation that I can form a conception of but no more.*[5]

It was Kierkegaard's mockingly triumphant view that the sublime dialectic of faith he had hit upon in the case of Abraham was the only dilemma Shakespeare had never ventured to speak about:

> *Thanks to you, great Shakespeare! You who can say*
> *everything, everything, everything exactly as it is—and yet*
> *why was this torment one you never gave voice to?*[6]

Yet here for once, Kierkegaard's judgment would seem to have proved wrong, for this dialectic would seem to be precisely the one Shakespeare glances at in *Othello*. Faced, on a new, transformed level, with the absolutely contradictory claims of death and life, Othello inherits a dilemma and an anguish that could only be resolved ultimately in the manner of Abraham with whom Othello appears to be conceptually linked:

> *The moment the knight resigned he was convinced of the*
> *impossibility, humanly speaking; that was a conclusion of*
> *the understanding, and he had energy enough to think it ...*
> *but ... On this the knight is just as clear: all that can save*
> *him is the absurd; and this he grasps by faith. Accordingly*
> *he admits the impossibility and at the same time believes*
> *the absurd; for were he to suppose that he had faith without*
> *recognizing the impossibility with all the passion of his soul*
> *and with all his heart, he would be deceiving himself, and*

his testimony would carry weight nowhere, since he would
not even have come as far as infinite resignation.[7]

The sudden emergence of the Abraham-conception from the midst of Othello's tragic experience will be conditioned, of course, by our knowledge of the tragic irony of Othello's case; and it will remain to decide Othello's actual relation to this suddenly invoked likeness. But certainly we could hardly imagine a potentially more dramatic *coup de theatre*. An invocation of the possibility of a turn of events such as that associated with the Abraham story would seem to be a measure of the power of re-awakened love that is now developing in Othello. Of course, there could be no question in the world of *Othello* of a direct intervention from heaven. But this circumstance would almost seem to cast the audience itself in the role of the angel of the Abraham story, the Abraham-conception appealing, as it does, to the condition we have borne throughout the play of hovering over these thwarted lovers with our superior knowledge. That we know we would not intervene could only heighten the psychological intensity of Othello's anguish for us; and that heightening, paradoxically, draws us into a still more immediate relation to the hope of an ultimate resolution, breeding in us a feeling that perhaps something might yet come to pass to interrupt the course of events, as Desdemona suddenly awakes from sleep and death.

It is an illuminating experience, if initially a somewhat oblique one, to look back over Othello's speech and except for the fact that Othello would kill Desdemona because he thinks she is guilty, except that is, for the one line (6) in which the fact is recorded, except also for the early reference to "chaste", to see Othello as Abraham. Simply on the basis of that extraordinary note of sublime elevation sounded at the beginning, the Othello of the opening could hardly be thought unworthy of the comparison:

It is the cause, it is the cause, my soul . . .

The idea of a Promethean re-kindling of life (in 1.12), which arises so naturally in this sublime context, would be also out of place, grandly expressive as *it* is of Counter-Renaissance "metaphysical ache" or the denial of limit.[8] But, however small, there are those intensely poetic touches—of "rose" and "tree"—that might well suggest the symbolic Biblical landscape of the Abraham story, containing in themselves as well that typological foreshadowing of Christ with whom, in line with Renaissance exegesis of the Bible, it would be only too easy to associate Isaac and Desdemona in their innocence. Even the possibility of comparison with the Abraham-Isaac story on a sensuous plane is an experience for which an Elizabethan audience would have had an immediate precedent. They would have been adequately prepared for that experience in the Brome representation of the sacrifice from among the great Mystery Plays that had, not so long before, been a current feature of the popular life. What this wonderfully humanized and in its own way intensely moving version would certainly have brought to the forefront in popular imagination of this story was a feeling for the pathos and the cost of the sacrifice, accentuated by Abraham's kissing Isaac clearly in the terms of sensuous life:

> *A, Isaac, Isaac, up thow stond,*
> *Thy fayere swete mowthe that I may kis.*

> *A, Isaac, my owyn swete child,*
> *Yit kisse me agen upon this hill!!*[9]

Then there are the lines, to which I have given some attention, that clinch the comparison on the level of the story's dialectic:

> *Be thus, when thou art dead, and I will kill thee*
> *And love thee after.*

And as we absorb the end of Othello's speech, the likeness to what might have inspired Abraham's own feeling would seem to present no difficulty at all:

> *So sweet was ne'er so fatal; I must weep,*
> *But they are cruel tears; this sorrow's heavenly,*
> *It strikes where it does love.*

A case might indeed be made for Shakespeare's having perhaps deliberately woven the Abraham-conception into Othello's situation, as an inevitable and irresistible development of the sublime pitch and direction of Othello's address to the sleeping Desdemona. What the implied likeness would seem to signify in the end (to draw on Kierkegaard's own terms) is a transcendental "movement" of the spirit that appeals directly to the unhappy sense we have of the inevitability of Desdemona's death at this late point in the drama. Desdemona will die, but the hope continues that she will live in spite of this. This is the implicit, subtextual import to the intention, well-noted of Othello in this scene, of sublime "sacrifice". However, when Desdemona awakes eventually to deny any share of guilt, the tenuous framework of her recovered innocence on which Othello has been building, within his own specialized frame of reference, is suddenly and ironically threatened with being shattered. The drama at this point shifts drastically from one term into the other, that is, from a potential resolution by way of a dialectic of faith along Kierkegaardian lines (into which the scene originally modulates) into the now actual irony of the case. Caught as we are between these two terms over the course of a scene that Dr. Johnson thought too "dreadful" to be "endured",[10] we are hardly spared any measure of "fear and trembling", both in Kierkegaard's sense, and also in a sense, beyond Kierkegaard, characteristic of Shakespearean tragedy. In sharpest contrast with the extraordinary hope that is so poignantly invoked, we are suddenly made shockingly aware of the brutally ironic paths along which even the most sublime efforts towards resolution are borne, when these run counter to the facts of the case. From the ultimate disposition of the play's events, it is clear that for Shakespeare, faced with the prospect of a transcendental resolution, it is the facts of human nature that take precedence: in this case, that dark, inculpating process between them over which Othello and Desdemona are unable to exercise control, and of which they fail to establish any conscious understanding. And indeed what we are made to witness in the end is the furthest thing from the Abraham-conception: brute "murder" rather than "sacrifice", the most horribly ironic of deaths experienced by one at the hands of the other of this most noble-minded of pairs:

Des. *Alas, he is betrayed, and I undone.*
Oth. *Out strumpet, weep'st thou for him to my face?*
Des. *O, banish me, my lord, but kill me not!*
Oth. *Down, strumpet!*
Des. *Kill me tomorrow, let me live tonight!*
Oth. *Nay, if you strive—*
Des. *But half an hour!*
Oth.   *Being done, there is no pause—*
Des. *But while I say one prayer!*
Oth.   *It is too late.*
Des. *O Lord, Lord, Lord!*

10

On *King Lear*

It all happens here instantaneously, in one extraordinary eruptive moment. Thus Lear rejects the daughter whom he loves best of all when she balks at expressing herself in the "ritual of love" he has devised as part of the ceremony of his political leave-taking. Much has been made by critics of Cordelia's truthfulness and of her courage in challenging Lear about the value of his farewell "ritual of love"; much has been made also of her exposure of the hypocrisy of her sisters' avowals. But important distinctions have been cast aside. Thus Goneril's reply is distinct from Regan's and, as a response to Lear's ritual, is not unfitting; it is quite in keeping with the spirit of the event, which is intended far more as a celebration than criticism of the play has allowed. Why should Lear not make of his political leave-taking, after a life-time of ruling as King, this kind of celebratory event? Had the ritual fared well—and it is Regan who takes it out of its proper sphere—the end-effect would have been more than charming, even moving. Lear's purpose in devising the ritual is to bestow *himself* upon Cordelia, after more or less advertising (on the map that lies on the ground before them all) that there will, in any case, be an equal distribution of the kingdom's wealth for everyone.

Here is the only riddle that underpins the ritual challenge, which is presented in the form of a witty game, as to who can profess to love him most. What Goneril replies is what almost anyone who was placed in that situation would have proffered in response: an admission that words cannot express the love, that her father is worth more to her than any material good, is the equal of any spiritual or social good—in short as much as it is possible for a child to love. All this would (should) be anyone's ideal and what almost anyone of us would wish to profess, if we had been asked to say what we believed. As a response Goneril's speech is altogether fitting for a ritual occasion, and no signs of hypocrisy can be detected from the content itself. Cordelia's aside at this point significantly does not address any hypocrisy in Goneril's speech but is entirely *self*-concerned. Cordelia expresses considerable anxiety rather about her own ability to speak in such a situation, and so:

What shall Cordelia speak?

It is only when Regan comes forward to say her part that hypocrisy manifests blatantly, for Regan pretends that her love for her father exceeds "all other joys", which she conceives of (in a rather limited display of intelligence) in purely sensory terms. Lear himself is not oblivious to what has infiltrated the ritual as pretense. He is perceptibly offended by it, quickly running over it in his response, which, in comparison with the long attention he bestows on Goneril, is slighting to say the least, if not openly insulting. He is bent on preserving the ritual and getting on at last to Cordelia, whose love and expressions of love for her father in the past have never been in doubt, or how could Lear have ventured himself in this public way? Cordelia's complete refusal, at this point, to offer a single thought in reply, except to say:

> *Nothing.*

comes from a sudden, inexplicable, very strangely challenging pride. Although stopped in his course, Lear is ready to overlook this deliberate balking, as one might ignore any sudden strange lapsing in a wonderful child. Another halting effort is then made by Cordelia in fact to profess love—she has gone that far in accepting the ritual—but it is crude

> *I cannot heave*
> *My heart into my mouth;*

and her sequel to this effort immediately re-invokes the note of challenge:

> *I love your majesty according to my bond, no more nor less.*

It is not the content alone that does not allow Lear to accept her speech but the spirit in which it registers, in spite of which again Lear bears with her; once again, he makes room for her to recover. Finally, when she does launch into her speech, she is at no loss for words. She has begun a speech that looks like it will now function in the ritual's terms, but then chooses to be diverted, back to her sisters' replies—and this because she cannot take her own speech any further, is unable to see it through:

> *Surely I shall never marry like my sisters,*
> *To love my father all.*

Here is the final humiliating reduction of terms, just the kind of thing that *will* go forth in an argument that has degenerated and now bases itself on excavating stupidities or on crude stretching of the truth. How could we not see in Cordelia's braving of Lear a case of extreme challenging spirit that has lost sight of differences? differences in the way her sisters' speeches have actually registered; differences as to who is responsible for the insincerity (it is not Lear who has been hypocritical), and yet it is, implicitly, Lear who is being accused of the stupidity of it all:

> *Good, my lord,*
> *You have begot me, bred me, loved me. I*
> *Return those duties back as are right fit,*
> *Obey you, love you and most honour you.*
> *Why have my sisters husbands, if they say*
> *They love you all? Haply when I shall wed,*
> *That lord whose hand must take my plight shall carry*
> *Half my love with him, half my care and duty.*
> *Sure I shall never marry like my sisters*
> *To love my father all.*

It is a classic, and sad, case of reverse psychology. The diversion from her own speech to what her sisters have proclaimed—in fact it is only what Regan has proclaimed—functions as a way *out* of speaking, and defiantly, as self-protection, makes Lear responsible for *their* insincerities and her insecurities. Her anxiety about speaking at all is what initially drives her to balk at professing her love. It is only later that Regan's hypocrisy becomes the reason Cordelia has been looking for to justify not speaking. In any case, Lear puts the question to her that *would* decide the whole matter, if only Cordelia's answer to it were sincere:

> *But goes thy heart with this?*

To which Cordelia's reply ("Ay, my good lord.") is a deliberate pretense, for it can hardly be said that she has genuinely represented herself (what she really feels about their relationship) by what she has spoken. Lear makes one last appeal to her better sense by suggesting that she can hardly wish to come across as cold-hearted:

> *So young, and so untender?*

but that appeal can only feed the fire of her proud opposition further:

So young, my lord, and true.

But Cordelia has *not* been truthful, has not been tender, pretending to truth in respect of the judgment of her sisters by falsely dragging Lear into it, and also pretending where she claims that how she has represented herself really conveys her feelings about Lear. One is astounded by the direction Cordelia's will takes here towards chaos. Her will is a runaway train, with which Lear has now to deal, and in next to no time it has become for Lear a matter of psychic survival. What can Lear truthfully affirm about himself, suffocated as he is in that moment by Cordelia's overpowering *un*-truth? And how to salvage himself emotionally when Cordelia is cold-heartedly denying what the love they have known between them has really been about, which had seemed to them both the most incontrovertible of all realities and to him was all? Lear's response in the circumstances is to strike out for his own psychological life. The power of depraved will in Cordelia, and all it has been aiming to effect, is now met with the same counter-measure of depraved will in Lear, only in terms that now fully expose the implications of her challenge. Cordelia's denial of love and her exclusive pretension to truth must *logically* signify her dispossession by Lear, an equation he himself pursues with a perversity of deduction that now matches hers. It is a hand which she has forced, and all that is now laid out in this truly awful moment expresses the horribly total way in which the depraved "will" manifests itself when freely released from its dark source:

> Lear. *Let it be so. Thy truth then be thy dower,*
> *For by the sacred radiance of the sun,*
> *The mysteries of Hecate and the night,*
> *By all the operation of the orbs*
> *From whom we do exist and cease to be,*
> *Here I disclaim all my paternal care,*
> *Propinquity and property of blood,*
> *And as a stranger to my heart and me*
> *Hold thee from this for ever. The barbarous Scythian,*
> *Or he that makes his generation messes*
> *To gorge his appetite, shall to my bosom*
> *Be as well neighboured, pitied and relieved*
> *As thou my sometime daughter.*

As Cordelia has been extreme in pretending to stand by the "truth", so Lear is now extreme in standing by his "dispossession "of her. It is a measure of the horrible *depth* of perversity that is expressed between them. For Cordelia's dispossession to mean that she will also be forever a stranger to Lear, and no more to be pitied and relieved than the cannibal who devours his own children, is a measure of how far the depraved "will" can go in its expression of itself. However, it is what Cordelia herself has in a sense masterminded, having forced the moment to that point of crisis. Lear takes things considerably further. In his own insistent perversity, he goes on to divide Cordelia's share of the kingdom between his other daughters, thereby setting himself up, ironically, for his own dispossession at their hands. It is how the play, in its immediate terms, measures the whole impact of "ingratitude" in this family, which now becomes the principal theme.

In the later confrontation with Goneril, Lear brings out the full effect of the violent self-regard that has up to this point determined relations among this family:

> *Ingratitude, thou marble-hearted fiend,*
> *More hideous when thou show'st thee in a child*
> *Than the sea-monster.*

These words spoken of Goneril could not, of course, literally apply to Cordelia, and yet *something* of the sort showed in her at the time. Lear's words

> *How sharper than a serpent's tooth it is*
> *To have a thankless child.*

must have *some* measure of retroactive application to the effect that Cordelia's stance had on him. There is an essential moral difference, of course, between Goneril and Cordelia, as Lear recognizes too well at this later point. He knows it was madness of him to have reacted to Cordelia as if she *were* another Goneril. But, in any case, could *any* of it have been different? Cordelia takes the problem of human perversity to Lear, Lear in a more frightful way to Cordelia, and his other daughters in turn, more frightfully still, to him. Inevitably, when cast out onto the heath in the raging storm, Lear returns to the play's main theme of hopelessly monstrous ingratitude:

> *all germens spill at once*
> *That make ingrateful man!*

Gratitude thus becomes the play's now highlighted theme. By it the whole human tragedy might have been averted, and no doubt it would have, if only this group of human beings had made gratitude the whole basis of their personal and social being. But the idea of a human society wholly based in gratitude, so appealing as this is as a projected ideal, pales before the evidence of perversity so deeply ingrained in human nature one has to wonder if a culture of gratitude or kindness ever had a chance. As it is, what drives human nature is a species of "will" that takes over to the point that all become immersed in its consequences, even those whom one would otherwise think un-implicated by nature. Thus Edgar, who in the meantime has been made a victim of by his father, appears as the overwrought and utterly dispossessed Poor Tom, to embody the main direction of energy that is now streaming through this world:

> *. . . the foul fiend rages . . .*
>
> *Who gives anything to Poor Tom? Whom the foul fiend hath led . . .*

Humankind has been, in one sense possessed, in another dispossessed by a power that rages in it, which has now taken over the scene. Along the way all the good or kind characters have put themselves into the hands of the evil or ruthless by their own frightful share in human perversity. It is "frightful" because their *smaller* measure of perversity, which is nevertheless no small thing though "error", is of no account in the universal reckoning. Edgar's "study" in the meantime has become, most urgently and fundamentally

> *How to prevent the fiend.*

But efforts, like Lear's 'judgment' of Regan in the hovel-scene, to bring justice to bear on those who have consciously applied themselves to evil are simply unavailing, and purely theoretical—tragically, but also grotesquely, so. The efforts of a civilization to maintain itself in the face of this evil have become likewise grotesquely marginal and unreal, as in Lear's symbolic point to Tom (see III.vi.) that he should be better dressed if he is to be one of his knights.

The power of human perversity that has overtaken this world eventually comes round to Gloucester who is now violently blinded. Every last effort of the good characters to prevail against the evil only leads to their violent persecution. All of their anger at the evil is as a sword turned upon themselves. And the task from there becomes simply: "how to cope?" Also, "what hope in stemming the tide?" Albany, in his appalled reaction to all that Goneril and Regan have done in the meantime, gives us the full measure of a totally extreme situation:

> *If that the heavens do not their visible spirits*
> *Send quickly down to tame these vile offences,*
> *It will come:*
> *Humanity must perforce prey on itself*
> *Like monsters of the deep.*

One last effort to recover the whole from a final chaos is made through Cordelia who returns to this scene, as she says, to reclaim her father's right, and from pure, gratuitous love. The effect of her re-entrance is as that of a great balm re-applied to the all-consuming *fever* of human perversity that, outside the charmed circle of her effect, continues unabated—and *will* make its way to her. This fever will strike at her as hard as it has anyone else and will make of her in the end so much dead earth, as Lear so very terribly presents it when he lays the strangled body of Cordelia down before everyone:

> *I know when one is dead and when one lives*
> *She's dead as earth.*

Impossible to do justice to *this* final effect of reversal and annihilation. We had seen great love affirming itself, with such courage and obliviousness of consequences, but are now confronted with the most appalling image of the fate reserved for it. The best and only hope of redeeming love is pre-empted, uprooted, and wiped out before it has had any chance to take effect. Already at the time of their apprehension, Lear's dream of a restored life together had appeared but as a fantasy of life and love, in the context of such overriding evil:

> *Come let's away to prison;*
> *We two alone will sing like birds i' the cage.*

Lear fantastically supposes that they will be allowed to be free to share their life in prison, and he confronts the facts of their apprehension with the same pretension to power, over those in whose hands they now lie, as he had entertained earlier:

> *He that parts us shall bring a brand from heaven,*
> *And fire us hence like foxes.*
> . . . .
> *The good years shall devour them, flesh and fell,*
> *Ere they shall make us weep!*

In the end all *are* devoured, Lear and Cordelia also, and even the idea of the redemption of Lear cannot make up for the spectacle of horror that finally overtakes the loving image of Cordelia, who has become mere fodder to this scene of uncontrollable perversity. Even *after* all are confronted with the horror of her death, there is the pretension, on Albany's part, to carry on with the order of the state. But Shakespeare comes back into it to insist at that very point on the now undisplaceable effect of that death and the completeness of the tragic fate with which *he* is overwhelmed and would overwhelm us:

> *No, no, no life!*
> *Why should a dog, a horse, a rat, have life*
> *And thou no breath at all?*

> *Thou'lt come no more,*
> *Never, never, never, never, never.*

APPENDIX
Tony Gash's Letter
about *Shakespeare's Muse*

Dear John,

At last my teaching year has drawn to an end and I am able to write a few lines about your excellent Shakespearean explorations. What I love about them is the Kierkegaardian sense of subjectivity that they manifest. Not only are you determined to write about Shakespeare as a subjective existing individual whose art is a manifestation of his own psychic development in time, but as you do so you exhibit a personal passion: so that one intuits that you are writing out of your own experience as you believe Shakespeare was writing out of his. (Nor am I saying that you are projecting your own concerns on to Shakespeare, for I believe that good interpretation can only come out of such a meeting of minds.)

The idea of Lutheran depravity without Lutheran grace or Lutheran-Calvinist justification is very strong and original. Amongst other things, it rebuts recently overstated claims about Shakespeare's Catholicism. I am also prepared to entertain your notion of a dark muse, which, I assume is intended to take us into the domain explored by Jung and many others, whereby the conscious mind receives messages from an unconscious store of energies and imagery, which are often experienced at first as dark and dangerous, but, when acknowledged ('and therefore as a stranger bid it welcome') can become sources of creativity and growth. (I assume, with Freud, that these forces may well have something to do with our recovery of and reassessment of our earliest childhood experience of our parents, as new relationships reproduce, comically or tragically, the intensity and hitherto unacknowledged ambivalence of those first loves.) Like you I sense that imaginative engagement with 'the worst forces in human nature' has been one of the redemptive vocations of art, and have noticed, incidentally, that when I work with North American students on the art of acting, they sometimes find it more difficult to entertain lust or hatred or what you call 'the will to power' than their British counterparts, because they have been more efficiently schooled in a generalized niceness.

Now of course you are implying something much more profound and historically specific than this: something like a Hegelian movement of spirit, in which Luther opened the tide of 'depravity' which Shakespeare, and Marlowe, dared to embody. This seems more than plausible, as long as one doesn't accept the term 'depravity' oneself or assume that Shakespeare did. One objection to its use is that the notion that sin is grounded in sexuality-'nothing can cure libido'—is neurotic—or heretical, a theologian might say. For sexual desire is necessary for reproduction, and, according to Plato and others, is an unconscious expression of higher desires such as the desire for immortality or the good, which is not at first recognized for what it is. (Most parents must have been surprised by the way in which the intensity of their sexual desires can seem in retrospect to have been a cunning device on the part of the next generation to get here. And with their arrival comes the birth of a new quality of love, quite different, pace Freud, from desire.) Love in other words is not reducible to libido, and it is on this point that Othello is tragically mistaken. You are very sensitive to this when you quote Desdemona at the end of your brilliant discussion of Othello: 'Unkindness may do much/ And this unkindness may defeat my life,/ But never taint my love.' 'Unkindness' seems to me to be a very important word for Shakespeare—'None can be call'd deform'd but the unkind'—and carries, I think, a very un-protestant thought.

And what are we to make of Angelo in *Measure for Measure* who does indeed seem to accept Luther's challenge ('Come accept! Be a sinner!') which you quote as the key to Shakespeare's great tragedies, but which in *Measure for Measure* he subjects to what is ultimately a comic decorum. (Your remark that Shakespeare grew too serious for comedy seems to me to be your only real mistake. But you'd expect me to say that!) Here if anywhere is a demonstration of how the incapacity to admit an experience of sexual desire as anything but sinful, and indeed excremental, 'pitch our evils there', leads towards damnation, while the sexual desire itself could potentially have been the germ of Angelo's salvation. This might be read as Shakespeare's critical rejection of the strand of Protestantism that you claim he succumbed to. I don't agree, either, that the play ends with 'severe moral repression': its theatrical day of judgment in the last scene is much more complex and funny than that: Isabella's hard-won plea for mercy, and the Duke's zestful impersonation of a ranting itinerant friar are both wonderfully liberating.

That brings me finally to the problem about psychobiography. You are asking us to read the plays in relation to each other, sequentially, as a journey. But of course each of the plays takes an audience on a journey too, and its meaning is internally relational: the balance of light and darkness is always in play. So it's hardly evasive or merely charming when Rosalind challenges Berowne: 'With all the fierce endeavour of your wit/ To enforce the pained impotent to smile.' Nor can I ultimately agree about *King Lear* marking 'the point of greatest devastation' in the tragedies, for here, after all, the tragic effect of Cordelia's death depends on Lear's final recognition of his absolute love for her. Nor does the play lead us to accept the doctrine of universal depravity. On the contrary, its cast is equally divided between the kind and the ruthless. It doesn't contradict your story that the mood of the last plays is already beginning to show here, but that's surely part too of its generic (tragi-comic) design. Even a purer tragedy like *Macbeth* which is, to my mind, more horrible because it enacts the spiritual death of a great soul, does not, I think, imply that what you call libido or the will to power is universal: the England scene is eloquent, for example, about the reality of the virtues which Macbeth's tyranny and self-blinding have hidden.

I'm tiring now. So I'll postpone comments on your piece on *The Tempest*. It gave me great pleasure, against a background of despondency, when I read it on a coach-ride some months ago. Memories of you, and delight in your persistence, lifted my heart.

Yours,
as always,
Tony

ENDNOTES

Foreword

[1] A good if challenging way to begin, to unravel Steiner's views on God and the Sophia, would be to compare Steiner's lecture cycle on *The Spiritual Hierarchies*, Hudson, NY: Anthroposophic Press, 1987, with the full-scale summary of his views on the Sophia as provided by the anthroposophist, Sergei O. Prokofieff, in *The Heavenly Sophia and the Being Anthroposophia*, London: Temple Lodge, 1996.

[2] Quotations from Shakespeare have, over the years, been variously from the Alexander, Oxford, Penguin, and Arden texts. With the exception of the Alexander text, past participial forms have been modernized and only those passages that are less familiar to readers have been cited.

Chapter 1

On Graves, Hughes, Shakespeare

The Mythic Ground

[1] See Appendix B in *The White Goddess*, ed., Grevel Lindop, London: Faber, 1999, 489-504.

[2] The review is directly brought up in Graves's lecture. It first appeared in *The Yale Review* in the 1956 Winter and Spring issues, and was later collected in Randall Jarrell's *The Third Book of Criticism*, Farrar, Straus & Giroux, 1965, 75-112.

[3] *The Third Book*, 112.

[4] *The Third Book*, 90.

[5] *The White Goddess*, 13.

[6] All references to *The Complete Poems*, ed., Dunstan Ward and Beryl Graves, London: Penguin, 2003.

[7] The further question will be raised how *woman* undergoes this grandiose destiny. As the one in whom the Goddess directly reflects something of

Herself (the Goddess being up to a point "incarnate in every woman") woman must necessarily experience the whole cycle of death and rebirth in her own way, though this matter is not gone into anywhere in Graves, as far as I know. As a male poet, clearly Graves narrates his "story" largely from his male perspective, although given his orientation towards the Goddess, he is necessarily involved in offering some highly subtle views of woman's own role and experience in this picture. For a more complete picture of these views than can be offered here, see my chapter on Graves in my book, *The Modern Debacle*, New York: IUniverse, 2007.

8   *The White Goddess*, 20.

9   As in the Indian mythology, for one. See, for example, the illustration provided by Joseph Campbell in *The Hero With a Thousand Faces*, Princeton: Princeton Univ. Press, 1973; orig. pub., 1949, between 228 and 229. Italian Renaissance art, drawing directly on ancient Roman models, bears further abundant testimony to this graphic mythical subject. See Edith Balas, *The Mother Goddess in Italian Renaissance Art*, Pittsburgh: Carnegie Mellon University Press, 2002, 6 and 120 *passim*.

  The lion, as a constant attribute of the Goddess, represented, generally, the savagery of the earth and the wildness of the brute—in Graves's own terms, human beastliness as well: *all* tamed by, or brought under the controlling power of, the Goddess originally (see Balas, 22-23 and 59n.26.) However, at a certain point—as we shall see when we turn to Shakespeare—humankind becomes fully responsible for *itself*, which is the occasion of great despair in the first place.

10   See Ivan Stenski, *Four Theories of Myth in Twentieth Century History*, Bassingstoke, Macmillan, 1987, 75.

11   *Myth and Reality*, New York: Harper and Row, 1963, 139.

12   *Myth and Reality*, 142.

13   *Myth and Reality*, 141.

14   *Myth and Reality*, 12.

15   *Myth and Reality*, 141.

16   See my study, *The Modern Debacle*.

17 *Myth and Reality*, 192-193.

18 Stenski, 128.

19 Stenski, 128.

20 *Myth and Reality*, 190: "Everything leads us to believe that the reduction of "artistic universes" to the primordial state of *materia prima* is only a phase in a more complex process, just as, in the cyclic conceptions of the archaic and traditional societies, "Chaos", the regression of all forms to the indistinction of the *materia prima*, is followed by a new Creation, which can be homologized with a cosmogony."

21 Stenski, 102. Nostalgia, of quite another kind, was an intrinsic feature of Camus's own philosophy, as in *The Myth of Sisyphus*.

22 *Myth and Reality*, 192.

23 *Myth and Reality*, 189.

24 *Myth and Reality*, 188.

25 Ernst Cassirer, *Language and Myth*, New York: Dover, 1953, 94.

26 *Language and Myth*, 99.

27 *Language and Myth*, 99.

28 *Language and Myth*, 99.

29 *Language and Myth*, 99.

30 *Language and Myth*, 37.

31 *Language and Myth*, 62.

32 Cassirer, *Language and Myth*, 45, expands upon this matter as follows: "some indirect relationship must obtain, which covers everything from the most primitive gropings of mythico-religious thought to those highest products in which such thought seems to have already gone over into a realm of pure speculation."

33 Among these one might put together the following synopsis: "Mythical thinking....is captivated and enthralled by the intuition which suddenly

confronts it. The ego is spending all its energy on this single object, lives in it, loses itself in it. Only when this intense individuation has been consummated, when the immediate intuition has been focused and, one might say, reduced to a single point, does the mythic or linguistic form emerge, and the word or the momentary god is created. At this point, the word which denotes that thought content is not a mere conventional symbol, but is merged with its object in an indissoluble unity. What significance the part in question may have in the structure and coherence of the whole, what function it fulfils, is relatively unimportant—the mere fact that it is or has been a part, that it has been connected with the whole, no matter how casually, is enough to lend it the full significance and power of that greater unity. Whoever has brought any part of a whole into his power has thereby acquired power, in the magical sense, over the whole itself." (*Language and Myth*, 32, 57, 58, 92.)

That "whole", that "greater unity", Graves might be thought to have himself brought forward in that great centre-piece of his poetic oeuvre, "To Juan at the Winter Solstice".

[34] Owen Barfield, *Poetic Diction*, London: Faber, 1962, 86.

[35] *Poetic Diction*, 92.

[36] *Poetic Diction*, 85.

[37] *Poetic Diction*, 34.

[38] *Poetic Diction*, 32.

[39] Owen Barfield, *Saving the Appearances*, London: Faber, 1957, 142.

[40] *Poetic Diction*, 32.

[41] *Poetic Diction*, 32. Durkheim is quoted from *The Elementary Forms of the Religious Life*.

[42] *Saving the Appearances*, 126. In my section on Barfield I am, of course, bound to reproduce his own homocentric terms, although it is clear that while "man" or "archaic man", as terms, will be accepted of a cultural past largely fashioned by men, they are hardly suitable for a future in which women, no doubt from quite another perspective, will also be doing much of that cultural-artistic fashioning or "creation" Barfield

anticipates happening. I myself offer a brief treatment of Sylvia Plath's unique production from this point of view, in *The Modern Debacle*.

[43] *Appearances*, 142.

[44] *Appearances*, 144.

[45] *Appearances*, 144.

[46] *Appearances*, 127.

[47] *Appearances*, 127. Contrast Cassirer's concept of the Word, above, **13**.

[48] *Appearances*, 131-132.

[49] *Appearances*, 144.

[50] *Appearances*, 121.

[51] See *Symbols of Transformation*, New York: Harper, 1962, 224.

[52] "Graves and the White Goddess" from *The Third Book of Criticism*, 107.

[53] *Symbols of Transformation*, 232.

[54] *Symbols*, 232.

[55] *Symbols*, 227.

[56] *Symbols*, 227.

[57] *Symbols*, 232.

[58] *Hero With a Thousand Faces*, 12.

[59] Cf. *The White Goddess*, 334: "an obvious difference between poems and dreams is that in poems one is (or should be) in critical control of the situation; in dreams one is a paranoiac, a mere spectator of the mythographic event".

[60] *Hero With a Thousand Faces*, 256-257.

[61] *Hero With a Thousand Faces*, 257.

[62] *Hero With a Thousand Faces*, 114.

[63] *Hero With a Thousand Faces*, 137.

[64] Cf. Barfield on Jung: "the traditional myths and the archetypes which he tells us are the representations of the collective unconscious, are assumed by him to be, and always to have been, neatly insulated from the world of nature with which, according to their own account, they were mingled or united....The psychological interpretation of mythology.... when it actually comes up against the nature-content of the myths...still relies on the old anthropological assumption of 'projection.'" *Saving the Appearances*, 134-135.

[65] In "Conjunction", for example, Graves intuits the final unity for himself.

[66] *The White Goddess*, 476. Contrasting with Graves in this quotation, Campbell himself assumes the possibility of *progression*, but there is also much relativity along the way: "As [a man] progresses in the slow initiation which is life, the form of the goddess undergoes for him a series of transfigurations: she can never be greater than himself, though she can always promise him more than he is yet capable of comprehending." *Hero With a Thousand Faces*, 116. "[T]he whole sense of the ubiquitous myth of the hero's passage is that it shall serve as a general pattern for men and women, wherever they may stand along the scale." *Hero With a Thousand Faces*, 121.

[67] How far this rationalizing element dictates to the modern theory of myth may be gathered from the extreme views of Levi-Strauss who, in insisting on "the unique cognitive status of myth", went so far as to see myth as possessed of "its own entelechy" and so "explained by nothing except myth". Thus myth is, in the end, its own "meta-language... as fully rational as any other communication", though, according to Levi-Strauss, it took the "super-rationalism" of Freud to allow us to see the possibility of reaching such "knowledge". See Stenski, *Four Theories*, 152-158.

   This insistent rationalizing of mythical consciousness has carried over also into the literary criticism on Graves, especially in more recent years, even among those who otherwise profess an intense admiration of his work. Thus we have watched Graves's life-long poetic effort to express himself in his relationship to the Goddess reduced to a matter of the deliberate cultivation of "ineffability"; his effort to present the Goddess in his book, *The White Goddess*, to a need to create "fixity", while his apparent renunciation of "the high mythopoeic mode" in his late poetry has been seen as a deliberate "effacement" and "erasure" intended to overcome a sort of Sisyphean repetition to which Graves must have felt condemned in continually re-stating the "one story":

> *the force of the accumulation of similes, metaphors, traces, marks, black and white of Graves's writings, is that it obliges readers to interpret the ineffability of the Triple Muse as a meaningful function within a larger semiotic system.*

> *Graves was certainly perceptive enough to know that the link between words and things can never be fixed, that poetry and truth make two—yet he chose to fix it, and to write within that fixity. The White Goddess is a monument to that fixity...*

> *the advent of the Black Goddess is marked in the verse by a deliberate effacement of the language of the high mythopoeic mode in favor of a discourse which strips away many of the outward trappings of myth....[It] spells possible release from the life-long obligation to write a muse-poetry which is condemned to do little more than generate restatements of the recurring monomyth. The Black Goddess exists, therefore, as in one sense the end of myth, the simultaneous completion and erasure of the single poetic theme,...*

In the case of the first and third quotations, see Robert A. Davis "The Black Goddess" from *Graves and the Goddess*, ed., Ian Firla and Grevel Lindop, Selinsgrove, Susquehanna Univ. Press, 2003, 109-111, in the case of the second quotation, Andrew Painter, "How and Why Graves Proceeded in Poetry", also from *Graves and the Goddess*, 149.

For my critique of the easy view of late Graves as voiced by Davis here, see my *Debacle*, 71-75.

[68] *The White Goddess*, 476.

[69] *The White Goddess*, 455.

70 *The White Goddess*, 6.

71 See, for example, "This Holy Month". The need to counterbalance the energy with some form of right consciousness is implied in Graves's qualification above concerning the Western disposition to rationalism: cf. "not *altogether* happy."

72 See Nick Gammage "The Nature of the Goddess: Ted Hughes and Robert Graves" from *New Perspectives on Robert Graves*, ed. Patrick J. Quinn, Selinsgrove: Susquehanna Univ. Press, 1999, 151.

73 Gammage, 151.

74 Gammage (151) quotes Hughes from his "Interview with Ekbert Fass" from *The London Magazine*, January, 1971: "If you accept the energy, it destroys you. What is the alternative? To accept the energy and find methods of turning it to good, or keeping it under control—rituals, the machinery of religion. The old method is the only one."

75 See, along with "The End of Play", "No More Ghosts" and "To the Sovereign Muse".

76 "To the Sovereign Muse":

> *This was to praise you, Sovereign muse,*
> *And to your love our pride devote,*

77 How much alone see *The Modern Debacle*.

78 *Goddess*, 496.

79 *Goddess*, 499.

80 *Goddess*, 398.

81 *Goddess*, 399.

82 According to Hughes we need to see our way beyond the conflict (for the moment theoretically) by embracing Shakespeare's projection of how it finally resolves: "Since this great Court case is, as it were, still unfinished, the reader (like Shakespeare, and like my book, I trust) will have to make efforts to surmount the quarrel, and embrace Shakespeare's

final judgement." *Shakespeare and the Goddess of Complete Being*, London: Faber, 1992, 44.

[83] *Shakespeare and the Goddess*, 15.

[84] *Shakespeare and the Goddess*, 15.

[85] *Shakespeare and the Goddess*, 50.

[86] See also Gammage (156-157): "Hughes...describes how...rejection of the diabolic—part of the Goddess of total unconditional love—is actually the rejection of [the hero's] own soul....The hero, Hughes argues, cannot separate the two aspects of the goddess—the creative and the destructive—and so ends up rejecting both..."

[87] Suggesting that there was no other way to see it for what it is than to live through the consequences of it.

[88] *Shakespeare and the Goddess*, 43.

[89] With this shift in my argument, following Shakespeare's lead, I now embark on a more radical view of our *general* implication in guilt, man's *and* woman's, even if the human tragedy, as Shakespeare saw this, is brought to our view by man. It is also clear, as we shall see, that for Shakespeare only woman can finally bring us out of this human tragedy as we have inherited it.

The Worst of Depravity

[1] It is typical of Graves's already advanced view of this situation that he does not even credit Macbeth with murdering Duncan. In his view it is Lady Macbeth who commits the murder under the influence of an avenging Goddess who is showing Herself again against the pretentious dominance of rational man and very naturally disposing of him: "for it is her spirit that takes possession of Lady Macbeth and inspires her to murder King Duncan". *The White Goddess*, 417.

Hughes has it literally the same way but is himself anxious to bring out the whole process by which man has gotten himself into that condition. He speaks "of Lady Macbeth as Queen of Hell. Possessed by the powers of the Goddess (who was rejected before the play began), her avenging fury has already marked down the rational 'ruler' of the Adonis world that rejected her....[N]ot only will Macbeth's Adonis persona have to die, but Duncan and Banquo too." *Shakespeare and the Goddess*, 246.

2   *Shakespeare and the Goddess*, 84.

3   See *If It Were Done: 'Macbeth' and Tragic Action*, Amherst: University of Massachusetts Press, 1986, 81. "Sacred to the gods", and, one must add, to the Goddess, as I suggest over the next few pages. Her own association with war is a staple of the lore about her. See Balas, 169 *passim*.

4   *If It Were Done*, 82.

5   *If It Were Done*, 79, 77.

6   *If It Were Done*, 84. Clearly a point on which Calderwood distinguishes himself from another great theorist of sacrificial ritual, René Girard, whose focus is precisely on the ritual value of "scapegoat victims". See his *Violence and the Sacred*, Baltimore: Johns Hopkins University Press, 1977.

7   *If It Were Done*, 89.

8   See "The Early Scenes of 'Macbeth': Preface to a New Interpretation", *English Literary History*, 47, 1980, 26: "Among the benefits that flow from the king to his subjects are bloody occasions. His vassals are under obligation to him for the chance to fight and kill, to die nobly, to show valor and loyalty, to contend with others in manliness, to compete for reputation and honors by which valor is rewarded....Bloodshed is the proof of manliness and the source of honor and reputation. Bloodshed, bloodiness, bloody-mindedness quicken the pulse of the social order and sharpen its edge."

9   Thus Berger says of the role of the king in *Macbeth*: "The more his subjects do for him, the more he must do for them; the more he does for them, feeding their ambition and their power, the less secure can he be of his mastery." (24-25) "All seem aware of the precariousness of the symbiotic relation to the king..." (28)

[10] See Johannes Huizinga, *The Waning of the Middle Ages*, London: Edward Arnold, 1955 (orig. pub., 1924) 18: "Pride...the sin of the feudal and hierarchic age..." See also *Homo Ludens*, Boston: Beacon Press, 1955, 111-112: "pride and vainglory, the desire for prestige and all the pomp of superiority."

[11] *The Waning of the Middle Ages*, 96. Cf. Jung, *Symbols*: "symbol-formation... has no meaning whatever unless it strives against the resistance of instinct, just as undisciplined instincts would bring nothing but ruin to man if the symbol did not give them form." (228); "the old brutality returns in force..." (230)

[12] *The Waning of the Middle Ages*, 40.

[13] "That reality has constantly given the lie to these high illusions of a pure and noble social life, who would deny? But where should we be, if our thoughts had never transcended the exact limits of the feasible?" *The Waning of the Middle Ages*, 94. "For the history of civilization the perennial dream of a sublime life has the value of a very important reality." (82)

[14] Cf. I.iv: "There if I grow, /The harvest is your own." It is significant in this respect that both in Holinshed/Boece and in Buchanan, the immediate sources on which Shakespeare drew for *Macbeth*, the murder of Duncan *involves* Banquo as an accomplice. Shakespeare clearly had his own emphasis to make.

[15] *If It Were Done*, 84.

[16] Thus, to adapt a phrase from Bradley, "the despair of a man who [has] knowingly made war on his own soul": A. C. Bradley, *Shakespearean Tragedy*, New York: St. Martin's Press, 1978, orig. pub. 1904, 359.

[17] See J. I. M. Stewart *Character and Motive in Shakespeare*, Longmans, 1949, 93: "The thought of murdering Duncan, first or new glimpsed in the recesses of his mind at the prompting of the witches, produces violent somatic disturbance, as the prospect of a ritual act of cannibalism may do in a Kwakiutl Indian."

[18] As in the banquet scene where the Ghost of Banquo appears to him. Cf., also, III.ii: "these terrible dreams/That shake us nightly."

[19] Cf. III.iv.

[20] See *Shakespeare*, London: Jonathan Cape, 1959, orig. pub. 1936, 325. The scene in question is II.ii, when Macbeth enters having just murdered Duncan.

[21] I develop this further below in my chapter from *Othello's Sacrifice*, Toronto: Guernica, 1996.

[22] Ferocity, a sensual quality, is a definite aspect of Cordelia's character which she shares with the whole of the Lear-family, qualified though the ferocity is in her case by a more deep-set goodness. Cf. V.iii: "Shall we not see these daughters and these sisters?"

[23] More on this below in my chapter, "Shakespeare's Muse", and my chapter, "On Luther".

[24] Another kind of love, of the spirit, will have to emerge from human nature. This is the ultimate end of the tragic process in Shakespeare, as I show in *Othello's Sacrifice*. Something of the pattern described there is presented below in the excerpt that appears as Chapter 4.

[25] See my chapter on "Sexuality" in *Otherworldly Hamlet*, Montreal: Guernica, 1991, from which I quote here, 50 *passim*: "At the heart of the outrage to Hamlet's father is the suggestion of a horrible inhumanity represented by a murder whose significance for Hamlet's father is that he was "Cut off in the blossoms of his sin" . . . What the phrase appears meant to convey, to the tragic confounding of Hamlet's aesthetic sense, is a judgment on the sinfulness of even the richest and noblest sexuality, what had formerly been assumed, that is, to be the expression of a noble beauty in nature fully embodied for Hamlet in the sexual splendour of his father as a man, but which metaphysical events have now revealed to be finally punishable in the otherworld." "It isn't merely that a bestial lust leads to (or is involved in) the inhumanity of murder; ultimately, the significance of such lust is to emphasize the lust in all love, involving a murder that is *itself* a violent arraignment of sexual love, leading to judgment in the otherworld for Hamlet's father."

[26] More on this in Chapter 2 and Chapter 3.

²⁷ I offer much more on Shakespeare's complex relation to Luther below, in Chapters 2 and 3. Clearly, Shakespeare goes on to deal with the fall into human nature in his own highly characteristic way, being his own tragic visionary.

²⁸ One needs to see for oneself how Hughes perceives Shakespeare's experience taking shape with every play that came from his hand from *Hamlet* onwards.

²⁹ In this understanding Shakespeare reflects what was perhaps the most dominant view of his age which could not forget, as Calvin framed the matter, that "while all these iniquities do not break out in every individual, [s]till it cannot be denied that the hydra lurks in every breast." "For did the Lord let every mind loose to wanton in its lusts, doubtless there is not a man who would not show that his nature is capable of all the crimes with which [St.] Paul charges it". From the *Institutes of the Christian Religion*, Edinburgh: The Calvin Translation Society, 1845, Vol.I. Bk.II, Chap. III, 338, 339.

³⁰ How the conflict of feelings between Graves and his beloved is handled in "Eurydice" is a case in point. In this poem Graves appears to be almost reached by the influence of passion as experienced by the Shakespearean (and the general Jacobean) hero. At some point the poet expresses himself in the same bitter contempt and hatred of the beloved, for her betrayal of their shared ideals:

> *Look where she shines with a borrowed blaze of light*
> *Among the cowardly, faceless, lost, unright*
> ....
> *She has gnawn at corpse-flesh till her breath stank,*
> *Paired with a jackal, grown distraught and lank*

The beloved has *wandered* from them, disloyal to their cause, and the poet has come to the limits of his endurance in watching their love betrayed. Even so, Graves cannot let himself be taken away with his feelings, abiding in the simplicity of his unshakeable allegiance to his Goddess, whom he will not allow to be forsworn—no matter what the cost. Graves is so persuaded that it is man who, even in such circumstances, fails to understand the beloved, is so given up to the idea that man must refuse his own demands on the Goddess, that he must see to it that himself is strangled in his own passion of revolt. But there is much ambiguity in "Eurydice". The poet speaks of a 'scene' of violent passion between himself and the beloved:

In a mirror I watch blood trickling down the wall—

confronted by which, the poet asks:

Is it mine?

This reads as suggesting that the poet remains superciliously unaffected by the beloved's violence and beyond its power to destroy his faith, as the rest of the line seems to clarify:

Yet still I stand here, proud and tall.

The destructive import of this passion is thus simply put away by Graves, as an affront to the incontrovertible will of the Goddess (to which the beloved's passion is thus referred). But has Graves not in this but denied a passion that might otherwise as validly have claimed his attention as evidence of a hopeless reality—which, we may suppose, has not gone away only because it has been thought away?

[31] Gammage, 151.

Chapter 2

Shakespeare's Muse

[1] As Sonnet 86 bears out: "I was not sick of any fear from thence."

[2] See Raymond Waddington, *English Language Notes*, Volume XXVII, No. 2, 1989, 27-42.

[3] An interesting comparison suggests itself with Jacques Maritain's appalled rejection of Luther's thought in *Three Reformers*, London: Sheed and Ward, 1932.

[4] In bringing this remarkable vision forward Marlowe was building on a bridge that links *Dr. Faustus* directly back to *Tamburlaine*. Faustus's quest, like Tamburlaine's emergence, is associated with a *general* emancipation of forces (political-historical forces in the case of Tamburlaine, the profoundest metaphysical forces in the case of Faustus). Marlowe's

context generally is the very great one of the *Counter*-Renaissance in which man appears in "the infinite capacity" of his universal faith. See Hiram Haydn, *The Counter-Renaissance*: New York: Harcourt, Brace and World, 1950.

5 Editorially it is far from clear that the first two lines I quote take question marks, as in the extant texts.

6 See his *Marriage of Heaven and Hell.*

7 The extent of their power over Faustus is finally measured with reference to his exaggerated expression of despair at the end of the play where he says:

> *The serpent that tempted Eve may be saved,*
> *But not Faustus.*

When, early on, Faustus speaks of offering "lukewarm blood of new-born babes" to Belzebub, he is already possessed by the dark forces with whom he has made contact. His talk of serving his own "appetite" at this point is also given to us in the context of his possession, having in fact no relation to the noble ends he serves in his own person. The later forms of escapist sensuality that Faustus chooses are likewise the expression of his subjected state, attractively individualistic though these may appear to us to be especially in the case of the invocation of Helen. Even Faustus knows that his involvement with Helen signifies the tragic collapse (on the pattern of the collapse of Troy) of that romantic Wittenberg he had projected as the symbol of a redeemed Europe when he first set out on his quest.

One might also mention here, to complete the account, that where Faustus appears to be willing evil upon the Old Man at the end, his words are intended as rhetorical bravado, to deflect the punishments threatened to him by Lucifer. Careful attention to the tone of these words will reveal that Faustus is not actually willing this action; the words are brought to bear upon the Old Man only because the forces that Lucifer represents choose to translate these words into deeds, as one expression of the phantasmagoria of despair Lucifer and company impose upon Faustus.

Close reading of Marlowe's text will indeed confirm the fundamental nobleness of his hero as this contrasts with the depravity that is wilfully thrust upon him, without his free choice, by the play's dark forces. On the other hand, Marlowe was not in the least minimizing the tragic awfulness of a humankind that thinks itself ready to deal with these forces.

8 It follows from what I have already argued about the Old Man that his destruction at the hands of Lucifer constitutes a highly subtle and complex action if, as I am claiming, the Old Man is himself a phantasmagoric creation of this Lucifer and his devils. He is like the Angels to whom Faustus never directly reaches out: a voice in Faustus' subconscious mind whose destruction spells the point at which Faustus passes beyond the possibility of hope. I.e., in the destruction of the Old Man we are confronted with the point at which Faustus is led to *believe* or *think* the destruction of his hope final.

9 I offer a detailed reading of the play in these terms in my book, *Otherworldly Hamlet*, 55 *passim*: "And it thus that we are given a sense of what has been lost and must be abandoned: belief in a love which ennobles nature characterized in the play by the love between Hamlet and Ophelia and that originally assumed of Hamlet's father and mother, what the play elaborates as the "rose" in love (III.iv) embodying "rose of May" (IV.v)—contrasting with "A took my father .../With all his crimes broad blown, as flush as May" (III.iii)—that itself held the "expectancy and rose of the fair state" (III.i), but which tragic events have revealed to be merely the "primrose path" (I.iii)—consider "the blossoms of my sin" (I.v)—to "sulphurous and tormenting flames" (I.v).

10 Matters that I deal with at length throughout *Otherworldly Hamlet*. Bound up with this effort of "justification" is the faith Hamlet continues to reserve in the moral probity of human nature (in spite of his new knowledge) which he seeks to vindicate especially in his confrontation with his mother, where he seems to offer a definite plan of recovery.

11 On this more below, in Chapter 3 in the section "On *Othello*".

12 Compare *Hamlet*:

>   Hamlet. *Ha, ha? Are you honest?*
>   Ophelia. *My lord.*
>   Hamlet. *Are you fair?*

Ophelia. *What means your lordship?*

Hamlet. *That if you be honest and fair, your honesty should admit no discourse to your beauty.*

Ophelia. *Could beauty, my lord, have better commerce than with honesty?*

Hamlet. *Ay, truly, for the power of beauty will sooner transform honesty from what it is to a bawd than the force of honesty can translate beauty into his likeness. This was sometime a paradox, but now the time gives it proof.*

* * *

Gertrude. *What have I done, that thou dar'st wag thy tongue*
In noise so rude against me?

Hamlet. Such an act
That blurs the grace and blush of modesty,
Calls virtue hypocrite, takes off the rose
From the fair forehead of an innocent love
And sets a blister there, makes marriage vows
As false as dicers' oaths—O, such a deed
As from the body of contraction plucks
The very soul, and sweet religion makes
A rhapsody of words. Heaven's face doth glow,
O'er this solidity and compound mass
With heated visage, as against the doom,
Is thought-sick at the act.

Gertrude. *Ay me, what act,*
That roars so loud and thunders in the index?

[13] See Nicholas Brooke, "The Ending of *King Lear*", from *Shakespeare: 1564-1964*, ed., Bloom, Providence, Rhode Island: Brown University Press, 1964, 86; 84.

[14] "The most withering indictment" because evil could no longer be thought to come simply from those of evil race.

Chapter 3

On Luther

1   Erik Erikson. See his *Young Luther: A Study in Psychoanalysis and History*, New York: Norton, 1993; first published 1958.

2   Violence against others in the form of iconoclasm and other forms of social and personal persecution; violence against oneself by suicide of which there was a suddenly higher toll in Luther's day. See the impressions from this time as conveyed by Jacques Maritain, who was, however, violently disposed against Luther (re: endnote 3 for **Shakespeare's Muse**). The psychological burden of this time is further reflected in the extraordinary self-indulgence that accompanied Luther's exhortations to the people to know themselves better as sinners. See, for example, Peter Manns, *Martin Luther: An Illustrated Biography*, New York: Crossroad Publishing, 1982, 180, where Manns speaks of "the patience and indulgence [Luther] showed his numerous friends, colleagues and brothers, who . . . were suddenly in very much of a rush to extinguish the "burning fire" . . ." Yet Luther was not altogether blameless in spawning this trend, as Hiram Haydn suggests in *The Counter-Renaissance*, 418, with reference to Luther's cry of "pecca fortiter" (as above, **54.**):

> *Luther's statement was. . . an exhortation to live shamelessly in the animal world of the naturalists—and so forthright a one that its qualifying reservations were often not even heard. And behind it—and here in conjunction with Calvin—lay, of course, another premise held in common with the animalists—that of man's badness. A premise held only with a theological reservation, but one pointing in the same direction, nevertheless.*

See also *Othello's Sacrifice*, 80-81.

3   Cf IV.i.39: "With whispering and most guilty diligence,/. . . he did show me/The way. . ."

4   Friar Peter and the Provost.

5   From *Otherworldly*, see 55-56: "Hamlet's behaviour in the nunnery-scene is ultimately explained by the knowledge that he could not from an otherworldly perspective have loved Ophelia with the innocence he

supposed; yet the knowledge itself is endowed with the full pain of a tragic discovery conflicting with the more immediate knowledge that he did and still does. And it is thus that we are given a sense of what has been lost and must be abandoned . . ." (re: endnote 9 for **Shakespeare's Muse**).

6   My *Myth, Depravity, Impasse.* See above, **36**.

7   *Othello, King Lear, Macbeth.*

8   The emergence of this "will" in *Macbeth* was described in Chapter 1. As for *King Lear*, see Chapter 10.

9   Cf. *Hamlet*, III.i: "Are you honest..."

10   Cf. *Hamlet*, III.i: "Are you honest..."

11   Cf. *Hamlet*, III.iv: "What have I done..."/"Ay, me, what act?"

12   Cf. *Hamlet*, III.iv: "Heaven's face does glow/O'er this..."

Chapter 4

Shakespeare's Tragic Progress

1   See the account by Hiram Haydn, 'Elizabethan Romanticism and the Metaphysical Ache', from *The Counter-Renaissance*: 'On the one hand, an assertive ideal of unlimited freedom, on the other the sense of transiency. And since most of these thinkers and writers among the Elizabethans applied the ideal of unlimited freedom to the limited goods of mortal life—especially the goods of sensuous love and beauty—they were really treating a naturalistic position with a romanticist attitude. The resultant conflict is everywhere apparent in Elizabethan literature', 61.

2   See Owen Barfield, *Romanticism Comes of Age*, Middletown, Connecticut: Wesleyan University Press, 1966, 110.

3   See *The Wheel of Fire*, London: Methuen, 1961; rpt.1972; orig. pub. Oxford University Press, 1930, 140.

4   See T. B. Tomlinson, *A Study of Elizabethan and Jacobean Drama*, Cambridge: Cambridge University Press, 1964, 27.

⁵ See *Johnson on Shakespeare*, ed., Walter Raleigh, London: Oxford University Press, 1959, 162-163; 200.

⁶ See "The Ending of *King Lear*", from *Shakespeare: 1564-1964*, ed., Bloom, Providence, Rhode Island: Brown University Press, 1964, 86; 84.

⁷ Much of Part Three of my *Othello's Sacrifice* concerns itself with this basic traditional attitude, and how it needed to be outgrown.

⁸ This, and all that follows, takes up again from Chapter 2, **69**, and is, no doubt, the elaboration the reader has been waiting for.

⁹ See my summary of Barfield's presentation of this point as given in *Romanticism Comes of Age*, in *Othello's Sacrifice*, 91-94; see also 105ff.

¹⁰ This emphasis links up to my general argument about Shakespeare's relation to any possible new mythical development such as might arise in our post-Renaissance age, as presented in Chapter 1.

¹¹ Thus we note, among other aspects, the extraordinary role that Cerimon, the doctor, has had in this story (a figure who, it has been thought, comes closest to bearing the character of the Rosicrucian of which we hear so much in Shakespeare's age, as in Frances Yates, *Shakespeare's Last Plays*, London: Routledge, 1975, 89). It is he who symbolically leads the characters out at the very end of the play, for it is he who possesses the further knowledge of how Thaisa was miraculously recovered, about which Pericles must now be informed.

¹² There is of course still more to the foregrounding of these characters. They seem to step out of their, dramatically, literal situation directly into our presence in the theatre, in keeping with the masque-like qualities of this play.

¹³ Other factors will explain why the mother is not restored, as hinted above, **71**. These factors are fully elaborated upon in Chapter 5.

¹⁴ See Steiner's cycle of lectures on *The Gospel of St. Luke*, London: Rudolf Steiner Press, 3ʳᵈ Edn., 1975, 23.

Chapter 5

Prospero's Powers

1 An end-point equivalent with the ending of *King Lear*, as we have seen above, **118**.

2 The great enigma in this process, of course, which for some will simply be an unacceptable postulate, is that woman must continually die while man will have continually brought death upon her or else simply abides her death as in the case of the innocent and evolved Prospero. This enigma I do not pretend to pronounce upon but must leave standing as unpenetrated for now, but one will note in the meantime this very same process in the life of Novalis whose beloved Sophie dies, tragically, so that he himself can evolve. It is clear that he himself would not have evolved precisely as he did, that is into the great spiritual visionary that he became, without the preternatural impact Sophie's death had on him, as if he had had to be taught about death or taken through a certain form of death, to be able to break through into a new life. In the end, it is death to a certain form of expectation of life and love.

3 Nor is Prospero the Presenter of these plays alone but of a great many that precede them, of *Hamlet* and *Macbeth* certainly, but also *Othello* and, most notably, *King Lear*. Certainly we need to entertain a new and more ambitious idea of Shakespearean dramatic production, one that would make any presentation of *The Tempest* contingent on a prior viewing at least of the two main plays that precede it as its informants, as well as some form of major rehearsal of Shakespeare's momentous progress through the tragedies.

4 Stephen Orgel, ed., *The Tempest*, Oxford: Oxford University Press, 1987, 106n.

5 In *The Golden Age of Chartres*, Edinburgh: Floris Books, 1987.

6 *The Golden Age*, 81

7 Querido provides us with a detailed chart, *The Golden Age*, 75: "The following table, read from below upwards, presents the ascent. The descriptions in brackets are based on the writing of the Chartres Masters:

Liberal Arts	leading to the sphere of	foremost representative
Astronomica (embodies the ritual of the stars)	Saturn	Ptolemy
Geometrica (measures)	Jupiter	Euclid
Arithmetica (counts)	Mars	Pythagoras
Musica (sings)	Sun	Pythagoras
Rhetorica (paints the words)	Venus	Cicero
Dialectica (teaches the true)	Mercury	Aristotle
Grammatica (speaks)"	Moon	Donatus

8   *The Golden Age*, 74, 93.

9   Lecture of 13 July, 1924, given in Dornach. Reprinted in *Karmic Relationships*, London, Rudolf Steiner Press, 1977.

10 Lecture of 13 July, 1924. For a remarkable account of the difference between the 'planetary' and the 'starry' worlds as these bear further on the structure of the zodiac, see the anthroposophist, Sergei O. Prokofieff, "The Starry Script as a Key" from *The Twelve Holy Nights and the Spiritual Hierarchies*, London: Temple Lodge Press, 1993.

Compare Graves's own more distant, allusive reference to these worlds in "To Juan", stanzas 2 and 3.

[11] Lecture of 13 July, 1924.

[12] In the case of Perdita, as described above, **126**; in the case of Miranda, see **128**.

[13] In his *Theosophy*, Hudson, N. Y., Anthroposophic Press, 1988, 122.

[14] 'Upper Devachan' in Steiner's account from *Theosophy*, and the 'World of Reason' in his account from *Theosophy of the Rosicrucian*, London, Rudolf Steiner Press, 1981.

[15] Robert A. Powell uncovers the same three-part structure to such spiritual progression, with reference to the great mystery experiences before the Christian era, respectively at Eleusis, at Ephesus and in Egypt: thus, "the sublime experience of the goddess holding a child", "experience . . . of the music of the spheres", and "the will to . . . serve the divine". See *The Sophia Teachings*, Great Barrington, MA: Lindisfarne Press, 2001, 20-21. Powell's account is otherwise somewhat blithely *dis*sociated from the whole drastic process of self-overcoming that we have inextricably associated with that progression here. Nevertheless, this book offers a wonderful outline of the Sophia tradition especially as this comes down to us in the West in relation to the Logos or Christ. The Sophia and Christ become two main aspects of my material, as it turns out.

[16] *Rosicrucianism and Modern Initiation*, London, Rudolf Steiner Press, 1982, 45.

[17] *Rosicrucianism*, 44.

[18] *Rosicrucianism*, 50.

[19] *Rosicrucianism*, 51, 53.

[20] Lecture of 24 December, 1920. Reprinted in *The Search for the New Isis, the Divine Sophia*, Spring Valley, NY: Mercury Press, 1983.

[21] Lecture of 24 December, 1920. Italics mine.

[22] The Sophia's form as Virgin is reflected, as we shall see, in the imagistic terms in which the candidate for initiation experiences his inner development *after* purification, e.g., as the Virgin Alchemy and the Virgin Theology—this as the candidate moves progressively through

higher and higher worlds along with the Sophia. The Goddess Natura is the form the Sophia takes when the initiate first meets Her in Her outer function in relation to the created world. (Here some form of comparison can be made back to Graves's experience of Nature, as described in Chapter 1.) All are inner and outer aspects of the Sophia Herself Who should thus be seen as encompassing the whole spectrum of inner and outer manifestations that accompany Her active influence in the life of the initiate who has known purification. *Until* this point the Goddess continues to appear in a darkly problematic form, as in the case of Shakespeare's dark Muse, reflecting the candidate's continued subjection to his dark nature, his relative ignorance of himself. One has thus to distinguish another, more refined condition for the Goddess when She is seen in relation to a further stage in the purifying process in which 'man' can partake. Such developments further substantiate that additional evolution of the Goddess *into* the Sophia as Erich Neumann himself once pictured this:

> *The dual Great Goddess as mother and daughter can so far transform her original bond with the elementary character as to become a pure feminine spirit, a kind of Sophia, a spiritual whole in which all heaviness and materiality are transcended. Then she not only forms the earth and heaven of the retort that we call life, and is not only the whirling wheel revolving within it, but is also the supreme essence and distillation to which life in this world can be transformed.*

All this is, what's more, also relative to what 'mankind' can make of itself:

> *The Archetypal Feminine in man unfolds like mankind itself. At the beginning stands the primeval goddess, resting in the materiality of her elementary character . . . at the end is Tara[-Sophia] . . . an eternal image of the redeeming female spirit. Both together form the unity of the Great Goddess who, in the totality of her unfolding, fills the world from its lowest elementary phase to its supreme spiritual transformation.*
>

The Great Mother, Princeton: Princeton
Univ. Press, 1955, 334-335.

23 She is the chaotic Goddess of the Underworld in Her own fallen portion shared with humankind, as in Gnostic lore; otherwise, She is the pure, heavenly Sophia. In Her fallen portion (which will be restored when humankind redeems itself), She is known as Achamot. See Hughes, *Shakespeare and the Goddess of Complete Being*, 351ff. Also, Sergei O. Prokofieff, "The Cosmic Aspect of the Sophia" from *The Twelve Holy Nights*, 89. For yet another view of this situation, see Robert Powell, *The Sophia Teachings*, 95-96.

24 Much of this last paragraph (including the second-to-last endnote) is inserted clearly to bridge over the material of the present volume and especially to connect the present chapter with the first chapter and the next, although all three chapters had their own separate contexts when first published. Needless to say, a whole other, full-length study of the relationship between the Goddess and the Sophia would be required which would extend far beyond the scope of the work I have attempted as a literary critic. That larger study, as I see the matter, would have to entail, centrally, showing how Rudolf Steiner's literal investigations fit into and radically affect the symbolic approach to the Goddess as made by Erich Neumann for one, for the latter was a Jungian not an anthroposophist. Clearly my own approach to this material already shows a decided disposition towards the insights of anthroposophy in my own considerations as a critic. One would need to show, at the same time, how literary authors themselves reflect, in the detail of their work, the many changes and issues raised by the historical evolution of the Goddess. Some seminal attempts have been made along these lines by Robert Graves and by Ted Hughes, in the latter case in his full-length study of Shakespeare and in his essay on Coleridge, on both of which I draw significantly in my work. I have myself offered a study along these lines in *The Modern Debacle*. However, close treatment of the extensive presence and influence of the Goddess in the work of literary authors remains to this day an undeveloped area of critical study, and would appear to await some future revolution in our conception of the possible scope of cultural poetics.

25 Andreae's *Chymical Wedding* was published in 1616—roughly four years after *The Tempest*, and on a textual basis, the historical influence would *seem* to run through John Dee, via the English dramatists including Shakespeare, *thence* to Andreae. However, in his record of the Chemical Wedding,

Andreae was building on a visionary experience he had had in his youth at the age of 18, and a manuscript of Andreae's *Chymical Wedding* it would seem was being "read" as early as 1604, according to Carlo Pietzner, who is the translator of Rudolf Steiner's essay on the *Wedding*, as published in *A Christian Rosenkreutz Anthology*, ed., Paul Marshall Allen, Blauvelt, N.Y.: Rudolf Steiner Publications, 1968. In any case, Andreae's *Wedding* purports to record an experience that takes place *over 150 years earlier*, and presumably there would also have been an *esoteric* development long before Dee, with its own influences, from the time of the actual Wedding of 1459. This is the situation I assume in my chapter, deferring to Rudolf Steiner's acute testimonial indications about the historical significance of the *Wedding* when one refers this work back to such an esoteric development. There had already been a long (Rosicrucian) alchemical tradition, before Christian Rosenkreutz undergoes the Wedding that was to re-establish alchemical practice on a different basis.

[26] See "The Chymical Wedding of Christian Rosenkreutz" from *A Christian Rosenkreutz Anthology*, 41. Steiner's essay was published in 1917.

[27] "The Chymical Wedding of Christian Rosenkreutz", 40.

[28] Lecture of 27 January, 1908. Cited by Prokofieff, *Twelve Holy Nights*, 88.

[29] Shakespeare's depiction of this 'death' should not be confused with the still greater and more complex death of the Sophia over a much longer period of time as this is given to us in Gnostic literature (see Hughes, *Shakespeare and the Goddess of Complete Being*, 351ff.) and in Anthroposophical literature (see Sergei O. Prokofieff, *The Heavenly Sophia and the Being Anthroposophia*, 182-183). The 'death' of the mother in Shakespeare reflects the *other* great, topical, event of this time—"the passage of the Sophia through man". *This* latter 'passage' is a purely supersensible event—experienced by Christian Rosenkreutz (from what we know) more or less without upheaval. However, as an event undergone by Shakespeare through his tragic heroes—with all the attachments to the world at that time which these heroes reflect to us—this 'passage' takes the form *in the plays* of a very great upheaval. In *Shakespeare the tragic visionary*, the passage is experienced as a great 'death', although, as we discover in the later romances, this 'death' turns out to be sacrificially 'borne' *by* the mother.

[30] Until Prospero's experience 'at sea', there is no indication of his having as yet acquired *magical* power from his 'studies', but he has certainly done so by the time he safely reaches the island he is to inhabit (as he says himself, with the help of 'providence divine;'—I.ii.159). There, his first achievement is to free Ariel from the pine tree to which the sorceress, Sycorax, has horribly confined this 'spirit' for 'a dozen years'—(I.ii.279). Clearly Prospero has come into his power of magic *as a direct result* of what he has, in the meantime, experienced 'at sea'.

[31] Powerfully dramatized in Peter Greenaway's film rendering entitled *Prospero's Books*.

[32] Ted Hughes (in *The Goddess of Complete Being*) traces the 'tragic quest' back literally twelve years, to Jacques in *As You Like It*. It is in the figure of Jacques, Hughes argues, that Shakespeare first makes the conscious decision to undertake the quest. My own reading (as given in the next sentence of my text) differs from Hughes's reading where he associates this beginning with Prospero's exile at sea.

[33] We must consequently assume that the twelve years that intervene—from the time of the sea-adventure to the tempest that is raised, represent a further *narrative* time additional to the autobiographical sequence, as if the action were being projected into the future, which is where we take up when the action begins. All this, though strange and unusual, would seem to be in keeping with the frankly utopian nature of this play.

[34] Lecture of 3 February, 1913, cited by Sergei Prokofieff in "The Cosmic Aspect of the Sophia" from *The Twelve Holy Nights*, 87-88.

[35] Rudolf Steiner, *Anthroposophical LeadingThoughts*, London: Rudolf Steiner Press, 1973, 108.

Two developments will thus be noted here: an old Goddess-based knowledge, from ancient times, that has by now lost its original integrity, and another Sophia-based knowledge that has itself evolved further, from a former time, as all sensual tendencies are left behind.

"[P]ure thinking directed towards the understanding of physical existence" equates with a new standard of *objectivity* by which we now look at human nature (and so, our sensuality) for what it really is.

[36] "The Chymical Wedding of Christian Rosenkreutz", 37-38.

[37] "The Chymical Wedding", 37.

[38] See the account as given by Paul Marshall Allen, *The Time Is At Hand! The Rosicrucian Nature of Goethe's "Fairy Tale of the Green Snake and the Beautiful Lily" and the Mystery Dramas of Rudolf* Steiner, Hudson, N.Y.: The Anthroposophic Press, 1995, 91.

[39] From *The Time Is At Hand!*

[40] Ferdinand's situation at this point might be referred to *Prospero's Books*, specifically to the scene where Ferdinand is lying halfway up the stairs as if crucified (cf. Ferdinand's 'wooden slavery'—III.i.62). In the film presentation, Prospero is at the top of the stairs, Miranda at Ferdinand's side.

[41] One can only speculate on the symbolism of the Tower, but I would propose that, in its seven-tier form, it is a recapitulatory emblem of the seven-part process of the Rosicrucian initiation, as outlined above.

[42] Rudolf Steiner identifies these Virgins as Theology and Alchemy in his essay "The Chymical Wedding" cited above, 43-44.

[43] This difference emerges immediately from a comparison of *The Wedding* with, for example, the *Anti-Claudianus* of Alain de Lille who was one of those Masters. The latter work will be familiar to English readers from C. S. Lewis' treatment of it in his *Allegory of Love*.

[44] See Frances Yates, *The Rosicrucian Enlightenment and Shakespeare's Last Plays*. I say 'uncanny' because Shakespeare's main focus on a daughter and her lover in his last plays anticipates by a few years the later situation of James's daughter, Elizabeth, and the Count Palatine. James himself does not appear to have had anything to do with the Rosicrucian scheme of that time and only wished to distance himself from it, for political reasons.

[45] In his essay on *The Chymical Wedding*, 45.

[46] Steiner's dates for these respective ages: The Sentient-Soul Age, to the time of the birth of the ancient Greek civilization (from 2800-700B.C.); the Intellectual-Soul Age, which includes the Middle Ages (from 700B.C.-1400A.D.), the Consciousness-Soul Age, beginning at the

time of the Renaissance (from 1400A.D.-3500A.D.). All approximative dates.

[47] C.A. Burland, *The Arts of the Alchemists*, New York: Macmillan, 1962, 141.

[48] Burland, 71.

[49] In *The Goddess of Complete Being*, 462.

[50] Burland, 71.

[51] Cf. Burland, 72: "The dews distilled and the flames reflected fell on the black mass, which reddened and glowed, and then whitened . . .Then came the Phoenix, the strange flashing white jewel, the flower, the expanding feathers of white fire."

[52] Miranda, the mother, and Prospero constitute the three.

[53] Burland, 72.

[54] IV.i.124.

[55] Burland, 142.

[56] Burland, 144.

[57] See *Esoteric Christianity and the Mission of Christian Rosenkreutz*, London: Rudolf Steiner Press, 1984, 39-45 *passim*.

[58] See Prokofieff, *The Twelve Holy Nights*, 90-91, also the chapter, "The Great Servants of the Sophia: Rudolf Steiner and Christian Rosenkreutz" from *The Heavenly Sophia and the Being Anthroposophia*, 125-128.

[59] This is Richard Ramsbotham's idea, shared privately. Cf. Prospero, with reference to Caliban: "This thing of darkness I/Acknowledge mine".

[60] Above, in several places.

[61] For a detailed account of this further development, see Sergei Prokofieff, *The Heavenly Sophia and the Being Anthroposophia*, 68ff.

[62] See endnote 46 for this chapter for the dating of these epochs.

[63] See Rudolf Steiner, *The Gospel of St. John and Its Relation to the Other Gospels*, Spring Valley, N.Y.: The Anthroposophic Press, 1982, 190-192; also 158 and 167. See also Prokofieff, *The Heavenly Sophia and the Being Anthroposophia*, 123-124.

Chapter 6

From *The New School*

[1] For more on these developments, see my *Modern Debacle*.

[2] Cf. Chapters 4 and 5, especially **122, 156-157**.

[3] For more on Wordsworth's experience in this regard, see my book *This Life, This Death: Wordsworth's Poetic Destiny*, Bloomington: IUniverse, 2011.

[4] See *The Thinking Spirit: Rudolf Steiner and Romantic Theory*, cited above.

[5] The four Mystery Plays are *The Portal of Initiation*, *The Soul's Probation*, *The Guardian of the Threshold* and *The Souls' Awakening*, each composed in successive years. Steiner's Plays were never intended as Literature as we know that discipline today, but they provide a singular point of view from which the idea of Literature may be re-evaluated and new directions set forth that represent a transformed prospect for Literature in the future.

[6] See Ted Hughes's Introduction to his *Choice of Coleridge's Verse*, London: Faber, 1996 for a full account of Coleridge's psychic struggle. Opium, it is well-known, Coleridge wrongly thought his way out, and it hurt him greatly both nervously and physically; hence the need to get away to convalesce.

[7] Cf. the situation of Marlowe's Faustus in respect of his experience of Helen of Troy, as described above, in endnote 7 for **Shakespeare's Muse**.

[8] As described above in chapter 5, "Prospero's Powers".

⁹ Though the matter is not explicitly raised at this point (it will be strongly suggested later), we surmise that, in abandoning the woman who once loved him, Johannes secretly transfers the object of his lustful nature to Maria.

¹⁰ For a full treatment of the demonic import of Coleridge's terrifying psychic imagination and his efforts to come to terms, see Ted Hughes's Introduction to his *Choice of Coleridge's Verse*, entitled "The Snake and the Oak". There are the following passages from "Christabel", for example:

> *Beneath the lamp the lady bowed,*
> *And slowly rolled her eyes around;*
> *Then drawing in her breath aloud,*
> *Like one that shuddered, she unbound*
> *The cincture from beneath her breast:*
> *Her silken robe, and inner vest,*
> *Dropt to her feet, and full in view,*
> *Behold! Her bosom and half her side . . .*

*   *   *

> *A snake's small eye blinks dull and shy;*
> *And the lady's eyes they shrunk in her head,*
> *Each shrunk up to a serpent's eye,*
> *And with somewhat of malice, and more of dread,*
> *At Christabel she looked askance!*
> *One moment—and the sight was fled!*
> *But Christabel in dizzy trance*
> *Stumbling on the unsteady ground*
> *Shuddered aloud, with a hissing sound . . .*
> *So deeply had she drunken in*
> *That look, those shrunken serpent eyes,*
> *That all her features were resigned*
> *To this sole image in her mind . . .*

¹¹ One thinks back to the case of Marlowe's Faustus, as discussed above.

¹² In *The Thinking Spirit*, cited above, my purpose is, precisely, to see the reader through the many, discrete stages of that process, as Steiner's work elaborates on these. The reader will find in the collection of texts

I offer from Steiner's work much of the theoretical background (with its roots in Romantic writing) he/she will need, to fill in the contextual import of Steiner's action in his plays.

The word "strength" is repeated five times in Benedictus's account of Johannes's progress: in the first three instances of the word, the actual thinking power underlying such strength is denoted, in the fourth instance (which is where my quotations begin) Johannes's success in coming into such strength, in the fifth the final element of re-inforcing support gratuitously offered by the initiate (in this case, Benedictus) to the candidate who has come this far.

[13] For a discussion of Coleridge's distinction between the two imaginative faculties, see Ted Hughes "The Snake and The Oak", cited above, 9.

[14] I intend this as a complex statement. Coleridge wrote the first part of "Christabel" before he met Sara. However, he took up the second part *after* their meeting, and it has been suggested (by Rosemary Ashton in her biography on Coleridge, *The Life of Samuel Taylor Coleridge*, Blackwell, 1996) that after this meeting "it became more impossible than ever for him to handle [his theme] in the poem." (185). There is at least that kind of basis for reading Sara into the poem, and an evolution in Coleridge's life-experience that suggests that at a certain point her identification with its theme had become the primal fact.

[15] See the Intro to *Coleridge's Verse*, 95.

[16] Hughes's Intro, 56.

[17] See the last pages of Hughes's Intro: his "Postscript", to which he gives the title "The Snake in the Spine", 90-96.

[18] In his *Women in Love*. Among other things, my purpose in these pages is to question Hughes's too easy championing of what is to be found in "the blood-stream", as if great danger did not lurk there: an issue addressed in more general terms in Chapter 1 of this volume. See, further, John Middleton Murry's penetrating critique of Lawrence's own misguided implication in this matter in *Son of Woman: The Story of D.H. Lawrence*, New York, Jonathan Cape, 1931.

[19] Coleridge himself quite fully understood that the process of Imagination was not one for "the sensual and the proud" (see "Dejection"); English

Romantic Imaginative production at its best is very consciously predicated on this understanding. It is in another respect that the English Romantics fail to take *their* explorations any further. Breaking in magnificently upon these "pure, and in their purest hour" (each in his varied way), the Imagination begins to disclose what can only be described as the inner content of the *outer* world. The *inner* world, remains, for its part, relatively unexplored, and we are as a result still removed from the discovery of an outer content to that world. See in this regard my chapter on Keats in *Myth, Depravity, Impasse.*

[20] This is Yeats's position in "Ego Dominuus Tuus" until the later descent into atavism.

[21] Cf. *The Waste Land:* "We think of the key, each in his prison/Thinking of the key, each confirms a prison/Only at nightfall . . ."; "for you know only a heap of broken images".

All quotations from *T.S. Eliot, Collected Poems 1909-1962,* London: Faber and Faber, 1963.

[22] Cf. *The Waste Land*: "And upside down in air were towers/Tolling reminiscent bells, that kept the hours/And voices singing out of empty cisterns and exhausted wells"; "These fragments I have shored against my ruins".

[23] See his "Introduction", 57.

[24] As per Hughes, "Introduction", 59n.

[25] Hughes, 6. For a full account of this cosmic process, in anthroposophical terms, see Steiner's *Egyptian Myths and Mysteries*, London: Anthroposophic Press, 1972, rpt. 1990.

[26] Hughes, 31. Compare Graves's own elaborate presentation of the Underworld and the Goddess's association with it in "To Juan", stanzas 5 and 7. The cosmology in which Graves asks us to believe is especially marked by emphasis on a literal connection, through Nature, to the great "sea" of death that the Underworld represents. In its darker, material aspect, Nature is seen as *continuous with* this Underworld, as, for example, in "The Sea Horse". Consider, however, Graves's own limitations in relation to his presentation as described on **41-42**, and **43**.

[27] Robert Powell in *The Sophia Teachings* has extensively argued the case for the Sophia breaking through especially in our time.

[28] Unconsciously driven by an *earlier* manifestation of the Anthroposophical Spirit, Shakespeare finds himself likewise contending with the seemingly inexpungeable problems of lust or self-love and the more general problem of greed that at a certain level also includes the problem of intellectual over-determination—in forms that are both well-meant (as in the case of Shakespeare's 'good' characters) and ill-meant (in the case of his 'evil' characters). Through his extensive meditations on this wide range of human experience, as dramatized by the characters of his creation, Shakespeare would seem to have been working out his own share in these problems insofar as they continued to determine his own essential human nature. In contrast with the problematic character of the development as dramatized between Johannes and Capesius, there is an indication in Shakespeare at a certain point of a very grand *expunging* of these inculpating tendencies and consequently a greater progress, which I associate with his unique experience of living *through* the ending of *King Lear* (as described above, **118**).

[29] On which more in *The New School of the Imagination*.

[30] I offer more speculation on this culminating experience, as one might *imagine* Shakespeare going through it, in the last pages of *Othello's Sacrifice* (from 109 onwards). Those pages will also return the reader to a main reference-point in my argument about Shakespeare's spiritual progress, namely Nicholas Brooke's reading of the ending of *King Lear* and the radical challenge he felt that ending presents. See also *The Thinking Spirit*, 112ff.

Chapter 7

Visionary Miraculism

[1] My main theme as explored above; see also *Othello's Sacrifice*, 108 *passim*.

[2] Hardin Craig, *The Enchanted Glass*, Oxford: Blackwell, 1935, 1. Attempts were made to rectify what seemed to some a gross confusion between the "corporal" and the "visible", in Pierre Charron, for example, by way

of allaying in "simple men" doubts that "spirits", themselves invisible, could be thought of as corporal:

> *But because many simple men under this word corporal, do*
> *imagine visible, palpable, and think not that the pure air, or*
> *fire without flame or coal are bodies, have therefore likewise*
> *affirmed, that spirits both separated and humane are not corporal,*
> *as in truth they are not in that sense: for they are of an invisible*
> *substance, but whether airy... or celestial... or whether... of a*
> *substance more delicate and subtile, yet they are always corporal,*
> *since limited by place, movable, subject to motion and to times.*
> (*Of Wisdome*, tr. Lennard, London, 1670, 23-24.)

Yet as J. B. Bamborough concludes:

> *It can be observed that although they spoke of the non-corporeal*
> *nature of the soul, many Elizabethans had difficulty in thinking*
> *of an immaterial substance. Often they appear to have in mind*
> *some kind of extremely rarified matter, something like the popular*
> *idea of ghosts at the present day. The tendency to think of the*
> *spiritual as a refined form of the material would follow naturally*
> *from the idea of gradation fundamental to the concept of the*
> *Great Chain.* (*The Little World of Man*, London: Longmans, Green and Co., 1952, 30.)

3 Herschel Baker, *The Image of Man*, New York: Harper & Row Publishers, 1961, first pub., 1947, 278.

4 Godfrey Goodman, *The Fall of Man*, London, 1618, 41-42.

5 D. G. James, *The Dream of Learning*, Oxford: Clarendon Press, 1951, 7-9.

6 As James continues:

> *There are new forms to which we must look; and these new*
> *forms are part of the proper study of metaphysic. But... as Bacon*
> *argues "Plato... lost the real fruit of his opinion, by considering of*
> *forms as absolutely abstracted from matter, and not confined and*
> *determined by matter..."* (*The Dream of Learning*, 11-12.)

7   Timothy Bright, *A Treatise of Melancholie*, London, 1586, 111.

8   L.B. Campbell, *Shakespeare's Tragic Heroes*, London: Methuen & Co. Ltd., 1961; rpt., 1970; first pub., Cambridge University Press, 1930, 77.

9   *Shakespeare's Tragic Heroes*, 74.

10   Peter Lowe, *The Whole Course of Chirurergie*, 1597, Sig. 2v; cited by Bamborough, *The Little World of Man*, 54.

11   Pierre Charron, *Of Wisdome*, 14. Cf. Donne in "The Funerall": "*the sinewy thread* my brain lets fall/Through every part,/Can tie those parts, and make me one of all", or in "The Extasie": "...our blood labours to beget/Spirits, as like souls as it can,/Because such fingers need to knit/ *That subtle knot*, which makes us man:" From *John Donne: Selected Poetry*, ed. John Carey, Clarendon: Oxford University Press, 1998, 120, 115.

12   Levinus Lemnius, *The Touchstone of Complexions*, London, 1581, 36.

13   Pierre de La Primaudaye, *The Second Part of the French Academie*, London, 1594, 251.

14   Andreas Laurentius, *A Discourse of the Preservation of the Sight*, tr., Richard Surphlet, 1599, London: Oxford University Press, 1938, 19-20.

15   John Crowe Ransom, *The World's Body*, Baton Rouge: Louisiana State University Press, 1968; orig. pub. Charles Scribner's Sons, 1938, 137-140.

16   *The World's Body*, 133.

17   Thomas Wright, *Passions of the Mind in Generall*, 1604, cited by Joseph, *Elizabethan Acting*, London: Oxford University Press, 1964, 9. Italics mine.

18   All quotations from Shakespeare in this chapter from *The Complete Shakespeare*, ed. Peter Alexander, London: Collins, 1952.

19   Cf. Ransom, *The World's Body*, 135:

     it is evident that the metaphysical effects may be large-scale
     or they may be small-scale. (I believe that generically, or
     ontologically no distinction is to be made between them.) If

> *Donne and Cowley illustrate the small-scale effects, Milton will illustrate the large-scale ones, probably as a consequence of the fact that he wrote major poems. Milton, in the "Paradise Lost", told a story which was heroic and miraculous in the first place. In telling it, he dramatized it, and allowed the scenes and characters to develop of their own native energy.*

20 From *Microcosmographia* 1618, 6-8, cited by J. B. Bamborough, *The Little World of Man*, 21; emphasis mine.

21 See *Anatomy of Melancholy*, ed., A. R. Shiletto, London, 1893, I.ii.II.iv; Shiletto I, 175, cited by Bamborough, 54.

22 *The Shape of Things Known*, Camb. Mass.: Harvard University Press, 1972, 2.

23 Howard Baker, *Induction to Tragedy*, Louisiana: Louisiana State University Press, 1939, 84, 99, 103.

24 Thomas Kyd, *The Spanish Tragedy*, ed. Philip Edwards, London: Methuen, 1959.

25 Rosemund Tuve, *Elizabethan and Metaphysical Imagery*, Chicago: Chicago University Press, 1947, 150.

26 *Elizabethan and Metaphysical Imagery*, 156.

27 See Hiram Haydn, *The Counter-Renaissance*, New York: Hartcourt, Brace and World Inc., 365-367.

28 In considering this matter, Tuve concludes (170-175) that "the Metaphysicals stood with their predecessors [the Elizabethans] in using images whose significancy committed them to generalized interpretations of experience or to evaluations with general implications", which is to say "evaluations conceptually stated".

29 "It is either stated or used as a premise by great numbers of critics who... write on Metaphysical poetry in its 'modern' aspects—examples are T. S. Eliot, F. R. Leavis, Allen Tate, Cleanth Brooks, C. Day Lewis, F. O. Matthiessen, Theodore Spencer, Herbert Read, George Williamson." (164n.)

[30] *Elizabethan and Metaphysical Imagery*, 166.

[31] All quotations are taken from the edition of Lily B. Campbell, *The Mirror for Magistrates*, Cambridge: Cambridge University Press, 1938.

[32] See 298-317 in Campbell's edition.

[33] See Alwin Thaler "Literary Criticism in *A Mirror for Magistrates*", *JEGP*, 1950, no.1.

[34] At the basis of this view is what Elizabeth Sewell has magnificently elaborated upon in *The Orphic Voice*, New Haven: Yale University Press, 1960, with special reference to the period under consideration through 71-91: "It is a vision of a method of thinking in which enfoldment and enlightenment are one and the same thing, in which there is no division between figure and meaning." (98). It is a major part of Sewell's intention in her book to insist on the momentous, if ambiguous, contribution to the propagation of this view also of Bacon (see particularly, 82-99).

[35] See *The Poetical Works of John Milton*, ed., Helen Darbishire, London: Oxford University Press, 1961.

[36] Sir Philip Sidney, *An Apology for Poetry* ed., Forrest G. Robinson, New York: The Bobbs-Merrill Co. Inc., 1970, 14, 16. Italics mine. See also Sewell on contradiction in Sidney, 71-81.

[37] *Elizabethan and Metaphysical Imagery*, 21.

[38] Forrest G. Robinson, *The Shape of Things Known*, 94.

[39] See John Lydgate *The Fall of Princes*, ed., Henry Bergen, London: Oxford University Press, 1967, BK I 1.477, 14.

[40] *Induction to Tragedy*, 111.

[41] From "The Theme of Damnation in *Dr. Faustus*", from Marlowe: '*Dr. Faustus*': *A Casebook*, ed., John Jump, London: Macmillan, 1969, 95.

[42] See "Appendix I", scene xii from the Revels edition, ed., John Jump, London: Methuen, 1962, 115-116. Further references to this edition.

[43] See Michael Levey, *From Giotto to Cezanne*, London: Thames and Hudson, 1962, 148.

⁴⁴ See particularly the chapter "The Denial of Limit: The Romanticists" where Haydn speaks in connection with the Elizabethans of that "susceptibility to the denial of limit...in terms directly reminiscent of Pico and Bruno...", *The Counter-Renaissance*, 365-367. For Haydn, the pronounced romanticists are "Spenser, Campion, Sidney, Raleigh, Chapman, Donne, Bacon, Marlowe and—in one aspect of his nature—Shakespeare".

⁴⁵ See Ransom, *The World's Body*, 142.

⁴⁶ Quotations from Yeats's "Byzantium" are taken from *The Collected Poems of W. B. Yeats*, London: Macmillan, 1973.

⁴⁷ A discussion of the "eternal blazon" from *Hamlet* is offered below (on 224.)

⁴⁸ See G. K. Hunter, *Dramatic Identities and Cultural Tradition*, Liverpool: Liverpool University Press, 1978.

⁴⁹ For an extensive consideration of dream-vision literature up to the reign of Henry VIII, see A. C. Spearing, *Medieval Dream Poetry*, Cambridge: Cambridge University Press, 1976. As for the Elizabethans, it would take Shakespeare, with his acute sense of its dramatic possibilities, to revitalize this material to greatest effect—as with Clarence's dream from *Richard III*, where the dream-vision structure merges with the material of the marvellous journey into hell (with its echo of Kyd) to serve the projection of a powerful representation of tragic guilt:

> *No, no, my dream was lengthen'd after life.*
> *O, then began the tempest to my soul!*
> *I pass'd, methought, the melancholy flood*
> *With that sour ferryman which poets write of,*
> *Unto the kingdom of perpetual night.*
> *The first that there did greet my stranger soul*
> *Was my great father-in-law, renowned Warwick,*
> *Who spoke aloud 'what scourge for perjury*
> *Can this dark monarchy afford false Clarence?'*
> *And so he vanish'd. Then came wand'ring by*
> *A shadow like an angel with bright hair*
> *Dabbled in blood, and he shriek'd out aloud.*

> '*Clarence is come—false, fleeting, perjur'd Clarence,*
> *That stabb'd me in the field by Tewksbury.*
> *Seize on him, Furies, take him unto torment!*
> *With that, methoughts, a legion of foul fiends*
> *Environ'd me, and howled in mine ears.*
> *Such hideous cries that, with that very noise,*
> *I trembling wak'd, and for a season after*
> *Could not believe but that I was in hell,*
> *Such terrible impression made my dream.*
> *(I.iv.43-63)*

50 *Hamlet,* it would seem, presents the case of a doubleness of intention in its unfolding structure that we shall ultimately come to see as appropriate to drama absorbed in what I describe below as the Counter-Renaissance 'conflict of consciousness'. For depending on the standard adopted, whether we see it from the point of view of the abstracted Hamlet of first acquaintance "seeking in the dust" and following the Ghost's disappearance, or that of the fully evolved Hamlet of the rest, the Ghost will appear both more real or less, 'miraculously' penetrated or frankly assumed.

51 For a critical, though not unappreciative, view of this mentality, one might quote Huizinga on medieval realism, with its further historical bearing on Shakespeare's play:

> *Instead of looking for the relation between two things by*
> *following the hidden contours of their casual connections, thought*
> *makes a leap and discovers their relation, not in a connection of*
> *cause or effects, but in a connection of signification or finality.*
> *Such a connection will at once appear convincing, provided*
> *only that the two things have an essential quality in common*
> *which can be referred to a general value. Expressed in terms of*
> *experimental psychology: all mental association based on a casual*
> *similitude whatsoever will immediately set up the idea of an*
> *essential and mystic connection. This may well seem a meagre*
> *mental function. Moreover, it reveals itself as a very primitive*
> *function, when envisaged from an ethnological point of view.*
> *Primitive thought is characterized by a general feebleness of*
> *perception of the exact demarcation between different concepts, so*

that it tends to incorporate into the notion of a definite something
all the notions connected with it by any relation or similitude
whatsoever...Nothing shows better the primitive character of
the hyperidealist mentality, called realism, than the tendency to
ascribe a sort of **substantiality** *to abstract concepts. (The Waning*
of the Middle Ages, London: Edward Arnold, 1948, orig. pub.,
1924, 184-199.) Emphasis mine.

[52] The association of the process of developing vision with an experience of death is a theme I also touch on, with reference to Graves and to Keats, in the last pages of *Myth, Depravity, Impasse,* as indeed in the first pages devoted to Graves in Chapter 1 here. See, also, as per Shakespeare, *Othello's Sacrifice,* 109ff.

[53] Louis Martz, *The Poetry of Meditation,* New Haven: Yale University Press, 1954, 27-30.

[54] Variously numbered, depending on the edition. It reads as follows:

> *At the round earth's imagined corners, blow*
> *Your trumpets, angels, and arise, arise*
> *From death, you numberless infinities*
> *Of souls, and to your scattered bodies go,*
> *All whom the flood did, and fire shall o'erthrow,*
> *All whom war, dearth, age, agues, tyrannies,*
> *Despair, law, chance, hath slain, and you whose eyes,*
> *Shall behold God, and never taste death's woe.*
> *But let them sleep, Lord, and me mourn a space,*
> *For, if above all these, my sins abound,*
> *'Tis late to ask abundance of thy grace,*
> *When we are there; here on this lowly ground,*
> *Teach me how to repent; for that's as good*
> *As if thou hadst sealed my pardon, with thy blood.*
> from *John Donne: Selected Poetry,* ed. John Carey, 201.

[55] *The Counter-Renaissance,* 366-367. See also Melissa Wanamaker, *Discordia Concors: The Wit of Metaphysical Poetry,* Port Washington, N.Y.: Kennikat Press, 1975, 20-22. Emphasis mine:

> *Originally poetic "invention" was thought to be the "discovery"*
> *of God's metaphors that readily lay at hand in his two books*
> *of Nature and of Scripture. When, however, skepticism had*
> *sufficiently undermined faith that images of the divine were*
> *immanent in visible nature, the source of metaphor's mediating*
> *function shifted more directly to the metaphysical poet's wit,*
> *which, in imitation of God, the first artist, now conceives,*
> *rather than merely finds, metaphors which assert an essential*
> *truth—analogous to God's reality, if not identical to it. Creation*
> *of such "conceptual" metaphors initially disturbs the poet, however,*
> *for how he is to know that his metaphors are analogous to God's?*
> ***Further, are they demonic or divine?*** *And most importantly, are*
> *they capable of asserting "essential" truths, for only such metaphors*
> *can draw the mind upwards to meditate upon God.*

56 Depths that I explore above (especially in Chapters 1-3). *How* things have become unreal I also explore above (from Chapter 4 onwards).

Chapter 8
Shakespeare's Richard II

1 All references to this play from the Alexander text (see endnote 18 for **Visionary Miraculism**).

2 An earlier play in the period on which it is thought Shakespeare's *Richard II* was based.

3 A pattern that Shakespeare will bring to great climax in *Macbeth*, as we have seen (in Chapter 1).

4 See Ure, "Introduction" to *Richard II*, Arden edition, London: Methuen, 1956, lxxv.

5 See Brents Stirling, *Unity in Shakespearian Tragedy*, New York: Columbia University Press, 1956; rpt. 1957, 32. See, too, R. F. Hill, "Dramatic Techniques and Interpretation in *Richard II*", *Early Shakespeare*, Stratford-Upon-Avon Studies 3, London: Edward Arnold, 1961, 112.

6 Cf. E. K. Chambers, *Shakespeare: A Survey*, London: Sidgwick & Jackson, 1925, 90; Richard D. Altick, "Symphonic Imagery in *Richard II*", *PMLA*, 62, 1947, 349-350; W.H. Clemen, *The Development of Shakespeare's*

Imagery, London: Methuen, 1961; first pub., 1951, 55; A.P. Rossiter, *Angel With Horns*, ed., Graham Storey, London: Longman Group, 1961; rpt., 1970, 39—all of whose opinions can be directly traced to Dowden's *Shakspere: His Mind and Art*, London: Kegan Paul, 1892; orig. pub., 1875, 195-196:

> *Instead of comprehending things as they are, and achieving heroic deeds, he satiates his heart with the grace, the tenderness, the beauty, or the pathos of situations… But when he has exhausted the aesthetic satisfaction to be derived from the situations of his life, he is left with nothing further to do. He is an amateur in living, not an artist.*

The other side of the traditional coin, which originates with the *fin de siècle* romanticism of Pater, Montague and Yeats, and which actually idolizes Richard's aestheticism, does not appear to me any more sensitive to the peculiar difficulty of Richard's position: cf. Walter Pater, *Appreciations*, London: Macmillan, 1890, 205; C. E. Montague. "F. R. Benson's Richard II", *Manchester Guardian*, 4 December. 1899, from *Specimens of English Dramatic Criticism*, ed., A.C. Ward, xvii-xx Centuries, London: Oxford University Press, 1945, 223-224; W. B. Yeats, "At Stratford-on-Avon", *Ideas of Good and Evil*, 1903, rpt., *Essays and Introductions*, London: Macmillan, 1961, 106. For modern appearances of this point of view, cf., *inter alia*, Mark Van Doren, *Shakespeare*, New York: Henry Holt, 1939, 89; H. B. Charlton, *Shakespearian Tragedy*, Cambridge: Cambridge University Press, 1948; rpt., Norwich: Jarrold & Sons, 1952, 46. Behind both points of view (romantic and 'anti-romantic') is the undying emphasis on Richard as a sentimentalist through and through.

7   See Ure, "Introduction" to *Richard II*, lxxvi.

8   See Nicholas Brooke, *Shakespeare's Early Tragedies*, London: Methuen, 1968, 124.

9   See S. T. Coleridge, *Coleridge on Shakespeare*, ed., Terence Hawkes, Harmondsworth: Penguin, 1969; orig. pub., as *Coleridge's Writings on Shakespeare* ed., Alfred Harbage, G.P. Putnam's Sons, 1959, 256. For Coleridge's elaboration of his idea of Richard's "intellectual feminineness", see 249.

[10] See Stirling, *Unity in Shakespearian Tragedy*, 36.

[11] See Brooke, *Shakespeare's Early Tragedies*, 126.

[12] *Coleridge on Shakespeare*, 256.

[13] See Stirling, *Unity in Shakespearian Tragedy*, 36.

[14] See Ure, "Introduction" to *Richard II*, lxviii.

[15] See Ruth Nevo, *Tragic Form in Shakespeare*, Princeton: Princeton University Press, 1972, 74-75.

[16] See Michael Quinn, "The King is Not Himself: The Personal Tragedy of Richard II", *Studies in Philology*, Vol. 56, 1959, 173. Cf., too, Arthur Sewell, *Character and Society*, Oxford: Clarendon Press, 1951, 45.

[17] Richard's sudden consciousness of death is also suggested (see above) in the line "Have I not reason to look pale and dead?" (III.ii.79)

[18] For a similar account of the 'humanity that cannot fulfil the divine image' see Nicholas Brooke *Shakespeare's Early Tragedies*, 113.

[19] This is John Crowe Ransom's term, from *The World's Body*, 137-140.

[20] See Samuel Johnson, *Johnson on Shakespeare*, ed., Walter Raleigh, London: Henry Frowde, 1908, 111. (Bold parts mine.) See, too, Holinshed's comments on Richard's fate, which appear to me to be generally representative of Shakespeare's judgment (the poet's treatment of the Bishop is of course somewhat subtler), from *The Historie of England*, 2nd ed., 1587, cited by Peter Ure, ed., *Richard II*, 189-190:

> ...and as it was reported, the archbishop willed him to be of good comfort, for he should be assured not to have anie hurt, as touching his person; but he prophesied not as a prelate, but as a Pilat. For, was it no hurt (think you) to his person, to be spoiled of his royaltie, to be deposed from his crowne, to be translated from principalitie to prison, & to fall from honor to horror. All which befell him to his extreame hart griefe (no doubt) which to increase, means alas there were manie; but to diminish, helps (Got wot) but a few...

21 See Ruth Nevo, *Tragic Form in Shakespeare*, 84: "The detailed, almost ritualistic specification with which he itemizes the idea of renunciation of the world suggests the intensity with which he is attempting to make a virtue of his necessity." This psychological 'movement', however, can be used either, as Nevo does, to insist on what Richard is trying to make of himself, or alternatively as I do, what in himself Richard is unable to escape.

22 See William Hazlitt, *Characters of Shakespeare's Plays*, London: Taylor and Hessey, 1818, 178-179.

23 See W. H. Clemen, *The Development of Shakespeare's Imagery*, 57-58.

24 See Peter Ure, "Character and Role from Richard III to Hamlet", *Hamlet*, Stratford-Upon-Avon Studies 5, London: Edward Arnold, 1963, 16: "The entire episode of the deposition as conceived by Bolingbroke and his party is by Richard wrenched awry in order to fulfill Richard's imaginative needs and to express the exact and individual character of his suffering." It is more or less this perception of Ure's that I am elaborating on here but in a much wider context of meaning, for it will be clear that I am ascribing to Richard's expression a more universal, radical character.

    See, too, Derek Traversi's conception of Richard's expression in these scenes as "psychological correspondence" to Richard's nature, *Shakespeare: From 'Richard II' to 'Henry V'*, Stanford: Stanford Univ. Press, 1957, 43; also, R.F. Hill's conception of that expression as "the rhetorical projection of psychological intensity", *Early Shakespeare*, 112. Neither Traversi nor Hill, however, take note of the radical implications of Richard's effort of expression along the lines I am pursuing here.

25 For a discussion of the *O vos omnes* lament, specifically from the point of view of the powers of Judgment available to Christ, see Rosemund Tuve, *A Reading of George Herbert*, Chicago: Chicago University Press, 1952; rpt., 1969, 74-75.

26 E.H. Kantorowicz, *The King's Two Bodies: A Study in Medieval Political Theology*, Princeton: Princeton University Press, 1957, 40.

27 Peter Ure, *Shakespeare and the Inward Self of the Tragic Hero*, Durham: Univ. of Durham, 1961, 8-9.

[28] Kenneth Muir, *Shakespeare's Tragic Sequence*, London: Hutchison, 1972, 31.

[29] Virgil Whitaker, *The Mirror Up To Nature: The Technique of Shakespeare's Tragedies*, San Marino: Huntingdon Library, 1965, 122.

[30] Michael Quinn, "The King Is Not Himself", 182-185.

Chapter 9

Othello's 'Sacrifice'

[1] Except for the first of the four quotes, for which I have favored the Lowrie translation, Princeton: Princeton Univ. Press, 1941, rpt.1970, 33, see Soren Kierkegaard, *Fear and Trembling*, ed., Alastair Hannay, Harmondsworth, 1985, 81, 58, 75.

[2] Ivor Morris, *Shakespeare's God: The Role of Religion in the Tragedies*, London: Allen and Unwin, 1972, 339.

[3] Helen Gardner, "The Noble Moor" from *Shakespeare's 'Othello': A Casebook*, ed., John Wain, London, 1971, 161.

[4] Gardner, 161.

[5] *Fear and Trembling*, 60, 65, 66.

[6] *Fear and Trembling*, 90.

[7] *Fear and Trembling*, 75-76.

[8] See Hiram Haydn, *The Counter-Renaissance*, New York: Harcourt, Brace and World, 1950, especially the chapter "The Denial of Limit: The Romanticists".

[9] David Bevington, ed., *Medieval Drama*, Boston, 1975, 308-321.

[10] Samuel Johnson, *Johnson on Shakespeare*, ed., Walter Raleigh, London, 1908, 200.

A CHRONOLOGY OF PRODUCTION

Shakespeare's Richard II, God, and Language (1975, rev.2008)
(published 2009)

"Hamlet and the Tragedy of Sexuality" (1977)
(published in *Hamlet Studies,*1988)

"Hamlet and the Fortunes of Sorrowful Imagination" (1979)
(published in *Cahiers Elisabethains*, 1989)

Visionary Miraculism in Shakespeare and Contemporaries (1981-1982, rev.2007)
(published 2008)

"And I Will Kill Thee/And Love Thee After": Othello's "Sacrifice" as Dialectic of Faith (1988-1990)
(published in *English Language Notes*, 1990)

Otherworldly Hamlet (1988-1990)
(published 1991)

Othello's Sacrifice (1990, 1994)
(published 1996)

The Thinking Spirit (1996)
(published 2007)

Prospero's Powers (1997-2002)
(published 2006)

Shakespeare's Muse, 2000.
(published 2007)

The New School of the Imagination (2001-2005)
(published 2007)

The Modern Debacle (2003-2006)
(published 2007)

Myth, Depravity, Impasse (2006-2007)
(published 2008, rpt. 2011)

On Luther, 'Measure for Measure', Good and Evil in Shakespeare (2008)
(published 2009)

On 'King Lear' (2009)
(published 2011)

Born in Montreal, Quebec, Canada, JOHN O'MEARA received his Ph.D from the University of East Anglia in 1986. He taught for over 20 years at the University of Toronto and the University of Ottawa.

CPSIA information can be obtained at www.ICGtesting.com
Printed in the USA
LVOW040853090312

272243LV00001B/12/P